Volumes previously published by the University of California Press, Berkeley, Los Angeles, London, for the Center for Chinese Studies of The University of Michigan:

MICHIGAN STUDIES ON CHINA

Communications and National Integration in Communist China, by Alan P. L. Liu
Mao's Revolution and the Chinese Political Culture, by Richard Solomon
Capital Formation in Mainland China, 1952–1965, by Kang Chao
Small Groups and Political Rituals in China, by Martin King Whyte
Backward Toward Revolution: The Chinese Revolutionary Party, by Edward Friedman
Peking Politics, 1918–1923: Factionalism and the Failure of Constitutionalism, by Andrew Nathan
Reform and Revolution in China: The 1911 Revolution in Hunan and Hubei, by Joseph W. Esherick

EDUCATION AND POPULAR LITERACY IN CH'ING CHINA

Michigan Studies on China
Published for the Center for Chinese Studies
of The University of Michigan

MICHIGAN STUDIES ON CHINA

China's Economic Development: The Interplay of Scarcity and Ideology, by Alexander Eckstein

The Chinese Calculus of Deterrence: India and Indochina, by Allen S. Whiting

The Presidency of Yuan Shih-k'ai: Liberalism and Dictatorship in Early Republican China, by Ernest P. Young

The Outsiders: The Western Experience in India and China, by Rhoads Murphey

The Concept of Man in Contemporary China, by Donald J. Munro

China Enters the Twentieth Century: Chang Chih-tung and the Issues of a New Age, 1895–1909, by Daniel H. Bays

Education and Popular Literacy in Ch'ing China, by Evelyn Sakakida Rawski

The research on which these books are based was supported by the Center for Chinese Studies of The University of Michigan.

Education and Popular Literacy in Ch'ing China

EVELYN SAKAKIDA RAWSKI

Ann Arbor The University of Michigan Press

Published in the United States of America by
The University of Michigan Press and simultaneously
in Rexdale, Canada, by John Wiley & Sons Canada, Limited
Manufactured in the United States of America

Library of Congress Cataloging in Publication Data

Rawski, Evelyn Sakakida.
Education and popular literacy in Ch'ing China.

(Michigan studies on China)
Bibliography: p.
Includes index.
1. Education—China—History. 2. Illiteracy—China—History. 3. China—History—Ch'ing dynasty, 1644–1912. I. Title. II. Series.
LA1131.R35 370'.951 78-15526
ISBN 0-472-08753-3

To my grandmother
Kiku Tanaka Sakakida
who chose music over literacy

Acknowledgments

The basic research for this study was conducted during 1972–74 with the aid of grants from the University of Pittsburgh, the American Council of Learned Societies, and the Center for Chinese Studies at the University of Michigan. Wei-ying Wan of the Asia Library, University of Michigan; George Potter at the Harvard-Yenching Library; and librarians at the Library of Congress, Tokyo's National Diet Library, Tōyō bunko, and Naikaku bunko helped immensely in the collection of materials. My debt to these libraries is clear in the bibliography.

Valuable comments and criticisms of the manuscript in its various drafts came from Cho-yun Hsu, Dwight H. Perkins, Andrew J. Nathan, and Thomas G. Rawski. Elling Eide read and helped improve chapters 5 and 6 with his trenchant comments. Karen Gottschang skillfully edited the final manuscript. I am of course responsible for what remains.

Contents

Tables

Figures

Map

Chapter 1

A Historical Survey of Popular Literacy in China

The Quality of Literacy

One of the most difficult problems confronting students of premodern literacy concerns the definition of the term. Modern systems of universal education have not obliterated all distinctions, yet life in modern industrialized society hardly equips us to imagine the great variety of reading and writing skills that existed in earlier times. European historians cite the presence of signatures on marriage registers as evidence of premodern literacy,[1] but signatures themselves tell little about the extent of an individual's literacy. Such a criterion is meaningless for evaluating the literacy of Chinese speakers, who were obligated to master a nonalphabetic language requiring knowledge of many distinct characters for reading and writing.

Full literacy in eighteenth and nineteenth century China was attained only after long study of the Confucian classics, and the large corpus of commentaries, histories, and literary materials handed down from previous centuries. Traditional China had no concept of mass literacy. Those who were educated were by definition educated in the orthodox classical curriculum, largely the monopoly of a small group of males who competed for examination degrees. Nonetheless, knowledge of a lesser order existed in traditional China, and proved very useful in everyday life.

The education, examination life, and writings of the elite, who may well be described as a small and specially trained group with command of the literate culture, have been studied by many modern scholars.[2] Lower levels of literacy, however, have generally been ignored. Indeed, historians of China have long argued that widespread illiteracy contributed to China's slow advance along the path of modernization. This study demonstrates that during the eighteenth and nineteenth centuries, a wide variety of educational opportunities provided large numbers of ordinary Chinese, who did not aspire to master the elite educational curriculum, with functional skills in reading and writing.

If literacy can be defined as the acquisition of some functional level of reading and writing abilities, there was a continuum of such skills in Ch'ing China. The educational achievements of examination candidates constitute one pole in this continuum. Techniques for teaching basic reading and writing skills within a fairly short time had been developed in the traditional educational system. Chapter 2 will show that the school curriculum could cram recognition of approximately 2,000 characters into a young boy within a year, along with the ability to write a considerable but smaller number of characters. This elementary phase of an elite education, which a boy in a well-to-do household would master before being assigned a formal tutor, could be acquired by the less fortunate in the charitable and clan schools, and marks the threshold of elite education.

A significantly large number of persons possessed reading and writing skills below this level. Abbé Huc, writing in the mid-nineteenth century, reported, "With few exceptions, every Chinese knows how to read and write, at least sufficiently for the ordinary occasions of life."[3] Many of Huc's pronouncements were exaggerated, but his impression of widespread basic literacy was echoed by other observers.

With a nonalphabetic language, individuals with knowledge of a limited number of characters possessed narrowly specialized vocabularies. The limitations as well as the pervasiveness of these elementary skills were noted by a missionary: "There is scarcely an adult male but can pick out a few characters here and there in a proclamation posted on the wall; but in the Chinese language, to know a few characters does not assist one in the least to understand the meaning of others. Multitudes can read the characters so as to know the names of hundreds of them, without being able to read a book. . . . "[4] Such people, while not fully literate, "know the characters they require in their business; it may be a hundred or a thousand. They can often read and write business letters, but they cannot read even a single book at sight."[5]

The practical value of such specialized vocabularies is confirmed by the goals of the twentieth century Mass Education movement, which aimed at teaching 1,200 basic characters in a four- to six-week course. Separate readers were developed for urban residents, farmers, and soldiers; completion of the readers allowed graduates to "read simple books, write letters, and keep accounts."[6] According to Sidney Gamble, "In a study of the characters used in various kinds of written material and their comparative frequency rates in a million and a half characters the Mass Education movement found that if a person could recognize nine characters he could read one out of seven characters in simple material. 78 characters would cover 50 per cent, 352 characters 70 per cent, and 1169 characters 91 per cent."[7]

Since the Mass Education movement selected characters from vernacular materials, these findings probably reflect the kind of vocabulary typical of vernacular materials in an earlier period. A limited reading vocabulary of several hundred characters thus permitted some comprehension of very simple materials, while knowledge of 1,200 characters gave a total vocabulary of "well over 2,000 words."[8]

Adult education programs supported by the Chinese Communist Party aimed at similarly modest levels of literacy. The spare-time schools (*shih-tzu pan*) designed to reach adults who could not attend the night schools, taught from 450 to 750 characters.[9] In June, 1950, a People's Congress directive on adult education defined literacy as the ability to read and to use 1,000 characters. Persons knowing fewer than 300 characters were counted as illiterate "even if able to count and write receipts," for they had not mastered the "basic tool of the culture."[10] Under this directive, semiliterates were defined as those knowing between 500 and 600 characters but unable to read or write on the elementary level. Later, standards were raised so that semiliteracy required mastery of 700 characters and literacy a knowledge of 1,500 characters.

The goals of the modern Mass Education movement and the

adult education programs of the People's Republic testify that persons with mastery of fewer than 2,000 characters could still possess functional literacy of a specialized sort. At the lower level of this continuum of reading and writing skills were those who recognized only several hundred characters, but might still be able to count and to write receipts. Popular or mass literacy as defined in this study begins with this lower level of abilities and moves up through higher levels of mastery to include the many Chinese who were exposed to the elementary elite curriculum in private and institutional schools but did not continue their education to advanced levels.

A consideration of the nature as well as the number of the characters learned is important for evaluating popular literacy. Many of the 2,000 characters that constituted the elementary phase of elite schooling were relevant to a Confucian education but of little use in everyday life.[11] On the other hand, the cheaply printed glossaries that introduced several hundred characters to nonelite readers emphasized concrete terms rather than abstractions. This important subject will be treated more fully in chapters 6 and 8.

The Problem of Popular Literacy

Most generalizations about Chinese literacy refer only to full mastery of the written language. One view holds that the nature of the language precluded widespread literacy: "When a virtually nonphonetic system of writing becomes sufficiently developed to express a large number of meanings explicitly, only a small and specially trained professional group in the total society can master it, and partake of the literate culture."[12] Such a statement ignores levels of knowledge below mastery of the elite written culture.

In the same way, the comment made by several scholars, that rural schools could not prepare students for the civil service examinations,[13] is not pertinent for the rudimentary levels of literacy studied here. Those who argue that rural poverty prevented sound and permanent private financing for education are vague about whether access to education refers only to preparation for the civil service examinations.[14] Traditional Chinese attitudes have had great influence, as Denis Twitchett notes: "We often make the mistake of accepting at its face value the Chinese literati's view that literacy is to be equated with a thorough grounding in Confucian learning. By this standard, the literate class was very small indeed. But undoubtedly there was always a very large number of persons who, although uneducated by the yardstick of classical scholarship, were nevertheless literate."[15]

The view that only a very small minority of Chinese were literate is especially surprising when considered in light of studies on education in Tokugawa Japan (1603–1867). Ronald Dore shows that by late Tokugawa the majority of town dwellers with settled occupations, and a good proportion of middle-level farmers, were literate, thanks to schools (*terakoya*) that developed in response to an effective economic demand.[16] If a stratified, status-fixed society such as Japan's experienced this great demand for basic skills in reading, writing, and arithmetic among townsmen and farmers, a relatively open society such as China's, where education was the key to upward social mobility, should have stimulated a similar if not greater effective demand for literacy. In the terms used by Carlo Cipolla, the investment and consumption demand for education should have been very high in China. Indeed, available information indicates that a relatively high degree of functional literacy, which provided the foundation for complex political, social, and economic institutions, existed well before the Ch'ing.

Literacy before the Ch'ing Period

Inscriptions on a wide range of objects dating from before 202 B.C. show that popular literacy, in this case among artisans, was important in ancient China, but there is no other evidence for determining the extent to which people below the ruling class could read and write. The Tunhuang manuscripts of the fifth to tenth centuries A.D., which "show every grade of literacy from the accomplished scholar down to the man who could only painfully scrawl the characters of his name," also support the notion of a wide range of abilities. Writing exercises and elementary textbooks were included in the Tunhuang finds.[17]

The most potent force for the dissemination of literacy must have been the expansion of printing after the thirteenth century. By 1644, large-scale printing, flourishing commercial book production, and the development of special types of materials for a fairly broad audience suggest the existence of a substantial degree of popular literacy.

China also experienced an expansion of educational opportunities, particularly during the Ming (1368–1644), when a network of elementary schools was established across China Proper. These schools, encouraged by the government, supplemented privately financed education, which had always been the major channel for literacy. The increase in schools and the wide availability of popular literature support the notion of a substantial increase in educational opportunities and popular literacy during this period.

Female Literacy

Before the twentieth century, formal education for women was neither approved nor systematically provided for in Chinese society. Joanna Handlin shows that certain sixteenth century literati promoted female education, but that there was an ongoing debate in Ming and Ch'ing times between these proponents and others who felt that in a woman, ignorance was a virtue.[18] Despite notable historical exceptions such as the female historian Pan Chao of the Former Han dynasty (206 B.C.–A.D. 23), and a few famous women poets, the majority of women were illiterate.

Early nineteenth century estimates placed the female literacy rate at only 1–10 percent. John L. Buck's survey of rural areas in the 1930s disclosed that only about 2 percent of the entire female population over age seven had ever attended school, and only half of these were considered literate. Although this figure should probably be taken as the lower range of an estimate of female literacy, since the rural areas surveyed by Buck would be predictably less favorable to female education than an urban milieu,[19] there is no evidence that female literacy rates ever rivaled those for males.

Regional variance in female literacy was probably great. Kwangtung, for example, seems to have had high levels of female literacy, as can be seen from the 1896 census statistics for Hawaii, where 25 percent of the Chinese female immigrants were literate.[20]

Female literacy was no doubt most common in the households of the literati. Special books for women, like the *Nü lun-yü* (Female's "Analects"), *Nü hsiao-ching* (Women's "Classic of Filial Piety"), and *Nü ssu-tzu ching* (Female's "Four-Character Classic") provided female versions of the textbooks used in male education. Yüan Mei, the eighteenth century poet, drew his female pupils from this social group, and such women occasionally organized poetry clubs like the men of their acquaintance.[21]

We learn about these literate women through chance references in writings about and by their male kin: T'ang Shun-chih's younger sister and sister-in-law; Yüan Mei's aunt, sister, and daughter; mothers of successful men, from Prime Minister Hsü Kuo's mother in the sixteenth century to the mothers of Liang Ch'i-ch'ao, Pa Chin, and Chiang Kai-shek, who guided their sons through their first lessons, in the nineteenth and twentieth.[22] These women not only enjoyed easier access to education, since their male relatives were literate, but once educated, their ability to keep accounts and records undoubtedly helped them fulfill their duties in managing large households.

Girls who were formally educated were offered a different curriculum from their brothers. Since women were barred from public life, and considered inferior to men as beings, there was no point in teaching them the Confucian classics. The female versions of the orthodox primers noted above were used instead. There was at the same time an inherent danger in overeducating women who might then no longer be able to tolerate their subordinate position in the Chinese family. Wu Ching-tzu's novel *The Scholars* satirizes the Chinese bluestocking in Miss Lu, a pampered daughter taught to write eight-legged essays just like a man.

There is evidence that some courtesans could write poetry, implying that they were probably given schooling. Some female professional entertainers, who were often known for their original renditions of narrative songs, may also have been literate.[23]

The extent of female literacy in ordinary households is difficult to evaluate. Joanna Handlin describes how the Ming scholar Lü K'un provided reading aids for the semiliterate in his *Kuei fan*

(Regulations for the women's quarters), a didactic work for women, suggesting that there was an audience to profit from such aids. Marjorie Topley's study of marriage resistance in certain parts of the Canton delta shows that young girls working in sericulture were not only taught to read, but that special works were written for them. The *pao-chüan* for women, which put female biographies into ballad form, had counterparts in other parts of China as well. Daniel Kulp tells us that in Phenix Village, the 3–5 percent of females who were literate were in great demand as readers among the village women, who enjoyed ballads "especially designed for women to read or sing."[24]

Village women who could read and write must have been in a distinct minority. For villagers who had enough difficulty financing the education of a bright son, educating a girl was "like weeding the field of some other man."[25] A son was forever a part of the Chinese patrilineal line, but a daughter was looked upon as a transient, someone who would soon marry and belong permanently to her husband's family. Educating a daughter was viewed as a waste of scarce resources by her natal family.

Female literacy in traditional times was thus hindered by conservative attitudes and values as well as by economic considerations. Literacy was probably most widespread among elite women and professional entertainers of various kinds, and least common among the rural women who constituted the bulk of the population—here literate women must have been few indeed. In keeping with traditional conditions, the rest of this study concentrates on male literacy.

Literacy in the Ch'ing Period

Ch'ing administrative regulations presupposed a significant degree of nonelite literacy. Several low status groups of government underlings, who were denied access to civil service rank, were literate. Clerks had to be able to read and write, but as one clan rule explained, "Officials are socially prominent, but clerks in the government office belong to an inferior class. Since the clerks are literate, people often address them as sir. However they have to crook their knees before the officials and wait upon the pleasure of the latter. It is a very humble vocation."[26]

In his study of Ch'ing government, T'ung-tsu Ch'ü estimates that the number of clerks serving at any one time ranged from a minimum of 100 in a small county to a maximum of 3,000 in a large one. This would suggest that a minimum of 300,000 literate clerks participated in local government at any one time, not including those serving in prefectural, provincial, and central government offices.[27] Since regulations prescribed a five-year limit on clerkships, even if the rule were not rigidly enforced, the pool of literates available for such positions in China could well have been at least double this figure if not more. The personal servants hired by magistrates to assist with local administration constituted another segment of nonelite literates, since they were barred from the examination system by their origins in the despised outcast groups.[28]

Merchants were also necessarily literate. At one extreme, the Yang-chou merchants, many of them multimillionaires, were patrons of the arts and letters, and sometimes bibliophiles. Moreover, since record-keeping was a mandatory part of their occupation, merchants on a humbler level were also at least functionally literate. The central government required that all gathering places for trade, urban or rural, as well as in ports, have official representatives. These brokers (*ya-hang*) and wharf heads (*fu-t'ou*) were to be appointed from "the households in the profession." The magistrate handed out an official seal and record book to these representatives, who were required to register the pass numbers, goods, and names of all traveling merchants or boats passing through their route. Records were to be checked at the county office each month.[29]

That enterprises as lowly in status as the porter's trade, which was said to be filled with landless men from the lower ranks of the peasantry, required tickets and schedules of carrying charges, is revealed by the local written regulations that have come down to us. Boat owners, who also used contracts in their businesses, both on the inland routes and in coastal shipping, could also read and write.[30]

Written contracts were used for purchasing or mortgaging real estate, for renting land, hiring laborers, borrowing money, and even for selling children.[31] These transactions took place not just in the large urban centers, but in the smaller periodic markets as well.

Popular Literacy in Town and City

Chinese cities and towns were natural centers for written communications of all kinds. First, there were communications with the government. Government proclamations were posted in cities, as when, for instance, the K'ang-hsi Emperor (1662–1723) wished to make an example of an official:

> And Chang P'eng-ko, whom I praised so often and kept in the highest offices, could write a memorial so stupid that I ordered it printed up and posted in major cities so that everyone could read it—for he claimed that the drop in the river's level was due to a miracle performed by the spirit of the waters, when the real reason was that no rain had fallen for six months in the upper reaches of the Yellow River.[32]

Written regulations for various enterprises were designed to protect the public. For example, when the government limited the interest rates that could be charged by pawnshops, it directed that the printed rules be posted in front of each shop.[33] Wage rates for various workers in Soochow were carved on stone in order to preserve the agreements reached.[34] For their part, the populace used placards posted on city walls to voice grievances against petty officials.[35]

News of official business was printed in the official gazettes (*i pao, t'ang pao*), and their commercial counterpart, the *Peking Gazette (Ching pao)*. There were also provincial gazettes printing official news from the governor's yamen.[36] The *Peking Gazette* and the provincial gazettes were primarily of interest to degree holders, officials, and others dealing closely with government, since their news was confined to official appointments, promotions, and the like. A type of newspaper with more widespread readership was the *hsin-wen-chih*. Sold on the streets for a few cash, these were small sheets usually devoted to one "extraordinary" event. Roswell Britton, writing on the Chinese periodical press, observed:

"The style of writing in original *hsin-wen-chih* stories . . . was consciously designed for the clerks, artisans, and tradespeople whose occupations required a small command of characters, and for the large numbers of men who had started on the road to scholarship and public office but stopped in elementary stages."[37] Special issues were illustrated, sometimes in color. Episodes of the Opium War found their way to north China through the *hsin-wen-chih*.[38]

Guilds, which displayed their regulations in shops, also printed and circulated market reports for their members. Talcott Williams reported coming across a forward exchange market in Ningpo in the 1850s, where Spanish dollars were being sold for copper cash, with quotations from Soochow, 200 miles away, brought in by pigeon post. The practice of using carrier pigeons, found among business firms, was supplemented by other modes of transport for conveying parcels, letters, and funds. The postal system in China, run by private firms, seems to have been quite efficient.[39]

Streets were full of written advertisements for medicines, doctors, theatrical performances, fortune-tellers, inns, and restaurants. Some basic literacy must be assumed among townsmen, when, in the late nineteenth century, the Swatow guild ostracized a powerful Foochow merchant by having anonymous placards bearing scurrilous accusations against him paraded around town.[40]

As foreign residents in the 1830s observed, "Of the whole population of Canton not more than one half are able to read. Perhaps not one boy out of ten is left entirely destitute of instruction; yet of the other sex not one in ten ever learns to read or write." Other estimates from the same period put male literacy at about 80 percent of the city's population.[41]

While the early pretreaty port foreigners debated among themselves whether one could say "that in China, there are more books and more people to read them, than in any other country in the world,"[42] they did agree that the Cantonese were remarkably fond of books, and that the numerous printing houses, bookstores, and circulating libraries for those who could not buy books carried on a very active business. One observer commented:

> I have often heard of "circulating libraries"; but before I reached this country I never saw them carried through the streets so as to

> accommodate every man at his own door. . . . some of the circulating libraries here are stationary, and every customer must go or send to the depository for the books which he wishes to obtain. Often, however, he is spared this trouble. The librarian, with an assortment of books in two boxes . . . sets off on his circuit, going from street to street, and from door to door. In this way he passes his whole time and gains his livelihood. He loans his books, usually for a very short time and for a very small compensation; they being generally short volumes and only a few in a set. The books thus circulated are chiefly novels, and sometimes those of a very bad character . . . . The librarian, whom I met at the door of the hong this afternoon, loaning books to the servants and coolies of the factories, said that his whole stock amounted to more than 2000 volumes. He had with him, however, not more than 300 volumes: the others being in the hands of his numerous customers.[43]

The existence of a specialized service supplying books at minimal cost to such persons as servants and workers supports the high estimates of male literacy previously cited.

In Canton, foreign trade and high rates of male literacy stimulated the printing and sale of books, modeled after Chinese reading primers, that were designed to teach Portuguese and English by writing the sounds of foreign words together with their meanings, both in Chinese characters. According to one writer: "Similar books are very common among the people of Canton, and it is deemed one of the first steps to the acquisition of English to copy out one of these manuscripts. Not only the names of articles, but idioms, phrases, and rules of etymology, are sometimes found in them, thus making a partial grammar."[44] The books, which cost "a penny or two," were "continually in the hands of servants, coolies, and shopkeepers"[45]—those who stood to profit in dealings with the foreign traders.

Such high levels of male literacy were not confined to Canton. In mid-nineteenth century Foochow, Justus Doolittle observed fortune-tellers who used methods requiring an ability to read—and not merely to consult books. One procedure consisted of selecting one or two sheets of paper from a box; each sheet had a character written on it, which was then analyzed to tell the customer's fortune.[46]

Literacy extended to members of secret societies. In the initiation ceremonies of a branch of the Triads, the novice was directed to "go to our secretary, and ask him for a book; in that book you will find all our rules and secret signs." Some Triad documents were in manuscript form, others in small paper books, "much thumbed."[47]

Susan Naquin's fascinating study of the Eight Trigrams Uprising of 1813 shows that sect leaders, who came from a wide variety of backgrounds, possessed scriptures that were treasured, illicitly printed, and passed on from one generation to the next.[48] Yu-wen Jen similarly finds that the mid-nineteenth century Taiping rebels emphasized publications. Between 1852 and 1862, forty-four official Taiping books were printed, most of them in large enough quantities to ensure distribution to the entire army as well as to the families of officers. Actually this concern for written propaganda dated from the 1840s, when the Taiping leader Feng Yün-shan recruited converts in his Kwangsi base to copy tracts. The Taipings also printed and distributed manuals, regulations, and registration forms for enlisted men.[49]

Popular Literacy in the Village

All of the groups discussed above may be classified as urban or at least as nonagrarian. What of the countryside? Here too the available information suggests that a sizable proportion of the male inhabitants could read and write.

The most obvious materials that point to popular literacy in rural areas are those derived from the government-instituted systems of police security and tax collection. The police security system (*pao-chia*) was based on an organization that grouped all households into units of 10, 100, and 1,000. Households were mutually responsible for police surveillance in their designated units, while unit heads supervised and updated household placards that listed all members of a residence. Similar registers were kept at hostels, temples, and shrines.[50] According to government regulations, the onerous tasks of keeping records and reporting to the yamen were to be entrusted only to citizens who did not hold one of the examination degrees; yet literacy was obviously required to carry out the job.

Did the rural village house enough people who could read and write to carry out the regulations? Kung-ch'üan Hsiao interprets a 1757 decree, directing that *pao-chia* heads be selected from persons who are honest, literate, and own property, to mean that students who had failed to pass the examinations for the *sheng-yüan* degree should be selected, since the ability to read and write was "rarely possessed by commoners in the villages"[51]—nonetheless the government regulations for tax collection also rested on an assumption of widespread rural literacy.

The tax collection (*li-chia*) system instituted in early Ch'ing was reformed in the late seventeenth and early eighteenth centuries. One eighteenth century system appointed a man (*chia-chang*) who was responsible for ten households. A list of the tax collections due from these households, with payment deadlines, was sent by the county office, which held him responsible for the total amount due. In another system, the local yamen sent a document listing each household's tax obligations to the head of a five- or ten-household unit. This document was passed from household to household; failure to circulate it was punishable by law.[52]

The police security and tax collection systems may sometimes have been mere paper structures in the Ch'ing dynasty,[53] but it is difficult for a student of Chinese government to accept the notion that they were totally divorced from social reality, or that the Chinese bureaucracy would have instituted such detailed regulations if their implementation were obviously impossible. Operation of the *li-chia* system assumed a certain degree of literacy: it is interesting to note that the regulations do not discuss the problems of communicating tax obligations to illiterates. Since both the police security and tax collection systems required some ability to read and write, the complete inability of a rural populace to do either would surely have been recognized in government documents. Moreover, Ch'ing rulers were not innovating when they established the *pao-chia* and *li-chia* systems, but were following historical precedent.

Methods used by the government to communicate with the populace provide further evidence of widespread popular literacy. Like its predecessors, the Ch'ing used publicly posted notices as a means of informing its citizens about new rules and regulations, or other matters of official concern. Doolittle noted that these proclamations were posted not only in towns but in country villages as well.[54]

Propagating information on new agricultural techniques through cartoons on yamen walls was a method used by magistrates as early as the Sung period (960–1278).[55] In many other written communications to citizens, the conscious use of rhymes echoed techniques prominent in elementary textbooks. For example, Chang Po-hsing, while governor of Fukien (1707–10), used three different versions of the *Sacred Edicts:* one for the literati, "one illustrated with popular sayings for those of medium intelligence and scholarly ability, and one with memorable jingles for the simple country folk."[56] Chang's attempts were among many efforts to render the difficult official style of the *Sacred Edicts* into colloquial form for popular consumption.[57]

Similar recognition of the problems inherent in official communications is found in one of Wang Hui-tsu's manuals on administration: Wang "recommends using simple and comprehensible language in all written public notices, since people usually find it difficult to understand the written language and soon tire of trying to read long-winded and verbose documents." Wang added that the notices should be written in "nice calligraphy, easy to read."[58] Attempts like these testify not only to the desire of some officials to promote effectively the flow of information to the people; they also recognize the various levels of reading skills in the Ch'ing population.

Lineage practices reinforce the thesis that written materials pervaded Chinese society. As Emily Ahern notes, genealogies that defined and supported lineage organization presupposed literate males within the lineage. Other clan activities also rested on written materials. For example, poor persons in the Yang clan of Kiangsu had to present certificates to receive their charitable rice allotments.[59] Hu Shih's father, Hu Ch'uan (1841–95), when supervising reconstruction of his ancestral hall in Anhwei, noted that he first visited the site where the lumber had been cut, numbered all the pieces, and recorded their weights in a book. Returning to the clan, he "sent two, four, six, eight or twelve men to each location, according to the size of the job. He gave each group a slip bearing the number of the piece of lumber they were to carry, so as to avoid conflict and confusion."[60] This took place in the slack agricultural season when "there was no work to be done in the fields," suggesting that the kinsmen sent to get the lumber (who were literate enough to read numbers) were farmers who still tilled their own land.

Even in areas of China without strong lineages, written documents were necessary for many occasions in village life: marriages, funerals, the division of family property, paying and allocating taxes, and sales transactions. As Myron Cohen notes, literacy was required "not only for scholarship and official administration, but for successful farm management and commerce, and it was extremely useful if not essential for those wishing to assume a greater than ordinary influence in the local affairs of their neighborhood or village."[61]

Many peasants in north as well as central and south China also participated in water control organizations. These systems increased in number during Ming times, and their financing and control moved into the hands of those cultivating the soil. Since irrigation systems often included several villages, coordinating maintenance activities and allocating water were quite complicated tasks. Records had to be kept of the schedule for drawing water, for assessing households to finance the work, and for mobilizing labor to repair the dikes and channels. The supervisory and record-keeping duties were rotated among landowning farmers.[62] Participation in water control systems thus gave some peasants experience in fairly complex organizations involving more than one village; such activities required a certain level of basic literacy.

We have already mentioned the government practice of posting notices and the use of posters in Swatow to drive a Foochow merchant out of town. Similar use of written polemic could be found in villages. Yu-wen Jen recounts an 1844 incident in Kwangtung, where the elders asked "the most learned men and best calligraphers" in the village, Hung Hsiu-ch'uan and Hung Jen-kan, to inscribe the customary lines on red paper in order to eulogize the gods. When they refused, "in the ensuing uproar harsh words were exchanged and denunciatory poems from both sides were posted on the walls of the village."[63] For this incident to have any meaning, there must have been villagers who could read and write.

Early nineteenth century observers found numerous schools in the countryside. "The First Annual Report of the Morrison Education Society" notes: "In the country, each village, or subdivision of a village, has its own school-room."[64] These observations were echoed by a Catholic missionary residing in the interior, and by missionaries in north and southeast China during the second half of the nineteenth century.[65] As Huc, writing in mid-century, recorded, "There is no little village, not even a group of farms, in which a teacher is not to be found. . . . "[66]

Perhaps one reason for the presence of so many schools and such widespread rudimentary literacy in rural areas is that village society was not exclusively agrarian. As Maurice Freedman points out, the countryside was not simply the home of the peasantry, but housed a "sizable fraction" of persons "engaged in occupations clearly not those of peasants." Despite great regional variations, twentieth century statistics support Freedman's view.[67] To the extent that Ch'ing village society was interpenetrated by nonagrarian activities, there was an added incentive to learn to read and write, since the rewards for basic literacy in the market and trades were high.

Despite the existence of a more literate populace in rural areas than previously supposed, the rate of male literacy was still probably lower in rural than in urban places. An early nineteenth century estimate from Kwangtung suggested that in rural districts "not more than four or five tenths" of the men could read, as compared with the estimated 80 to 90 percent male literacy rate within Canton itself.[68] These missionary estimates are sustained by data on Cantonese immigrants who came to Hawaii during the late nineteenth century from rural districts in the delta. In 1896, a census revealed that slightly under 50 percent of all Chinese in Hawaii over six years of age were literate; over half the males could read or write in one language, usually Chinese.[69]

Literacy in the Early Twentieth Century

If we compare late nineteenth century estimates from Maritime Customs regional offices with data for the early twentieth century, we find that literacy rates do not seem to have changed markedly from late Ch'ing to Republican times. The Maritime Customs estimated that slightly less than half of all males over school age had received some schooling in the 1880s, while the largest Republican survey, conducted by John L. Buck in the 1930s, showed that 45 percent of all males over the age of seven had received schooling, and that 30 percent were considered literate.[70]

These figures concealed great regional disparities. The *Chinese Recorder,* which sent out questionnaires in 1918 to 127 places in sixteen provinces and Manchuria, using the ability to read the New Testament in Chinese as a criterion of literacy, found that male literacy ranged from 10 percent to almost 100 percent, and that female literacy ranged from zero to 85 percent. In all, the report complained that half the members of Christian churches could not read the New Testament "with ease."[71]

In another survey, when 215 villagers between the ages of nineteen and seventy were questioned near the Kiangsu provincial school of education, over 40 percent had some degree of reading ability.[72] This figure is similar to one for the mid-1930s for 214 villages in Kiangsi, where Kuomintang programs for rural education had been organized in 1934. Here only 21.9 percent of the population was literate.[73] Cornelius Osgood, who studied a Yunnan village in the late 1930s, reported that 22.9 percent of the population over six years of age was literate. This figure included a transient population of boat people who were at the bottom of the socio-economic hierarchy, as well as females. When only the settled village population was counted, 31 percent was literate.[74]

Japanese investigators surveying north China villages in the 1930s and 1940s found that every village had some men who could read and write, but the size of this group ranged from "only a few" up to 80 or 90 percent who could write their names and 30 percent who could read a newspaper.[75] Many writers report the existence of schools, some with a modern curriculum, others teaching traditional lessons. A study of Ten Mile Inn, a poor village in north China, shows that even here, most village boys attended school "during the couple of years when the boy was able to absorb something but was still of little help to his parents."[76] Regional disparities in literacy persisted in China after 1949. Although there

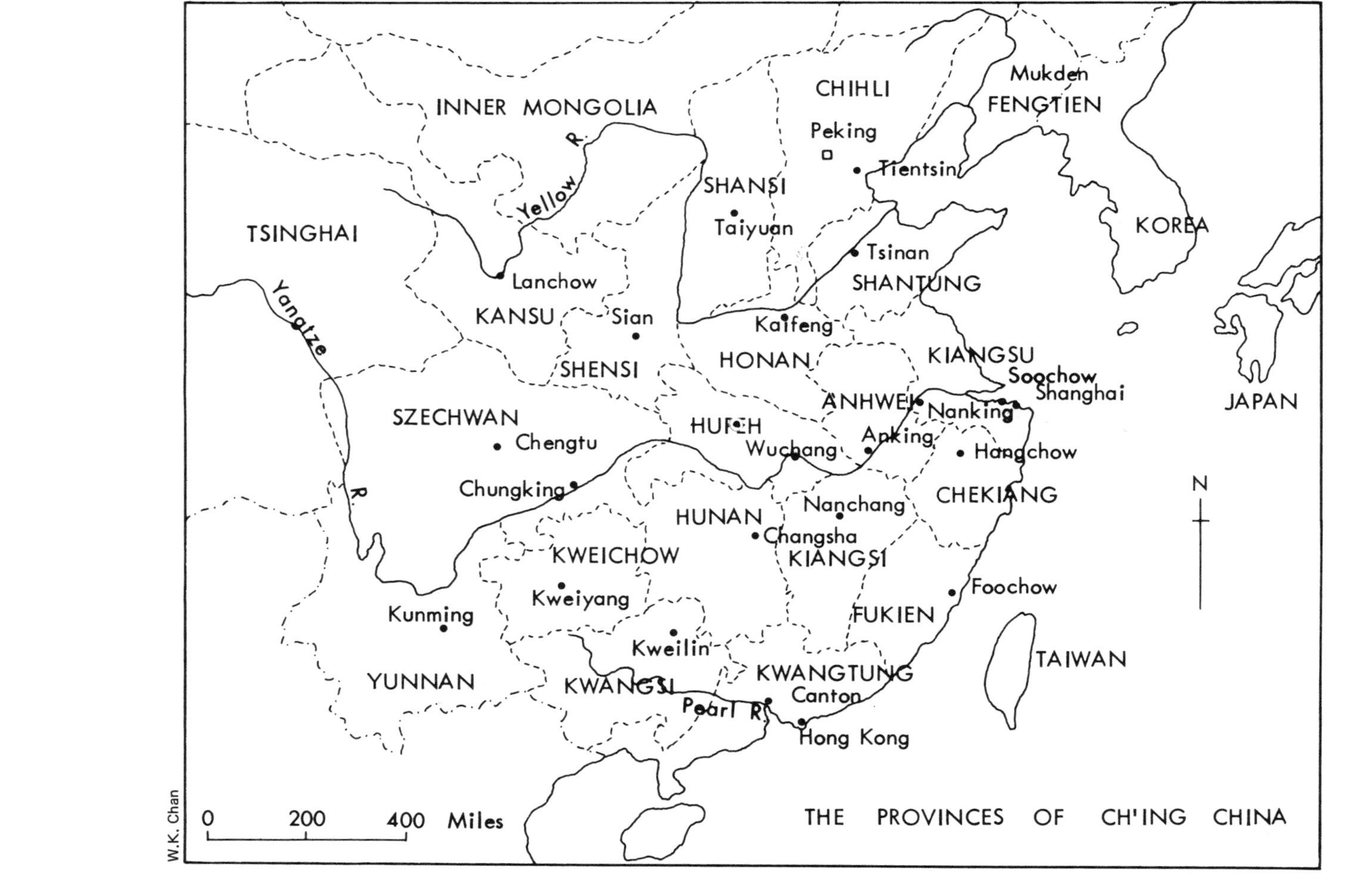
INNER MONGOLIA
CHIHLI
Mukden
FENGTIEN
Peking
Tientsin
Yellow R.
SHANSI
Taiyuan
KOREA
TSINGHAI
Tsinan
SHANTUNG
Lanchow
KANSU
Sian
Kaifeng
Yangtze R.
SHENSI
HONAN
KIANGSU
Soochow
Shanghai
JAPAN
ANHWEI
Nanking
SZECHWAN
HUPEH
Anking
Chengtu
Wuchang
Hangchow
Chungking
N
Nanchang
CHEKIANG
HUNAN
Changsha
KWEICHOW
KIANGSI
Foochow
Kweiyang
Kunming
FUKIEN
Kweilin
TAIWAN
YUNNAN
KWANGSI
KWANGTUNG
Canton
Pearl R.
Hong Kong
W.K. Chan
0
200
400
Miles
THE PROVINCES OF CH'ING CHINA

was 66 percent literacy in Fukien as early as 1952, some areas reported literacy rates as low as 30–40 percent in 1957.[77]

Literacy was closely linked to wealth and occupation. Edgar Snow found that 60–70 percent of First Front Army soldiers were literate in 1936. Even the ordinary soldiers of various warlord armies seem to have had a relatively high rate of literacy, when one considers that they were recruited from the poorest segments of the population. James Yen's study of Fengtien troops in the 1920s shows that 16.6 percent of the soldiers were literate, and T'ao Meng-ho's 1929 study of a Shansi brigade shows a literacy rate of 13 percent. In Ting county, Hopei, in the 1930s, 71 percent of persons engaged in education, government, or military professions were literate; so were 48 percent of merchants, 33 percent of farmers, and 18 percent of manual laborers.[78]

There was also a fairly high literacy rate among urban workers. In 1949, on the eve of the establishment of the People's Republic, 30 percent of workers at Anshan's #1 Sheet Mill and 35 percent of Shenyang workers were literate. In the industrial center, Shanghai, 54 percent of those employed in the city in 1950 were literate, a figure far above the estimated 20–30 percent for China as a whole during this period. Indeed, although basic literacy for adult workers was a major goal in the People's Republic during the 1950s, discussions in educational journals as early as 1951 show that because many workers already knew how to keep accounts and write simple letters, literacy programs had to provide advanced materials to sustain their interest.[79]

Motives for Education

"Profound reverence" for schooling is a trait reported not only in China Proper but among Chinese living in Manchuria, northern Thailand, and other parts of the world.[80] During the Second World War, the first labor hero in Ten Mile Inn was awarded the title of "First Scholar" for increasing the efficiency of manual labor, because this was still the highest honor the villagers knew.[81] This title, customarily reserved for the scholar with the highest marks in the official examinations, exemplifies the primary motivation for education in traditional times, namely that education was the key to prestige, power, and wealth through government service.

Ping-ti Ho and others have written enough about the civil service examinations to make it clear that they were genuinely competitive, requiring strenuous effort and study. Since only a very few were able to obtain degrees, it behooved families to select their brightest sons for the prolonged education that was a prerequisite to sitting for the examinations. Talent could not be identified, however, without exposing a much greater number of young boys to elementary schooling. Students who were not successful in the examinations could still help their families financially by finding careers in other fields, as Ho demonstrates in his case studies of social mobility.[82]

Because education was for so long the key to success in a bureaucratic society, the process of study itself acquired respect, even among villagers. To have his sons in school enhanced a peasant's "face" and his status in the community. To this was added the more practical motive of defending his family from being cheated by others. Ho cites an example of Anhwei agricultural tenants, cheated by a villager over a land deal, who supported a young son through school, "for without an educated man the family could not defend itself against local sharpers in the future."[83] The family of the Red Army leader, Chu Teh, who were Szechwan tenants, sent their sons to school for the same reason: "Since tax collectors, officials, and soldiers respected or were afraid of educated men, my family decided to send one or more sons to school."[84]

Literacy brought other practical advantages. Kiangsu peasants who were asked, "What are the advantages of literacy?" replied, "to keep accounts" (27 percent); "to read and write letters" (26 percent); "to avoid being cheated" (10 percent); only 6 percent replied more generally, "to read newspapers and books."[85] As Martin Yang explains:

> The villagers regard education as a means by which a family can raise its position. Children are taught to read names, to understand the content of land deeds, and to recognize the different kinds of paper money orders so that they will not be cheated in business transactions. . . . Calligraphy, account keeping, the use

> of the abacus, and the learning of the terms for farm implements, domestic utensils and manufactured commodities also held an important place in the curriculum. . . . [86]

This was even more true of families in business or trade. Morton Fried, describing an Anhwei county, writes, "It is the normal procedure for a boy of any commercial or artisan family whose investment and return in business is more than minimal, to be educated formally, though this education rarely continues beyond elementary school or a few grades of middle school."[87]

Recognizing the everyday usefulness of literacy is the key to understanding the motivations underlying popular literacy, not just in the early twentieth century, but in the eighteenth and nineteenth centuries as well. The economic demand for literacy, or the investment demand for literacy, was high, not only in the cities but in the Chinese countryside.

Just as access to markets and cheap transportation separated economically advanced from more backward areas, the economic demand for literacy was stronger in some regions than in others. Peasant resistence to education in the communist-held border regions during the war with Japan, as reported by Peter Seybolt, stands in sharp contrast to the positive attitudes reported above for areas of the lower Yangtze.[88] Such contrasting views toward education, perhaps less marked in the imperial period when regional examination quotas gave backward regions opportunities to compete with central and south China, probably became more evident after the abolition of the examination system and the fall of the dynasty, which gave rise to new power situations and new equations for career advancement, unimpeded by a centralized bureaucracy that allocated status on a regional basis.

Summary

Ch'ing China inherited a means for cheaply reproducing and widely disseminating printed materials, along with a tradition of supporting elementary schools in both rural and urban areas. Fragmentary anecdotal and circumstantial evidence has been cited in this chapter to support the thesis that the extent of functional literacy during the eighteenth and nineteenth centuries was greater than has previously been supposed. Basic literacy was unevenly distributed between males and females, with perhaps 30 to 45 percent of males and only 2 to 10 percent of females possessing some ability to read and write. The distribution of literacy was also affected by location, occupation, and wealth.

Chapters 2, 3, and 4 describe institutionalized alternatives to private tutelage, the clan and charitable schools, which educated children at little or no charge. Chapters 5 and 6 treat the subject of popular literacy from another perspective, first by examining the literature that could be purchased, then the simple glossaries, the *tsa-tzu,* which were available for use as aids in character recognition. Chapter 7 discusses the role of popular literacy in Ch'ing society, and the contribution of literacy to China's modernization. Finally, chapter 8 describes some continuities in elementary education from the traditional period to the present.

Chapter 2

Elementary Education

The Ch'ing dynasty, like its predecessor, the Ming, instituted a state-sponsored hierarchy of schools, which was integrated with the examination system of bureaucratic recruitment. This hierarchy extended from schools at the lowest administrative levels, the county or department, to the Imperial Academy (*Kuo-tzu-chien*) in the capital.[1] The state schools were more a reward for high literacy than a place where one learned, since admission was based on a series of competitive written examinations, which presupposed a thorough knowledge of the Confucian classics.[2]

Their private counterparts, the academies (*shu-yüan*), were never really institutions for elementary education. Instead, as one writer pointed out: "The *shu-yüan* is a place which nurtures talent. All offspring of scholars and the *hsiu-ts'ai* (first degree winners) from among the people study here. But children do not."[3] *Shu-yüan* prepared literate students for the higher degrees. In earlier periods and in some regions during the Ch'ing, they served as nuclei for historically important philosophical schools and political cliques. Again, their significance remains outside the sphere of elementary education.[4]

Privately Financed Education

A broad segment of the Ch'ing population personally financed their children's elementary schooling. Although the most important channel for acquiring basic skills in reading and writing, the private nature of this sector precludes extensive documentation of its size.

We can only estimate, from descriptions of private tutors and schools, the extent of elementary education in this category.

Beginning from the ages of two to five, boys born into the households of degree holders, officials, and wealthy men began learning to read and write at home. Since their parents or relatives were literate, instruction was informal, and sometimes carried out by women. The eighteenth century poet Yüan Mei recalled how his Aunt Shen helped him pronounce words that he did not know, and as noted earlier, mothers are frequently cited in this role.[5] In these early years a boy learned to recognize approximately 2,000 characters, and to write a smaller but significant number, so that by the time he was enrolled in formal studies with a tutor (between the ages of five and seven) he had already passed through elementary schooling.[6]

While boys of elite families typically studied with a private tutor, sons from households in more modest circumstances could be sent to schools run by teachers in their own homes or in nearby temples. Doolittle commented on such schools in nineteenth century Fukien:

> There are numerous primary schools in China, supported by the people of a neighborhood who choose to send their children. There are no school-houses, schools being commonly held in a spare hall or room belonging to a private family, or in a part of the village temple. There is no village tax nor any aid from government received for the support of schools. Each parent must pay the teacher for the instruction of his children.[7]

Sometimes these students were taught by famous scholars. We know, for example, that the philosophers Yüan Yen (1635–1701), and Tai Chen (1722–77) taught in village schools at some point in their careers. Chang Chung-li's biographies of 173 degree-holding scholars mention many who accepted students at home.[8]

Villagers could also get together and invite a teacher to set up classes. That engaging a teacher in this way was a common practice is suggested by the inclusion of contract forms for this purpose in the popular "encyclopedias of daily use," almanac-like compendia that circulated widely in China from late Ming times. In these forms, appropriate spaces were left so that the necessary information regarding specific names, dates, and wages could be filled in. One example reads:

> ___________ persons establishing a school: Now so that our sons and nephews (will) expound books, we cordially invite ___________ (*hao*, surname) in ___________ year to take the teacher's seat on a lucky day, to guide the students, taking care that they seek the good, leading them throughout to achievement and to be grateful for beneficence, to respect virtue without limit. Respectfully, with our names and the salary all stated below.[9]

The enrollment of pupils in such schools varied a great deal, from one or two students up to as many as forty. The ages of students also covered a wide range, from boys six or seven years old to those aged sixteen or eighteen.[10] As Arthur Smith's description of Shantung in the late nineteenth century shows, these schools enrolled boys from peasant families of average means: "This young Confucianist is the bud and prototype of the adult scholar. . . . His brothers are all day in the fields, or learning a trade, or are assistants to someone engaged in business, as the case may be, but *he* is doing nothing, absolutely and literally nothing, but study."[11]

To establish a village school was a goal widely shared in Ch'ing China. Smith observed: "It is far from being the fact that every Chinese village has its school, but it is doubtless true that every village would like to have one. . . . "[12] Schools for village children were found even in pioneering regions like Ch'ing Manchuria, where the Japanese moving into the region in 1905 discovered "*shu-fang*" (schools; literally "study") still holding classes.[13]

The expenses involved in operating a school were not very great. Smith wrote that "renting a place for a school seems to be almost or quite unknown."[14] The student's parents furnished his table and stool, so furniture was not a necessary cost to the school as a unit; moreover, although salaries of private teachers varied considerably, they could be quite low.

Chung-li Chang presents a biography of Li An-li, a native of Kweichow, who received only ten taels in his first year of teaching, and three years later, with eight students, only 24 taels supplemented with food payments.[15] Doolittle found in Fukien that 'literary men who are poor, and who fail of acquiring goverment employment, are frequently glad to teach school at almost a nominal price.''[16] The same phenomenon was noted in Shantung, where ''one of the most honorable of callings is at the same time one of the most ill-paid. . . . the country schoolmaster, who can compete for a situation within a very small area only, is often remunerated with but a mere pittance—an allowance of grain supposed to be adequate for his food, a supply of dried stalks for fuel, and a sum in money frequently not exceeding ten Mexican dollars [approximately 6.6 Haikwan taels] for the year.''[17]

In some areas, village education might be interrupted by poverty:

> The population grows daily. Those who till the soil manage to keep themselves alive with congee and gruel. Even if they have talented sons and younger brothers, they cannot prevent them from losing the chance to attend school. In the private schools a teacher gathers several tens of children and teaches them, in an ancient building. . . . Those who come back in the ninth month (of the lunar year) are no more than 30 to 40 per cent of the original numbers. Owing to the fact that the fees the teacher receives are insufficient to support himself he often has to announce that the school is temporarily closed. This state of affairs may continue for several years.[18]

Village schools were open most of the year, but responded to the agricultural cycle by closing during the busiest harvest season to permit students to help their families in the fields. Kulp observed that the old-fashioned schools in Phenix Village, Kwangtung, had two vacations of a month each, during the summer and the late autumn harvests; and Lillian Li finds that Kiangnan schools closed during the silkworm season when labor demands were at their peak. For those who could not afford to attend year-round schools, there were short-term courses, with fees paid daily instead of monthly or annually, which also provided instruction in reading. The classes held in the villages for farmers' sons during the winter months were one version of such schools.[19]

Privately financed education was thus available to villagers as well as to elite households. Although it was said that ''village children when they reach age nine or more begin to look toward selecting an occupation," the assumption was that "children, unless they are very poor, must go to school."[20] Or, as a seventeenth century writer put it, "In . . . areas of culture, the well-to-do hire teachers for family schools, or the town or village households gather pupils for instruction in elementary schools. . . . thus the children of scholars, farmers, artisans and merchants can all follow a teacher."[21]

The length of schooling a boy received varied with the means of his household. In the early nineteenth century, missionaries reported:

> The better course of common education occupies the student five, six, or seven years; others are continued at their books for three or four years; while some remain only a few months, or at most one or two years. The rich generally give their sons the advantage of a full course. . . . The middling classes, of the better sort, usually give their children every aid in their power. The poor, for the most part, are restricted by their poverty from giving their children any education, or from continuing them in school beyond two or three years.[22]

Boys from families too poor to pay for schooling were not necessarily barred from the classroom: the clan schools and the public charitable schools in Ch'ing China were often established primarily for this group. Such schools therefore marked the lowest boundaries of educational opportunity for poor boys. By studying them, we can gauge the extent of elementary education from yet another perspective.

Clans and Education

Family injunctions articulated a lineage's motives for promoting the education of its members whenever possible. Clan members who passed the civil service examinations and held office brought glory to their clan; they could also help protect lineage interests and the interests of individual kinsmen. In addition, inculcation of family principles and rules of ethical conduct through the education of children ensured the perpetuation of clan unity and strength. The tone of a clan's concern is nicely expressed in the 1880 edition of *Ching-chiang Chang-shih tsung-p'u* (6.7b), which specifies that all children six *sui* and above should be taught to read; between the ages of fifteen and twenty *sui,* their potential could be evaluated and decisions made on their futures. Those with ability are enjoined to prepare for the civil service examinations, but the others are urged to know at least some *li* (ritual) and *i* (principle, morality).

It was therefore in the interest of the clan to encourage the education of its talented members; nor could this responsibility be left to individual parents. Many lineage rules observed that the lack of correlation between birth and talent implied that wise fathers could have stupid sons, or that poor fathers might have bright sons.[23] A few clans established rules for reprimanding and fining parents who refused to pay school fees for bright boys when they could afford to do so.[24] The Hsiangs of Chekiang even stipulated that "those who cannot read the *Classic of Filial Piety,* the *Hsiao-hsüeh* (Elementary primer), the family injunctions, the Four Books, and the family genealogy, will not be permitted to enter the ancestral hall for the rites."[25]

Besides the numerous injunctions encouraging education, many clans provided more concrete support by financing clan schools, and by distributing stipends to students. The most common scholarships were those given to candidates for the civil service degrees; many clan rules show that cash awards were presented to successful degree winners as well as to students sitting for the examinations.[26] Some clans, however, also allotted stipends that either fully covered or partially subsidized elementary education.

The Yaos of Chia-hsing, Chekiang, gave students in their clan school 160 cash a month while in the lower division, and from 200 to 300 cash monthly when they entered the upper division, depending on their stage of study. Even when separate divisions did not exist, some clans distributed stipends according to the subject matter studied. The P'an genealogy stipulated that students first learning characters be granted 1,000 cash a term, those studying the classics 1,500 cash, and those studying composition 2,000 cash.[27]

Lineages that did not give cash often aided students by providing school supplies as well as free tuition. In schools that boarded pupils, meals and gifts of clothing might also be made available. More commonly, clans distributed textbooks, paper, brushes, and ink stones, either uniformly, or as prizes for good conduct and academic performance, as judged on regular tours of inspection. The T'u clan gave each student a book bag, the squared character blocks and books used in elementary instruction, and writing equipment.[28]

Many of these grants and gifts were reserved for students in clan schools, but some lineages gave money to those unable to attend the clan school. The Yaos had regulations providing children in this category with grants that varied in size with the level of study, but could be as high as 10,000 cash a year for students in advanced writing composition. The Fangs of Nanking gave four ounces of silver to children who could not attend their school. Another clan in Ch'ang-shu that awarded three ounces of silver to fatherless boys suggested that those living near the private lineage school study there, while still another clan stipulated that a separate school should not be established. Instead, the parents were to select a teacher; if the boy were fatherless, the choice was to be made by the manager of the clan's charitable estate.[29]

Most of the aid described above was designed to reach the poor, but some clans provided more general educational help. The Tsengs of Hunan awarded grants differentiated according to family wealth: households owning thirty *mou* or less were designated "middle" families and their sons received larger amounts of grain than those in households with more than thirty *mou* of land.[30]

Clan Schools

Unlike other schools within the lineage whose teachers were paid by individual households, clan school costs were met by revenues from corporate property. Held most commonly in part of the ancestral hall or charitable estate building,[31] clan schools were of two types: those open to all boys in the lineage, and those founded especially for the instruction of fatherless boys or the sons of poor households in the lineage. The schools were known by a variety of names, among them *chia-shu* (family school), *tsu-shu* (clan school), and *i-hsüeh*.(charitable school). The available information shows no clear demarcation in purpose between the types of clan schools: *chia-shu* or *i-shu* (charitable school), for example, could denote a school open to any member in one clan or a school intended only for the poor in another.[32]

Most clan schools limited admission to members although the Yao clan, for example, allowed exceptions for the sons of daughters who had married into impoverished clans.[33] The usual age of admission was seven years.[34] In some lineages, instruction was divided between an elementary division (*meng-shu*) for six- to seven-year-olds and an intermediate division (*ching-shu*) for older students. These divisions were flexible, permitting students to be shifted to the appropriate classrooms on the basis of classroom performance. The upper division of the Yao family school was reserved for bright boys over ten *sui;* those under ten *sui,* and slow learners over ten *sui,* were sent to the lower division. Students who became eleven *sui* and showed promise were to be exchanged with slow learners in the upper division.[35]

Classes were generally small. "Since we are only hiring one teacher at present, we cannot have too many students; the number is fixed at ten," stipulates one clan rule. Another, which also limited classes to ten, notes that "if there are too many, the teacher will not be able to look after them all, and the teaching will be ineffectual." The largest class allowed in available clan rules was twenty.[36]

Clan rules emphasized moral character as well as scholarship in selecting a teacher. Some stated that if there were no qualified clan member available, an outsider should be hired: "It will not do to be swayed by favoritism" into hiring a nonentity.[37] Teachers were not given complete independence in the classroom. Clan representatives were appointed to supervise the school and to conduct periodic examinations of pupils. In some clans, these duties fell to the manager of the charitable estate, while in others, they were the responsibility of a specially designated school head or a group of "supervisors of lessons."[38]

Both students and teachers were enjoined to regular attendance at school, which continued throughout most of the year. The school year began in the first month after the New Year festivities, and holidays were given during the important festivals. For example, the Ku family school had three-day holidays for seven festivals during the year.[39] Many schools stressed that, outside of these holidays, students required special permission for absences, which could only be justified by illness or grave family affairs. Students in the Yao family school were boarders and allowed only one visit home a month. Teachers who were absent for more than a few days were expected to find a substitute.[40]

In addition to supporting elementary schools, some clans maintained more advanced schools for students, and tried to identify and promote bright youngsters through the clan school hierarchy. The Fan clan directed students wishing to study classical style (*ku-wen*) to apply for admission to the academy, while the Ma clan had similar provisions for promotion into the ancestral hall school.[41]

Students who did not show academic promise were encouraged to turn to trade or farming. Many clans terminated dull students at age fourteen, but some established more complex rules for households in different financial circumstances. The Hsiangs of Chekiang made decisions on the future of boys from poor families at age twelve, and for youths of rich families, at age nineteen. Another lineage, the T'us of Kiangsu, ruled that those without great academic promise should go out to learn a livelihood after the age of ten.[42] This clan and others provided cash grants to aid those turning to trade or farming. The Fangs of Nanking provided thirty ounces of silver to fatherless youths at this point in life.[43]

Funds for grants, teacher's salaries, school supplies, and the like were taken not only from the rental of school lands but from ritual and charitable land revenues as well. This willingness to spend more on education than strictly earmarked funds would permit reflected the belief that educated clan members were the key to lineage prosperity. The Fans of Soochow directed that ten percent of the revenues from charitable land be set aside to pay for educational grants. The Wus of Kiangsu, who had school lands, noted that other clan income should be used if the school land revenues proved insufficient.[44] Still other clans stipulated that the schoolteacher's salary could be taken from the funds set aside for the ancestral hall.[45]

Charitable Schools: *I-hsüeh* and *She-hsüeh*

Clan schools were usually limited to members; private and village schools required that individual households pay their share. These types of schools thus limited entry, either by kinship ties or by requiring payment of fees. In addition to elementary education of this sort, the eighteenth century witnessed a revival of free public elementary education. From 1652 on, the Ch'ing government encouraged the development of lower level community schools (*she-hsüeh*) and charitable schools (*i-hsüeh*). Neither was new; both were continuations of much earlier institutions.

Government Policies on Elementary Education

Although the history of free public elementary education in China goes back to very early times, the Ch'ing government had to look for precedent only as far as the preceding Ming dynasty, when community schools in particular flourished with government encouragement.[46]

Community schools were established in the Ch'ing dynasty following a government order of 1652 requiring that every rural area set up a school and select persons of "honest and sincere character" to serve as teachers. This order was shortly followed by a decree that envisaged opening schools for non-Han Chinese in frontier areas, and directed local officials to provide the necessary funds.[47] Although civil disorders in many regions must have made it difficult to implement these early directives, subsequent emperors continued to endorse the establishment of free elementary schools within the empire and on the frontier.

Imperial sponsorship of education was consonant with the ideological and practical dimensions of ruling China. On the one hand, such a policy was the outward manifestation of the profound reverence for letters and love of scholarship expected of a Confucian monarch. Added to this was the notion, expressed by the K'ang-hsi Emperor and others, that the best way to influence popular mores was through education.[48] Furthermore, in frontier areas populated by non-Han minorities, schools were a means of assimilation and could be used to dampen potential unrest. Through the early Ch'ing, there was a consistent policy of allocating government funds for elementary schools in frontier regions, while officials within China Proper were usually directed to set up schools without being given funds for this purpose.[49]

The policy of creating schools in frontier regions begun by the Shun-chih Emperor (1644–61) was continued by his successors through the first half of the eighteenth century. The K'ang-hsi Emperor's decrees of 1705 and 1706 creating schools in Kweichow and Yunnan were followed in 1720 by an edict establishing similar schools in frontier areas of Kwangsi. Subsequent decrees from the 1720s through the 1750s not only supported Yunnan and Kweichow schools but extended government-funded elementary schools to frontier regions in Szechwan, Hunan, and eastern Kwangtung.[50]

The elementary school network within the settled parts of the empire was also expanded by a series of imperial decrees. In 1702, the K'ang-hsi Emperor directed that charitable schools be opened outside one of Peking's main gates, at government expense. An order in 1713 that such schools be established throughout the empire was followed by an observation in 1715 that the habits of the common people, glimpsed on the imperial tours, were still coarse; charitable schools should therefore be extended to poor and isolated regions.[51] The concern that schools were concentrated in towns and did not reach rural citizens was echoed by the Yung-cheng Emperor who, in 1723, ordered that all youths between the ages of twelve and twenty who wished to learn should be admitted to school. The same notion, without age limits, was stated by the Ch'ien-lung Emperor (1736–96), who also directed officials to use government funds for school expenditures.[52]

Imperial policy in the early Ch'ing thus promoted the creation of elementary schools for the poor. For their part, civil officials also supported the effort to spread elementary education—as Confucians they shared the emperor's belief in the power of education to accomplish moral transformation. More to the point, without the rudiments of instruction in ethical principles, the common people "do evil things without consciousness" of the import of their actions. Imperial rescripts placed the responsibility for moral education on the district official, but as one magistrate stated, this was a difficult task to carry out.[53] Elementary schools, conveniently dispersed, were one solution to the problem. These schools were often viewed as channels for what Hsiao terms "ideological indoctrination," not just through the recitation of the *Sacred Edicts* at prescribed intervals,[54] but by virtue of the fact that the textbooks used in the schools conveyed Confucian ethical principles.

The literati waxed enthusiastic over the benefits of indoctrinating boys from poor families with the values of filial piety, loyalty, and righteousness: "When a boy understands righteousness he can transform the elders of his household, and can transform a neighborhood."[55] The social effects of education were potentially very great, lending elite promotion of schooling not just the virtue of being in accord with Confucian values, but the hope of generally improving public mores. It is not surprising that degree winners in China supported free elementary schools in both their private and official roles.

Free elementary schools existed under a variety of names in Ch'ing China. Some scholars have argued that *she-hsüeh,* community schools, were different from *i-hsüeh,* charitable schools;[56] but there seems to have been no clear and consistent distinction in the nature of schools bearing these names. The community and charitable schools were not sharply distinguished from one another in the imperial edicts. The Shun-chih Emperor used the term *she-hsüeh,* most of the K'ang-hsi Emperor's pronouncements referred to *i-hsüeh,* and the Yung-cheng and Ch'ien-lung Emperors used both terms in their edicts on the subject.[57]

Data for various provinces in China show that in practice, however, regional distinctions in names did exist. Throughout north and central China during the Ch'ing dynasty, free elementary schools were generally called *i-hsüeh,* but in the southern provinces of Kwangtung, Fukien, Kiangsi, and Chekiang, the same schools were known as *she-hsüeh.* There were also changes in names over time. In north China, as one gazetteer points out: "What the Ming used to call *she-hsüeh* are today's *i-hsüeh.*"[58] The names of the free elementary schools of the Ming dynasty were thus different from those of similar Ch'ing institutions.

Liu Po-chi argues that in Kwangtung, early Ch'ing *i-hsüeh* were more advanced than the elementary *she-hsüeh* and were akin to academies in their educational level.[59] Further variant names for free elementary schools—*i-shu* (charitable school) and *kuan-shu* or *kuan-hsüeh* (official school)—also appear in local records, but the most widely used terms were *she-hsüeh* and *i-hsüeh*.[60]

Students

Despite differences in names, community and charitable schools shared certain characteristics. They were all explicitly devoted to elementary education: the regulations of one school stated that those who had already taken the examinations for the civil service degrees would not be admitted.[61] The detailed regulations on teaching reading, writing, and sometimes arithmetic, assumed that beginning students had received no prior instruction.

Community and charitable schools varied in the range of instruction that they provided. Occasionally, they were divided into an elementary division (*meng-kuan*) and an upper division (*ching-kuan*), but most of the time, beginning and advanced students were taught in one school. In some areas, the educational level of advanced students in the community and charitable schools seems to have been similar to that of students in the academies. A Shansi provincial gazetteer states, for example, that after 1733, when imperial policy shifted to encourage the establishment of academies, charitable schools no longer took advanced students and thus became "merely elementary schools (*meng-shu*)."[62]

The ages of students attending these schools also varied. Although a 1736 decree stated that adults as well as children should be permitted to enroll, and a 1723 edict declared that community schools should educate those between the ages of twelve and twenty, schools usually accepted pupils aged six or seven, and occasionally even younger. One school ruled that young children who required supervision in getting up and going to bed would not be admitted; neither would boys over the age of eleven who had not yet learned to read.[63]

Upper limits on pupils' ages also varied. Some schools chose thirteen or fourteen as the maximum, although poor children would probably have to drop out before then.[64] The rules of one school suggested that by age fifteen, bright students should be pushed into an academy for advanced schooling, while dullards should concentrate on learning how to earn a living. Another recommended that students over nineteen years of age who still could not recite the classics or were truant without permission for three months be expelled. None of the schools provided for students after the age of nineteen or twenty.[65]

Imperial injunctions defining community and charitable schools as facilities for the poor were implemented in many schools. One school regulation warns: "Those with the ability to hire a teacher will not be permitted to force their way in"; another, that "those with parents who can themselves pay will not be admitted."[66] Others expressed the same policy positively; according to one magistrate, the schools were established so that the sons and grandsons of poor people, from generation to generation, could study without spending a cent.[67]

The general principle of free tuition was occasionally modified. Regulations for several schools allowed parents to pay all or as much of the fees as they could afford, while noting that free education was available. One school asked parents to provide only the monetary "presents" customarily bestowed on teachers at special festivals and ceremonies, sums that most schools incorporated into the total salary paid to the teacher.[68] Some schools required that students bring their own benches and desks; others supplied all furniture as well as meals, bedding, and school supplies.[69]

The preceding discussion suggests that most students in community and charitable schools were boys from respectable families of modest means, aged seven to thirteen or so, who received a free, or almost free, education. Despite the general emphasis on open admission, there are some hints of discrimination against the socially outcast groups in Ch'ing society. A charitable school in Shang-jao county, Kiangsi, though noting that all poor boys who were bright and wanted an education could register for admission, added that "children of prostitutes, actors, and lictors will not be admitted." Another school in Hsü-chou, Kiangsu, stipulated that menials such as woodcutters, servants, and others of "low abilities" should not be admitted.[70] The lack of further information makes it difficult to estimate how widespread such discrimination may have been. Even with such restrictions, however, the majority of the poor population was eligible to attend school.

Financing and Management

In the absence of direct government funding, schools were established by local officials, local elite families, and sometimes by guilds and groups of villagers. Detailed studies of school founders show the importance of officials and degree holders in promoting elementary education. More than half of the charitable schools in Shantung from the late seventeenth to the early nineteenth centuries were founded by officials, and information on donors for forty-two charitable schools in Shang-ch'eng, Honan, shows that 65 percent were either officials or lower degree holders.[71]

While data from other sources, presented in table 1, corroborate these findings, they also reveal the important contribution made by people who were neither officials nor degree holders. Some of the "private citizens" listed in the table were villagers of ordinary status. In I county, Anhwei, the households (literally, "massed surnames") founded the local school. One of the schools in Luan-ch'eng, Chihli, opened after three villages petitioned for a school.[72] A third of the charitable schools founded in Ch'ü-wu, Shansi, were built from funds contributed by village residents, and similar examples exist for areas in Hupei, Shantung, and Szechwan.[73] There were also some schools founded by guilds and merchants, and several that were esablished by the famous Wu Hsün, a poor Shantung peasant who ended his life as a benefactor of charitable schools.[74]

The most vital task in establishing a school was to secure the funds needed to allow it to open its doors year after year. Schools were endowed with money, land, and buildings. Details on the costs and sources of school finance are the subject of chapter 3.

When a school was founded, its affairs were put into the hands of a school manager (called *tung-shih, chang-chiao, ssu-hsüeh,* or *ching-li*) selected from the local residents, generally from among

TABLE 1
Founders of Charitable Schools

Place	Number of Schools	Percentage Founded by					Reference
		Officials	Lower Degree Holders	Private Citizens	Other	Unknown	
Lo-ch'ing, Chekiang	21			52.4		47.6	HC, 4.49b–51a
Luan-ch'eng, Chihli	34	61.7		14.7		23.5	HC, 6.17a–19a
T'ang, Chihli	16	100.0					HC, 4.40a–42a
Wen-an, Chihli	6	100.0					HC, 2.36ab
Yeh, Honan	39	56.4	2.6			41.0	HC, 2.11a–16b
Huang-kang, Hupei	17	52.9	23.5		17.6[a]	5.8	HC, reprint 1882 ed., pp. 733–36
Ch'ung-yang, Hupei	29	17.2		34.5	27.6[a]	20.7	*Hupei* TC, 59.55b–56a
Fang, Hupei	7	100.0					Ibid., 59.62b
Ku-ch'eng, Hupei	23	17.4	52.2	13.0	4.3[a]	13.0	Ibid., 59.61b
Lo-t'ien, Hupei	13		46.2	38.5		15.4	Ibid., 59.57b–58a
Nan-chang, Hupei	8	25.0	37.5	25.0		12.5	Ibid., 59.61a
Yun, Hupei	12	16.7	41.7	25.0		16.7	Ibid., 59.62ab
Sung-chiang, Kiangsu	20	20.0	15.0	25.0	25.0[a]	15.0	FC, reprint 1817 ed., pp. 682–714
Chao-ch'eng, Shansi	10	20.0		70.0		10.0	HC, 17.22a–23a
Ch'ü-wu, Shansi	24	25.0		33.3		41.7	HC, 8.28b–29a
Fen-yang, Shansi	9	11.1		77.8		11.1	HC, 3.14ab
Lin-fen, Shansi	8		12.5	75.0		12.5	HC, 5.6ab
Feng-hsiang, Shensi	20	40.0		5.0		55.0	FC, 6.8b–38b
Fu-p'ing, Shensi	10	70.0		30.0			*Shensi* TC, 37.22b
Liu-pa, Shensi	7	28.6	14.3	42.8		14.3	*T'ing-chih,* 4.8ab
Teng-ch'eng, Shensi	19	26.3		73.7			*Shensi* TC, 38.7a
Ch'eng-k'ou, Szechwan	25			100.0			*T'ing-chih,* 10.70a–76a
Ch'ung-ch'ing, Szechwan	138	34.0	2.9	32.6		30.4	FC, 5.6b–15a
Feng-chieh, Szechwan	25		56.0	24.0		20.0	HC, 18.3a–5b

[a]Clan schools.

the elite (*shen-shih*).[75] One school regulation describes the post more precisely: "One must select an upright and well-to-do person who can succor the various charitable schools. The major thing is that the head scholar be one who contributes money in the locality. If he cannot manage it all, then ask one or two men in the village who are honest and upright to do it."[76]

The manager was paid for his services. In one school his term of office was limited to two years, and such a provision may have existed elsewhere as well. He was responsible for everything from hiring the teacher, supervising the curriculum, making periodic inspections of the students, and handling school finances, to greeting and escorting the local official on his tours of inspection.[77] Sometimes the manager's tasks were divided between two people. In other cases, supervisory duties were delegated to the county Confucian school or to the county Sub-Director of Studies.[78] In two Chihli counties, the manager of the local academy also supervised the charitable school.[79]

School Size

When a community or charitable school was established, it was often given a building in which classes could be held. Sometimes, when the magistrate founded a school, he ordered that a school building be erected near the county school or on sites adjacent to academies. Since buildings required expenditures for construction, if not for land purchase, another frequent choice was to use structures already standing. One writer advised: "If we first build the schools, I fear the expenses of building will exhaust the funds and there won't be enough to open the school. It is better first to choose public places in the locality, either the places for rural lectures, or Buddhist nunneries or temples, which have several empty rooms that can be swept out."[80] A Kiangsi gazetteer suggested that founders should "select a quiet place, far from the hustle and bustle. A market street is clamorous and no place for study. In mountain districts there are out of the way places. In the city select the city god temple, the Dragon King temple, and set up a charitable school in each."[81]

In Shantung, almost one-fourth of the charitable schools in the early nineteenth century met in temples. Many Chihli counties housed over half of their elementary schools in this fashion, and information from other areas suggests that this practice was widespread.[82]

The size of school buildings varied according to whether or not they boarded students. Many schools provided lecture halls, book rooms, study rooms, personal living quarters for the teacher, and a kitchen or two. An elementary school in Wu-chou prefecture, Kwangsi, had three lecture halls, twenty study rooms, kitchens, and other rooms, while one in Nanning boasted eight lecture halls, twenty-four studies, and personal living quarters. Elementary schools in Soochow sometimes had twenty, twenty-seven, or even twenty-nine rooms in all, while Shantung charitable schools were said to have about twenty rooms per building.[83]

Most schools were probably much smaller. The average size of forty-three elementary schools in one Honan county was 4.5 rooms; in sixteen schools in a county in Szechwan, it was 5.1 rooms. One Chihli county had schools with three or four rooms each, while another had schools with an average of almost seven rooms each. The size of the building did not always reflect the size of the student body: in six urban charitable schools in a Shansi county, the number of students per room ranged from two to more than six.[84]

Direct information on what amounts to a student-teacher ratio provides a better basis for estimating average class size. Most school regulations stipulated the appropriate size of the class. It was most common to cite upper limits beyond which enrollments should not rise, since a teacher could not effectively instruct more than a certain number of pupils. One school, however, set a minimum, and suggested ways of compensating teachers who taught more than "their share" of students.[85]

There was usually only one teacher, and according to the available figures, presented in table 2, an average of twenty-three students per elementary school. The general range of class size does not seem to have changed markedly over time, or to have differed too greatly from one region to another.

TABLE 2
Students per School

Place (county, province)	Date	Students per School	Number of Schools	Reference
Lin-kuei, Kwangsi	1685	20+	1	*Kuang-hsi* TC, 133.21a
T'ai-chou, Kiangsu	1800	30	2	*T'ai* CC, 8.19ab
Ku-ch'eng, Hupei	1826	20–30[a]	70	*Ku-ch'eng* HC, 3.34b
Cho-chou, Chihli	1830	20[a]	1	*Chi-fu* TC, 114.47b
T'ai-ku, Shansi	1833	20[a]	1	*T'ai-ku* HC, 6.48b
Chih-chiang, Hunan	1837	10–20[a]	10	*Chih-chiang* HC, 1870 ed., 12.35a
Chih-chiang, Hunan		15+	12	Ibid., 12.41a
Kwangtung	ca. 1860s	11–16[a]		Yü Chih, *Te-i lu,* 10.4.5b
Shang-jao, Kiangsi	1867	20[a]	1	*Shang-jao* HC, 7.74b
Yung-ch'ing, Chihli	1872	16	1	*Yung-ch'ing* HC, 14.16b
Tan-t'u, Kiangsu	1873	40	1	*Tan-t'u* HC, 19.44b
Hsü-chou, Kiangsu	1874	10[a]	1	*Hsü-chou* FC, 15.18a
Ch'ü-wu, Shansi	ca. 1880	35[b]	6	*(Hsü-hsiu) Ch'ü-wu* HC, 8.28a
Huang-kang, Hupei	1880	20	6	*Huang-kang* HC, 5.57b
Yen-ch'ing, Chahar	ca. 1881	30[a]	1	*Yen-ch'ing* CC, 4.41a
Chiang-tu, Kiangsu	ca. 1883	30	1	*Chiang-tu* HC, p. 900
T'ang-i, Shantung	1895	20	1	*Wu Hsün li-shih tiao-ch'a chi,* p. 45
Luan-chou, Chihli	1896	15[a]	1	*Luan* CC, 1898 ed., 12.83a

[a]These are fixed limits in enrollment in school regulations.
[b]Average.

Schoolteachers

The selection of a teacher was a most important task. As one school regulation notes, "The charitable school is established to nurture moral transformation, so the business of hiring a teacher is grave." This conviction appears in many discussions on establishing elementary schools: several regulations caution against favoritism in selecting a teacher, since a man in this position could spread great harm. It was believed that the teacher should be a person of moral rectitude as well as a scholar—put more specifically, he must not gamble, get drunk, or stir up trouble.[86]

Elementary schoolteachers were usually chosen from among the local degree holders, particularly *sheng-yüan* (holders of the first examination degree) and *t'ung-sheng* (students eligible to compete in the examination for the *sheng-yüan* degree). As Ping-ti Ho explains, since *sheng-yüan* could not hold office, they had to earn a

living if they were not from wealthy families.[87] Imperial edicts directed that *sheng-yüan* be hired for these teaching posts and that good teachers be rewarded by facilitating their progress to higher degrees.[88] Numerous references to the hiring of *sheng-yüan* in school records, and data summarized in table 23, indicate that this group furnished many local teachers.[89]

A discussion of hiring practices in Ku-ch'eng, Hupei, gives a more detailed picture of the considerations involved. The school manager is first cautioned to look for a strict teacher of good reputation from among the local *sheng-yüan;* if there are no eligible candidates, then the teacher can be selected from the local *t'ung-sheng*. Someone from the locality is preferable: "It does not do to carelessly hire some *t'ung-sheng* from the outside, with no reputation." This is because "the day-to-day character and conduct of a local *sheng-yüan* or *t'ung-sheng* is easily ascertained; he is familiar with local pronunciations, and he will be easily understood by the students. If we take an outsider, there is no way of knowing the details of his character, his speech will be different, and his phrases unclear to the students."[90] Yet another regulation emphasized that the teacher's writing must be in the regular script and his style clear: "It will not do to select an old *t'ung-sheng* who has not sat for the exams for a long time, just to fill the post."[91]

Teachers were hired for one-year periods, and rehired if they performed satisfactorily. Regulations limited the holidays that they could take and many decreed the length of the school day. Performance was evaluated through regular inspection tours by the school manager or educational officials.

The School Calendar

As in the clan schools, classes in the charitable schools began in the first month after the New Year celebrations had ended (somewhere between the fifteenth and twentieth day of the month) and continued, with occasional holidays during the major festivals, until the fifteenth or twentieth day of the twelfth month. Students were not allowed to take extra holidays beyond an allotted number of "home visits," except for weddings, funerals, or personal illness. One regulation stated that it was not permissible to dismiss classes for dramatic performances and similar entertainments. Schools could, however, release students to help in the fields during the peak of the agricultural season.[92] Classes in both clan and charitable schools lasted from dawn to dusk, with a break for lunch. In some schools, students went home for this meal, but in others, it was served at school expense.[93]

The daily class schedule included a great deal of review, recitation, reading, and writing. For one school, regulations state: "For each student create a lesson book, one a month; each day carefully note in it the few characters to be learned, the few lines of text to be learned, the several pages to be reviewed, the few characters in the 'regular style' to be written, and the several pages of text to be explained."[94] The class day began with a review of previous work. New reading lessons were introduced in the mornings when there would also be recitation. Lunch was followed by writing practice and lectures by the teacher, as well as by more reading instruction and review.

Lectures were a means of providing moral instruction. In one school, the teacher was told to expound selected passages from morality books. A teacher should sit at a table where students could gather around to look and listen: children like illustrated books and while delighting in the pictures the moral of the story slips easily into the ear and the mind. In another school, selected daily passages providing moral instruction were then assigned as writing lessons. The teacher took the best written example to paste on the classroom walls.[95]

The School Curriculum

What did students learn in the clan and public elementary schools? And how did they learn? Although the discussion in this section focuses on the acquisition of basic skills in reading, writing, and arithmetic, Chinese education consisted of much more than that. Like most schools, the first lessons concentrated on classroom behavior: "At five or six *sui,* when a child first enters school, have him first learn to sit, to be quiet, to recognize characters; these are the lessons for the youngest in the elementary school."[96] More importantly, the curriculum was infused with heavy emphasis on the ethical principles expressed in ritual observances and written texts.

Ceremonies honoring Confucius, and in some cases, the Neo-Confucian philosopher Chu Hsi, were conducted at regular intervals by the teacher and his students. A permanent tablet could be hung in the classroom for the ceremony, but sometimes a slip of paper was put up.[97] Clan schools occasionally substituted reverence before ancestral tablets for the Confucian ritual. In a charitable clan school for fatherless boys, the ritual, appropriately enough, was conducted at the "chaste widows' hall."[98]

A basic element of the Confucian teaching conveyed in the elementary schools concerned filial piety and proper behavior toward family members. Stories of model filial sons were used along with other tales that furnished concrete rules for ideal deportment. Some schools encouraged parents to report badly behaved children to the schoolteacher for punishment.[99] As Frederick Mote notes, "That the education was authoritarian, inculcated morality, and made surrogate parents of teachers need not be doubted. But neither are those exclusively Chinese characteristics. Has education in traditional, even in modernized societies, not frequently displayed similar characteristics?"[100]

Learning to Write

Unlike boys of elite families who entered school knowing how to read and write, students admitted into elementary schools of the kind considered here were generally assumed to be illiterate. The first lessons in school, learning the elementary skills of literacy, used methods essentially the same as those used in elite households.

Learning to write was more complicated in Chinese than in an alphabetic language. Not only did pupils first have to learn to grind ink, they also had to practice handling a brush, which involved learning the correct positions for the hand, wrist, and elbow with respect to the writing surface.[101] The holding of a brush was demonstrated by the teacher, who would grasp the child's hand and go through the motions of writing. Children first inked over large characters written in red, then traced over them, a pedagogical method that went back to the Sung period.[102] It was at this stage that stroke order was taught. One clan regulation observes that many young students did not hold the brush correctly: "Strokes are upside down, the character is confused, so at the beginning when tracing characters, one must look at the work and correct it."[103] The materials used for tracing seem to have been rhymes made up of simple and commonly used characters.[104]

In the next stage of writing, written models were copied, often on "squared paper," so that the proper proportions of character elements within a given character could be learned. Students were taught to write in the regular style (*k'ai-shu*), generally considered the basic foundation for writing. The number of characters assigned gradually would be increased as students progressed, to perhaps one hundred a day.[105]

In addition to writing on paper, students could practice with a "whiteboard," a method described by Doolittle: "The Chinese have boards of various sizes and thicknesses, painted white, which they often use to write upon. . . . Pupils in schools use such boards, of only about half an inch thick, and six or eight inches long, by three or four inches wide, on which they practice writing Chinese characters . . . or on which the teacher writes characters for them to see or copy."[106] Such boards, found in private houses, offices, shops, and stores, could be readily wiped clean with a wet cloth or paper.

Learning to Read

One method of reading instruction presented children with characters that were pictographs, like those for "sun" and "moon," and progressed gradually to more complex characters and grammatical constructions, but this method does not seem to have been widely used.[107] A more popular method of instruction, which went back to T'ang times, was the use of "square blocks" (*fang-tzu*). Originally, these were small lacquered wooden boards, inscribed with the *Thousand-Character Classic (Ch'ien tzu wen),* with one character per block. The child could learn a few characters a day; the advantage of the blocks was that they could be shuffled, arranged in different sequences, and reviewed as an educational game.[108] In one clan school, the blocks were inscribed with the twenty-four models of filial piety. A common alternative was a book in which the initial characters to be learned were written in ruled squares, with common homophones on the back.[109]

The number of characters that could be absorbed in one day ranged from ten to several tens of characters. Even assuming the lower rate of ten new characters a day, a student progressing through the elementary curriculum could learn 2,000 characters within the first year of school.[110] These characters were learned partly by using the "square blocks" described above, and partly by reading elementary textbooks designed to teach character recognition.

Elementary Texts

Three books dominated elite elementary education from Sung times on: the *Thousand-Character Classic,* the *Trimetrical Classic,* and the *Hundred Names.*[111] The oldest of the trio was the *Thousand-Character Classic,* which was written in the sixth century. It consists of 1,000 characters, organized into couplets of four characters each, with no repetitions. By Ch'ing times, numerous versions of the text were in circulation, all retaining the organization by four-character couplets.[112] The *Trimetrical Classic,* which goes back to Sung times, was also available in many versions. Organized into three-character couplets, it included about 1,200 characters in all. The *Hundred Names* consisted of 400 family surnames, but since some names were more than one character long, the book actually contained over 400 characters.[113]

Put together, these three books—or the "*San-Pai-Ch'ien*" as they were popularly called—provided a student with knowledge of about 2,000 characters (eliminating repetitions), which was the vocabulary acquired by boys from elite families before enrolling in formal studies with a tutor. These books were not very difficult. The *Hundred Names,* merely a list of surnames, posed no problems in understanding. The *Trimetrical Classic* told a story, but the *Thousand-Character Classic* was made up of couplets which frequently bore little relationship one to the other. The primary asset of these books was not a story but the convenient form in which they introduced characters to beginning readers.[114]

The use of what were essentially collections of characters in the beginning phase of the elementary curriculum is explained by one scholar as reflecting the nature of the Chinese language. Without an alphabet, there was no way a child could begin to read immediately; characters had to be learned one by one. In this first stage, emphasis was put on character recognition rather than complete understanding, and interest was a secondary consideration. To begin by teaching character recognition through complete sentences, thus improving the content of early lessons, would expose the child to many repetitions of characters but relatively few characters within a limited time span. At the same time, the content of the materials would have suffered from the restricted reading vocabulary the child had mastered. The use of the *Thousand-Character Classic*, the *Trimetrical Classic*, and the *Hundred Names* made possible a "crash course" for learning a certain number of characters within a short time. The student was then equipped to handle materials where content was important.[115] At the rate of learning ten new characters a day, these three books could be finished in less than a year.

Somewhat similar considerations help explain why the reading and writing lessons were not integrated. Chinese students did not write the characters they used in character recognition lessons, but used other materials that presented very simple characters. The characters in the *San-Pai-Ch'ien* were of varying difficulty, and they were certainly not selected on the basis of their simple construction. Learning to write Chinese was difficult and to expect beginners to write directly from the text of the *San-Pai-Ch'ien* would have made the writing lessons much harder. Moreover, the initial pace of learning to write is slower than the pace that can be achieved in character recognition. At a later stage, progress in these areas, and in explication and understanding, which was not emphasized in the beginning phases, might be reversed.[116] Traditional methods of reading and writing instruction thus recognized certain problems inherent in the nature of the language, and compensated by presenting materials in a sequence that shifted emphasis among the goals of reading, reading comprehension, and writing.

After learning the first 2,000 characters, at age seven or so, a boy in an elite household was enrolled in formal studies under a tutor. He would begin study of the Four Books: the *Analects,* the *Great Learning, Mencius,* and the *Doctrine of the Mean.* These would be followed by the Five Classics: the *Book of Changes,* the *Book of History,* the *Book of Songs,* the *Book of Rites,* and the *Spring and Autumn Annals.* These texts were the heart of a Confucian education.[117]

Elementary schools run for children of the poor varied a great deal in the extent to which they followed the elite curriculum. It was relatively unusual to find schools like the Yün clan school which had boys of seven studying the Four Books.[118] Many schools interposed other elementary texts to supplement or replace the *San-Pai-Ch'ien,* and envisaged instruction in the Four Books and the Five Classics as the very end phase of schooling. In part, this reflected the different clientele of the charitable schools and the different goals of their founders; in part, it reflected widespread practices in Ch'ing education.

The elementary schools taught students who were not usually going on to prepare for the examinations. As one writer pointed out, "Farmers and the poor do not have far-reaching ambitions; they do not expect their sons to do more than several hundred characters and roughly know the meanings."[119] Especially bright students could be pushed into more advanced study, but for the most part these were not classrooms for future degree holders.

As we have pointed out, there was a strong impulse to view schools as convenient and effective channels for ideological indoctrination, but for such purposes the elite curriculum presented some problems. Poor children could not spend the long years of study necessary for the Confucian education which so effectively inculcated Confucian values into the elite.[120] The question was how to transmit Confucian values to the general populace in clear and easily understood terms, within a relatively short time. For this task, the classical texts were inappropriate.

The Four Books and the Five Classics were books of profound

philosophical import, written in difficult language and expressing concepts that children could not be expected to understand. None of these classics was written for children or for specific use as an elementary textbook. It is not surprising, then, that when they were first studied, emphasis was put on memorization rather than on understanding.[121] For those who were concerned with elementary schools as channels for effecting moral improvement, the deficiencies of using the classics as primers were apparent. As one writer observed, "Recently when children enter school, their elders and the teacher instruct them in the Four Books; in talking about *jen, i, hsing-ming, li,* and *yüeh,* the tongue of the lecturer is fatigued and the listeners titter."[122]

Since study of the Four Books was extremely slow, in sharp contrast to the brisk pace at which recognition of the first 2,000 characters was taught, there was a need even in the elite curriculum for texts that would provide simpler readings to review characters already learned, as well as to teach facts and ethical principles. By Ming and Ch'ing times, a wide range of books was available to fill this need—and, unlike the classics, they were generally written in easily understood language, some in the vernacular. Many were organized in rhymed couplets, or in matching paired phrases, which could be chanted and readily memorized. As school regulations in Chih-chiang, Hunan, note: "These books are clear and easily understood so that ignorant people's children can all know the principles in them and adopt these in their conduct."[123]

Such books were often used to modify the elite curriculum. For example, late seventeenth century school regulations from Chihli, after pointing to the importance of moral indoctrination among the young, suggested that a text called *Hsien-hsien hsiao-hsüeh* (Primer of virtuous men from the past) be used, because it was so easy to read and understand. Along with this book, the child studied the *Trimetrical Classic,* the *Thousand-Character Classic,* the *Hsiao-hsüeh* (Elementary primer), and finally the Four Books.[124]

The Ma clan school of Anyang directed that after a student had mastered 1,000 characters, he would study a group of six elementary texts, only one of these being part of the *San-Pai-Ch'ien* trio. After these had been mastered, it was advised that the Four Books be assigned.[125] A set of regulations for public elementary schools in Hupei assigned the *Hsiao-erh yü* (Children's discourse), a popular work presenting proverbs in rhyme, many in the colloquial language; the *Hsiao-hsüeh shih-li* (Confucian primer), another rhymed work; and the *Sacred Edicts* as the beginning texts.[126]

There was considerable divergence in the actual difficulty of the assigned books. Some, like the *Hsiao-hsüeh,* included passages from the classics, using many difficult words; even rhymed versions like the *Hsiao-hsüeh yün-yü* (Rhymed primer) were hard.[127] A work like the *Ti-tzu kuei* (Rules for youths), a popular elementary text cited by several schools, seems to have combined the virtues of conciseness, relatively few characters, and catchy rhymes with easily understood texts.[128] Still other works, not written specifically for children, were the popular morality books that had attracted a wide audience since late Ming times.[129] However written, most books were selected for their ethical content, and were sometimes provided free of charge by officials.[130]

If the need to use "shallow and easily understandable books" to ease the task of moral indoctrination did not always result in the selection of the easiest books,[131] the stress on explanation and repetition must have helped close some of the gaps in understanding. "In elementary education, it is most important to explain; this method avoids learning without comprehension; when [texts] are explained in detail, there will be benefits."[132] This emphasis on reading comprehension was the dominant theme in the schools.

First of all, as one clan regulation pointed out, all books used in the classroom should be punctuated and carefully written so that the characters are clear.[133] It was commonly held that " . . . there are three stages in reading books: to the mind, to the eyes, to the mouth. If it has not reached the mind, then the eyes will not read with care. If the mind and eyes are not together, the recitation will be wild and it will not be retained, or if it is retained, it will not be for long."[134] The teacher was enjoined to make sure that each character was clearly enunciated, and the correct meaning understood: "In all recitations, whenever there is a doubtful point . . . take advantage of the opportunity to look into it. Make sure it is understood before letting it go. If it is not answered at once there is the worry of forgetting. It is best to write it down when it occurs in a book on doubtful points which students can use for explanations."[135]

Repetition was emphasized, with the notion that "one must read it over so many times that it naturally rises to the mouth, and will not be forgotten for a long time."[136] This called for regular review of materials. One regulation notes, "Take care that the readings are thoroughly familiar, the meaning understood. Every morning explain the general meaning, have them [the students] repeat it; after three days have them repeat it again, to see whether or not they remember."[137]

One method used to bridge the gap between the written language (*wen-yen*) and the vernacular (*pai-hua*) was to assign students the task of rendering materials from one style to the other: "It is not necessary that they first compose: merely take one or two simple phrases and cause them to be lengthened or shortened. Take characters which have been taught and have them rendered into the vernacular; or take colloquial sayings and have these put into the literary style. Take *wen-yen* and have it put into colloquial language, or point out an object or incident to write up."[138] By this means, the Four Books and the other classics could more easily be taught to students.

Arithmetic

"Arithmetic is one of the basic six arts which one must know"[139]—this was certainly true for peasants as well as for urban dwellers in Ch'ing China, though few school regulations say anything about teaching arithmetic, and it does not seem to have been generally taught. Regulations for schools in Hsü-chou, Kiangsu, direct that after the initial phase of concentrated character recognition, arithmetic should be introduced: from multiplication, conversion of catties to *liang,* the 9-times-9 tables, up to learning the extraction of square roots. Teachers were recommended to use *Suan-fa ju-men* (Introduction to arithmetic) which "can be understood at a glance."[140] In one clan school, a specialist was called in to teach arithmetic to students who were not bright enough to go on to prepare for the civil service examinations[141]—these were the boys destined for careers in the trades and commerce.

Although Kulp reports that old-fashioned schools in Phenix Village, Kwangtung, gave some instruction on the use of the abacus, this was more commonly reserved for shop apprentices.[142] According to John Burgess, all apprentices in commercial guilds had to learn to use the abacus, keep accounts, and read and write. Ch'ing records of the Peking fabric store *Jui-fu-hsiang* indicate that the first year of a three-year apprenticeship was partially spent learning how to write and use the abacus. The apprentices were supposed to practice on their own during slack periods and at night, under journeymen supervisors.[143] A nineteenth century manual for pawnbrokers also exhorts apprentices to spend every spare moment in study: in their spare time at night, they should take up the abacus and request instruction, for "the abacus is man's [i.e., the pawnbroker's] foundation."[144]

Summary

Ch'ing China provided elementary education through privately financed schooling, clan schooling, and charitable schooling. Education was thus available to a very broad cross-section of the Ch'ing male population, from those who could afford to pay to those from poor families. Provisions in some charitable school regulations directing that parents in slightly better economic conditions contribute to school fees, and descriptions of village schools paid for by private persons, suggest that there was a range of schools, from the free school on up.

A small minority of outcast groups was barred from entering the free schools. As for the children of peasants who could not spare their labor from the fields, the opportunity cost of keeping a seven- or eight-year-old child from field work was quite low, and short-term classes, held in the winter season, furnished learning opportunities for even these children.

What the average child could learn at a free school is also pertinent for evaluating this elementary educational system. Despite a highly moralistic bias, instruction concentrated on reading and writing. As many as 2,000 characters might be acquired as a reading vocabulary within a year, and a start made on writing characters. Boys who went to school for two or three years were thus equipped to read and write simple materials.

Chapter 3

Costs in Institutional Education

Chapter 2 described the clan and charitable schools, which were intended to provide instruction for poor boys. This chapter studies the cost of founding such schools, an important element in analyzing their availability and geographic distribution, the topic of chapter 4.

Private individuals could consider the costs of hiring a tutor an annual and temporary expenditure, but most charitable schools had to be endowed to ensure that they could provide a free education on a permanent basis. The endowment was necessary to finance a teacher's salary, a manager's salary, and the funds to maintain a school building. This chapter investigates costs of institutional education, modes of investment, and sources of funds. From the standpoint of cost and financing, it was possible for every part of Ch'ing China, including rural areas, to have charitable schools.

Teachers' Salaries

The largest expense for both the clan and the charitable school, claiming from 50 to 100 percent of the annual budget, was the teacher's salary;[1] this was the irreducible minimum cost involved in running a school. Funds for buildings and maintenance, salaries for managers and servants, meal provisions, books, and even furniture could be omitted if necessary; but without a teacher, the school could not open its doors.

The traditional relationship between teacher and student was one of the most sacrosanct in the Confucian world, and education in Confucian ethics included learning the proper modes of respect toward one's teacher. This respect was expressed in daily ceremonies at the beginning and end of classes: "Every morning when the scholar enters the room, he bows first before the tablet [of Confucius] and then to his teacher."[2]

A more concrete expression of this feeling was accomplished by the presentation of "gifts." By Ch'ing times, a teacher received monetary offerings at the beginning and end of the school term, and "mat," "wine," or "food" cash, along with other gifts during major festivals throughout the school year. In the T'u clan school, established in 1856, the teacher received a basic sum of 30,000 cash for the year. In addition, he was given 400 cash as an opening school gift, 1,000 cash "mat" gift, 700 cash apiece for three festivals, and a closing school and "mat" gift of 1,000 cash—resulting in a total salary of 34,500 cash for the year.[3] Regulations for the Ku clan, printed in 1894, list a basic sum of 40,000 cash, supplemented with a food allowance (24,000 cash), and opening and closing ceremony cash (2,000), bringing the total salary up to 66,000 cash for the year.[4]

The extra monetary gifts in these examples amounted to 13 percent of the teacher's total salary in the T'u clan school and 39 percent in the Ku clan school. Similar supplementary payments made by public charitable schools in Anhwei, Shansi, and Chihli provinces constituted from 9 to 25 percent of the total salary.[5] Some schools did not separately itemize these "gifts," but simply lumped everything together into an annual payment. When free room and board were provided, the actual value of the salaries received exceeded the cash payments.[6]

Most schools paid teachers in grain or money, although in the seventeenth century a few gave them fields to cultivate as recompense for their services.[7] The available information on teachers' salaries, presented in table 3, shows that payments in grain were limited to the seventeenth century, when economic conditions were generally unsettled, or to isolated regions. Grain payments do not appear in the Yangtze delta except in the early Ch'ing, whereas they persisted in Shang-ch'eng, Honan, an area which was "amidst the myriads of mountains, spread over more than two hundred li, where carts do not pass and merchants do not come."[8] The Shensi and Szechwan areas that paid salaries in grain were in the Han River highlands, a relatively remote area that attracted large numbers of migrants in the eighteenth century. Yung-sui, Feng-huang, and Chih-chiang, which after 1800 paid salaries exclusively in grain, were located in western Hunan, a frontier region partly inhabited by non-Han Chinese groups.[9]

TABLE 3
Elementary Teachers' Salaries in Ch'ing China, by Province

Place	Date	Number of Schools	Salary: Grain (*shih*)	Salary: Cash (x1,000)	Salary: Silver (in taels)	Reference
Anhwei						
Huai-ning	1671	1	36.0[a]			TC, 70.6a
	1714	6			36.0	Ibid.
She	1821–50	3			38.9	HC, 2.10b
Chekiang						
Chia-hsing	1880s	1		60.0		Taga, "Shinmatsu kakyo," p. 118, n. 26
Chihli						
T'ung-chou	1701	4			24.0	CC, 1873 ed., 5.21ab
Tientsin	1729–31	2			60.0	FC, 35.11b
Huo-lu	1736	2			12.0	HC, 1736 ed., 6.11b
Shu-lu	1757	1		20.0		HC, 1799 ed., 5.64b
Ch'ang-yüan	1810	3			12.0	HC, 6.18a
Wu-ch'iang	1831	1			24.0	HC, 5.14a
Pao-an	1835	5			24.0	CC, 3.21a
Luan-ch'eng	1836	1		30.0[b]		HC, 1872 ed., 6.11b–12a
	1839	4		30.0		HC, 1846 ed., 3.19b
Ching-hai	1870	1		60.0		TC, 115.49ab
Ts'ang-chou	1880	1		78.0[c]		*T'ien-chin* FC, 35.31b
Huo-lu	1881	5			48.0	HC, 1881 ed., 8.49b
Ting-hsing	1881	1		60.0		HC, p. 102
Nan-pi	1882	1		110.0		HC, 4.34a
Ts'ang-chou	1886	1		68.0[c]		*T'ien-chin* FC, 35.32a
Luan chou	1896	1		96.0[d]		CC, 12.82b
Honan						
Shang-ch'eng	1802	12	33.1			All Shang-ch'eng data from HC, 6.18b–25b
	1802	3			24.0	
	1802	6	24.5	6.75		
	1802	22	21.6		8.6	
An-yang	1886	1		50.0		Taga, *Sōfu no kenkyū*, p. 584
Kuang-chou	1887	2		80.0		CC, 1.27b
Hunan						
Feng-huang	1704	6			16.0	*T'ing-chih*, 11.50b–51a
Pao-ching	1730	4			16.0	HC, 4.9b

TABLE 3 (*cont.*)

Place	Date	Number of Schools	Salary: Grain (*shih*)	Salary: Cash (x1,000)	Salary: Silver (in taels)	Reference
Hunan (cont.)						
Yung-sui	1733	12			16.0	*T'ing-chih,* 2.12a
Kan-chou	1738	1			40.0	*T'ing-chih,* 4.69b–70a
	1738–41	6			16.0	Ibid.
Yung-sui	1800	7	24.0			*T'ing-chih,* 2.12a
	1807	13	16.0			Ibid.
Feng-huang	1807	25	16–24			*T'ing-chih,* 11.50ab
Chih-chiang	1837	22	40.0			HC, 12.35a, 41a
Hupei						
Ch'ang-lo	1735–45	4			16.0	*I-ch'ang* FC, 6.15b–16b
Hao-feng	1754	2			24.0	Ibid.
Ch'ung-yang	19th c.	2			22.0	HC, 4.51b
	19th c.	6		32.0		Ibid., 4.52a
Huang-kang	1880	6		44.0[e]		HC, 5.57b
Wu-ch'ang	1884	6			18.0	TC, 59.53ab
Kiangsi						
Shang-jao	1867	1	50.0			HC, 7.75a.
Kiangsu						
Wu clan sch.	1648	1	15–17			*Wu-shih chih-p'u,* 12.9a.
Sung-chiang	1744	1			60.0	FC, p. 682.
T'u clan sch.	1856	1		34.5		Taga, "Shinmatsu kakyo," p. 120, n. 32
Tan-t'u	1866–9	6		58.3		HC, 19.43a–44b
Ku clan sch.	1894	1		68.0		Ogawa, "Chūgoku zokujuku," p. 543
Li clan sch.	1894	1		60–80		Chung-li Chang, *Income of the Chinese Gentry,* pp. 100–101
Kwangsi						
Lo-ch'eng	1737	2			12.0	TC, 166.15a.
Lai-pin	1766	1			10.0	Ibid., 166.16a
I-shan	pre-1800	1			20.0	Ibid., 166.17a
Lin-kuei	pre-1800	11			24.0	Ibid., 166.13b
Wu-lu	pre-1800	1			16.0	Ibid., 166.17ab
Kweichow						
All schools	1740				20.0	*Hsüeh-cheng ch'uan-shu,* 64.7b
Shansi						
T'ai-p'ing	1699	1			8.0	HC, 1725 ed., 2.45a
	1775	1			20.0	HC, 1775 ed., 2.13b
T'ai-ku	1833	1			44.0	HC, 6.48a
Shantung						
Ch'ang-ch'ing	1821–50	1			5.0	Nakamura, "Shindai Santō nōson
Lin-i	1821–50	1			10.0	no gigaku," p. 33
T'ai-an	1821–50	1			30.0	(for all 3 items)

TABLE 3 (*cont.*)

Place	Date	Number of Schools	Salary: Grain (*shih*)	Cash (x1,000)	Silver (in taels)	Reference
Shensi						
Chiao-i t'ing		1			20.0	TC, 37.3b
Lüeh-yang	1833	27		12.0		HC, 2.32a
Ting-yüan	1866	1	11.0			HC, 11.30a
	ca. 1879	2		30.5		Ibid., 11.30b–31a
Mien	ca. 1883	1		24.0		HC, pp. 142–143
Ning-ch'iang	ca. 1888	4	7.0			HC, 2.20ab
Szechwan						
An-yüeh	1783	1			80.0	TC, 79.34a
Ch'iu-chou	1801	4			24.0	CC, 9.30b–31a; TC, 79.39a
Shih-chu chou	1803	1		30.0		TC, 79.46b
Ta-i	ca. 1816	4			12.0	TC, 79.39b; HC, 9.33ab
Ch'ien-chiang	1821–50	1		30.0		HC, 3.51a
Ch'eng-k'ou	1827	1	20.5[a]			*T'ing-chih,* 10.72a
	1827	4		32.2[f]		Ibid., 10.71a–75a
	1827	12			33.8	Ibid.
	1840	1		48.0[f]		Ibid.
Feng-chieh	ca. 1893	6			30.0	HC, 18.3a–5b
Manchuria						
Ninguta	ca. 1690	1			15–30	R. Lee, *The Manchurian Frontier,* p. 88

[a]In unhusked rice.
[b]Unless otherwise stated, copper cash figures are in *chih-ch'ien.* This figure is marked *ta-ch'ien,* but since big cash did not exist until the 1853–61 period, it is taken here to mean *chih-ch'ien* as opposed to *chung-ch'ien* which was the normal system in Chihli: see Frank H. H. King, *Money and Monetary Policy in China* (Cambridge, Mass., 1965), p. 65, 245.
[c]Originally in *ching-ch'ien* (metropolitan cash), converted to *chih-ch'ien* at rate of 2:1 (see ibid., pp. 58–61).
[d]Originally in *tung-ch'ien* (eastern cash) converted to *chih-ch'ien* at rate of 6.25:1. See ibid.
[e]Computed from montly salary, assuming school year of eleven months.
[f]Originally in maize, converted at 300 cash per *tou: Ch'eng-k'ou t'ing-chih,* 6.14ab.

In frontier regions like Kweichow and Kwangsi, teachers were paid in silver (unlike the remote areas mentioned above) because the schools were officially funded. Some areas with large minority populations offered higher salaries: for example, teachers in western Hunan schools dominated by minority students received higher salaries than those teaching in areas of Han Chinese settlement.[10]

Rural-Urban and Other Variables in Teachers' Salaries

Data in table 3 suggest that salaries were higher in the cities than in the countryside.[11] One would expect that since the supply of literates who formed the pool of potential teachers was greater in urban than in rural settings, lower wages would have prevailed in cities. But the higher cost of food and housing in cities might offset this downward pressure on urban teacher salaries; that urban salaries were instead higher appears to reflect qualitative differences in teaching personnel. Urban schools could choose more highly educated or better qualified teachers, who could command greater salaries than unemployed literati in the countryside.

In 1738, schools in Kan-chou, Hunan, paid forty taels to a teacher in the city school and sixteen taels to teachers in the rural schools. A school that opened in 1754 outside Hao-feng's south gate paid thirty-two taels, while a rural school founded in the same year offered a salary of only sixteen taels. A similar comparison of rural and urban Shantung salaries is weakened by the fact that the rural salary comes from one district, Ch'ang-ch'ing, and the urban salaries from the other two areas in the province. The possibility that these salaries reflected regional differences is strengthened when the two urban salaries are compared: they show a greater contrast than the data from Ch'ang-ch'ing and Lin-i. The case of Luan-ch'eng, Chihli, also suggests that rural-urban differentials did not always exist: here the city school, founded in 1836, provided a salary of 30,000 cash, the same amount paid by rural schools founded in the county just three years later.

Salaries could also vary according to a location's rank in the central place hierarchy. Table 3 shows a salary of sixty taels for two city schools in Tientsin, Chihli, in 1729–31, and a much lower salary of twelve taels for two schools in the Huo-lu county seat about six years later. These differences, related to the size and importance of the urban places in question, are also evident in other parts of China: in Tan-t'u, Kiangsu, teachers' salaries in the late nineteenth century ranged from 30,000 cash at schools in market towns to 100,000 cash in one school located just outside the west gate of the county seat.

Table 3 also shows that the differences in salary levels among regions was as great, if not greater, than the salary differences between town and country in a given region. A comparison of urban school salaries in Kan-chou, Hunan (in 1738), and Huo-lu, Chihli (in 1736), shows that in Hunan, salaries inflated by a government policy that used elementary schools as a means of assimilating non-Han minorities were three times greater than those for Chihli. The Sung-chiang, Kiangsu, salary in 1744 was 1.5 times higher than the Hao-feng, Hupei, urban school salary a decade later.

There were thus three factors affecting teachers' salaries: urban-rural location, rank in the central place hierarchy, and a region's economic status in China as a whole. Although there may have been some cases where free housing and meals added substantially to the salaries listed in table 3, these sums usually represent total payments to teachers. Table 4 examines teachers' salaries over the eighteenth and nineteenth centuries. Despite a gradual rise in salaries, a comparison of salary trends with price movements in the same period, as shown in figure 1, indicates that there was no increase in real salaries. While salaries did not respond as quickly as prices to changing economic conditions, and seem to have resisted the sharp downward fluctuations shown in price movements, their behavior roughly parallels long-term price trends.

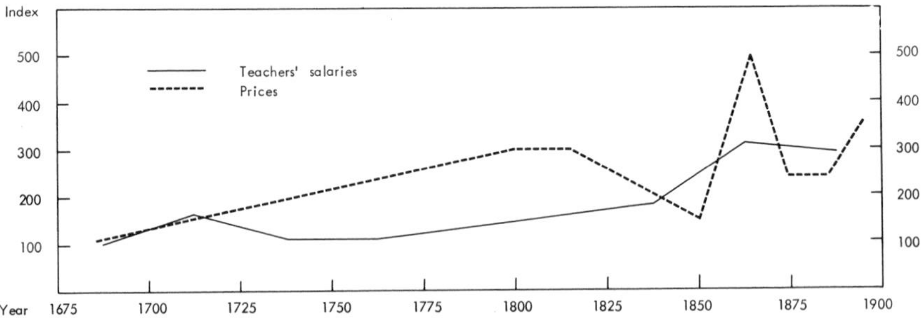

Fig. 1. Long-term behavior of teachers' salaries and prices, 1675–1900. (*Sources:* Median teachers' salaries from table 3, with 1675–1700 = 100. Prices from Yeh-chien Wang, "The Secular Trend of Prices during the Ch'ing Period [1644–1911]" [Chinese University of Hong Kong] *Journal of the Institute of Chinese Studies* 5.2 [1972]:361, table 6. Wang's index is based on 1682 = 100.)

TABLE 4
Changes in Teachers' Salaries, 1675–1900

Period	Salary (in taels)						Number of Items	Median (in taels)
	Less than 10	10–19	20–29	30–39	40–49	50+		
1675–1700	1		1				2	15.0
1700–1725		6	4	6			16	24.0
1725–1750		30			1	3	34	16.0
1750–1775		1	2				3	16.0
1775–1800			2			1	3	20.0
1800–1825		7	7	1			15	24.0
1825–1850	1	34	26	2			63	27.0
1850–1875				4		4	8	47.3
1875–1900		6	2	6	12	11	37	44.0

Sources: All salary items presented in table 3 that were dated and given in money were used for this table, the cash salaries being converted to silver at 1,000 cash = 1 tael.

Other Salaries

Some schools reported information on salaries paid to school managers, while others do not seem to have made any provision in their budgets for this post. One school in Yen-ch'ing, a county beyond the Great Wall in what is now Hopei province, paid its manager thirty strings of cash, or about one-third the teacher's salary. Another in Jung county, Kwangsi, lists a salary of twenty-six taels of silver for a manager in 1690, but omits information for teachers' salaries.[12] Similar information from Liu Po-chi's study of Kwangtung academies indicates that a manager's salary was slightly less than half the salary for lecturers, and this may also have been true for elementary schools.[13] In clan schools, the school manager was often also the manager of the charitable estate and paid from estate funds rather than out of the school budget. Paid managers, thus, probably received from one-third to one-half the amount offered to teachers—but many schools did not pay managers.

Wages for servants are rarely found in school budgets, and many schools probably employed none. One school in Ts'ang-chou, Chihli, paid study attendants 12,500 cash each, a sum that represented 18.4 percent of the teacher's salary.[14]

Building and Maintenance

Although the cost of buying a schoolhouse varied considerably from region to region and over the course of the eighteenth and nineteenth centuries, everyone agreed that it was expensive. In the Soochow area, a magistrate buying a house for a school in 1743 spent 518.7 taels of silver, a sum equivalent to 30 to 50 percent of his annual *yang-lien* (salary supplement). Much of the cost was undoubtedly linked to the high price of urban real estate: in 1746, the purchase of a house in the city of Soochow cost 800 taels, as opposed to only 226 taels needed to renovate a temple in the nearby town of P'ing-wang chen the same year.[15]

Soochow, in one of the most highly urbanized parts of eighteenth century China, was at one end of the spectrum; Ch'eng-k'ou county, in the mountainous northeastern part of Szechwan province, occupied a position close to the opposite pole. In Ch'eng-k'ou, the purchase of a three-room house for a school in 1827 cost 63,900 cash, a sum only slightly higher than the cost, 56,300 cash, of renovating a building of the same size in the area that year. Although these sums seem modest when compared to building expenditures in Soochow eighty years earlier, the relative burden, considering the wealth of the two regions, was equally heavy. For example, a Ch'eng-k'ou charitable school spent 170,000 cash, or 42.5 percent of its total funds, to purchase a thirteen-room building in 1832;[16] this can be compared with the 1743 Soochow purchase cited earlier, which used up 50.8 percent of the school's total funds.

Building costs were high everywhere. In T'ai-ku, Shansi, when a building used for elementary classes collapsed, the cost of rebuilding it in 1833 came to over 430,000 cash, a sum more than eight times the annual income of the school. Similarly, the 1867 purchase and renovation of a house in Ching-hai, a county seat near Tientsin, cost over 38 percent of the school's total endowment. In Huang-kang, Hupei, where the magistrate donated funds to repair and convert buildings in 1830, the cost was twice the annual income of the school.[17] If school founders decided to buy or erect a special building for classes, they were thus adding considerably to the capital required. The cases cited above show that these costs ranged from one-third to over one-half the total funds possessed by a school. Renting a house was cheaper, but still not negligible in cost: rents in Tan-t'u, Kiangsu, totalled 20,000 cash a year, or 20 percent of the school's annual income.[18] Maintenance expenses came to about 10 percent of the annual income for some schools.

Since purchase and rental were both expensive, many schools chose to hold classes in public buildings. Clan schools, of course, had ready-made facilities in ancestral halls; occasionally, public elementary schools were also permitted to use an ancestral hall for classes.[19] Temples of various kinds—Buddhist and Taoist temples, the city god temple, or the military temple, which stood conveniently dispersed around the rural landscape—were used by many charitable schools. When floods or other disasters destroyed the building, the school usually closed—unless a new fund drive gathered enough money to rebuild.[20]

Stipends and Supplies

Student stipends, when given, added considerably to a school's expenditures. The Yao clan of Chekiang, for example, provided students in the lower division with 160 cash a month, and upper division students with 200–300 cash a month. For a normal class of eight to ten students in the lower division, students' stipends over the year amounted to a sum that was from 23.5 to 29.3 percent of the amount paid to the teacher, while expenditures on upper division stipends were equivalent to 20.6 percent of the teacher's salary.[21]

Clan schools were not alone in spending large sums on student grants. A charitable school in Ta-i, Szechwan, set aside a sum equal to 75 percent of the teacher's salary for student stipends.[22] Other schools awarded prizes: in Lo-ch'eng, Kwangsi, a fund equivalent to 41 percent of the teacher's salary was set aside for this purpose.[23] Even when no cash payments were made, stipends could take the form of free meals:

> It is best to determine provisions according to locality. If there are ample funds, then students themselves can eat in school, two meals a day. It is best to practice economy; each month give meat three times. If there are people who won't eat fat, intestines and stomach, give them the money [equivalent]. If there are students who wish to take the pork home to present to their parents, since this reveals filial intent, let them suit themselves. The schoolteacher and manager should eat together. In their diet one should also not prevent frugality. If finances are insufficient the students definitely cannot stay for meals, but the schoolteacher and manager are not also prevented from eating.[24]

Some clan schools provided congee with pastries or vegetables only at certain points in the school year—during the long summer days or in the cold winter months. The menu could be trimmed or expanded as finances permitted.[25]

The cost of free meals varied a great deal. A poor character in the eighteenth century novel *The Scholars* subsists in Nanking on eight cash a day, which buys only four "cakes of unleavened bread."[26] On the other hand, in the 1760s, a Buddhist vegetarian sect in Chekiang with hostels for boatmen charged the sailors only four cash a day for food. In Canton, about 1834, the cost of a meal of rice and greens was estimated at less than three cash per person, while a more elaborate meal cost twenty cash.[27] A class of twenty-three students and their teacher could thus dine for perhaps 72 cash a meal, or 21,600 cash a year, assuming that they were given only one meal a day during the school term. While well-to-do schools could afford expenditures on this scale, most schools could not. And, with late nineteenth century inflation, the cost of providing free meals rose greatly: an 1870s charitable school regulation alloted 60 to 70 copper cash a day per person for food.[28]

Chapter 2 described how concern for ethical instruction motivated officials and school founders to provide textbooks free of charge. School supplies were also sometimes distributed as prizes, either out of charitable estate funds in the case of clan schools, or from prize funds in other schools. Furniture was not included in school budgets, although part of the reason may have been that clan schools, which were more likely to supply benches and tables, probably drew on charitable estates for this purpose.

In addition to regional differences and intertemporal changes, a school's operating costs thus depended on the condition and ownership of its buildings, whether or not managers and servants were employed, and the presence or absence of stipends in the form of cash payments, free meals, or prizes. Schools purchasing or building their own classrooms required from 40 to 50 percent more funds than those using public buildings. Those with paid managers added 33 to 48 percent to their wage bills. If servants were hired, operating costs were further increased. Finally, stipends in the form of cash or kind could also add substantially to the annual expenditures. Since these frills could be eliminated, however, the only essential cost linked with founding a school was the teacher's salary.

Fiscal Resources

Another way of looking at the cost of institutional schooling is to examine the available information on school holdings and resources. Table 5 presents information on the annual income of various charitable schools, and related information on total school endowments is provided in table 6. Both tables show regional differences in wealth. When the annual incomes of Kiangsu schools are compared with teachers' salaries found there, it is clear that these schools operated well above the margin of existence. The annual income of Chen-tse's school, 114 taels in the mid-eighteenth century, for example, was almost double the teacher's salary of 60 taels for the same period; and while salaries throughout Kiangsu ranged from 34,000 to 58,000 cash in 1850–70, annual school incomes ranged from 63,000 to 600,000 cash.

Modes of Finance

The relationship of income to endowment was determined by the form in which a school held its resources. Although these could be extremely varied,[29] four basic modes of financial management can be identified: investment in school lands and urban real estate, investment of capital at fixed rates of interest, and regular government payments. Table 7 presents information on the relative importance of these categories of school financing. The government support considered in this table is limited to direct annual commitments to pay school costs. The table excludes instances of villagers paying school expenses.

In almost all parts of China, schools relied heavily on landholdings as a means of perpetuating corporate wealth and obtaining fixed annual incomes. Although urban rentals were negligible as a source of revenue for most schools, cash investments and government funding assumed considerable importance for some areas. Cash deposits with pawnbrokers and merchants were made not just in highly urbanized regions but also in remote sections of the Han River highlands such as Ting-yüan, Shensi; and Ch'eng-k'ou, Szechwan.

School Lands

The institution of permanent endowments in the form of land stretches far back into Chinese history, and the Ch'ing use of land-

TABLE 5
Annual Incomes of Charitable Schools, by Province

Place	Date	Number of Schools	Annual Income: Cash (x1,000)	Annual Income: Silver (in taels)	Reference
Chihli					
Hsüan-hua	1757	1		20.0	TC, 116.76a
Shu-lu	1757	1	20.0		TC, 114.95b
Shu-lu	1799	1		36.0	HC, 1799 ed., p. 594
Ts'ang-chou	1828	1	75.0		*Ch'ung-hsiu T'ien-chin* FC, 35.31a
Ching-hai	1870	1	60.0		TC, 115.49ab
Yung-ch'ing	1874	2	77.5–113.4[a]		HC, 14.16a–18b
T'ung-chou	1879	1		75.0–150.0	CC, 5.25a
Ts'ang-chou	1880	1	156.8		*Ch'ung-hsiu T'ien-chin* FC, 35.31b
Chü-lu	1886	1	15.0–17.0		HC, 4.47a
Ching-hai	1891–3	10	57.2[b]		*Ch'ung-hsiu T'ien-chin* FC, 35.18a–20b
Hunan					
Liu-yang	ca.1873	1	30.0[c]		HC, 8.24b
Kiangsu					
Chen-tse	1746	1		114.0	HC, p. 313
T'ai-chou	1800–18	4		117.5	CC, 8.19ab
Tung-t'ai	1817	1		200.0	HC, p. 528
Shanghai	1843	1	97.5		*Chinese Repository* 15 (1846):426
T'ung-shan	1821–50	10	63.4–82.4		HC, p. 929
T'ung-shan	1855	1	72.0		Ibid.
P'ei	1866	1	600.0		*Hsü-chou* FC, 15.11b
Shanghai	1868	9	81.3		*Shanghai hsien hsü-chih,* pp. 653–57
Wu-hsi, Chin-kuei	1866–1900	3	60.0		HC, pp. 117–18
Shansi					
T'ai-yüan	1865	4		50.0	TC, 76.34b
Shantung					
Tsou-p'ing	1795–1820	1		47.0	Nakamura Jihei, "Shindai Santō nōson no gigaku," p. 33 (for all 5 items)
Chi-ning	1821–50	1		19.0	
Lin-i	1821–50	1		30.0	
Hui-min	1821–50	1		50.0	
T'ai-an	1821–50	1		100.0	
Shensi					
Ning-ch'iang	early 19th c.	4	32.5		CC, 2.20ab
Mien	1877	1	24.0		HC, pp. 142–143
Ting-yüan	ca. 1879	2	30.0,60.0[d]		HC, p. 464
Szechwan					
Sui-ning	1743	1		27.0	TC, 79.33a
Pa chou	1762	1		50.0	TC, 79.13a
An-yüeh	ca. 1783	1		80.0	TC, 79.34a
Ch'eng-k'ou	1844	1	14.4		*T'ing-chih,* 10.75a
Pa	ca. 1867	1		51.5	HC, 2.40b

[a]higher sum for urban school, other for rural school.
[b]converted from *chin-ch'ien* (Tientsin cash) to *chih-ch'ien* at ratio of 2:1 (Frank H. H. King, *Money and Monetary Policy in China,* p. 61). All copper cash entries are in *chih-ch'ien.*
[c]strings of cash.
[d]lower sum for lower division, higher sum for upper division.

TABLE 6
Total Charitable School Endowment, by Province

Place	Date	Number of Schools	Total Endowment: Cash (x1,000)	Total Endowment: Silver (in taels)	Reference
Chihli					
Hsüan-hua	1757	4		100.0	TC, 116.76a
Shu-lu	1799	1		200.0	HC, p. 594
Cho chou	1831	2	225.0[a]		TC, 114.47b
Nan-kung	ca. 1831	7		328.5	HC, 3.33a–34a
Ching-hai	1870	1		260–270	TC, 115.49ab
T'ung chou	1882–3	5		600.0	CC, 5.25a
Honan					
I-yang	1828	36	300.0[a]		HC, 5.9b
Kiangsu					
Wu-chiang	1732	1		300.0	*Su-chou* FC, 1824 ed., 25.37a
Chen-tse	1746	1		950.0	HC, p. 313
Ju-kao	1774	1		760.0	HC, 1873 ed., p. 749
Ju-kao	1816	1	1600.0+[a]		Ibid.
Wu	1819	1	550.0		*Su-chou* FC, 1824 ed., 25.24b–25a
T'ung-shan	1821–50	10	500–650.0		HC, p. 929
Shensi					
Ning-ch'iang	early 19th c.	4	193.7[a]		CC, 2.20ab
Tzu-yang	1824, 1833	6	200.0[a]		HC, 2.5a
Mien	1877	1		80.0	HC, pp. 142–43
Szechwan					
Ch'eng-k'ou	1827–40	19	303.4[a]		*T'ing-chih,* 10.70a–76a

[a]Strings of cash. All cash in *chih-ch'ien*.

TABLE 7
Modes of Finance of Elementary Schools

Place	Date	Number of Schools	Percent with Primary Income from[a]				
			Land	Urban Rent	Cash Invest.	Govt. Funds	Unknown
Chihli							
1. Luan-ch'eng	1838	18	77.8	0	0	22.2	0
2. Ching-hai	19th c.	16	0	0	6.2	62.5	31.2
3. Ts'ang-chou	19th c.	6	25.0	0	41.7	33.3	16.7
Honan							
4. Shang-ch'eng	1803	43	93.0	0	0	6.9	0
5. Yeh	19th c.	39	97.4	0	0	0	2.6
Hunan							
6. Liu-yang	ca. 1873	28	71.4	0	3.6	0	25.0
Hupei							
7. I-ch'ang	18th c.	7	7.1	0	0	78.5	14.3
8. Ku-ch'eng	1826	19	31.6	15.8	52.6	0	0
9. Lo-t'ien	ca. 1876	22	100.0	0	0	0	0
10. Huang-kang	ca. 1882	17	47.0	0	11.8	35.3	5.9
Kiangsi							
11. Wu-ning	19th c.	24	87.5	4.2	8.3	0	0
Kiangsu							
12. Feng-hsien	19th c.	8	87.5	0	0	0	12.5
13. Hua-t'ing	1854–55	15	33.3	0	0	40.0	6.6
14. Ju-kao	1863–72	7	14.2	0	42.9	0	42.9
15. Ch'ing-p'u[b]	to 1871	16	43.7	0	0	37.5	6.2
16. Tan-t'u[b]	to 1874	11	0	0	0	27.3	27.3
17. K'un-shan	1868–77	7	85.7	0	0	0	14.3
18. Wu-hsi, Chin-kuei	to 1871	20	60.0	0	5.0	20.0	15.0
Shansi							
19. Ch'ü-wu[b]	18th c.?	24	4.1	0	0	29.2	33.3
Shensi							
20. Ting-yüan[b]	19th c.	23	21.7	0	17.4	21.7	34.8
Szechwan							
21. Ch'eng-k'ou	1827–40	25	50.0	0	50.0	0	0

Sources:
1. *Luan-ch'eng* HC, 6.18a–19a.
2. *Ch'ung-hsiu T'ien-chin* FC, 35.18a–20b.
3. Ibid., 35.30b–32a.
4. *Shang-ch'eng* HC, 6.4b–25b.
5. *Yeh* HC, 2.11b–16b.
6. *Liu-yang* HC, 8.25ab.
7. *I-ch'ang* FC, 6.15b–16b.
8. *Ku-ch'eng* HC, 3.39b–42a.
9. *Lo-t'ien* HC, 4.46b–47b.
10. *Huang-kang* HC, pp. 733–36.
11. *Wu-ning* HC, 16.29a–36b.
12. *Feng-hsien* HC, pp. 343–49.
13. *Ch'ung-hsiu Hua-t'ing* HC, pp. 409–12.
14. *Ju-kao hsü* HC, pp. 181–83.
15. *Ch'ing-p'u* HC, pp. 709–19.
16. *Tan-t'u* HC, pp. 354–55.
17. *K'un-Hsin liang-hsien hsü hsiu ho-chih,* pp. 81–82.
18. *Wu-hsi, Chin-kuei* HC, pp. 117–18.
19. *Hsü hsiu Ch'ü-wu* HC, 8.28a–29a.
20. *Ting-yüan* HC, 11.29a–31b.
21. *Ch'eng-k'ou t'ing-chih,* 10.70a–75a.

[a]Schools receiving more than half their income from a given source; if exactly half the income was received from each of two sources, the school was divided into two half-shares for the computation.

[b]In these cases, there was an additional source of financing: in Kiangsu, financing by charitable foundations, in Shansi, annual funding by villagers, and in Shensi, funding by clans was involved.

holdings to finance schools was very traditional. School lands, like other corporate property, differed from privately owned plots in that they could not be sold freely. This was a great advantage for those seeking to provide a stable fiscal base, since it made dissolution of a school's assets more difficult. And, of course, land could not disappear into commercial bankruptcy. As one magistrate wrote, "Concerned that if we put out the funds to merchants and collected interest, it could not be maintained in the long run, we therefore purchased top quality land and invited tenants to till it."[30] School lands might disappear through gradual encroachment by tenants, or through floods,[31] but most investors regarded land as more safe, stable, and enduring than cash investments.

Schools obtained land through donations from private citizens and from officials, who transferred confiscated plots, untaxed lands, or temple holdings to schools in their jurisdiction. The lands were rented out to tenants; rents, after taxes,[32] were paid either in kind or converted into money, which was then used for salaries and other expenses.

Clan schools in general were better endowed with lands: take, for example, the difference in landholdings between charitable schools and clan schools in Liu-yang, Hunan, where the average holding for the 89 percent of charitable schools with land was 45.3 *mou,* as compared with the 1,000 *mou* average for the 63 percent of clan schools whose landholdings were listed. In Wu-hsi and Chin-kuei counties, Kiangsu, average holdings for the 36 percent of public schools with land was 59.5 *mou,* while clan schools, 72 percent of which owned land, possessed an average of 331.5 *mou.*[33]

As noted in chapter 2, still other clan schools drew funds from the clan charitable lands (*i-t'ien*) and occasionally from the revenues of ritual lands (*chi-t'ien*). These were rich resources: the average charitable landholding for forty-eight clans in Wu-hsi and Chin-kuei was 654.7 *mou,* or almost double the holdings of clan schools in the same area. Even in the deflationary 1850s, these holdings represented a cash income of 573 taels a year.[34]

Table 8 presents information on school lands in Kiangsu province. When clan schools are excluded from the calculations, we find that the average holding was 65.1 *mou.* In the 1870s, this represented a cash income of 97.97 taels a year, or approximately

TABLE 8
Size of Average Landholdings for Schools in Kiangsu

Place (county)	Date	Schools with Land: Number	Percentage of all Schools	Average Holding (*mou*)	Reference
Wu-hsi, Chin-kuei					
public schools	19th c.	4	36.4	59.5	*Wu-hsi, Chin-kuei* HC, pp. 117–18
clan schools	19th c.	8	72.7	331.5	
Ch'ing-p'u	1850–71	8	50.0	39.5	*Ch'ing-p'u* HC, pp. 709–19
Feng-hsien	1836, 1870	7	87.0	98.9	*Feng-hsien* HC, pp. 343–49
Hua-t'ing	1850–73	5	33.3	97.8	*Ch'ung-hsiu Hua-t'ing* HC, pp. 409–12
Ju-kao	1863–72	2	28.6	17.5	*Ju-kao hsü* HC, pp. 181–83
K'un-shan, Hsin-yang	1868–77	6	60.0	52.3	*K'un-Hsin liang-hsien hsü-hsiu ho-chih*, pp. 81–82

96,206 cash per school, assuming a rent paid in rice that was converted to cash.[35] This figure compared with information in table 5 on incomes shows that schools endowed with land tended to be more prosperous, even in Kiangsu. Holdings of this size could easily pay the salaries noted in table 3, and do not represent the minimal holdings needed to sustain a charitable school. In order to pay the salaries listed in table 3, for example, only 25 to 28 *mou* would have been required by the Wu clan in the seventeenth century;[36] to pay a salary of 60 taels in the mid-eighteenth century, 50 to 53.6 *mou* would have been needed;[37] and, in the period 1866–69, due to the high price for rice, less than 39 *mou* would have yielded enough rents to pay a salary of 58,300 cash.[38]

Schools with access to the rice markets of the lower Yangtze could obtain relatively high prices for their rice. This meant that high incomes could be gained from fairly small landholdings. Even in less urbanized regions, however, landholdings of modest size were able to support schools. In Shang-ch'eng, Honan, forty of the forty-three schools established in 1802 were endowed with land, although only twelve paid for all school expenses out of land rents. The average holding for these twelve schools was 22.9 *mou*.[39] Although most of the parcels were either donated or transferred from temple or untaxed lands to the schools, two of the land purchases noted cost 5.56 and 9.30 taels per *mou*. If these prices are applied to the average holding cited above, from 127.3 to 213 taels of silver were required to establish a charitable school based on landholdings in Shang-ch'eng during this period.

TABLE 9
Average Landholdings for Charitable Schools in Chihli

Place (county)	Date	Schools with Land: Number	Schools with Land: Percentage of all Schools	Schools with Land: Average Holding (*mou*)	Reference
Man-ch'eng	1660s	16	100	49.9	*Chi-fu* TC, 114.68ab
Li	1680s	38	100	47.9	Ibid., 114.87b–88b
Kao-ch'eng	1703–19	5	23	47.0	Ibid., 115.91a
Wan	1707	6	60	55.0	Ibid., 114.84b–85a
T'ang	1715	14	100	11.5	*T'ang* HC, 4.40b–42a
Tung-kuang	1715	7	100	98.6	*Chi-fu* TC, 115.40a
Chi-chou	1661–1721	6	67	44.2	Ibid., 117.21b–22a
Yüan-shih	18th c.	4	57	44.4	Ibid., 115.84a
Ta-ming	18th c.	10	77	78.1	*HC,* 16.6b
Shu-lu	pre-1799	15	100	36.2	*Shu-lu* HC, 1799 ed., pp. 798–800
An-su		9	90	33.7	*Chi-fu* TC, 114.71b–72a
Nan-kung	pre-1831	15	100	37.9	Ibid., 117.25b
Tsao-ch'iang	pre-1803	14	100	33.3	*Tsao-ch'iang* HC, 10.23b
Tsao-ch'iang	pre-1850	25	100	31.4	*Chi-fu* TC, 117.32b–33a
Jao-yang		8	57	40.9	Ibid., 117.64b–65a
Luan-ch'eng	1820–50	15	83	38.1	*Luan-ch'eng* HC, 6.18a–19a
T'ien-chin (fu)	1871	10	37	51.0	*Chi-fu* TC, 115.46a
Yung-ch'ing	18th–19th c.	3	100	476.7	Ibid., 114.21ab
Ting-hsing	17th–19th c.	14	73	151.2	*Ting-hsing* HC, pp. 98–103

Table 9 presents information on landholdings in Chihli schools. Here the average landholding was 55 *mou*. Cash rents, which varied widely according to the quality and location of land, determined the minimal holdings required to endow a school. In Yung-ch'ing, for example, untaxed wasteland given to the charitable school in 1874 yielded an average rent of only 240 cash per *mou,* while rents of 714 cash per *mou* were being collected in Ts'ang-chou, a district near the city of Tientsin, in 1880, and 1,500 to 2,000 cash per *mou* in Ting-hsing, a county near Yung-ch'ing, in 1873.[40]

Teachers' salaries also varied: in Ting-hsing, they received 60,000 cash in 1873; and in Ts'ang-chou, 78,000 cash in 1880. The minimal landholdings that would yield enough revenue to pay these salaries were 30 *mou* in Ting-hsing, but 109 *mou* in Ts'ang-chou. In Ts'ang-chou, the cost of 109 *mou* would have been 374.9 taels.[41] At

Yung-ch'ing rents, at least 250 *mou* were needed to pay a salary of 60,000 cash, and 325 *mou* to pay a salary of 78,000 cash. This seems to fall within the range of total endowments per school recorded for late nineteenth century Chihli in table 6, but table 5 indicates that charitable schools in other areas of the province, including Ching-hai, a county near Tientsin, and Chü-lü, in the southwest, did not have annual incomes on this level.

Despite average holdings of 55 *mou,* early nineteenth century schools in many parts of Chihli could survive financially with the income from 30 to 35 *mou*. This can be compared with Nakamura Jihei's estimate that city schools in Shantung required at least 10, and rural schools at least 20 *mou* of land to pay teachers' salaries in the period 1821–50, despite larger average holdings of 79 to 97 *mou*.[42]

Investment in Real Estate

Purchases of stores or houses to establish a source of income for schools were expensive and the rents derived from urban properties relatively low; this may help explain why income from urban real estate played a minor role in financing schools. Low rents were noted by foreigners: one writer in the 1830s calculated that the poorest Cantonese paid rents of 150 to 714 cash a month.[43] This agrees with information on rents in Tung-t'ai, Kiangsu, where a four-room house in the rice market fetched .21 taels (about 210 cash) a month in the early nineteenth century. In late nineteenth century Tientsin, the net income from fifty-eight rented rooms came to only .47 taels a room for the year.[44]

Investment of Capital

Investment of funds with shops, pawnbrokers, and merchants was a very popular method of financing schools. As table 10 shows, monthly interest rates varied between .8 and 2.45 percent, resulting in annual rates of return of 10 to 33 percent. The rates tended to be lower than the maximum, indicating that schools chose security over maximizing returns.[45] Indeed, fear of possible bankruptcy was the major constraint against this means of endowing schools.[46]

TABLE 10
Returns on Invested Capital for Schools, by Province

Place	Date	Interest Rate per Month (in percent)	Reference
Chahar			
Yen-ch'ing chou	ca. 1881	1.5	*Yen-ch'ing* CC, 4.40a
Chihli			
Hsüan-hua	1757	1.6	*Chi-fu* TC, 116.76a
Shu-lu	pre-1762	1.4	*Shu-lu* HC, 1762 ed., p. 594
Ts'ang-chou	1820	1.65	*Ch'ung-hsiu T'ien-chin* FC, 35.31a
	1880	1.6	Ibid.
T'ung-chou	1882–83	1.2	*T'ung* CC, 5.25a
Ching-hai	ca. 1891	1.0	*Ch'ung-hsiu T'ien-chin* FC, 35.20a
Honan			
Shang-ch'eng	1803	1.0	*Shang-ch'eng* HC, 6.18b.
I-yang	1828	1.0	*I-yang* HC, 5.9b.
Kiangsu			
Chen-tse	1746	1.0	*Chen-tse* HC, p. 313.
Wu-chin	early 19th c.	0.8	*Wu-chin, Yang-hu* HC, 3.9b–10b; 5.7a–8b.
Kwangtung			
Canton	early 19th c.	1.0	Hunter, "*Fan Kwae*", pp. 39–40; rate on running account with the best security
Shantung			
General average,	18th c.–1850	1.0	Nakamura Jihei, "Shindai Santō no shoin to tentō," *Tōhōgaku* 11(1955):100–109
Shensi			
Mien	1877	2.45	*Mien* HC, pp. 142–43
Ning-ch'iang	ca. 1888	1.3	*Ning-ch'iang* HC, 2.20ab
Szechwan			
Ch'eng-k'ou	1827	1.8	*Ch'eng-k'ou t'ing-chih,* 10.75a

Government Aid

Official aid for financing charitable schools extended from direct personal contributions from magistrates and other local officials to allocations of funds from provincial and county treasuries. Funds could be collected from local market taxes or from resources earmarked for Confucian schools. Indirectly, officials also aided schools by granting requests to transfer property from temples or by donating confiscated lands and untaxed lands to local charitable schools.[47] Official aid to charitable schools could be put on a regular annual basis, covering all or part of the school expenses. When given in the form of land or a cash gift, it could either partially or totally provide for a school's permanent endowment. As table 1 shows, officials played a major role in founding schools, and it is therefore not surprising to find that government aid in the form of direct subsidies (see table 7) was also an important element in school finance.

Rates of Return

Information on rates of return from investments in land, urban real estate, and commerce can help us evaluate the form in which school endowments were held. Yang Lien-sheng presents information on varied rates of return from an early nineteenth century Hunanese source, which shows that the annual rate of return on land was 6.4 percent, as compared with a rate of 10.5 to 11 percent on store rentals and 15 to 18 percent on deposits with a silversmith. Yang concludes that the rate of return from land was the lowest and the rate of return from commerce the highest among investment alternatives open to Chinese of the period. Of course, the greater security of land balanced higher returns from commerce.[48]

In Tsao-ch'iang and Ts'ang-chou, Chihli, annual rates of return in the late nineteenth century were 6.25 and 12.9 percent, respectively; some schools in Ch'eng-k'ou, Szechwan, obtained returns of 10.2 to 21.4 percent on purchases of "mountain land" in 1827.[49] Late nineteenth and early twentieth century figures comparing values of annual output and land show similar rates of return for parts of Chihli and Kiangsu provinces.[50]

In the same period, slightly higher returns could be obtained from deposits with pawnshops or merchants. The annual rate of return on such deposits in late nineteenth century Ts'ang-chou, Chihli, was 21 percent at a time when returns from land were 12.9 percent. In Ch'eng-k'ou, cash endowments provided returns of 23.9 percent (see table 10), as compared with 10.2–21.4 percent from land.

Differing local rates of return from land and commercial investments significantly affected the sums that schools required as a permanent endowment. Land endowment in late nineteenth century Ts'ang-chou would have cost a minimum of 374.9 taels, as compared with 232.7 for a cash endowment for commercial investment. In Shang-ch'eng, Honan, endowing a school with land in 1802 cost 159 to 408 taels of silver, while endowing the same school with cash for investment would have cost 189.3 taels.[51] Areas in Ch'eng-k'ou getting returns of 21.4 percent from land did not have to raise substantially more money than was needed to obtain the same income from deposits with pawnshops, but those getting only 10.2 percent returns would certainly have had to do so.[52] A survey of comparable information on rates of return shows that while returns from land ranged from 6.2 to 21.4 percent, returns from deposits with pawnshops yielded 10 to 30 percent a year. Higher rates of return were balanced by greater risk, but, in general, schools paid a significant cost in preferring land as a mode of school endowment.

Minimum Costs

In view of the regional variance in school endowments, what can be said about the minimum required to establish a charitable school? Schools sometimes closed down because of insufficient funds. In 1755, the magistrate of Liu-an chou, Anhwei, tried to revive a charitable school in the town, but the effort lasted only ten years due to financial troubles. A subsequent reopening of the school in 1772 failed within two years for the same reason, and it was not until 1824 that the school was successfully reestablished on an adequate financial base.[53]

When the magistrate of I-yang, Honan, established thirty-six schools in 1828, he provided 300 strings of cash as capital for each school, with the proviso that deficits would be made up. In fact, many of these schools failed to survive for lack of sufficient funds.[54] Here is a precise measure of the minimum endowment required in I-yang at the time: the annual income of 36 strings, derived from an investment of 300 strings of cash, enabled some schools to break even while others could not.

Table 6 shows that in 1831, schools in Shensi province and Cho-chou, Chihli, required much smaller endowments than I-yang schools at almost the same time. In Ch'eng-k'ou, Szechwan, schools were founded with only slightly more than 300 strings of cash each between 1827 and 1840. Schools in Shang-ch'eng, Honan, founded twenty-six years earlier than I-yang's, required less than 300 strings of cash per school.[55] Indeed, schools in Cho-chou each generated enough surplus with an endowment of 225 strings of cash to start a third school a few years later.[56]

Considerable regional variation in the amount needed to keep a school operating can be expected when the principal cost, the teacher's salary, varied so greatly. The rise of salaries in money terms, particularly in the second half of the nineteenth century, combined with declining rates of return in landed and commercial investment to raise the sums required to endow charitable schools. According to Chung-li Chang, rates of return on landed investment declined from 10 percent a year in the late eighteenth century to less than 2 percent in some areas a century later.[57] Information on school (and other) lands in the nineteenth century suggests that the latter figure may be an underestimate, but even if the overall decline in rates of return were less drastic, the real cost of endowing a school with land probably increased. Funds deposited in pawnshops also faced declining returns, as average monthly interest rates fell during the eighteenth and nineteenth centuries;[58] this also raised the endowments needed to open a school.

Smaller endowments were needed to found rural schools because teachers' salaries were lower in the countryside than in the cities; and, because interest rates on cash investments were higher in rural and less developed economic regions, these areas were also sometimes favored with higher rates of return. This situation is revealed not only in the rates presented in table 10, which were highest in economically backward parts of Shensi and Szechwan, but in the urban rates charged by the Shansi banks in the early nineteenth century, which were as low as .4 to .5 percent a month.[59] In the same vein, the highest rates of return were obtained not from prosperous rice paddies but from mountain slopes in Ch'eng-k'ou, Szechwan, where marginal lands had been brought into cultivation.

This does not imply that raising funds was easier in rural areas than in cities. Teachers' salaries might be considerably higher in cities, but cities were also more prosperous. As one commentator explained, "In the rural areas, collecting funds is especially difficult, and cannot be compared with the provincial capital. There may be two or three wealthy households, but they differ in virtue. The virtuous will do all they can to contribute, while the benighted ones will largely be on guard to tighten the purse strings; they view their wealth as their life."[60] Because of the relative concentration of well-to-do families in cities and towns, the lower endowments needed for schools in rural areas might have been at times more difficult to raise than the higher amounts necessary for urban schools. On a national scale, similar contrasts could be drawn between the richer lower Yangtze and coastal areas with large numbers of wealthy households on the one hand, and the poorer northwest and extreme southwest regions. These are the same contrasts that produced marked regional differentiation in social mobility, as noted by P. T. Ho.[61]

Elite and official participation could modify the bias produced by regional and rural-urban differences in wealth. On the one hand, urban residents were sometimes solicited for funds to support rural schools,[62] and on the other, government aid and official sponsorship were important factors in the founding of many schools. As noted earlier, frontier regions in the eighteenth century received community and charitable schools at government expense. Elsewhere, magistrates and other officials donated large sums of money, allocated annual subsidies from government coffers, or otherwise provided the necessary school endowments. Perhaps the most outstanding example of the impact a vigorous official could have on a region's education is Ch'en Hung-mou's successful founding of over 650 charitable schools while financial commissioner of Yunnan province (1733–37).[63]

Another element that ameliorated rural fund-raising efforts was the wide range of participation in founding schools. At one extreme, there were gifts of several hundred *mou* or hundreds of taels from one donor, but there were also land gifts as small as half a *mou*. Villagers also banded together to provide the necessary funds for schools, as shown by examples from Hupei, Shantung, Shansi, and Szechwan.[64] And degree holders who gave donations were not always well-to-do: in Shang-ch'eng, a *sui-kung-sheng* (annual tribute student; a degree holder) who donated a house for the school was compensated "because of the poverty of the family."[65] Yet another solution to the problem of raising funds was a nineteenth century proposal to establish short-term charitable schools, with a curriculum to cover two months' instruction rather than the normal school year of ten to eleven months, and requiring only ten strings of cash to pay expenses.[66] There is no indication that schools with this type of schedule were numerous, although it was a common practice in privately financed education.

Conclusion

The endowments required to found charitable schools were fairly modest. In most parts of China through the eighteenth and nineteenth centuries, schools endowed with land survived on less than fifty *mou,* and some managed with considerably less land. Not only was it possible to accumulate school land through small contributions, but the total required was not very large when compared with the estimated average gentry holding of 150 *mou.*[67]

Declining rates of return and concomitant increases in required endowments during the nineteenth century do not seem to have taxed the ability to found schools to any significant degree. This can be illustrated by examining required endowments for commercial investment, which as we have noted, rose from less than a hundred taels in the early eighteenth century to 346.5 taels by the period 1865–1900. The relatively modest size of even the latter sum is revealed by comparing it with the 12,200 taels raised annually to support a local defense corps in Kuei-yang, Hunan,[68] or the "several hundred taels" spent on dramatic performances during the annual local religious festivals;[69] the latter sum was little more than 1 percent of the estimated annual income of district and departmental magistrates, who often helped finance schools.[70] From the standpoint of cost and financing, it was thus possible for even poor rural areas in China to have charitable schools.

Chapter 4

The Availability of Elementary Education

> . . . despite distinctions in size, all schools have the same significance for molding people. Talent flourishes under prosperity. According to county records, formerly when lists of successful candidates placing first or second on the examinations were posted, those from towns were numerous, but few from the country were on it. This does not stem from differences in ability, but truly depends on whether or not teaching has reached a place.
>
> —*Wen-an* HC, 1703 ed., 2.36b

This chapter investigates the availability of elementary education in late Ch'ing China. It begins with a study of institutional facilities for education. As pointed out in chapter 2, charitable, community, and clan schools served limited populations: the first two were designed to educate the poor, while the latter usually reached only lineage members. Chapter 4 will show that the number of charitable and community schools increased over the eighteenth and nineteenth centuries, although their growth did not keep pace with population expansion during this period. Clan schools must also have served as important institutions for education, especially in central and south China. Despite problems with sources of information for clan schools—a difficulty that will be treated in this chapter—and inadequate information on lineage distribution, the probable impact of clan schools merits discussion.

The second part of this chapter focuses on privately financed education. Neither clan nor charitable schools were intended to replace privately financed schooling, which throughout the period constituted the most important channel for acquiring literacy. Although we have no quantitative information for China as a whole, local records for three south Chihli areas in the late nineteenth century (discussed in appendix 2) show that an extensive network of private schools covered the rural as well as the urban landscape. In these areas, private schools—together with the less numerous charitable schools—provided sufficient facilities to teach basic literacy to between one-third and one-half the males of school age.

Indirect evidence must be used to assess the importance of private schooling in other parts of China. Information on the supply of potential teachers provides a means of estimating the size of this sector by establishing its upper limits. A comparison of the number of potential teachers with the estimated number of boys of school age shows that there were enough teachers available to educate far more than the 30–45 percent of the eligible male population suggested by late nineteenth and early twentieth century estimates of school attendance. Data concerning incomes from employment other than teaching for *sheng-yüan, t'ung-sheng,* and *chien-sheng,* and evidence of the humble occupations that many of them pursued, not only support the statistical conclusion that the supply of available teachers was very large, but suggest that there was, if anything, an oversupply. The modest incomes of private teachers leads to a look at comparative incomes to determine what groups in Ch'ing society could afford tuition fees for their sons. The results of this analysis clearly support anecdotal evidence that opportunities for schooling were present for a sizable portion of the Ch'ing population.

Sources of Information

Local gazetteers, the major sources of information for charitable schools, vary widely in quality and availability, precluding a collection of standardized information for all of China at any one point in time. It is possible, however, to evaluate the accuracy of information presented in the available gazetteers and to arrive at a qualified estimate of the number of schools in the late Ch'ing.

Almost all gazetteers, whether on the county, prefectural, or provincial level, include a section on schools. Most of them present some information on charitable schools, although compilers were primarily interested in more advanced institutions of learning. These compilations were undertaken on local initiative and used local funds; therefore some areas compiled gazetteers frequently while others did not. For example, Shansi issued a provincial gazetteer in 1734, 1811, and 1892; but Kiangsu printed only a 1737 edition; and Kansu, a 1736 and a 1909 compilation. Similar gaps occur in the prefectural and county publications, making it difficult to use these gazetteers to fill gaps in provincial editions.[1]

An instance of the ways in which gaps in coverage can influence results can be demonstrated by comparing information in the major provincial gazetteer for Szechwan, compiled in 1816, with a prefectural gazetteer dated 1843. The provincial gazetteer lists only 2 charitable schools for Chungking prefecture, while the 1843 prefectural gazetteer records 138.[2] In this case, the provincial gazetteer probably omitted or lacked data. Identical school listings for Pao-ning prefecture in the 1816 provincial and 1821 prefectural gazetteers, however, indicate that the provincial gazetteer accurately recorded the state of affairs in this region. An alternative explanation for the discrepancies in the figures for Chungking is that 136 schools were founded there between 1816 and 1843, in line with the expansion of schools elsewhere in the province, shown in table 11. Regardless of the cause, the lack of a provincial gazetteer for Szechwan dating from the late nineteenth century results in a significant underestimate of schools in this area.

Even when gazetteers were compiled more frequently, they did not always provide additional information. The 1811 Shansi provincial gazetteer is supposedly a revision of an earlier work, but actually presents exactly the same data on charitable schools given in the 1734 compilation—despite the fact that county gazetteers show that changes did indeed occur between 1734 and 1811. Thus, repetition of data often nullifies the value of having numerous editions of a gazetteer.

Sometimes information was omitted because it was unavailable to compilers, a problem confronted in gazetteers of higher administrative units, where data had to be obtained from counties and departments. At other times, compilers apparently were not interested in charitable schools and did not list all of them;[3] a

TABLE 11
Information on Schools in Szechwan Province

Place (by prefecture)	Number of Schools[a] In Provincial Gazetteer[b]	In Lower-Level Gazetteers	Reference
Ch'eng-tu			
Hua-yang	0	0	1816 HC, 15.43b–44a
Chungking	2	138	1843 FC, 5.6b–15a
Pa	0	8	1867 HC, 2.40b–41a
Hsi-yang chou			
Ch'ien-chiang	0	6	1894 HC, 3.51ab
K'uei-chou			
Feng-chieh	0	25	1893 HC, 18.3a–5b
Wu-shan	1	0	1715 HC, schools section
Yün-yang	1		1854 HC
Wan	1	14(2)	1866 HC, 11.10b–11b
K'ai	0	(1)	1746 HC, school section .lb
Ta-ning	0	(15)	1885 HC, 4.7b–8b
Pao-ning	7(4)	7(4)	1821 FC, 27.2a–3a
Sui-ting			
Ta	0	(2)	1815 HC, 15.2a
T'ai-p'ing	0		1795 HC, school section
Ch'eng-k'ou	0	25	1844 *t'ing-chih*, 10.70a–76a

[a]Schools include *i-hsüeh*, *she-hsüeh*, and *i-shu*. Active schools are recorded; those in parentheses are defunct.
[b]1816 *Ssu-ch'uan* TC, chüan 79.

comparison of these sources with others indicates that unfortunately such omissions were not confined to compilers conscientious enough to point them out.

Similar problems arise in trying to accumulate quantitative information on lineage schools. Here the obvious source is the clan genealogy, but this also has significant weaknesses. The first problem is that there are more genealogies available for areas that were not the regions of greatest lineage strength in the twentieth century, namely the lower Yangtze region, than for Fukien and Kwangtung. Whether this disproportionate regional distribution reflects an inverse correlation between lineage strength and willingness to sell genealogies, or is indicative of the role genealogies play in forming organized kinship groups,[4] a mere counting of schools in these sources, even if they were accurately recorded, would produce a distorted picture of their distribution. An equally serious drawback to genealogies is that they frequently omit information, not only on lineage schools, but on their required financial base—corporate landholdings—as well. Since some lineages drew on ancestral hall funds to support schools, the absence of lands specially earmarked for schools need not indicate that they did not exist.[5] More broadly, as Johanna Meskill points out, genealogies frequently do not record corporate property.[6]

Clan Schools

Any effort to quantitatively estimate the contribution of clan schools to Ch'ing elementary education is frustrated by scattered information indicating that such schools were widespread and of considerable importance, on the one hand, and a distressing lack of systematic or supporting data on the other.

The distribution of clan schools throughout China was probably related to the regional distribution of lineages. As Jack Potter states, however, the prevalence of strong lineages in south and central China does not preclude their existence in the north.[7] While single-surname villages were rare in north China, statistics for three counties in Hopei show that from 24 to 48 percent of the villages were dominated by a surname group to which half or more of the households belonged. This information can be added to Makino Tatsumi's finding that 89 percent of one rural area in Feng-hua, Chekiang, was similarly dominated by one surname, or Hsien-chin Hu's example of Kao-an, Kiangsi, where 86.6 percent of the villages were single-surname villages.[8] Statistics on the regional origins of genealogies held in major library collections support the thesis that strong lineages were present in almost all parts of China. Since compiling a genealogy required resources, it is significant that every province in Ch'ing China, with the exception of Kansu, is represented in these collections. Investigation of the available genealogies produces direct information on the existence of clan schools even in Shantung and Honan.[9]

Lineage schools were not limited to villages inhabited by families of the same surname. In Taitou, Shantung, the largest lineage maintained a village school; eventually a second school was opened by two other surname groups. Although intended primarily for clan members, both schools admitted outsiders. There were clan lands in Ten Mile Inn, a Honan village dominated by three surname groups, and classes were held in the ancestral halls.[10]

Further examples of the existence of clan schools in north China come from local histories. There was, for example, the charitable school of the Wangs, founded by Wang Ch'ao-chung and his son in Tung-chang chia-chuang, Chihli.[11] In Ting-yüan, Shensi, three out of twenty-two charitable schools were clan schools, with two of the three holding classes in the ancestral hall.[12] In the local history of Shu-lu, Chihli, the well-to-do Shang lineage was mentioned for having achieved the extraordinary feat of "living together for eight generations." In addition to ritual and marriage lands, this lineage held school lands supporting two schools, a lower and an upper division.[13] Corporate estates in north China could be quite large, although this was rare. The Yins of Po-yeh in Pao-ting prefecture, Chihli, had almost 800 *mou* of lineage land, including school lands of 150 *mou* and charitable school lands of 100 *mou*. Like clan estates in the south, these were modeled on the Fan clan estate.[14]

In central and south China, where local lineages are said to be strongest, analysis of genealogies provides meager information about clan schools. Hui-chen Wang Liu, who studied the twentieth century rules of 151 clans primarily from Kiangsu, Chekiang, and Anhwei (in the lower Yangtze area) discovered that 116 held corporate property; of these, only 15 listed charitable schools, and only 6 had school or educational lands. But 75 clans provided funds for the reward and relief of clan members, and of this group 24 maintained funds to aid schooling, while an additional 35 had special grants for those taking the civil service examinations or their modern equivalent.[15] Scrutiny of Kiangsu genealogies dating from the eighteenth and nineteenth centuries reinforces Hu's finding that there is little information on clan schools in these materials.[16]

Information on the landholdings of lineage schools in the lower Yangtze provinces, presented in chapter 3, indicated the wealth of these institutions. Yet in this area where "those of the same surname extend to several tens of households or to several hundred households,"[17] few gazetteers list clan schools. From Soochow, the site for the famous Fan clan school, for example, there are records of only two such schools attached to clan charitable estates, although seven others are mentioned in genealogies from this prefecture.[18] Sung-chiang local histories list six clan schools; and eleven, or half of the schools listed for Wu-hsi and Chin-kuei counties, were in this group.[19] Records for Chin county, Chekiang, show twenty-eight clan schools, or 70 percent of all the elementary schools listed for the area.[20]

Clan schools must have served an important educational role in central China. As the local gazetteer for Liu-yang, Hunan, records, "Clans which are large must separately build a temple. At Ch'ing-ming and the Winter Solstice they gather to sacrifice. . . . The elite households sometimes use sacrifice land for charitable estates or charitable schools to educate clan members. This is an asset of local custom."[21] The incomplete listing of nineteen charitable schools run by lineages in this county can be compared with the nine public charitable schools cited for the same period.[22] In Hupei, clan schools recorded in local gazetteers amounted to 23 percent of the schools in Huang-kang county, and from 27 to 47 percent of those in Ch'ung-yang county.[23]

Kwangtung and Fukien were the regions of greatest lineage strength. In Kwangtung, where 80 percent of the peasants were estimated to live in lineage groups, clan assistance to elementary education, whether through the support of clan schools or the granting of financial aid, was probably very important. About one-third of the cultivated land in this province was held by lineages, and education seems to have received a major part of the revenues derived from such corporate properties.[24]

Schools were sometimes used to protect lineage interests. When visiting Kwangtung in the 1920s, Shimizu Taiji found many ancestral halls had the characters for "Study" (*shu-fang, shu-shih, shu-wu*) inscribed on their doors. This partially reflected the frequent use of ancestral halls as classrooms, but Shimizu learned that in the past, when permission was sought to erect ancestral halls during periods when the government discouraged clans, the stated purpose of building a "Study" had successfully circumvented government restrictions.[25]

During the mid-nineteenth century, community schools or *she-hsüeh* became foci for a local militia movement led by the Kwangtung elite, who used the schools to legitimize their organizational activities. Indeed, Frederic Wakeman believes that the militia movement itself revived many local schools that had ceased to function in the first half of the century.[26] Wakeman's point suggests that the *she-hsüeh* were no longer fulfilling a genuine educational role in late nineteenth century Kwangtung, yet firsthand accounts indicate that clans did not forsake elementary education during any part of this period.

Reports from the 1830s (cited in chapter 1) describe how each village had its own school, with many boys studying for two to four years before entering a trade or craft.[27] Even when clans did not actually support the village schools, they often provided free classroom space for schools run by kinsmen; since the teacher and his pupils belonged to the same clan, fees were low. In Sheung Shui, the New Territories village studied by Hugh Baker, fees were apparently low enough to allow most males in the lineage to attend the clan school.[28]

Some Fukien clans had corporate property designated for providing scholarship aid: Liu Hsing-t'ang cities such lands in T'ing-chou prefecture,[29] but there is no information that would permit an assessment of such provisions for the whole province. At the same time, whether in Fukien or elsewhere, clan ties helped poor students. This was true even in Ch'u county, Anhwei, an area with few outward manifestations of clan strength, as noted by Fried: "The importance of kinship in the educational process cannot . . . be under-rated. Those boys who were most certain of a formal education were the children of richer families. Many poor boys who received educations did so because they were sponsored by their clans. The financial backing was invariably based on family ties and even the teacher was often some relative of the richer boys."[30] This survey should indicate both the probable importance of the clan schools, and the serious lack of information, not only on the schools themselves, but also on the distribution of the lineages on which they were based.

School Expansion in the Ch'ing

Scattered statistics from local histories, shown in table 12, indicate that the number of charitable and community schools generally increased during the eighteenth and nineteenth centuries: the number of schools rose in twenty-five areas, and declined in only seven. Other regions with expanding school systems were Szechwan (shown in table 11) and Shantung.[31]

Imperial interest in education influenced the establishment of schools in the eighteenth century. In Chihli, 42.9 percent of all the charitable schools listed in the provincial gazetteer were founded during the reign of the K'ang-hsi Emperor (1661–1722), a ruler who vigorously promoted education, while the second highest number were established in the subsequent Yung-cheng reign (1723–35).[32]

The nineteenth century saw some extraordinary disasters, in addition to the vicissitudes inflicted on agriculture by flood or drought. By far the most serious were the breaking of the dikes in the 1850s, when the Yellow River changed its course to the sea,[33] and the Taiping, Nien, and Moslem rebellions, which affected the majority of Chinese provinces during the period 1850–68. Along with the homes and properties of citizens, school buildings and lands were frequently ruined or destroyed during this unrest. In response to this destruction, many areas in China witnessed a major effort to revive and expand elementary schools during the T'ung-chih (1861–74) and Kuang-hsü (1875–1908) reigns.

During the T'ung-chih Restoration, the period of Confucian revival following the suppression of the Taiping Rebellion, provincial officials naturally emphasized support of local schools as a means of restoring the Confucian order. Mary Wright discusses the encouragement of academies and the printing of official editions of the classics that accompanied this program;[34] the literati were also encouraged to support charitable schools, which could serve to transmit the Confucian restoration to the nonelite populace.

Kiangsu officials were especially active in promoting elementary schools in this era. Governor Ting Jih-ch'ang in 1867 ordered magistrates throughout the province to establish schools.[35] Efforts had already begun in some areas: in Yangchow, where all of the city's charitable schools had been destroyed by Taiping rebels,

TABLE 12
Active Community and Charitable Schools, 1700–1900, by Province

Place	Number of Active Schools[a]				Direction of Change
	1700–50	1750–1800	1800–50	1850–1900	
Chihli					
1. Cheng-ting fu		87		133	+
2. Han-tan		10		12	+
3. Kao-ch'eng	22			22	0
4. Man-ch'eng		13		16	+
5. Nan-kung			15	15	0
6. Shen-chou	1[b]			7	+
7. Shu-lu		16		27	+
8. Ta-ming		7		13	+
9. Tung-ming		2		10	+
10. Tz'u-chou	14			10	–
11. Wen-an	6			6	0
12. Wu-chi		13		19	+
Chekiang					
13. Hsi-an			0	7	+
14. T'ai-shun	22			12	–
15. Jui-an			0	3	+
16. I-wu			2	9	+
Fukien					
17. Ch'üan-chou fu		108	116		+
18. Shao-wu fu			22	12	–
19. T'ing-chou fu			69	68	–
20. Yen-p'ing fu			68	68	0
21. Lung-yen			6	10	+
Honan					
22. Ho-nei			8	9	+
23. Shang-ch'eng			43	1	–
24. Wu-an	10			10	0
Hunan					
25. Li chou		14		6	–
26. Li-ling	1			4	+
Hupei					
27. Hsiang-yang fu		1		45[b]	+
28. Chu-shan		1		3[b]	+
Kiangsi					
29. Wu-ning			15	19	+
Shansi					
30. Shansi province	203			367	+
31. Chao-ch'eng	1		10	0	+, –
32. Lin-fen	2	8		10	+
33. T'ai-p'ing	1	1		9	+
Shensi					
34. Chen-an		1		2[b]	+
35. Feng-hsiang fu		20		42[b]	+
36. Han-yin			1	1[b]	0
37. Lo-nan		0		3[b]	+
38. Shang-nan		2		1[b]	–
39. Sian fu		45		113[b]	+

TABLE 12 (*cont.*)

Sources:

1. 1762 FC, 8.64a–68a; all Chihli items in 1850–1900 column are from *Chi-fu* TC, 1884 ed., chüan 114–17.
2. 1756 HC, 3.56a.
3. 1720 HC, 2.19b–20b.
4. 1780 HC, 4.30b–31a.
5. 1831 HC, 3.31b–34a.
6. 1697 CC, 3.2b–4b.
7. 1799 HC, pp. 798–99.
8. 1790 HC, 16.5a–7a.
9. 1756 HC, 2.12b.
10. 1703 CC, 6.25b.
11. 1703 HC, 2.36ab.
12. 1757 HC, 2.3ab.
13. 1811 HC, 10.48a; all Chekiang items in 1850–1900 column are from 1899 TC, chüan 25–29.
14. 1729 HC, 3.13a–15a.
15. 1809 HC, 2.50b–53a.
16. 1802 HC, 3.33a.
17. 1763 FC, 14.32b–33a; 53b–54a; 66ab; 15.20b–22b; 65a. All Fukien items in 1850–1900 column are from 1829 TC, chüan 62–66.
18. 1900 FC, pp. 209, 213, 216, 219.
19. 1867 FC, pp. 178, 180, 181, 182, 183, 184, 185.
20. 1873 FC, p. 176.
21. 1890 HC, p. 105.
22. 1825 HC, 16.13ab; all Honan items in 1850–1900 column are from 1914 reprint of 1869 TC, 43.46a–49b.
23. 1803 HC, 6.18b–25b.
24. 1739 HC, 7.32a.
25. 1752 *Li-chou chih-lin*, 9.28a; all Hunan items in 1850–1900 column are from 1885 TC, chüan 68–70.
26. 1744 HC, 6.45b.
27. 1760 FC, 8.24a–26b; all Hupei items in 1850–1900 column are from 1921 TC, chüan 59.
28. 1785 HC, 15.12b–13a.
29. 1824 HC, 97.14a–16b; 1881 TC, *chüan* 81, 82.
30. The 1811 TC, chüan 35–36, presents, unrevised, data from the 1734 edition; 1892 TC, chüan 76. Information for all Shansi areas in the 1850–1900 column is taken from the latter source.
31. 1827 HC, 17.22a–23a.
32. 1779 HC, 5.6ab.
33. 1775 HC, 2.13b.
34. 1753 HC, pp. 358–62; all Shensi data in 1850–1900 column are from 1934 TC, chüan 37–38.
35. 1767 FC, 6.8b–38b.
36. 1818 *t'ing-chih*, 3.4ab.
37. 1746 HC, chüan 6.
38. 1752 HC, 8.18a.
39. 1779 FC, 19.10a–20.13a.

[a]Only active *i-hsüeh* and *she-hsüeh* were counted.
[b]Exceeds the time period; see sources.

four schools were opened in 1866. In P'ei county, in northwest Kiangsu, Tseng Kuo-fan allocated 600 *mou* of lake land to support two charitable schools in that same year. Feng Kuei-fen, a native of Soochow, established a charitable bureau in Yüan-ho with a school attached to it.[36]

Large sums were raised for Kiangsu schools: according to one writer, over 500,000 taels were raised in Soochow and Sung-chiang prefectures.[37] Schools newly established or revived during the T'ung-chih reign included all of the schools in Tan-t'u and Tan-yang, Chen-chiang prefecture, 72 percent of the active schools in Soochow, 40 percent of those in Ch'ang-chou prefecture, 30 percent of those in Yangchow, and smaller numbers in other parts of the province.[38]

Similar efforts were made elsewhere. In Chekiang, donations as large as 900,000 taels of silver were raised for schools.[39] Lung Ju-lin, a district magistrate in Shansi, established over 120 charitable schools in his area during the 1860s.[40] Help also came from central government officials: in Wen-an, Chihli, a Hanlin scholar and a secretary at the Board of Works contributed funds to revive schools in their native districts. These efforts continued into the subsequent Kuang-hsü reign.[41]

Urban-Rural Distribution of Schools

The K'ang-hsi and Yung-cheng emperors expressed concern about education in poor and isolated regions, since wealthier urban areas were naturally endowed with more favorable educational opportunities. During the preceding Ming dynasty, *she-hsüeh* had penetrated into rural areas: a study of 472 administrative units from the prefecture down to the county shows that of the 3,837 schools listed, 26 percent were in towns and 73 percent in the countryside.[42] The ideal of favoring rural schools was put into effect in varying degrees in different parts of China during the Ch'ing dynasty.

The provinces of Hupei, Chihli, and Honan differed on the question of rural emphasis, with Hupei and Chihli favoring rural schools and Honan continuing to have more urban schools—only one-third of Honan's schools were in the countryside. Szechwan, like Honan, had a preponderance of urban schools: 44.6 percent were situated in urban locations and only 21.4 percent in rural areas. This was not the case in Chekiang, where 32.6 percent of schools were in rural areas and 21.2 percent in urban places.[43]

Both community and charitable schools in Hupei were found most frequently in villages: 37 percent and 54.9 percent, respectively, as opposed to 9.7 and 22.2 percent in the urban areas.[44] Community schools, representing 12.7 percent of all Chihli public elementary schools, were fairly evenly distributed between town and hamlet (37.7 percent urban, 34.8 percent rural), but the charitable schools, which formed the majority, were mostly rural: 62.6 percent as opposed to 33.9 percent in towns. The counties of Yeh, Shang-ch'eng, and Wu-an in Honan; and Chao-ch'eng, Ch'ü-wu, and Lin-fen in Shansi, were other areas where from 74 to 87 percent of the schools were located in villages.[45]

Nakamura's study of Shantung schools shows that their spatial distribution could change dramatically from one period to the next. In Shantung, where *she-hsüeh* dominated in the eighteenth century, only 20 percent of the 104 *she-hsüeh* recorded were in the country, as were 8 percent of the *i-hsüeh*. During the K'ang-hsi reign (1661–1722), sixteen schools were founded in towns as opposed to ten in villages, but by 1723–35, only three schools were established in towns as compared with nine in the countryside. Emphasis on rural schools continued through the late eighteenth and early nineteenth century, and by 1843, there were 60 percent more rural than urban schools in this province.[46] A similar trend may have occurred in Szechwan. The two schools listed for Chungking prefecture in the 1816 provincial gazetteer, for example, were both located in the city. In the 1843 prefectural gazetteer, however, 74.8 percent of the 131 active schools listed were rural and only 12.2 percent urban.[47]

Discrepancies in wealth affected the siting of schools within the rural sector itself, since it was easiest for prosperous areas to raise the required endowment. The most striking evidence of marked regional difference resting on local economic strength comes from Liu Po-chi's study of Kwangtung academies. During the Ch'ing, academies and *she-hsüeh* were concentrated along the inland rivers and the Pearl River Delta, the loci for marketing activity; 42.4 percent of Kwangtung *she-hsüeh* were located right in Canton prefecture itself.[48] In this instance, the pattern of private and public educational opportunities coincided, since the wealthiest areas were also most likely to have the largest numbers of private tutors and private schools.

But Kwangtung was exceptional in the extent to which public elementary schools were concentrated in the most prosperous regions. In Chihli, for example, the ideal of widespread educational opportunity seems to have been successfully implemented. Only 6 percent of Chihli counties had no schools. No one region dominated. The median number of schools in a county was five, as compared with an average of 6.7 that would have prevailed had the schools been equally divided among all the counties.[49]

In Gilbert Rozman's classification of Chihli's central place hierarchy, the four largest urban centers after Peking were Tientsin, Pao-ting, Shun-te prefectural city, and T'ung chou. These were all major commercial cities, with Tientsin and T'ung chou situated along the important Grand Canal route, and Pao-ting and Shun-te serving as major stops along the overland route from Peking to the west. The number of schools in three of these cities was well above the median, but of the nine next largest cities, five fell below the median. These five cities were Cho-chou, Chi-chou, and Ch'ang-p'ing chou, located on major transport routes into Peking; Ts'ang-chou, an important center along the Grand Canal route; and Lin-yü, located at the pass of Shan-hai kuan, the principal route to the area north of the Great Wall.[50]

It might be argued that Chihli was a special case because of its proximity to the national capital and its sensitivity to imperial and central government policies, but patterns of school distribution in other provinces also contrast with those found in Kwangtung. T'ing-chou, a prefecture in southwest Fukien, had more schools than the much larger and richer region in Foochow prefecture.[51] In Hunan, the commercially bustling prefecture of Ch'ang-sha, which included the cities of Hsiang-t'an and Ch'ang-sha, supported fewer charitable schools than the western sub-prefecture of Shui-sui, where schools had been used by the state to assimilate non-Han populations.[52]

Availability of Institutional Education

We can see from the preceding discussion that institutional education expanded in many parts of China during the late nineteenth century, as schools became more numerous in both rural and urban areas. At the same time, data in appendix 1 indicate that population growth had outpaced school facilities by the mid-nineteenth century. Table 19 shows that when the number of schools is compared with the number of boys of school age, the availability of (nonclan) institutional education was limited. Even Yunnan province, which had the most favorable ratio of schools to school-age population, could accommodate less than 5 percent of the potential student body. In other provinces, the ratio was even more unfavorable.

This bleak general picture is somewhat qualified when one examines specific counties. By establishing over 120 schools in Lung county, for example, the Shansi magistrate referred to earlier provided for at least 14 percent of the male school-age population. In addition, if the rule restricting admission to poor boys were observed, the ratio of schools to eligible boys would rise for this and all other regions.

A final evaluation of the availability of institutional education in Ch'ing China must include clan schools. Throughout central and south China, clan schools probably added significantly to the educational opportunities for poor but bright boys. Even in the north, where clan strength was weaker, the outstanding student sometimes obtained financial aid from his lineage. When clan schools are added to community and charitable schools, institutional education must be counted as a marginal but significant force in the Ch'ing period.

Supply of Teachers

Privately financed education constituted the major channel of schooling in Ch'ing times. One reason for this situation is that, in comparison with other premodern societies, China had an unusually large pool of potential teachers, more than enough to teach the 30 to 45 percent of the male population cited in estimates of school attendance.

The most likely candidates for elementary teaching positions were unsuccessful competitors for the lower examination degrees, who were fully literate, but not qualified to hold government posts. Prominent in this group were the large numbers of *sheng-yüan, chien-sheng,* and *t'ung-sheng* who failed to earn higher academic degrees. As table 23 shows for several areas of Chihli province, these men filled a major proportion of elementary teaching posts.

Ch'ing history provides many examples of poor scholars who eked out a living by teaching while preparing for the examinations. Famous historical figures such as Hung Hsiu-ch'üan and the fathers of Tseng Kuo-fan, Liang Ch'i-ch'ao, and Li Tsung-jen, all fall into this category, and there are many other examples of *sheng-yüan* who earned a living by teaching.[53] Five out of eight "outside students" at the advanced level charitable school founded by Wu Hsün in the 1890s were *sheng-yüan* with jobs as elementary schoolteachers; when a lower division was added to the school, its teachers were also *sheng-yüan.*[54] Chung-li Chang estimates that there were about 1.1 million degree holders above the *t'ung-sheng* level in the early nineteenth century. Only a few of these, approximately 11 percent, acquired higher degrees. This left approximately .9 million *sheng-yüan* and *chien-sheng,* or 0.2 percent of the total Chinese population.[55]

T'ung-sheng, who also taught in elementary schools, were much more numerous. Chang estimates that they may have totalled two million. When taken together with *sheng-yüan* and *chien-sheng,* this group of highly literate potential teachers constituted .6 percent of the total Chinese population. This amounts to an upper limit of six potential teachers per 1,000 people, a figure far above the "crucial point" for the development of general literacy that Carlo Cipolla identified as lying between one and three formal teachers per 1,000 population.[56]

If we compare the supply of potential teachers (2.9 million) with the estimated number of school age boys (40.3 million)[57] in about 1850, we find that it was theoretically possible to teach every male child with a class size of only sixteen. Since estimated levels of male school attendance were below 50 percent for China as a whole, the same conclusion would be reached even if only half of the potential supply of teachers actually adopted teaching as an occupation. As we know from chapter 2, actual average class size was larger than sixteen, so a yet smaller number of teachers could accommodate the students. Hence, there seems to be no doubt that it was possible to educate broad segments of the Chinese population using the talents of the available number of failed scholars.

Alternative Sources of Income

Comparison of teachers' salaries at the elementary level with the income alternatives open to them provides a perspective on the relative attractiveness of teaching as an occupation for unsuccessful scholars. It also provides information on the direct cost of schooling to parents, and a basis for evaluating the relative price of an elementary school education. This analysis supports descriptive evidence of the importance of privately financed education in the Ch'ing period.

Academy Stipends

Sheng-yüan and *chien-sheng,* not to mention lower status *t'ung-sheng,* were advanced students who were already highly literate. As P. T. Ho has shown, Ch'ing population growth, coupled with inflexible degree quotas, meant that it became more and more difficult during the eighteenth and early nineteenth centuries to win the higher degrees that qualified one for government office. More and more men remained lower degree holders throughout their lives. Recruited from a fairly broad social base,[58] these failed scholars were frequently compelled to support themselves while pursuing success in the official examinations. One obvious alternative open to such persons was enrollment in an academy (*shu-yüan*).[59]

In Ch'ing times, academies, famous as philosophical centers, were increasingly oriented toward preparing students for the examinations. Privately endowed, they provided stipends and prizes for a fixed number of students, differentiated on the basis of performance in regularly scheduled examinations.[60] Some academies admitted only *sheng-yüan* and *t'ung-sheng,* but others let in *chien-sheng* and *kung-sheng* as well.[61]

TABLE 13
Annual Stipends Obtainable from Academies, by Province

Place	Date	Maximum Annual Stipends (in taels)		Reference
		Class A	Class B	
Chihli				
T'ung chou	ca. 1783	18.0		CC, 5.19b
Yen-ch'ing	ca. 1829	90.0[a]	20.0[a]	CC, 4.32ab
Luan-ch'eng	1836	8.0[b]	5.0[b]	HC, 6.9a
T'ang	1841	10.0	5.0	HC, 4.33a
Huai-an	1876	32.0[c]	32.0[c]	HC, 3.1a–2a
Ch'ang-p'ing	ca. 1886	24.0[d]	12.0[d]	HC, 12.14b–15a
Luan chou	ca. 1898	12.0	6.4	CC, 12.78b
Hunan				
Chih-chiang	ca. 1870	30.0[e]	30.0[e]	HC, 12.32ab
Feng-huang	ca. 1881	12.0	8.0	HC, 6.19a
Kiangsi				
Lin-ch'uan	ca. 1870	6.0	6.0	HC, 28.5b–6a
Ch'ung-jen	ca. 1848	8.0	8.0	HC, 43.4b
Nan-ch'ang	ca. 1849	10.0	10.0	HC, 8.14b–15a
Hsin-ch'eng	ca. 1870	2.4	2.0	HC, 4.6a
Wu-ning	ca. 1870	6.0	6.0	HC, 9.1b
Shansi				
P'ing-yao	ca. 1883	12.0	8.0	HC, 4.36ab
Shensi				
Lüeh-yang	ca. 1833	12.0	8.0	HC, 2.26a

Note: Monthly stipends for *sheng-yüan* and other lower degree holders eligible for admission were multiplied by the number of months stipends were awarded to arrive at annual stipends for Class A. The same procedure was followed for stipends awarded *t'ung-sheng* to arrive at annual stipends for Class B. Stipends in grain and money outside the copper cash and silver tael system were excluded. Copper cash was converted at the rate of 1 tael=1,000 cash.

[a]Only for first-ranked student.

[b]*Ta-ch'ien* (literally, "big cash") is taken to mean "standard cash" before the Hsien-feng period; see Frank H. H. King, *Money and Monetary Policy in China*, pp. 61, 245.

[c]Local cash strings, which may be half the value of standard-cash strings; see ibid., p. 60. The stipend might thus be half the amounts recorded in the table.

[d]*Ta-ch'ien*, here converted at the rate of 2,000 cash to 1 tael; see ibid., p. 61.

[e]*Ch'uan*(string), translated into taels at 1 string = 1 tael.

Table 13 presents information (which supplements Liu's data for Kwangtung) on the annual stipends that could be obtained by lower degree holders and *t'ung-sheng*. Because prizes, which could equal the monthly stipend, were awarded to only the very highest ranked students, they have been excluded from this table.[62]

TABLE 14
Median Levels of Academy Stipends and Teachers' Salaries, 1750–1900

Period	Class A Stipends							Number of Items	Median Stipend (in taels)	Median Salary (in taels)
	under 5	5–9	10–14	15–19	20–24	25–29	30+			
1750–1775		2						2	6.8	16.0
1775–1800		2		1				3	7.2	20.0
1800–1825		2	3	3	2			10	14.7	24.0
1825–1850		4	4		1			9	10.0	27.0
1850–1875	2	3	2	1	2		2	12	9.5	47.3
1870–1900	1	2	3	1	2		2	11	12.0	44.0

Sources: Information on *sheng-chien* (Class A) stipends is taken from table 13 and from Liu Po-chi, *Kuang-tung shu-yüan chih-tu,* pp. 319–21 (computed for the school year). Stipends paid in kind or outside the copper-cash/silver-tael system were omitted. Median salaries for teachers are taken from table 4.

Table 14 shows that stipends were significantly smaller than teachers' salaries. This statement holds true even in the unlikely event that a student doubled his stipends from an academy by placing first in every examination.[63] Direct comparisons of academy stipends with teachers' salaries tend to bear out this observation. In 1836, when *sheng-yüan* at the academy in Luan-ch'eng, Chihli, were being awarded stipends amounting to 8,000 cash a year, one *sheng-yüan* was appointed to teach at the charitable school for over 30,000 cash a year.[64] The highest ranked *sheng-yüan* in Luan chou, Chihli, during the late 1890s received an annual stipend of twelve taels from the academy, while a charitable schoolteacher received perhaps eight times this figure.[65] Only in Lüeh-yang, Shensi, did the combined prizes and stipends amount to more than the elementary schoolteacher's salary, and even here a *t'ung-sheng* would have done better by teaching than by accepting an academy stipend.[66]

The modest scale of academy stipends is evident when they are compared with the salaries paid to academy employees. In Lüeh-yang, Shensi, the gateman at the academy was paid 7.2 strings of copper cash a year, while *t'ung-sheng* got only 8 strings. The academy clerk, who was required to keep attendance records, was paid 9.6 strings—more than a *t'ung-sheng* received.[67] In Nan-ch'ang, Kiangsi, the Tung-hu Academy paid its cook 7.2 taels, only slightly less than the 10 taels received by *sheng-yüan*.[68] The gateman and tea boy in an academy in T'ung chou, Chihli, each received salaries amounting to two-thirds of the *sheng-yüan* stipend, while the personal servant and cook at the academy in Ch'ang-p'ing earned more than the *sheng-yüan*.[69]

In addition to giving students an opportunity for full-time study, academies gave travel grants to aid candidates making their way to the examination centers. They had libraries, and sometimes the attraction of famous scholars,[70] so there was considerable competition for admission to some academies. In Luan-ch'eng, Chihli, for example, an average of seventy-five to eighty-seven persons appeared for the semimonthly examinations to fill the Lung-kang Academy's twenty positions.[71] The size of an academy's endowment limited the number of students to whom it could proffer aid. For this reason, enrollment in an academy was not always a real alternative open to a failed student.

Alternative Occupations

In a period when it became more and more difficult to win an examination degree, scholars of modest means had to contrive to keep themselves alive while competing in the examinations. An example of the kind of strategy that many might have used is presented in *The Scholars*. Yu Yu-teh, the third generation of a line of poor teachers, has been left to his father's former employer, Mr. Chi, to raise: " 'You are a poor scholar, Master Yu,' said Mr. Chi. 'And poetry alone will be of no use to you. You must learn some skill by which you can make a living. In my youth I studied geomancy, and learned how to tell fortunes and select sites. I will be glad to teach you all I know, for it may serve you in good stead some day.' "[72] For such a person, the lower degree represented not only an opportunity for advancement to higher level examinations, but a better paying teaching post: " 'You should buy a few collections of *paku* essays to study too,' advised Mr. Chi. 'Then later, if you pass the examinations, you'll find better teaching jobs.' "[73]

As Ho points out, economic pressures on failed *sheng-yüan* and other students were so great that many ignored statutory restrictions against engaging in such "degrading" occupations as store bookkeeper, clerk, local broker, and even government runner.[74] Perhaps some became lawsuit specialists, the Ch'ing equivalent of modern lawyers, whom emperor and officials viewed with hostile suspicion. Though condemned as "unscrupulous characters" who incited people to lawsuits in order to make money, these professionals performed a function long carried out by degree holders in China, the settlement of local disputes. Although none of the three litigation specialists in cases presented by Derk Bodde and Clarence Morris was a degree holder, another case cites a military *sheng-yüan* who "prepared public notices, announcing plans for establishing an office for himself, wherein he hoped to fish for profit by handling taxation matters for people and settling their litigations."[75]

The preparation of legal documents for lawsuits required education and skills that went far beyond those attained in the elementary school curriculum, so that failed degree candidates might logically be suspected of participation. Doctors and fortune-tellers were also considered educated enough to prepare such documents. According to the *Sacred Edict:*

> Everybody in the country dreads men of this sort, and styles them "Masters of Litigation." And yet, if the magistrate begins thoroughly to investigate as to the writer of the indictment, these imbecile people still shield them, and provokingly refuse to betray them, merely saying, "It is an indictment drawn up by some strolling fortune teller or physiognomist, or travelling doctor." They hoax you into deep waters, ruin your family, waste your money, flog you, and still you shield them.[76]

Of course, medicine and the medical profession were not disreputable pursuits in and of themselves; Chang cites many cases of degree holders who were doctors.[77]

Some kinds of fortune-telling were also quite respectable. In nineteenth century Foochow, for example, the most common and popular fortune-teller made predictions on the basis of his client's birthdate. While blind practitioners worked in the streets, there were also specialists with sight, who not only had shops, but the advantage of also being able to consult books that gave omens according to the precise time of birth. Doolittle noted that these were "men wearing good apparel, and conducting themselves with propriety."[78]

Indigent *sheng-yüan* and other failed students might engage in fortune-telling, which in its more prestigious forms, like geomancy, was respected as a highly developed science. After all, *sheng-yüan* could sink much lower: it was not only in novels that they collected night soil for a living.[79] The Taiping leader Feng Yün-shan was at one time reduced to work as a harvest laborer; he also carried earth and gathered pig and buffalo manure for sale as fertilizer.[80]

In addition to teaching, a poor *sheng-yüan* or *t'ung-sheng* could thus work in a wide variety of occupations. He could use his education to settle lawsuits or to practice as a doctor or fortune-teller; he could accept employment as a bookkeeper or clerk; or sink to becoming a laborer or government runner. The humble nature of many of these occupations strikingly supports the statistical evidence that there was a large supply of potential teachers in

Ch'ing China. Teaching was an honorable profession for a scholar, certainly preferable to employment as a clerk or, worse still, a hired laborer. Both the statistical and anecdotal evidence reinforce nineteenth century reports of a general surplus of teachers.[81]

Teaching versus Other Occupations

By trying to place teachers' incomes in the context of other wages and incomes, we can evaluate the relative status of this occupation and indirectly measure the cost of private schooling for average households. In 1747, as a young *sheng-yüan,* Wang Hui-tsu taught village boys for a salary of twelve strings of cash a year. In Canton in the 1830s, a field worker or a workman in an urban shop earned about as much as porters and "menials," about .1 liang a day. If he were fortunate enough to find steady employment, he could thus obtain as much as 2.8 taels a month, which was equivalent to the low range of salaries for personal servants, clerks, master workmen, and the like, who earned from 2.8 to 7.1 taels a month. Over a year, a steadily employed field worker or urban workman, porter, or "menial" could thus earn 34.3 taels, or more than the median salary of a charitable schoolteacher in this period.[82] A highly paid clerk or master workman could earn as much as 85.7 taels a year, which was three times the median salary of charitable schoolteachers in the period, and approximately what a private urban teacher might have earned in Canton at the time. Private teachers in rural areas seem to have earned from one-half to two-thirds the income of their urban counterparts, which would place them above urban workmen and porters in annual earnings.[83]

Doolittle presented a similar account of relative incomes in mid-nineteenth century Foochow. He found that steadily employed carpenters and masons might earn as much as hired field laborers and personal servants. The latter, receiving wages and board, earned from 9 to 27 taels a year, which was about what clerks and accountants earned. If board is counted, both groups may have earned as much if not more than teachers, whose annual income was only 22.5 to 45 taels, without board. Doolittle's estimates are slightly lower than the median salary of 47.3 taels for charitable schoolteachers around 1850–75. As Doolittle noted, "Literary men who are poor, and who fail of acquiring government employment, are frequently glad to teach school at almost a nominal price."[84]

Even lower incomes for rural schoolteachers in Shantung were cited in chapter 1; a schoolmaster might be paid a small grain allowance, some fuel, and only 6.6 taels a year. Things could have been worse: Smith wrote, "It is not very uncommon to meet teachers who have but one or two pupils, and who receive for their services little or nothing more than their food."[85] Another late nineteenth century observer estimates that teachers earned from 2.5 to 12.5 times more than laborers, but could earn as little as 30 taels. According to Chang, the average income of "commoner" teachers, including *t'ung-sheng,* was less than 50 taels a year. This was not very different from the median salary of charitable schoolteachers in the period 1875–1900 (see table 4), which was 44 taels a year.[86]

Of course, not all schoolteachers were so poorly paid. Chang indicates that the average income of a "gentry" teacher, including *sheng-yüan,* could be about one hundred taels a year, but the range was broad. He cites one man who earned only ten taels in his first year, while another averaged several hundred taels a year from teaching.[87] Only wealthy and degree-holding households could pay teachers fees of a hundred or more taels a year, but it is the lower end of the income range for teachers that is pertinent to an inquiry into the accessibility of private instruction to ordinary citizens. The fact that clerks and accountants, persons with specialized but limited skills, could earn as much as teachers, who needed much more education, testifies to the relative abundance of qualified persons seeking a livelihood by teaching. The modesty of teachers' salaries at the lower end of the income scale suggests the extent to which nonelite groups in Ch'ing society could afford to educate their sons.

Tuition Fees

Tuition fees for elementary schooling could be very modest. One report from the 1830s estimated that boys attending a city school could pay 3 taels a year, as opposed to 1.4 to 2.1 taels in a village school.[88] Li An-li, the poor teacher cited by Chang, collected 3 taels a year and food from each of his eight students, but this seems to be a comparatively high fee. Hsü T'e-li, later a Communist Party commissioner of education, charged less than 1 tael a year when he taught school in Hunan during the 1890s, and Chu Teh, who attended a private school in rural Szechwan in the same period, paid only 200 cash a year.[89]

With ten pupils, tuition charges for the Foochow teachers cited by Doolittle would range from 2.2 to 4.5 taels per student. If there were twenty-three students, the average number in a charitable or community school, fees would drop to less than 1 to 1.9 taels. In Smith's example, a teacher with ten pupils collected .6 taels from each, with additional gifts of food and fuel, and the fees per student would have decreased as the number of pupils rose. The cost per student deduced from these citations of teacher income thus varies inversely with the number of pupils, although the high range of tuition fees of 4 taels and more would scarcely agree with Doolittle's remark that instruction could be obtained at "almost a nominal price."

What is the standard by which we can evaluate these fees? In Canton, fees of 3 taels a year represented slightly more than one month's wages for field workers, porters, and menials, but only 3.5 percent of the annual income of a well-paid clerk, accountant, or master workman. Such schooling would thus have been within the reach of these more highly paid urban residents. In Foochow, by Doolittle's account, the better paid carpenters, masons, accountants and clerks could probably pay the school fees too.[90]

Tuition fees in rural schools, ranging from 200 cash to over one tael, obviously had varying significance for peasants in different parts of China. Evaluating the relative importance of these sums for a peasant in the late nineteenth century really requires more information than we possess. For that reason, it is important to remember the judgements of observers on the scene: Smith, for example, stated that the fees were minimal, and Doolittle echoed the same opinion. Of course, the evaluations of foreigners, viewing rural and urban China from the outside, were of necessity different from those of poor Chinese who lived within the social system. Here, case studies provide illuminating support for foreign opinions.

Chu Teh, born in 1886 in Szechwan, was one of three sons in a family of tenant farmers who were "too poor to eat rice except on rare occasions."[91] Yet Chu and his two older brothers were sent to a private school, which charged 800 cash as tuition for the eldest son, and 200 cash each for the two younger boys. Thus, this poor tenant family, straining every resource, was able to pay approximately 1.2 taels for educating its sons. When Chu Teh and one brother continued their lessons at a better school, run by the wealthy landlord and boasting a teacher who was a *sheng-yüan,* the same fees were charged.[92]

Chu Teh's story reminds us of the great motivation that stimulated family sacrifice—Chu's family was willing to use its savings to educate its sons. This means that analysis of the relative cost of schooling, which tries to answer the question of how many peasants could pay fees, cannot rest solely on considerations of current income, but must look at the financial resources, sometimes not just of the family, but of the extended kinship group to which it belonged. The case studies presented by Ho illustrate family strategies of mobility too well for this point to require further discussion.

In the process of identifying the most promising candidate for advanced schooling, other sons were also educated for a few years. Thus Chu Teh was pushed on for further education while one of his brothers attended school for less than a year, and the other for a total of three years. Chu Teh's two cousins also attended school for two years each.[93]

Ch'ing biographies indicate that education was available to a broad cross-section of Ch'ing society. We have cases of men who obtained an education despite starting life as sons of farmers, agricultural tenants, and even army privates. The leaders of the Taiping Rebellion, which swept China in the mid-nineteenth century, were failed scholars from farm households. Yu-wen Jen, writing of Hung Hsiu-ch'üan, the son of middle-level Kwangtung peasants, states that, "Though it meant sacrifice, his family did not deprive their son of an education. At seven (by Chinese count) the boy entered a primary school in his own village and there proved to be a very bright and diligent student with a strong memory."[94] Hung studied for five or six years, became a *t'ung-sheng,* and eventually returned to his native village to teach. A distant cousin, Feng Yün-shan, had a similar educational background.[95]

Of course, farmers varied a great deal in resources and status. Chang Chien, the late Ch'ing industrialist, came from a middle-level farming family, but his grandfather and father both attended village schools as youths, and the four sons in Chien's generation were all sent to school. This kind of solidly respectable farming family is also found in the backgrounds of the Kwangsi warlords Pai Ch'ung-hsi, Li Tsung-jen, Huang Shao-hsiung, and Huang Hsü-ch'u. These families had a tradition of literacy to which they could point with pride, and occasionally counted failed scholars among their members.[96]

On a lower level, there were farmers who had attended school for only a few years or were self-taught and semiliterate. Ch'i Po-shih, the painter, came from such a household in rural Hunan, and learned his first characters from a semiliterate grandfather. The family could afford to send Po-shih to school for only one year.[97] Mao Tse-tung's father, who began life as a "poor peasant," still managed to attend school for two years, and knew enough characters to keep accounts. Mao himself, born in 1893, attended a traditional village school from the age of eight, and had already had five years of schooling when his father urged him to leave the classroom for full-time work in the fields.[98]

Hsü T'e-li, born in 1876 near Ch'ang-sha, Hunan, the son of an illiterate "half-farmer, half-coolie," attended school from the age of nine until he was fifteen, when he left to become a teacher. Wen T'ao, born to poor Kwangtung peasants in 1907, was sold to a rich landlord, yet he attended primary school until the age of eight. Wu Liang-p'ing, from coastal Chekiang, recounts how his grandfather, who ran a grocery store, learned to read and write by himself.[99]

We know from case histories that charitable schools played a role in educating poor students. Wang Shou-tao, born into a poor Hunanese peasant family in 1907, attended a free primary school. Later, he obtained a patron through kinship connections, and was aided in seeking further education.[100] Chiang Ch'ing, born in 1914 to a handicraft workshop owner in Shantung, managed to go to school even though her mother was working as a servant in a landlord household: "I was able to complete that stage of primary school only because tuition and books were free," she recalled.[101]

The lives of famous men who rose from poor and humble backgrounds do not prove that education was available to every male in Ch'ing China. Examples like these undoubtedly magnify the possibilities for schooling that existed, since such persons were far more determined and talented than the average person. Yet we should also consider the evidence of relatively high rates of literacy among Cantonese immigrants to Hawaii, cited in chapter 1. Immigrants may be a highly selective group, above average in ambition and ability, but they came from ordinary rural backgrounds. What these anecdotes suggest is that those with ambition could obtain an elementary education in late Ch'ing times, perhaps more frequently than has previously been assumed. Investigation of the institutional and private educational sectors supports the descriptive and statistical evidence of widespread literacy presented in chapter 1.

Chapter 5

Popular Literature

A major barrier to literacy in premodern Europe, the great expense of books, was absent in China, the country where printing was invented. The availability of cheap books was an important condition that not only permitted widespread popular literacy in China but promoted upward social mobility as well. In this chapter, we first study the increased supply of printed materials in historical perspective. We then examine popular literature in the context of the range of materials printed during the Ch'ing, and finally assess its availability to ordinary citizens by investigating book prices and printing costs. A subsequent chapter examines a particular kind of book designed for a nonelite readership, the *tsa-tzu* or character glossaries, which were used as aids for elementary instruction.

Historical Development

Mass printing may not have had the same "revolutionary" impact in China that Elizabeth Eisenstein argues it had in Renaissance Europe,[1] but its repercussions on Chinese social structure, scholarship, and literature were profound.

Since the Sung period, Chinese rulers and government agencies tried to preserve the Confucian canon in pure form by sponsoring numerous projects of scholarship, compilation, and reprinting. The Chinese government had always been a major book producer, financing the printing of dynastic histories, Confucian classics, and commentaries;[2] massive official undertakings such as the Ch'ing compilation of the *Ssu-k'u ch'üan-shu* (Imperial manuscript library)[3] were part of a very long tradition.

Although commercial printing appeared in the Northern Sung (960–1126), its vigorous development dates from the thirteenth century, when private printing houses flourished in the urban centers.[4] P. T. Ho argues that true large-scale printing did not emerge in China until the sixteenth century. During the Yüan dynasty (1279–1368), for example, major publications by government agencies were printed in amazingly small quantities: in some cases only fifty and in others one hundred copies were produced at one time.[5] Movable type was known to the Chinese since Sung times, but block printing continued to dominate the industry. Since the wooden blocks from which most books were printed constituted a fixed cost, the small quantities produced represented comparatively high costs for the publisher. In the sixteenth century, the volume of publications increased and printing costs seem to have declined. By the Ch'ing period books were more plentiful and more inexpensive than ever before.[6]

The growth of the publishing industry, in particular the private sector, took several forms. Individual titles were printed in larger quantities than before; in addition, both the number of titles and the variety of genres seem to have increased markedly. The impact of these changes can be seen by examining the stratified market for both elite and popular literature in Ch'ing China.

The Elite Book Market

As producers (authors, patrons, printers) and consumers, the highly literate Chinese elite continued to dominate the book market. The pinnacle of the market was an active trade in rare books, characterized by high prices and occasional bankruptcies among wealthy men competing to build personal libraries. Many of these connoisseurs were more than mere dilettantes—the same men who boasted of having "one hundred Sung (editions) under one roof" often contributed to learning by carefully selecting and editing rare works for reprinting.[7] Famous bibliophiles like Huang P'ei-lieh, Mao Chin, and Pao T'ing-po were motivated by the concerns of the historiographical school of Ch'ing scholarship, which laid down methods for the analysis and critical examination of texts.[8]

From the mid-sixteenth century, Confucian texts became available in greater quantity and variety than ever before. Indeed, the printing of books dealing with the Confucian classics expanded so greatly that it may have had adverse as well as favorable effects on social mobility, as P. T. Ho explains.[9] There is no doubt, however, that mass printing was an important factor in widening the circle of potential competitors for civil service degrees. Examination questions and answers, more practical aids to success, were now cheaply printed and available for purchase.[10]

At the same time there were yet cheaper books that served an expanding reading public. New developments in popular literature itself reflected historical changes in Chinese social structure.

Popular Literature

Literature from the Sung period onward reveals the influence of social change and the advent of large-scale printing. Poetry, formerly the exclusive province of degree holders and officials, was now also written by merchants, bookdealers, and even farmers' sons. Subjects that "according to earlier, more aristocratic canons of taste would have been considered undignified, mundane, or intrinsically prosy for discussion in verse"[11]—rats, lice, and the harshest, meanest aspects of life—were treated in Sung poems. The limited education of many minor poets in the period was also reflected in the tendency of Southern Sung (1127–1279) poetry to return to simpler T'ang models in style. Yoshikawa Kōjirō suggests that anthologies like the *San-t'i T'ang-shih* were intended as a type of handbook for such amateur poets. A popular commercially produced genre, books of "remarks on poetry" (*shih-hua*)[12] appealed to the same audience.

The beginnings of vernacular literature and the emergence of the novel in China were both stimulated by an urban milieu. Vera Hrdlickova has described how the literati would select and work up stories that they heard recited or sung by the professional storytellers in the marketplace. Vernacular fiction reveals its links with earlier improvised and spoken performances in its use of the spoken language and certain storytellers' conventions. In turn, the printed stories influenced the professional storytellers, who adopted turns of speech and dialect from the written language and its historical and religious themes.[13]

The printed editions of vernacular fiction extant from the Sung and Yüan periods, with their copious use of illustrations and simplified characters, must have attracted a fairly wide readership.[14] The purpose of the illustrations, according to Liu Ts'un-yan, was "to elucidate the story." In some Yüan and Ming editions, every half-folio was illustrated, with captions printed horizontally above the illustrations. By late Ming, the illustrations were reduced in number, but they still often occupied a full folio in a chapter.[15]

Vernacular fiction had an especially lively development during the sixteenth and seventeenth centuries, culminating in the novels of the eighteenth century. For Jaroslav Prusek, this period "appears more and more clearly to us as the dawn of a new era in Chinese literature. . . . During this time narrative prose came to occupy the dominant place in Chinese literature, while the character of this genre was undergoing a profound change. . . . From the eighteenth century onwards, . . . great artists began to cultivate narrative prose, seeing in it the most significant literary instrument and expressing through it their emotions and opinions. It thus began to take the place formerly held by the predominant genres of lyric poetry and the literary essay."[16] Although the eighteenth century saw the artistic and literary culmination of the novel in China, earlier works such as *The Romance of the Three Kingdoms* and *Water Margin* were still extremely popular with Ch'ing readers. Literature and drama often received inspiration from the same historical sources and from each other; numerous incidents from these novels were dramatized in various forms. Drama itself was divided into two types: the elite forms, which had developed with heavy dependence on the Ch'ing court and the wealthy patrons of the lower Yangtze cities, and popular drama, which was supported by theatrical performances at village religious festivals, clan ancestral sacrifices, and guild meetings, as well as by performances in urban theaters.[17]

Besides the plays themselves, Ch'ing publishers printed versions of street entertainment connected with the theater, such as the *t'an-tz'u* verses from the Soochow region which were sung and narrated with instrumental accompaniment, and the *ku-tz'u* from the Peking area. There were also versions in Cantonese. Scrutiny of some of the Cantonese ballads dating from the eighteenth and nineteenth centuries indicates that the books were usually small, printed on low quality paper, and ranged in length from two or three pages to booklets arranged in sets. According to Wolfram Eberhard, these ballads "are written *by* simple writers, not by scholars, and *for* simple folk to be read by them or to be listened to. . . . the ballads contain . . . details on customs in the Canton area; and the values which the ballads represent are often not the so-called 'Confucian' values."[18]

Immense collections of popular songs, some of them written by women, were published, especially during the second half of the Ch'ing dynasty.[19] Late Ming and Ch'ing readers could also choose from a wealth of printed diversion in the form of short stories, ranging from detective tales and ghost stories to accounts of heroic knights-errant.[20] Collections of jokes, essays, travelogues, and even salacious pseudohistories of the imperial household, were also written and offered for sale.[21]

The vast range of commercially printed literature for amusement was paralleled by an equally diverse group of materials for aid in self-improvement and practical affairs. Morality books (*shan-shu*) articulated popular religious sentiments. These books, studied by Sakai Tadao, became popular in Yüan times, but actually go back much earlier. Incorporating notions from popular Buddhism, Taoism, and Confucianism, the *shan-shu* prescribed meritorious behavior for individuals. One type, the "Ledgers of Merit and Demerit," presented lists of good and bad deeds to which points were assigned, so that one could tot up one's own moral net worth. Yet another kind of morality book, exemplified by *Meritorious Deeds at No Cost,* emerged, according to Sakai, in response to a demand for moral guides suited to the needs of the ordinary citizen.[22] The morality books served many different social groups: many specify behavior appropriate for each group, sometimes delineating occupational categories beyond the traditional four classes. W. L. Idema notes that a new emphasis on the possibility of individuals to shape their own destinies is expressed, not only in these morality books but in late Ming novels as well.[23]

Another category of books linked to popular religion were the *pao-chüan* (precious scrolls), Ming and Ch'ing materials named after Buddhist stories, and used by heterodox religious sects to propagate their beliefs. These late Ming and early Ch'ing *pao-chüan,* usually handwritten, were banned,[24] but in the nineteenth century, book publishers in lower Yangtze cities began printing *pao-chüan* that often presented literary rather than religious themes, including tales of knights-errant and other popular stories.[25]

In the fifteenth and sixteenth centuries, the demand for books relating to practical affairs stimulated the printing of popular encyclopedias, the *jih-yung lei-shu* (encyclopedias of daily use). These encyclopedias were offshoots of earlier compendia, dating back to the T'ang dynasty, which had been originally intended for the literati. The new versions published in the Ming treated topics of concern to ordinary citizens: the compilers often proclaimed their purpose in prefaces stating that the books were written for the use of all four classes in society.[26]

Popular encyclopedias catered to specialized interests. Some were essentially collections of sample forms for drawing up official documents or for writing various kinds of letters. Others dealt with elementary education, and still others focused on household affairs. Most encyclopedias included sample contract forms, of obvious importance to ordinary citizens: there were forms for selling or mortgaging lands, houses, or livestock; tenancy contracts; loan agreements; and forms for hiring porters or boatmen. Some editions provided the proper form to use when reporting a theft; the object named as stolen on the sample form in one encyclopedia was the most expensive item in a farmer's household—his ox.[27] Sakai has noted that none of the letter and document forms in these popular encyclopedias involved procedures for official correspondence or for communications with the emperor.[28]

The range of topics treated in popular encyclopedias was far wider than their titles suggest. One could find model clan and household regulations; detailed descriptions of the rites to be performed at birth, marriage, coming of age, and death; expositions of astronomy, astrology, agriculture, and craft techniques; illustrated sections on foreign barbarians; and information on wines, foods, clothing, and travel routes. In some respects, popular encyclopedias resembled Western almanacs, crammed with odds and ends of information and advice oriented to the interests and concerns of a nonelite readership.

Still another kind of popular material was the cartoon, the forerunner of the modern comic book. The *lien-huan t'u-hua* have been studied by Ch'ien Hsing-ts'un, who dates the beginnings of this form from the Six Dynasties period (222–589). From the sixth century to the Sung dynasty, the cartoon, which originated as a single illustration for a story, grew in length so that a complete story might be illustrated with as many as ten, twenty, or even thirty drawings. Short stories and plays were frequently accompanied by such illustrations.[29]

By the eighteenth century there were single-page cartoons, called *nien hua,* which were dominated by illustrations rather than by text and printed in one or many colors.[30] Like the comics, the *nien hua* presented sequential drawings, with explanatory writing placed beside certain characters in the pictures. From the *nien hua* to the comic books printed in Republican China and in the People's Republic today, one can trace a direct line.[31] In addition, there was in the Ch'ing period a form of tabloid newspaper that relied heavily on illustrations—the *hsin-wen-chih* (mentioned in chapter 1), which was printed to report unusual events.[32]

Illustrated materials also played a role in the dissemination of technology. Cartoons were used to convey information on agricultural techniques as early as the thirteenth century. The most important instance of such use during the Ch'ing was the publication of the *Keng chih t'u* (Pictures of plowing and weaving).[33]

Some popular literature was specifically educational in intent. Two types, the arithmetic books and the character glossaries, will be discussed in detail in the next chapter.[34] The richness and variety of printed literature in the Ch'ing provides eloquent testimony of the dominant role played by writing in this culture.

Printing Houses

As the volume of printing increased, elite publishing became separated from more mass-oriented printing. Scholarly texts and personal writings were brought out under literati sponsorship, and the printing of educational texts was sponsored by academies. Then, from the Yüan period on, there were commercial printers who specialized in producing reading materials of a vulgar bent. One outstanding commercial printing center of this sort was located in Chien-an and Chien-yang counties in northwest Fukien.

Ma-sha chen in Chien-yang and "Booktown" (Shu-fang chen) in Chien-an were filled with bookdealers who printed books for profit. In the Yüan dynasty, there were forty-eight known private publishers in Chien-an county alone, but until the destruction of Ma-sha by fire in 1500, the greatest commercial book output came from Chien-yang. Quality production, on the other hand, was centered in Soochow, Nanking, and Hangchow during the Yüan period.[35]

Profit was the criterion for selection of works to be published in Fukien: a decree issued in 1532 by the Office of the Provincial Judge in Fukien indicates that Chien-yang firms were printing poorly edited, cheap editions of the Confucian classics.[36] The increasing volume of printing encouraged specialization. Some houses specialized in color printing, others in specific categories of books such as medical texts or popular encyclopedias. The Fukienese printer Yü Hsiang-tou, a member of an old Chien-yang firm, was known for his illustrated novels, plays, and popular encyclopedias.[37]

During the Ch'ing dynasty, printing for the elite market was dominated by Kiangsu firms; Nanking, Soochow, and Hangchow remained as the major centers of quality commercial book printing. The producers of cheap popular editions, however, were more dispersed; and books were also printed by bookstores with regional branches.[38] For example, an early Ch'ing firm, the Shan-ch'eng t'ang, printed and sold popular fiction in branch stores in Kiangsu, Chekiang, and Fukien.[39] According to one source,

> For size of printings, Kiangsi and Kwangtung are the greatest. Kiangsi's printing is in Chin-hsi county's Hsü-wan; Kwangtung's is in Shun-te county's Ma-kang. Both have prospered from large numbers of printings.[40]

Other printing centers in Nan-ch'ang, Kiangsi; Ch'ang-sha, Hunan; and parts of Yunnan were active in early Ch'ing times.[41] Later, after the Taiping Rebellion of the mid-nineteenth century, the government opened printing bureaus in Nanking, Yangchow, Hunan, and Hupei. Shanghai also grew as a printing center when lead type was adopted.[42]

The procedure for printing at the Kwangtung center of Makang, situated on the Pearl River Delta, is described in a local gazetteer:

> Now woodblock editions cut at Ma-kang virtually encircle the forest of letters. Women and children can all do it; the men only carve the text on the blocks, according to the handwritten manuscript. The rest is done with female labor. Because of their cheapness, the books go everywhere. When the Soochow merchants come into Kwangtung to sell to the shops, they pick up Ma-kang imprints. Books they wish printed do not bear an imprint when done. The books are taken to Kiangnan and sold there with a Kiangsu imprint. Those within the empire who see them take them to be Soochow books.[43]

Another Kwangtung printing center was located at Fo-shan, a short distance from Ma-kang.[44] Despite occasional evidence of higher technical skills, these printers, like those at Chien-yang, were known primarily as producers of low quality, cheap books. Their use of unskilled female labor may account for the poor quality and low prices of these editions, as was the case at Ma-kang and at Hsü-wan, the Kiangsi center of popular publishing.[45] Cost advantages of cheap labor, paper, and ink also encouraged the establishment of clusters of printing houses in Hunan and Fukien.[46]

The marketing of books in urban areas seems to have been dominated by merchants from the lower Yangtze centers and Kiangsi. As already noted, it was Soochow merchants who exported Kwangtung books out of the province. The central location of Soochow as a book entrepot may explain why the Peking book quarter of the eighteenth century was dominated by merchants from Huchou, Soochow, and Kiangsi. It was not until the late nineteenth century that book traders from Chihli emerged as an important element in Peking's Liu-li-ch'ang book district.[47]

Government prohibitions provide further information about the distribution and printing of popular literature. Works of fiction and drama, songbooks, and unorthodox versions of the Confucian classics were all banned from production and sale because it was feared that they stood in the way of improving public mores.[48] The outraged sentiments of local officials are well expressed by the Soochow prefect who issued a ban on "lascivious paintings" after a visit to the book quarter:

> Each shop has lascivious books and pictures to sell for profit and to inflame people with lust. The filth extends into the women's quarters, increasing evil and licentiousness. There is nothing worse than this. The pictures that stimulate heterodox licentiousness are worse than lewd books, since books can only be understood by those with a rough knowledge of letters, while the pictures are perceptible to all.[49]

Efforts in Soochow to prevent the sale of such books reveal that they came from two sources: bookstores that printed the books themselves and traders who brought them into the city from elsewhere. In one agreement, dated 1837, sixty-five Soochow bookstores agreed to turn in banned books and the woodblocks from which they were printed for compensation. Outside traders bringing in such books were threatened with punishment.[50] The frequent repetition of prohibitions in many areas suggests that official controls were ineffective; that instead, the dissemination of popular printed materials in the cities continued; and that bookstores and book rental agencies were full of "lascivious" works. It was further cautioned that since there were also "lascivious" songbooks that "spread their poison very broadly" in the countryside, constant vigilance was required.[51]

Book Prices

Most recorded Ch'ing book prices are for the rare book market, which was especially active in lower Yangtze cities like Soochow and Hangchow. A hint of the prices offered in this market is given in the notice posted by the eminent seventeenth century bibliophile, Mao Chin:

> For a printed Sung edition, the owner of this house will be willing to give as much as 200 cash per leaf; for a manuscript

> copy, as much as 40 cash per leaf. For one good modern edition, if others offer 1,000, the owner here will be willing to pay 1,200 [cash].[52]

Some information on rare book prices in the late seventeenth century can be gleaned from an inventory of Mao Chin's collection of 500 titles, which lists the price he paid for each.[53] Mao and other bibliophiles searched out Sung and Yüan editions, which were far beyond the reach or interest of ordinary citizens. Yet a glance at the prices he paid for such rare books shows relatively modest levels of expenditure: many of Mao's books were purchased for a few hundred cash. The most expensive item cost a hundred taels, but the average price he paid for printed books was only 4.9 taels.[54]

Popular fiction and other materials produced for the mass market were cheaper, poorly printed, often with errors, and on paper of low quality. The prices charged for such works are rarely recorded. A Ming edition of the novel *Feng-shen yen-i* (Investiture of the gods) in 20 chüan with 100 chapters, sold for two taels of silver, a fairly high price.[55] Popular encyclopedias, which were often a hundred or more chüan in length, are said to have cost one tael in the sixteenth century. This amounts to a price of 8 cash per chüan for one such work, published in 1611 in 125 chüan.[56] Subsequent editions of poorer quality may have cost only one-tenth this sum. The *tsa-tzu,* which were very short, may have cost less than 100 cash.[57]

Although there is no direct information on the prices of other popular books during the eighteenth and nineteenth centuries, the low prices cited for scholarly works of better quality suggest that popular literature continued to be inexpensive.[58] This view is supported by the low cost of printing during the Ch'ing.

Printing Costs

The process of woodblock printing was a very simple one that did not change radically during the Ming and Ch'ing periods. According to a description furnished by Thomas Carter:

> The material used is generally pear wood. The wooden plate or block, of a thickness calculated to give it sufficient strength, is finely planed and squared to the shape and dimensions of two pages. The surface is then rubbed over with a paste or size . . . which renders it quite smooth and at the same time softens and otherwise prepares it for the reception of the characters. The future pages which have been finely transcribed by a professional person on thin transparent paper, are delivered to the block cutter, who, while the above mentioned application is still wet, unites them to the block so that they adhere; but in an inverted position, the thinness of the paper displaying the writing perfectly through the back. This paper being subsequently rubbed off, a clear impression in ink of the inverted writing still remains on the wood. The workman then with his sharp graver cuts away . . . all that portion of the wooden surface which is not covered by ink, leaving the characters in fairly high relief. Any slight error may be corrected . . . by inserting small pieces of wood. . . . The printer holds in his right hand two brushes at opposite extremities of the same handle; with one he inks the face of the characters, and, the paper being then laid on the block, he runs the dry brush over it so as to take the impression.[59]

The major expenses involved in printing included the cost of raw materials (paper, ink, and woodblocks) and the cost of labor for transcribing, carving, printing, and binding (sewing the sheets together). There were almost no capital costs: as a Western source noted, no foundries for casting type and no complicated machines for printing or binding were needed. Indeed, all of the essential tools could be packed and carried on a workman's back.[60] The woodblocks themselves, once carved, could last for as many as 30,000 printings; they could be stored for reprinting, or if used to print popular fiction, sold to another printer in the same city or elsewhere.[61] With actual woodblocks in hand, the printing was swift; one man could produce several thousand copies of a block in a day.[62] There were no significant scale economies in this kind of production.

Raw materials were a relatively minor factor in the total cost of producing a book. Prices varied according to the quality of the paper, ink, and wood from which blocks were carved. Pear wood was the standard material, but printers making cheap editions resorted to a softer wood that was easier to carve but produced a blurred imprint.[63] Ink and paper were relatively small components of the total cost. The ink used in a 1773–74 printing of a Kiangsu clan genealogy cost .22 taels per catty, or 5.8 taels in all, out of a total cost of over 300 taels.[64] Paper, purchased for the same purpose in 1789–90, cost 1.6 cash for a large sheet out of which several folios could be cut.[65] Estimates of the cost of printing the early Han dynasty *Shih chi* (Historical records), drawn up in the late eighteenth century for the *Ssu-k'u ch'üan-shu* project, allocated 167.5 taels for the purchase of the necessary pear wood blocks, less than one-fourth the cost of labor for carving them.[66]

Charges for carving woodblocks depended on the size and style of the characters used. In one example from the 1840s, the cost was sixty-eight cash per hundred characters,[67] but this may not have been a minimum price. Since the blocks had to be carved regardless of whether ten or ten thousand copies were to be printed, the relative expense of a book fell as the number of copies to be printed rose. This is illustrated by comparative figures for the two texts presented in table 15. The carving cost of the woodblocks required to print Text A, the rules for a free school run by the Hall of United Benevolence in Shanghai, represented 49.7 percent of the total cost of production, while the carving cost for the much longer regulations (Text B) represented only 30.4 percent of the total cost. When the relative difference in length is accounted for by calculating the printing cost per character (item 6 in the table), the effect of increased volume of printing costs is obvious.

According to Yeh Te-hui, the cost of carving woodblocks gradually increased during the Ch'ing period, from a charge of twenty cash per hundred characters in the late seventeenth century to fifty to sixty cash per hundred in the late 1870s.[68] Most of this increase, however, reflected the inflationary trend of the times, and the real cost rose only slightly.[69] Furthermore, costs could be reduced by using female labor, at 16 to 23 percent of the normal wages.[70]

It was thus possible to produce books for well under a hundred cash. As we have noted, a short text, if produced in sufficient volume, might cost just a few cash a copy—less than the cost of a bowl of noodles.[71] Except in regions with access to inexpensive water transport or in centers of book printing, however, the price

TABLE 15
Printing Costs in the 1840s

	Text A	Text B
Number of characters	726	25,666
Carving cost (cash)[a]	493.68	17,452.88
Total cost (cash)	994.0	57,453.0[b]
Number of copies printed	50	500
Cost per copy (cash)	19.9	114.9
Cost per character (cash)	0.0274	0.0045

Source: Text A: Reports of the twenty-first and twenty-second years of the Hall of United Benevolence in Shanghai, contained in "Regulations, etc., of Hall of United Benevolence for the relief of widows, the support of aged, providing of coffins, burial-grounds, etc.," *Chinese Repository* 15 (1846):424. Text B: Rules of the Free School operated by the Hall of United Benevolence, in ibid.

[a]The charge for carving was 68 cash per hundred characters.

[b]The total cost minus 400 cash spent on distributing the completed volumes.

of certain books could be considerably higher. Smith observed that in rural Shantung, the cost of Chinese books was "practically prohibitory to teachers who are poor," and that a good edition of the *K'ang-hsi Dictionary,* new, might cost as much as a village teacher's annual salary. This was a high quality edition, however, with "clear type and no false characters," of a work that was aimed at the literati market. Such books were rare in rural Shantung, but there were small, cheap pocket dictionaries in general use, and textbooks available in the village schools.[72] These shorter works not only cost less to transport, but could also be inexpensively printed by itinerants.[73]

It was always possible to copy a text by hand, although this was an onerous task with a long manuscript. Fees for professional copyists were low: Yeh Te-hui estimated that a "skillful scribe" in Hunan charged seventy to eighty cash per thousand characters, presumably a high figure consonant with the standards imposed by his bibliophilic interests.[74] Handwritten copies were sometimes used as textbooks in charitable schools, as in a Honan county where students could either buy a printed text or study from a handwritten copy.[75]

Ch'ing readers had another alternative to outright purchase—the use of the circulating libraries mentioned previously. These could be set up in shops or stalls, or by peddlers moving from place to place with their collections of books. The fee for borrowing a book was probably only a few cash.[76]

Summary

A survey of printing costs indicates that it was possible to produce cheap books selling for a few cash in the Ch'ing period. Books could also be copied by hand or borrowed from libraries. The range of alternatives available suggests that reading material in printed form could be obtained by one means or another throughout most parts of China. This view is corroborated by the persistent popularity of vernacular fiction into the twentieth century, when ordinary peasants, artisans, and factory workers, as well as more prosperous persons, were included among the readers of these materials.[77]

Indeed, China's development of popular culture is comparable in many respects with that of Europe. Leo Lowenthal has defined "mass media" as "the marketable cultural goods produced for a substantial buying public," and claims that the eighteenth century in England was the "first period in history where it can meaningfully be applied."[78] He argues that lowered production and distribution costs in the eighteenth century supplied new kinds of works, such as popular novels, newspapers, and magazines to an audience which included women, merchants, and shopkeepers. The larger market permitted a professionalization of writers and independence from the old system of patronage by the elite. There was a concomitant increase in the channels for distributing materials: the rise of the circulating library and the expansion of the bookselling trade exemplify this trend.[79]

In England, Lowenthal identifies the emergent middle class as the stimulus for the growth of popular culture. In China, which lacked a middle class as normally defined, the development of written forms of popular culture rested on low production costs and a printing technology that permitted small-scale production. New genres reflecting nonelite interests, the emergence of an identifiable group of printers specializing in the production of popular works, and even circulating libraries are found in the Chinese as well as the English context. Criticism of low literary standards in

English popular literature is paralleled by official Chinese denunciations of novels, drama, and fictional works as harmful to public mores.

In China, however, the estrangement of elite and popular cultures was more apparent than real. Chinese of all backgrounds united in an appreciation of popular fiction and its related arts, popular drama and songs. Influenced by the oral tradition, yet often written by highly educated men, literary works in these fields combined elements from both worlds. In turn, it was through these channels that simplified and transmuted versions of historical events and personages, of religious dogma and philosophical doctrine, created initially in the elite world, filtered down to the ordinary Chinese. An old man, reminiscing about his boyhood in the Canton delta in the late nineteenth century, recreates this transmission:

> The front porch of our home was paved with granite, and we used to gather there in the evenings after supper to listen to our elders. Someone would start off with a story from the Three Kingdoms period, perhaps one of the many stories of K'ung Ming. . . . And the story-teller, whenever the action became exciting, would burst into lines of poetry that said so much in so few words, often chanting the words in sing-song fashion that appealed to us. And that night, before we could fall asleep, we must repeat those lines of poetry until they too became a part of our being. We had become heirs to our great literary tradition.[80]

Chapter 6

Popular Educational Materials

When Mao Tse-tung recalled his boyhood and early education, he remembered vividly the pleasure he had derived from reading great Chinese novels like *The Romance of the Three Kingdoms* and *Water Margin*. There is no denying the hold these works had on the popular imagination. Mao's father, however, sent him to school for a more prosaic reason—so that he could learn enough to help with the accounts. If the primary motivation for many ordinary parents educating their sons was the hope of eventual success in the civil service examinations, a second and more easily realizable goal was that they learn to read, write, and do enough arithmetic to function in daily life. Throughout the Ch'ing period, there was concrete evidence of the advantages of even limited literacy, whether in the marketplace or when coping with kinsmen, officials, and tax collectors. Some of these advantages were described in chapter 1.

Occasionally in Ch'ing records one discovers self-educated persons such as Wu Liang-p'ing's grandfather and Yang Hsiu-ch'eng, the Taiping leader. How did these men learn? How did boys who attend school for only a year or two consolidate what they had learned? Two kinds of educational aids, the arithmetic guides and the *tsa-tzu*, are the topic of this chapter. Both were available in cheaply printed editions. Both belong to the realm of popular rather than elite literature, and both gave practical aid to those seeking to learn basic skills.

Arithmetic Guides

Anyone familiar with the work of Joseph Needham is aware of the rich mathematical heritage possessed by the Chinese.[1] Although the advanced accomplishments of Chinese mathematicians were probably little known or appreciated by ordinary citizens, arithmetical ability was of obvious value to the merchant, artisan, and peasant as well as to the tax-collecting bureaucracy. As Arthur Smith observed,

> There is scarcely a man, woman or child in China, who will not spend a considerable fraction of life in handling brass cash, in larger or smaller quantities. It is a matter of great importance to each individual, to be able to reckon, if not rapidly, at least correctly, so as to save trouble, and what is to them of far more importance, money.[2]

Although, as noted in chapter 2, some clan schools hired specialists to teach arithmetic to students preparing for careers in trade, it was not generally taught in the schools. The absence of arithmetic from the curriculum does not mean, however, that people did not know how to perform simple calculations. Smith, who bemoaned the lack of arithmetic in the classroom, suggested that people learned arithmetical operations from others.[3]

Those who wished could also consult certain popular books, which had existed from late T'ang times and were fairly numerous by the thirteenth and fourteenth centuries. These texts contained problems, with expositions of the correct methods to arrive at the solutions, and simplified methods for multiplication and division, expressed in rhyme.[4] Later arithmetic guides also presented diagrams and explanations for using the abacus, which was commonly adopted by tradesmen in Ming and Ch'ing times.[5]

Most popular books on arithmetic also presented methods that did not require an abacus. There was a multiplication table, identical to that used in the West, which went up to the familiar "nine times nine." For solving more complex multiplication problems, rhymes were used as aids. Rules expressed in rhyme could also be memorized to simplify the computation for lengthy problems of long division. The *chiu-kuei* and *kuei-ch'u* division tables are examples of such simplified methods.[6] Arithmetic guides also included tables with units of measurement for capacity, weight, length, acreage, and money. They supplied characters for large numbers as well as for fractions.

The techniques of arithmetic, particularly multiplication and division, vary a great deal even in our modern age. European immigrants to North America, for example, persist in using methods they learned as children, and find it difficult to comprehend those taught their children in American schools. Our difficulty in comprehending Chinese methods does not, therefore, mean that they were useless or ineffective. That many Chinese could perform rather complicated calculations is affirmed by observers like Arthur Smith:

> A country villager with whom the writer is well acquainted had too little land to support his family, so he accepted the offer of a neighbor to help him with the business he had lately undertaken. This consisted of sending four wheel-barrows to different villages daily to sell meat at the markets. . . . On the return of the barrows at night it was necessary to weigh what was left from the sales and compare it with the return of cash. This must be gone through with for each barrow. The assistant to the meat-dealer had to keep in all *fourteen different account books*.[7]

Smith and the villager were both taken aback at the enormous number of account books involved in the record-keeping. As Smith points out, each entry had to be checked on the abacus.

For our purposes, this anecdote is significant for its description of the ability of a marginal farmer, without enough land to support his family, to keep fairly complex accounts and to use an abacus. Smith's acquaintance had not been trained in a shop, yet his ability to keep books does not occasion further comment from the missionary. Similarly, Mao Tse-tung's father, with only a minimal education, kept his own account books until Mao was old enough to help him. Wu Liang-p'ing's grandfather, who taught himself to read and write, ran a grocery store and must have been able to do simple calculations.[8]

These examples point to the likelihood that the simple rhymed methods presented in arithmetic books, and perhaps some familiarity with the abacus, were fairly widespread even among ordinary citizens who lacked the specialized training given to apprentices in large commercial establishments. Multiplication and division tables that eliminated laborious computations and could be memorized were obviously useful in the lives of citizens who not only paid taxes, but participated in a marketing network that utilized a complex money system. Knowledge of the basic units of measurement was similarly essential for daily life.

Character Books

The term *tsa-tzu* (literally, "miscellaneous characters") is applied to a broad range of popular educational literature that consisted essentially of collections of characters used to teach reading recognition. According to Sakai, the *tsa-tzu,* which included words and phrases useful in daily life, were a kind of pocket dictionary for the beginning student.[9] But unlike dictionaries, *tsa-tzu* usually did not define the characters presented; they are perhaps more accurately described as reading primers.

Tsa-tzu had long been popular among ordinary householders. The Sung writer Lu Yu observed that *tsa-tzu* were called "village books" because they were studied in the short-term winter schools attended by farmers' sons, and the early eighteenth century writer P'u Sung-ling described a work called the *Farmer's Character Book (Chuang-nung tsa-tzu)* that many village youths in his native Shantung recited.[10]

The *tsa-tzu* circulated among the lower strata of society. They were not usually accepted into the orthodox elementary curriculum. As the regulations of one charitable school state, "Generally what pertains to orthodox studies should be made primary; all *tsa-tzu* and vulgar books must not be studied."[11] Since they were regarded by the elite as vulgar books, it is not surprising that few *tsa-tzu* were signed by their authors. Generally not dated, and considered too lowly to be kept in libraries, they are rare books today. *Tsa-tzu* were printed as separate volumes, usually only a few pages in length, on cheap paper. Sometimes they were included in larger compendia, the popular encyclopedias. Although they had existed from very early times, *tsa-tzu* became especially numerous beginning in the late Ming.[12]

As noted in chapter 2, a popular method of teaching beginners to read was to use square blocks which were inscribed with one character per block. A variant of the square blocks was a book that brought together the initial characters to be learned, each written in a ruled square. Such books could be called *tsa-tzu*.[13] The simplest kind of *tsa-tzu* consisted of just such collections of characters. Often each character was accompanied by an illustration that facilitated identification of the character. Such *tsa-tzu* were not grouped explicitly into categories, and there was no attempt to make meaningful phrases or stories from the characters.

Chang Chih-kung divided the *tsa-tzu* into four groups on the basis of their increasing complexity of organization and content. Most of these books were not illustrated at all. First, there were the *tsa-tzu* that presented collections of words, in single- or multiple-character compounds, divided into categories such as the names of animals, plants, household implements, clothing, parts of the body, objects in nature, and so on. The characters were neither rhymed nor presented in meaningful phrases. *Tsa-tzu* in Chang's second group were also organized into categories, but written in rhymes of four or more characters. Group three consisted of *tsa-tzu* written in rhymed couplets to form meaningful phrases. Finally, the books in the fourth group, often compiled for a special region and purpose, were sometimes written in local dialect.[14]

The *tsa-tzu* were thus collections of characters that, like the square blocks, were meant to serve as aids for beginning readers. Used to teach character recognition, their primary emphasis was on introducing a given number of characters, and content was usually sacrificed to further this aim. In this respect, the *tsa-tzu* resembled the orthodox primers, which also slighted content while stressing the memorization of a large body of characters within a comparatively short time.

Illustrated Reading Primers

The simplest character books were those in which each character was accompanied by an illustration. As shown in figure 2, the illustration enabled the reader to grasp the meaning of the character easily. Such illustrated reading primers, published in separate volumes or incorporated into popular encyclopedias, can be called

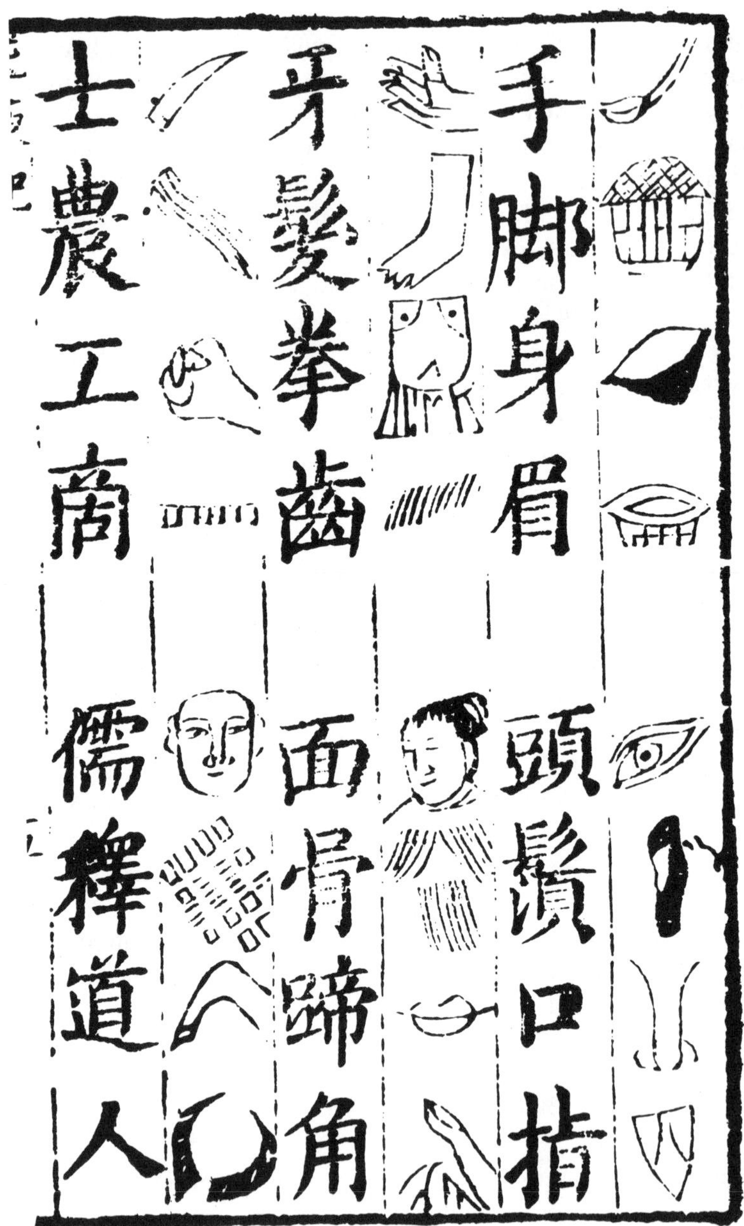

Fig. 2. Page from the *Tui-hsiang ssu-yen* (Illustrated four-character glossary). This page is typical of those in illustrated glossaries, with the character placed to the right of its accompanying illustration. (Courtesy of the Naikaku bunko, Tokyo)

illustrated glossaries, although unlike glossaries, the characters and character compounds presented are not defined.

Three glossaries published in single book form and three that are included in popular encyclopedias will be described here. The three illustrated books are: (A) *Tui-hsiang ssu-yen tsa-tzu* (Illustrated four-character glossary), said to be a 1371 edition;[15] (B) the fifteenth century *Hsin-pien Tui-hsiang Szu-yen* (Newly compiled illustrated four-character glossary);[16] and (C) the *Tui-hsiang ssu-yen* (Illustrated four-character glossary), which seems to be a Ch'ing edition.[17]

These three works, organized in identical fashion, appear to be related to each other. Each consists simply of illustrated one- and two-character terms, without explanatory notes or comments, and with no grouping of characters into categories. As shown in table 16, each presents a relatively small number of characters, especially when compared to the orthodox primers discussed in chapter 2. A large majority of the characters in each work, totalling 322 different characters, are common to all three. This figure represents 81.9 percent of the characters in Text A, 82.7 percent of those in Text B, and 92.7 percent of the ones in Text C.

TABLE 16
Comparison of Illustrated Glossaries

Text	Number of Leaves	Number of Illustrations	Number of Characters[a]	Number of Distinct Characters
Group I				
A	10.0	308	392	346
B	8.0	306	388	344
C	6.0	272	346	307
Group II				
A	22.5	360	480	435
B	30.0	360	480	437
C	15.0	360	485	441

Sources: Group I: Text A: *Tui-hsiang ssu-yen tsa-tzu*; Text B: *Hsin-pien Tui-hsiang Szu-yen*; Text C: *Tui-hsiang ssu-yen*. Group II: Text A: *Tseng-kuang yu-hsüeh hsü-chih ao-t'ou tsa-tzu ta-ch'üan*; Text B: *Tseng-pu i-chih tsa-tzu ch'üan-shu*; Text C: *Tseng-ting yu-hsüeh hsü-chih tsa-tzu ts'ai-chen*.

[a]In Group II, only the primary characters—not the homonyms—were counted, but repetitions were included.

The second group of illustrated reading primers includes those printed as parts of popular encyclopedias. Four examples will be studied. These are (A) the *Tseng-kuang yu-hsüeh hsü-chih ao-t'ou tsa-tzu ta-ch'üan* (Augmented and complete annotated glossary of knowledge essential for elementary schooling), a Ch'ing work;[18] (B) *Tseng-pu i-chih tsa-tzu ch'üan shu* (Augmented complete easy glossary), which is part of an undated popular encyclopedia entitled *Hsin-tseng yu-hsüeh i-chih kao-t'ou tsa-tzu ta-ch'üan;*[19] and (C) the *Tseng-ting yu-hsüeh hsü-chih tsa-tzu ts'ai-chen* (Expanded selected glossary of knowledge essential for elementary schooling), which has a Ch'ing date.[20] Another illustrated primer to be discussed is (D) the *Hsin-tseng yu-hsüeh i-chih kao-t'ou tsa-tzu ta-ch'üan* (Newly enlarged and complete easy glossary for elementary instruction). This work is part of the *Yu-hsüeh i-chih chia-li tsa-tzu,* a popular encyclopedia that probably dates from Ch'ing times, and is in any case identical with (B) in text, illustrations, and format.[21] In subsequent discussions, all generalizations applied to (B) thus cover (D) as well.

The illustrated primers incorporated in the popular encyclopedias cover only the upper third or quarter of each page. The rest of the page is printed with a separate, unillustrated glossary that is quite independent of the illustrated primer. Unlike the illustrated primers, the glossaries that occupy the bottom portion of the page are organized into categories. The illustrated primer has no definitions or commentaries, although the one- and two-character phrases are followed by a homonym in the same tone as the primary character. By contrast, the glossaries printed on the lower portion are accompanied by notes that comment on the meaning of each character.

As table 16 shows, the illustrated primers in Group II contain more characters than those in Group I. Again, a high percentage of the characters presented is common to all three works. These books share a total of 473 out of the 480 to 485 characters that appear in their pages.

When the characters used in the books of Groups I and II are compared, a common link between illustrated primers of both types is evident: 279 characters, or more than 80 percent of those presented in Group I texts and more than 60 percent of those in

Group II texts, appear in all six books. The six books together present 267 one-character terms and 156 two-character compounds. If repetitions are eliminated, these works introduced a total of 504 distinct characters.

Types of Terms

L. Carrington Goodrich noted that the obvious purpose of the illustrated glossary was "to teach people how to read everyday terms."[22] The majority of the words in the six texts are concerned with concrete objects and matters relevant to daily life, as is shown in table 17, which presents a summary of the various terms found in these works.

TABLE 17
Types of Terms Found in Illustrated Glossaries

	Characters in Each Category			
Category	Number in One-Character Terms	Number in Two-Character Terms	Number	Percentage of Total
Abstractions	0	6	6	1.0
Adjectives	5	0	5	0.9
Animals	48	16	64	11.0
Buildings and parts	15	26	41	7.1
Clothing and accessories	17	64	81	14.0
Cosmetics and hygiene	2	16	18	3.1
Food	0	8	8	1.4
Furnishings	11	14	25	4.3
Games and toys	1	6	7	1.2
Military weapons and armor	12	8	20	3.5
Minerals and materials	10	10	20	3.5
Musical instruments	14	0	14	2.4
Nature and geography	13	4	17	2.9
Parts of the body	18	0	18	3.1
People/social statuses	11	8	19	3.3
Tools	62	80	142	24.5
Transport	3	4	7	1.2
Unit measures	5	0	5	0.9
Vegetables and all plants	20	42	62	10.7
Total	267	312	579	100.0

Sources: Taken from the six texts cited in table 16.

Even the few words (1 percent of the total) that could be classified as abstract are homely in nature. It is not surprising in view of what we know about popular religion that *feng-shui,* the Chinese art of geomancy, is included in these glossaries, as is the compound for a method of divination (*pa-kua*)[23] and the one for numerals (*suan-tzu*). The illustrated glossaries completely ignore Confucian concepts, and omit the characters for "righteousness" (*i*), "rites" (*li*), and "virtue" (*te*).

It is perhaps natural that nouns dominate the elementary glossaries; these *tsa-tzu* contain no characters that function primarily as verbs in Chinese. There are also very few adjectives; only the most common descriptive words—round, square, tall, thin, and fat—are included.

The lists of animals, birds, insects, fish, and shellfish give not only the names of commonplace domestic species but those for fanciful mythological creatures like the dragon and the unicorn as well. Characters for real but exotic animals that would not normally be seen by any Chinese, such as the elephant, are also included. The suggestion that there might be a linguistic reason for their inclusion is supported by the persistence of such characters, which can be found even in post-1949 illustrated reading primers printed in the People's Republic.[24]

There are many words for articles of clothing, ranging from socks, jackets, trousers, and hats, to the garb of Buddhist monks. Among items of cosmetics and hygiene, the toothbrush appears alongside the razor, comb, and face powder. In the lists of words for buildings and architectural elements (gate, window, wall) are included names for animal pens. The agricultural importance of paddy rice, wheat, hemp, and beans makes the category of plant names obviously relevant to everyday life. Similarly, the usefulness of listing terms dealing with domestic furnishings (pillow, bed, table, stool, and such), parts of the body (ears, eyes, mouth), and transport (boats, wheelbarrow, sedan chair, carrying pole) needs no explanation.

There is also an abundance of words for tools and utensils. Many of them are for dishes and pots: there are twenty-five entries comprising thirty-four characters dealing with items of this nature. Agricultural implements, military weapons, and tools useful for artisans are also present. There are terms for implements used in milling, metalwork (anvil, tongs, and so forth), fishing, and textile weaving (shuttle, reed of a loom). The wheel and the abacus are presented in all six books. Tools for literary pursuits—the ink, ink-slab, brush, and paper—are also named.

Through the illustrated glossaries, a reader could learn to recognize characters for important flora and fauna, buildings, clothing, parts of the body, transport, and tools for domestic, field, or shop use. One could learn the names of metals, including gold and silver; unit measures for capacity (*tou, sheng*) and length (*ch'ih*); and the character for copper cash (*ch'ien*), the coin of everyday transactions. Despite their limited size, the illustrated glossaries present an impressive array of detailed information for many areas of everyday life.

Each glossary includes characters for major natural phenomena: heaven, clouds, thunder, rain, sun, moon, stars, mountains, rivers, and water. They deal with man-made creations such as roads, wells, and buildings—but here they stop. The traditional institutions that scholars regard as central to Chinese society do not appear in these glossaries: missing are terms for the family, the extended family or lineage, filial piety, the ancestors, gods, and ghosts.[25] Words for the village as an entity, not to mention guilds and government, are also absent from these pages.

All of the texts give the character for man (*jen*), but only those in Group II include woman (*fu-nü*), male child (*nan-erh*), and grandfather (*lao-tieh*). "Mother" is represented only in Group II texts, and then as part of a two-character compound for mica (*yün-mu*). The character for son (*tzu*) appears only as part of two-character compounds for various objects, never by itself or in a social context. The only terms relevant to social status are those that designate the traditional four classes (scholars, farmers, artisans, merchants), supplemented by characters for scholar (*ju*), Buddhist monk (*shih*), and Taoist priest (*tao*).

The boundaries of character recognition for readers of illustrated glossaries are thus exceedingly concrete and utilitarian. Religion and philosophy appear only in the guise of geomancy or divination, as names of temples, monasteries, and religious halls, or as names for the religious and philosophical specialists. The world of the imagination is ignored except for some mythological and exotic animals, some luxury items, and names of instruments and games of chance from the realm of entertainment.

Tsa-tzu versus Orthodox Primers

To fully appreciate the nature of the characters collected in the illustrated glossaries, they should be compared with those given in the orthodox elementary primers—the *Trimetrical Classic (San-tzu ching)* and the *Thousand-Character Classic (Ch'ien tzu wen)*.

The *Trimetrical Classic* was the text with which many children began their studies. It consists of 356 lines of three characters each, introducing about 500 characters after repetitions are eliminated. This total approximates the number of distinct characters (504) found in all six glossaries listed in table 16. The tone and emphasis of the *Trimetrical Classic* are evident from its opening lines:

> Men at their birth are naturally good. Their natures are much the same; their habits become widely different. If foolishly there is no teaching, the nature will deteriorate.[26]

A large part of the book contains hortatory injunctions, interspersed with historical anecdotes and information about such topics as the four seasons, the four points of the compass, and the Confucian Three Bonds (*san-kang*). Students are enjoined to study diligently: "Make a name for yourselves, and glorify your father and mother; shed lustre on your ancestors, enrich your posterity."[27] The characters "to study" (*hsüeh*), "righteousness" (*i*), and "to teach" (*chiao*), none of which appear in the glossaries, appear fifteen, seven, and six times respectively in the *Trimetrical Classic*.[28] The differences between this text and the popular illustrated glossaries in emphasis and interests are apparent when the characters common to both are counted: only sixty characters, about 12 percent of the total number in the classic and the same percentage of those in all six of the illustrated glossaries, are shared.

The *Ch'ien tzu wen,* perhaps China's "oldest primer,"[29] presents 1,000 characters, loosely organized into a narrative. In length, it is thus two to three times the size of an illustrated glossary. Like the *Trimetrical Classic,* it is a rhymed work that presents basic information interspersed with Confucian lessons on the universe and its components, China's past, its great men, and moral precepts for proper conduct. Even the section introducing characters related to agriculture presents the lesson in a didactic context and from the perspective of the elite:

> Good government is rooted in agriculture;
> Devote attention to it, sow and reap.
> Beginning work in the southern fields,
> I sow glutinous and panicled millet.
> Taxes are paid in ripe grain, tribute in new grain;
> And let there be exhortations and rewards, dismissals
> and promotions.[30]

Despite its size, the *Thousand-Character Classic* includes only 125 of the characters found in the illustrated glossaries: this figure constitutes only 12.5 percent of the characters in the classic and about 25 percent of those in the six glossaries.

The *Trimetrical Classic* and the *Thousand-Character Classic* occupied a central position in orthodox elementary education. The illustrated glossaries departed considerably from these standard texts in their complete lack of narrative and their method of inducing character recognition through pictures. These organizational differences were coupled with a vocabulary that deviated significantly from that introduced in the orthodox texts, one which was oriented to nonelite concerns and activities.

As the simplest kind of *tsa-tzu,* the illustrated glossaries represent what is perhaps an extreme form of separation from elite culture. Other kinds of *tsa-tzu* came closer to reproducing the outlook of the standard elite texts. An example is the *Chü-chia chin-yao jih-yung tsa-tzu* (Householders' essential glossary for daily use), a Ming work "newly printed and greatly enlarged" by a Fukien firm, the Wan-chüan lou.[31] This work, in one chüan, presents two- and three-character compounds designating objects in twenty-one categories. Although it was also basically just a list of characters, it includes many terms for family relationships, occupations, and words describing emotions—such as fear, sympathy, and worry—as well as verbs and adjectives.[32]

A book such as the *Chü-chia chin-yao jih-yung tsa-tzu* was still probably closer to the illustrated glossaries than to the orthodox texts in its basic orientation. When we examine *tsa-tzu* that were written in rhymed couplets to form meaningful phrases, there is discernible movement toward elite concerns. An example is an eighteenth century *tsa-tzu* called *Chin-yao tzu* (Important words), a work of one chüan written in five-character rhymes. Like the others, this glossary imparts vocabulary of a practical nature, but its perspective is much broader; the work introduces the Sage, albeit in a much more prosaic style than the orthodox primers: "Bean sauce is what Confucius required."[33] Unlike the illustrated glossaries, it also gives the names of various administrative units, from the county (*hsien*) to the state (*kuo*). It cites Confucian texts, and includes hortatory sentiments concerning filial piety and relations between siblings.

The most complex *tsa-tzu* tell stories that are frequently aimed at special audiences, and some employ local dialects. Chang Chih-kung described several examples: the *Shan-hsi tsa-tzu pi-tu* (Shansi essential glossary), which seems to be written for an urban mercantile readership; the *Liu-yen tsa-tzu* (Six-character glossary), aimed at children of fairly prosperous households dwelling at or near an urban center; and the *Shan-tung nung-chuang jih-yung tsa-tzu* (Shantung farmers' glossary for daily use), for children of "middle peasants."[34] This glossary for farmers presents terms for agricultural implements and processes in rhymed five-character couplets:

> When the ice melts, bring out the manure,
> Prepare it with a hoe and shovel.[35]

The work also discusses festivals, marriage customs, and other matters pertaining to the everyday life of the people, and thus combines the presentation of characters with a narrative meaningful to its reading public.

The *tsa-tzu* written in dialect provided a meaningful content that was far removed from the simple illustrated *tsa-tzu* described earlier. Even *tsa-tzu* that were simply lists of characters varied in complexity. A work like the *Hsin-k'o shih-i ch'ün-shu liu-yen lien-chu tsa-tzu* (Newly edited annotated glossary in six-word phrases for a host of books),[36] for example, which included lists of homonyms with brief definitions, was probably better suited to meet the needs of intermediate or advanced students than those of beginners. In their elaboration of content and their degree of difficulty, the *tsa-tzu* thus accommodated a wide range of reading skills. If we confine our attention to the simple illustrated glossary, how useful was it as an aid to literacy?

The long popularity *tsa-tzu* have enjoyed suggests that they were useful. We have earlier noted that they were utilized in Sung times. A missionary report in the 1830s observed that popular "miscellanies" that included illustrated glossaries had an "extensive circulation among the people" because of their small size and cheapness.[37] Pa Chin, who was born in 1904, used such a primer, the *Tzu-k'o t'u-shuo* (Illustrated reading primer) in his early schooling; he liked the pictures.[38] This kind of simple illustrated glossary continues to be published in the People's Republic today.

The *tsa-tzu* were not intended to be the sole written reference available to persons with limited education. They were mainly intended for children and were used in the early phases of instruction, supplemented by other materials.

Used alone, the *tsa-tzu* would not have presented enough material to teach a person to read and write. But adult needs could be met by a variety of information incorporated into the popular encyclopedias. These *jih-yung lei-shu,* which have been extensively described by Niida Noboru and Sakai Tadao,[39] included many items directly relevant to everyday life. An example is the *Tseng-kuang yu-hsüeh hsü-chih ao-t'ou tsa-tzu ta-ch'üan* discussed earlier. In addition to an illustrated glossary, this popular encyclopedia contained a section on arithmetic, with instructions for the abacus; form letters appropriate to various situations; contract forms for hiring laborers, buying land and houses, and so on; suitable forms of address for various persons; information on the provinces in China; travel routes throughout the empire; a historical record of the successive dynasties and emperors; an essay on Confucius and another on his disciples; the text of the *Thousand-Character Classic;* and other items. A man of limited education probably would have sought the help of those who were better educated than he for his more complicated transactions; but at some stage references such as the popular encyclopedias could have provided the necessary language and forms for written communications.

Chapter 7

Popular Literacy in Perspective

In previous chapters we have studied the institutional and private channels for elementary education in Ch'ing China, and some of the voluminous educational materials available to students during that period. Evidence of the large number of potential teachers and the widespread distribution of private schools led us to conclude that it was possible for a broad cross-section of Ch'ing males to attain some degree of literacy in private and charitable schools. Information from the mid- and late nineteenth century suggests that 30 to 45 percent of the men and from 2 to 10 percent of the women in China knew how to read and write. This group included the fully literate members of the elite and, on the opposite pole, those knowing only a few hundred characters. Thus loosely defined, there was an average of almost one literate person per family.[1]

The significance of this finding rests on an analysis of the role of literacy in Ch'ing society and, more broadly, on a comparison of Chinese conditions with those of preindustrial Europe. China emerges from such a comparison as an advanced society, with many modern characteristics that helped ease its transition to modernity in the twentieth century. This point is highlighted by an assessment of the contribution of literacy and education to the modernization process during the Industrial Revolution in England and Meiji industrial development in Japan, along with a discussion of the qualities required for modern life from a social-science perspective.

The Role of Popular Literacy in Ch'ing Society

In addition to its obvious practical uses, the ability to read and write was enhanced by the special Chinese attitude toward writing—the belief that Chinese characters had a certain "magic quality":

> In ancient times the Chinese characters undoubtedly had magical values. . . . Prayers in Chinese were not spoken to the gods but were written. . . . In East Asian civilization the written word has always taken precedence over the spoken; Chinese history is full of famous documents—memorials, essays, and poems—but lacks the great speeches of the West. The magic quality of writing is perhaps one of the reasons why the peoples of East Asia have tended to place a higher premium on book learning and on formal education than have the peoples of any other civilization.[2]

Mark Mancall has noted the importance of the written word as a "conveyor of virtue" and, on the popular level, its ritual importance in religion.[3] The magical properties of writing itself and the uses of written materials for religious activities can be distinguished for analytic purposes. Both were present in China.

During the Ch'ing, there were societies devoted to saving from destruction papers on which characters had been printed or written. Although the elite generally led such groups, reverence towards written materials was a more general Chinese trait, which Doolittle described as a "national characteristic."[4] This veneration was transmitted to others when Chinese settlers moved into areas inhabited by non-Han peoples. According to Yunnanese migrants in northern Thailand, the Lisu and Yao hill tribesmen honored Chinese writing; Yao shamans even recited incantations from Chinese texts.[5] Presumably, for these tribesmen, some of the magical aura linked with characters still lingered.

The doctrinal texts of Buddhism and Taoism and the manuals of geomancy and other practices were not intended for ordinary citizens, but extensive use was made of written materials at the lower levels of Chinese religious activity. In some instances, the written name of a god or spirit was all that was needed to create a shrine.[6] Communications with the gods were written: requests for rain, personal aid, or foreknowledge frequently took forms paralleling official communications within the bureaucracy. Charms and spells, viewed in this light, were "written orders sent into the world of spirits; in this quality they mostly bear, as is the case with terrestrial official orders, the impress of a seal.''[7]

When the gods replied, they also often had recourse to writing. We have already described various forms of fortune-telling based on Chinese characters. Divination, another popular religious activity, could also take on written form.[8] C. K. Yang observes that "in the traditional days, it was not the Confucian classics that enjoyed the widest sale, but the *li shu,* the almanac, that gave not only climatological information for agriculture but also magical guidance for activities in daily life.''[9] Such books listed lucky and unlucky days for specific activities: from weddings, funerals, opening businesses, and travelling, to digging the foundations for a new home.[10] Unlike the specialized doctrinal texts, this information was available to all in cheaply printed editions.

The ordinary citizen was thus a participant in a religious system that used written materials on the humblest levels. Even the religious rebel had recourse to written materials as an integral part of prophecies of doom and restoration, frequently built on cryptograms or puns.[11] Moreover, records and written manuals were part of the organizational fabric of the secret society.[12]

Chinese were also surrounded by writing used for decorative effect. Of course, calligraphy was an elite art form, but the use of written couplets to adorn homes was not confined to the elite. Auspicious couplets were displayed on doors and walls; characters were inscribed on windows, rocks, clothing, fans, snuff-bottles, tobacco-pouches, and fan-cases; and characters ornamented cups, saucers, plates, chopsticks, teapots, incense-burners, and cabinets. The appreciation of Chinese characters as decorative elements thus extended deep into the mainstream of Chinese culture.[13]

The religious and aesthetic dimensions of Chinese writing should not obscure its more mundane values. Not only did education offer a means of moving upward through the competitive civil service examinations into the political and social elite of Ch'ing society, but the very existence of this system of recruitment for office lent prestige to those who were lettered. The "perfume" of books and ink enhanced the status of families with educated members, although it was the acquisition of an elite education, not the basic tools of literacy, that conferred social respect.

The benefits of literacy were not confined to the elite. The prevalence of written contracts and communications and of specialized skills in this complex society meant that those with any ability to read and write were rewarded. Thus members of the elite who sponsored popular education saw it as a means of social indoctrination, but parents sending sons to charitable schools hoped for social and economic advance, either through the selection of a son for advanced study, or through the more modest gains possible with limited reading and writing ability.

In chapter 1, we reviewed some of the utilitarian ways in which literacy and written materials affected the life of the city dweller and the rural householder. The ubiquitousness of writing can be seen in the activities of various organizations in Ch'ing society: whether religious, political, social, or economic in nature, all used written materials both in their attempts at external communication with other groups and in their internal communications and organizational writings (rules and regulations, membership rolls, and so on). If government was the home of the literati, the same cannot be said for the guild, the secret society, and the lineage, whose membership included substantial numbers of persons outside the elite.

The crucial events in an individual's life—marriages and funerals, the naming of children, or entrance into groups—were marked by recourse to written materials. In Ch'ing times, a rural villager also encountered the written word in his economic exchanges at the market, in his activities in an irrigation organization, in his role as a tenant or a landlord, in his relations with the government through household registration and taxation, and in his dealings with his brothers in the division of family property. A villager's view of his culture and its past was formed in part from historical novels, short stories, plays, and popular songs—which were all enshrined in written form. When he tried to manipulate supernatural forces for his own benefit, the villager also used written communications. It is difficult to think of any sphere of life that was not affected in some way by writing. Under such conditions, the ability to read and write had obvious practical value.

In an urban milieu, the presence of commercial activities enhanced the rewards of literacy. There were correspondingly richer materials available to city dwellers such as gazettes, circulating libraries, and the plethora of written notices found on city streets.

Different groups placed varying degrees of reliance on literacy. The highly educated literati class can be placed at the top of the spectrum, with both scholars who tried unsuccessfully for degrees and the lucky few who won them falling into this category. Literacy was fundamental to most aspects of literati life, from philosophical beliefs to attitudes toward religion and self. The education of sons was mandatory, for an individual's prospects rested on acquiring an advanced education.

Below this group were the men who had attended school for several years: respectable merchants, artisans, shopkeepers, landlords, and well-to-do peasants who still tilled their own land, as well as some priests and monks, fit into this very large category. Following the orthodox elite curriculum, they studied the Confucian classics, at least in an elementary form. Some were forced to abandon their studies for want of funds, while others were sent into business because of their poor academic abilities. Whatever the cause of their interrupted education, persons in this group could probably read and write several thousand characters, enough either for business or for land management and commercial investment. These men recognized and partially subscribed to elite values. They tried, as their means permitted, to educate one or more of their sons for the civil service examinations. Their mastery of the basic skills of literacy provided them with a sound basis for amassing sufficient wealth to plot strategies that would ensure future upward mobility for their families. Along with the failed scholars and degree holders, they supported the market for popular literature of all kinds.

Then there were those who had enjoyed much briefer periods of schooling, either in rural winter schools, urban short-term schools, or similar programs that used such materials as the *tsa-tzu*. Unlike the previous group, who might be described as "rejects" from the elite schools, these men had not even been offered the prospect of moving into the elite that enrollment in the orthodox curriculum implied. Their limited schooling did not provide a sufficient basis for educational advancement and, since many of them did not read the elite primers in school, they were less likely to know more than the rudimentary Confucian values included in their textbooks. Their curriculum provided mastery of probably only a few hundred characters. Their limited reading skills, and even lower levels of writing ability, must have enabled some to keep simple accounts and to cope with the transactions involved in their daily lives: sales at their standard markets, the rental of lands to till, and the like. Probably many in this group consulted the more educated members of their communities for help in matters that required more advanced skills in reading and writing.

Finally, there were many men and women who were illiterate. While their inability to read and write left them at an obvious disadvantage in Ch'ing society, these individuals were not isolated from their educated neighbors. Through contact with literate family or community members, they had access to information contained in written materials.

As Carlo Cipolla has pointed out, even today there are substitutes for literacy in the form of radio, television, and movies.[14] In Ch'ing society, writing was just one of several channels of communication: the cultural counterparts of radio, television, and movies were the popular street entertainers and drama troupes who performed not just in cities but also at village festivals and rural periodic markets. Economic and political information percolated through the marketing hierarchy, with the teahouse and the travelling peddler serving as major vehicles for communication between the general populace and the ruling elite. Guilds and lineage organizations as well as the arbitrarily defined units in the *li-chia* and *pao-chia* systems were used by officials to disseminate regulations as well as to collect information. Occasionally these organizations also acted as voices of protest against government policies. In the underworld, boxing masters and secret societies were effective channels of communication that cut across a variety of social groups.[15]

Several factors suggest that the Chinese communications network as a whole was quite efficient, especially when compared with other premodern societies. The tendency of the elite members of Chinese society to continue their identification with their rural native places[16] ensured close interaction and a high level of communication among different social strata. Strong kinship organizations, especially in south and central China, united households of disparate status with a common interest in upholding lineage wealth and strength. When one considers the social organization of feudal Europe or Japan, the significance of these Chinese characteristics is evident. Added to this were the benefits associated with a large bureaucracy that circulated elites to various parts of a far-flung empire, maintaining control over these regions through written rules and regulations. The Chinese system of rotating officials and prohibiting them from serving in their native places ensured that localities could benefit privately and extra-governmentally from the observations and experiences of these officials. To a lesser degree, the same advantages were derived from merchants who engaged in long-distance trade.

Yet another factor strengthening the Chinese communications network was the geographical mobility of its citizens. In contrast to Tokugawa Japan (1603–1867), where internal migration was hedged with official restraint, Ch'ing history records several major migrations into the Yangtze highlands, the Han River highlands, southwest China, and Manchuria.[17] Diffusion of technology was but one of the many by-products of these movements of thousands of peasants.

Chinese Literacy in Comparative Perspective

How important is literacy in shaping a preindustrial society? And what are its effects? This section first examines studies of the impact of literacy on other societies in order to interpret the significance of fairly widespread literacy in traditional China. The related question of the importance of literacy for modernization in the twentieth century is then explored through comparative literature on the subject.

In the broadest sense, changes in the extent of literacy are tied to the advent of printed materials as a dominant form of written record and to the increased distribution made possible by advances in printing technology. In Europe, the advent of printing was linked with the scholarly revival that stimulated the Renaissance; rare or unique texts could now be duplicated in large enough numbers to ensure their survival, while new ideas enjoyed greater diffusion and served as the basis for further advances.[18] Of course, many of the effects of printing were felt in China at a much earlier period in its history: a recognition of literacy as an indispensable tool for the ruling elite and an understanding of the importance of printed matter in preserving texts and disseminating information predate the Ch'ing by many centuries.

But printing was also at the heart of Ch'ing intellectual developments. Ch'ing compilation projects and the printing of rare texts under private and imperial aegis sought to bring together the accumulated knowledge of the past and, in doing so, raised questions concerning the interpretation and significance of theretofore accepted texts. Printing thus played an important role in the rise of the historiographical school of Ch'ing scholarship.[19]

In England, the impact of expanding literacy on the production and distribution of printed materials was manifested in an emerging popular literature. As the reading audience increased, authors could earn a living from writing alone. Freed from dependence on aristocratic patrons, they responded to the interests of their new readership. Increased book production also made possible greater specialization in distribution. The rise of the circulating library in eighteenth century England, like the new newspapers, reflected the growth of literacy in that society.[20]

As discussed in chapter 5, a similar response occurred in China. Although popular literature appeared much earlier there, the vigorous ongoing activity of Ch'ing publishers attests to a large market for popular works. In urban areas, circulating libraries, much like those in England, may have catered to a broader cross-section of the urban population than their English counterparts.

Natalie Davis, studying sixteenth century France, asks if printing was responsible for setting up new networks of communication, opening new options, and providing new means of social control. In France, the expansion of urban presses and the increased circulation of books during the century encouraged artisans, tradesmen, and even such semiskilled workers as urban gardeners and fishermen to own books. Thus, the urban publics to whom authors and publishers addressed themselves had broadened to include more social strata, and artisans, tradesmen, and even women could now be found among the ranks of authors.[21]

The French countryside was largely isolated from this cultural surge. This was due not just to low levels of literacy, although that was also the case: only about 3 percent of the agricultural workers and 10 percent of the more prosperous peasants in late sixteenth century Languedoc could sign their full names, as compared with a third of the artisans in the town of Narbonne.[22]

Peasants were hindered from reading since most books were written in nonvernacular forms that they could not comprehend and, as Davis demonstrates, there was little practical incentive for reading in the form of new information useful in agriculture or daily life. There was no system for distributing books to the rural areas. Despite some modifications when Protestantism provided a new incentive for selling books in the countryside, these elements all combined to limit the impact of printing on the French village.

Rural isolation and low levels of literacy were thus mutually reinforcing conditions in sixteenth century France. The underlying causes of weak demand for literacy skills and books can be found in the separation of the rural and urban economy. French society had to become more integrated, socially as well as economically, before this rural isolation could be breached. Until economic relations pulled localities into larger market networks, the demand for both information and literacy remained low.

In the absence of such change, oral culture dominated the French countryside and "transformed everything it touched." In sharp contrast to what we have seen in China, "those who wished to control the countryside and bring it to order by means other than sheer force—whether bishop, seigneur, or king—would have to send not books but messengers, whose seals would not be mock and who would disclose verbally the power behind the papers that they read."[23]

The significance of Chinese institutions is underlined by a comparison of sixteenth century France and China. A society with an aristocracy is one where birth, residence, and class often produced sharp social and cultural divisions, as in France. Chinese society provided ordinary citizens, even villagers, with access to education and through it, entry into the elite. Because of local place and kinship ties which cut across occupational lines, elite interaction with other social groups was much greater than in

France. Since Chinese elites lived in villages as well as in cities, and since the elite curriculum was well defined, there was a demand for the Confucian classics in the countryside as well as in the cities, and the demand was large enough to stimulate the mass printing of such works. The rewards for high literacy were evident even to villagers, and there was thus a demand for schooling in rural as well as urban areas. As the sophisticated and complex economic organizations of late Ming and Ch'ing China suggest, the economy had developed to a point where reading and writing skills paid their way in practical matters as well. Indeed, China was so advanced in relation to the France of this period that Chinese emperors could conceive of "ideological indoctrination" on a massive scale.

Printing and literacy in China marched hand in hand with the evolution of economic and social institutions. The real development of local schools, the expansion of printing, and the rise of popular literature, together with the heightening of social mobility, all began in Ming times. When we consider the implications of these trends, it is hard to describe China as anything but an advanced, complex society, not stagnant but developing in a manner that requires further analysis and examination. From this perspective, China was remarkably modern in many respects.

Literacy and Modernization

Despite the assumption that literacy is an important foundation for industrialized societies, there is little agreement concerning the historical role of literacy in promoting industrialization. Those who argue that literacy played an important part in England's Industrial Revolution, for example, point to the importance of education in training skilled workers for the new factories. Others conclude that since schooling was of poor quality during this period, education was irrelevant to the Industrial Revolution. They assert that factory work did not require literacy, and debate whether education kept pace with population growth or economic development in England during the eighteenth century. Since children could now earn an income, the opportunity cost of sending a child to school was raised, and there may actually have been a disincentive to educate children at least in the short run.[24]

The argument over the contribution of literacy to industrialization moves into the broader question of its contribution to modernization. A recent study by Alex Inkeles and David Smith attempts to analyze "individual modernization" and the contexts in which this transformation of attitudes and behavior is accomplished. Inkeles and Smith contend that the school and factory are both powerful inculcators of individual modernization. The school imposes impersonal rules and a routine on students, teaches them skills that heighten a sense of personal efficacy, reinforces its lessons with rewards and punishments, and provides a model in the person of the teacher.

Similarly, the factory can be considered a "school for modernity" because it presents an objective standard of productivity, strict requirements of profitability, models of efficacy in the persons of the engineers, technicians, and skilled workers, reinforced by a system of rewards and punishments. Strict planning, time regimens, and rules give one "training in new ways of orienting oneself toward man, nature, and the social order."[25]

The contribution of literacy to modernization thus lies not so much in specific knowledge gained and transmitted by an ability to read and write, but in the transformation of attitudes and behavior—in developing an interest in the outside world, putting positive value on education and technical skills, encouraging persons to aspire to get ahead in the world, and giving them confidence that they can do so.

Modernization also instills the ability to appear and to act on a schedule. Sidney Pollard comments that one of the most critical and difficult transformations required in English industrialization was "the adjustment of labor to the regularity and discipline of factory work." The new machinery necessitated coordination of the entire work force, and the factory form of organization gave employers direct control over the production process. Employers were plagued by absenteeism, frequent feast days that closed the factories, and the difficulty of enforcing "time-thrift" on workers. They sought to inculcate the proper qualities of obedience, industry, ambition, sobriety, and thrift into the working class through schooling.[26]

The difficulties of English employers with their work force and their continuing efforts through the early Victorian period to determine the patterns of thought, feeling, and behavior of the working class by controlling education, point to a cultural gap between the elite and the workers that extended to the European continent. Philippe Aries describes the separation of education by age and social class as a phenomenon of the eighteenth century in France as well as in England. Thenceforth, "it was considered that education should be confined to the rich, for, if it were extended to the poor, it would turn them against manual labor and make social misfits of them."[27] Once education was denied the lower classes, it was natural that a greater separation of culture would ensue, one that proved to be a hindrance when the Industrial Revolution required that middle class virtues be instilled in the new labor force.

Discussion of the significance of Tokugawa education for Meiji modernization reinforces the view that changes in attitudes and behavior were crucial to the process. According to Ronald Dore, Tokugawa education provided the Japanese with "training in being trained," a valuable asset in the Meiji period, when national policy required mobilization for industrial development and modernization. The demonstrated ability to rise through education, which underlay the expansion of commoner demand for schooling during the Tokugawa, paved the way for the transference of similar expectations to the Japanese nation as a whole during Meiji times.[28] Some historians have been tantalized by the similarity in male literacy rates in Tokugawa Japan and England on the eve of industrialization.[29] Literacy rates are thus taken as an indicator of attitudinal and cultural transformations that were conducive to industrialization in these two societies.

Historians comparing Meiji Japan's rapid modernization with China's much slower response have listed Japanese rates of literacy as an explanatory variable. Yet Japanese levels of male literacy closely resembled those for China in the same period, the late nineteenth century. In late Tokugawa Japan, perhaps 27 to 35 percent or more of the population attended school. Ronald Dore estimates that 43 percent of Japanese boys received some sort of schooling.[30] According to Sydney Crawcour, "The rate of literacy in Japan was probably approaching 30 percent in the 1860's, if we define literacy as ability to read and write at a fairly elementary level. When conscription was introduced in 1873 it was found that 30–40 percent of the conscripts had some education, which they would have received in the 1860's."[31] Subsequent data suggest that this schooling was brief: in 1900 only 19.9 percent of males and 3.5 percent of females in the working-age population had completed the compulsory schooling of four years.[32]

The finding that Chinese rates of male literacy approximated Japan's during the late nineteenth century suggests that literacy is a necessary but certainly not a sufficient condition for modernization. It questions the use of high literacy rates to explain Japan's rapid mobilization and points to the analysis of differences in Chinese and Japanese geography, social structure, political institutions, and modes of interaction in explaining the contrasting Chinese and Japanese responses during the late nineteenth century.

A look at the Chinese process of modernization from a broader time perspective, however, permits one to argue that China and Japan resembled each other closely in certain significant respects. First and most importantly, both societies placed positive value on education as a means of social mobility. The oft-quoted Meiji Education Act, which stated that "learning is the key to success in life,"[33] echoed similar precepts found in innumerable clan injunctions in China and principles epitomized in the civil service examination system. Thus, official policy promoted popular education in both countries.

Despite dissimilar social structures, China and Japan educated their elites with the same Confucian texts. Samurai sons learned Chinese as part of the curriculum in fief schools, and Chinese influence was not confined to the texts studied by the elite. Popularized Chinese hortatory books were adopted by Japanese *terakoya,* which also used a Japanese version of the *Thousand-Character Classic.*[34] A recent study traces the importation of a popular book, written in vernacular Chinese, into Japan via the Ryukyus in the eighteenth century and its eventual adoption in a Japanese version by *terakoya.*[35] Detailed comparisons of texts used in Japanese and Chinese schools would probably uncover more instances of such transmission.

Diffusion of technology through books, as well as the demonstrated importance of obtaining and disseminating information through the written word, characterized both Tokugawa Japan and Ch'ing China. In both countries, the public notice board was an accepted means of communication between government and the populace.[36]

Thus, in the crucial areas of promoting positive attitudes toward acquiring knowledge, enabling wide recruitment of talent, permitting social mobility of a significant order, and inculcating the populace with political rule through the written word, the educational systems of China and Japan were more similar than dissimilar.[37] In addition, the already existing schools, teachers, and curriculum provided a basis on which new governments built in both societies.

The agricultural technology of China and Japan, based on wet-rice cultivation, bred a type of peasant unlike Europe's. Submission to routine and participation in a complex organization with regulations were nothing new to those who worked in intensive cultivation involving the creation and maintenance of irrigation systems. The Chinese peasant, who had lived under and gossiped about a bureaucracy for centuries, did not require adjustment to impersonal rules. Nowhere in the industrial history of China and Japan does one read of problems of absenteeism and maladjustment to factory routine as serious as those Pollard cites for England. Obedience, industry, ambition, sobriety, and thrift—the virtues English employers sought to inculcate into their workers—were qualities native to Chinese and Japanese peasants. The required transformation of values and behavior in China and Japan was eased by the nature of their traditional cultures.

China enjoyed other advantages. As Dwight Perkins notes, traditional China already had a high degree of agricultural commercialization, a complex farm technology, a national banking system, and a large urban sector, as well as private ownership of land and written contracts. This premodern development nurtured attitudes and behavior that made the Chinese effective entrepreneurs and workers when given an opportunity, as illustrated by their economic success in Southeast Asia, Taiwan, and the mainland.[38]

In examining the course of Chinese and Japanese history over the last century, one can thus argue that their traditional educational and cultural heritage provided both countries with advantages in planning for and moving toward the goals of industrialization and modernization. The differing speed of the Chinese and Japanese response during the late nineteenth century remains to be explained. The similarity of Chinese and Japanese educational systems during the Tokugawa and Ch'ing periods suggests that education per se cannot be considered a crucial factor in accounting for this difference.

Some will argue that the Japanese, who could view Confucianism as an external ideology, were able to reject its values without drastic changes in self-identity, while the Chinese, whose Confucianism was central to their cultural identity, found it understandably more difficult to jettison. This line of thought points to the different sources of legitimacy accepted by each culture, and the unique patterns of political relationships that characterized Tokugawa Japan and Ch'ing China. More concretely, these differences help explain the vastly greater revenues available to the Meiji state when it came to power,[39] revenues that could be applied directly to the tasks of economic development and modernization. An explanation of the greater speed of the Japanese response can probably be found in these areas, as well as in the elementary but vital fact of its smaller size and different geographical situation.

Chapter 8

Continuities in Modern Chinese Elementary Education

Education continues to play a primary role in transforming society in modern China. Beyond the need for training literate workers to fill the new occupations created by an industrializing nation, Chinese leaders see education as a means of molding desired social and cultural values and behavior. In this they echo the Ch'ing elite, for whom education was the foundation for a morally correct (and hence Confucian) social order, one resting on the conviction that persuasion was a more durable and an ultimately more successful tool than coercion.

Reliance on socialization is of course not unique to China. As Levi-Strauss notes, all governments have recognized this aspect of education: "The primary function of writing as a means of communication, is to facilitate the enslavement of other human beings. . . . The struggle against illiteracy is indistinguishable at times from the increased power exerted over the individual citizen by the central authority."[1] What has been distinctive in China is the greater emphasis placed on the normative function of education, not only in traditional times but in the twentieth century as well.

When Chinese reformers and revolutionaries began to consider the prerequisites for successful modernization, education remained foremost in their programs. For Liang Ch'i-ch'ao, writing after the turn of the century, the creation of a nation-state depended on the birth of a "new citizen," one who was equipped with the values and attitudes that were essential for a popularly based constitutional government.[2] In the 1930s, when Kuomintang (KMT) "Blue

Shirts'' sought to inculcate a fascistic model of citizenship, education was still considered the means by which the new citizen was to be created. In post-1949 China, this emphasis has led to the notion that education or ''remolding'' can create the correct class consciousness, even in persons of the ''wrong'' class origin. Stuart Schram has commented that Mao's ''approach to revolution stresses the importance of cultural change, and education, in the broadest sense, is the instrument by which he seeks to create new men and women.''[3]

Governments with such goals must look beyond education as a system for training technicians and elites to the broader task of schooling the masses in and out of the classroom. The Chinese educational reforms of the late nineteenth and early twentieth centuries, which by 1905 culminated in the abolition of the civil service examinations, were essentially measures affecting only the elite school system and its values, as were subsequent regulations aimed at establishing a national school system, curriculum, and teacher training program. Although the orthodox educational system underwent radical change, at least on paper, it was unable to meet the challenge of educating all the people. Effective in bringing new values and knowledge to only a very small fraction of the population, it could not handle the task of transforming China's millions into ''new citizens'' capable of participating in the creation of a modern nation-state.

By the 1920s and 1930s, various groups were turning their attention to formulating and implementing programs designed to bring these changes to the still traditional countryside. The disparate political commitments of men like Y. C. James Yen (leader of the Mass Education movement), Liang Shu-ming, and Mao Tse-tung did not preclude a shared recognition of the urgent need to transform values and behavior in the countryside where the majority of the population lived. Here, they all believed, lay the key to ultimate success in China's modernization efforts.

As various groups became interested in mass education, they confronted similar problems. The level of literacy existing in the villages was low when judged by the standards of industrialized countries, and the content of written materials inappropriate for transmitting modern concepts. The abolition of the examination system confused some people about the objectives of the new education, while regional indifference to the usefulness of literacy (reported in chapter 1) persisted.[4] In view of the size of the problem and the scarcity of personnel, money, and time, a limited course of study suitable for adult illiterates had to be devised. As mass education groups worked with villagers, they became more sensitive to the factors that shaped peasant response to their programs. These perceptions in turn helped modify the programs themselves.

In educational work, accommodation to peasant needs and demands resulted in a movement toward the use of traditional popular methods and materials: this was a way in which the past could serve the needs of the present. But the contribution of the traditional system to modern education also included both the physical plants and teachers bequeathed to the new schools that emerged after 1905 and the old-fashioned village schools that continued to form an important part of rural education into the 1940s. The twentieth century thus saw no abrupt discontinuities in the system of education that actually existed in China.

Reform of the Educational System

The extension of Western educational content and methods to elementary instruction came relatively late to China. Certainly it received no official attention in the nineteenth century. As late as 1902, Chang Chih-tung, who had been instrumental in creating new schools for Hupei province and had led a national movement for educational reform, was content to leave elementary education in private hands. This came out of Chang's feeling that to achieve educational reform by beginning with the elementary level would take too long. In a memorial written the year before, he had recommended that initial emphasis be placed on the establishment of new middle and high schools. The imperial edicts of September, 1901, which had ordered counties and departments to open primary schools and kindergartens with a Sino-Western curriculum, were not actually implemented; and a 1906 edict revealed that the state did not intend to finance primary schools.[5]

With the exception of missionary efforts, early attempts to

create modern elementary schools were confined to private citizens. The Meishee School, which opened in Shanghai in 1876, was probably the first modern elementary school.[6] By the turn of the century, it had been joined by schools in Shanghai, Peking, and parts of Chekiang and Chihli.[7] Most of these schools were created with the active support of the reform-minded elite. In Chekiang, it was Sun I-jang who founded over 300 primary and middle schools in Chuchow and Wenchow prefectures in the late 1890s.[8] Perhaps the most famous prototype of the educational reformer in this period was Chang Chien, a degree holder from Nan-t'ung, Kiangsu, who used profits from his cotton mill to finance schools. Chang Chien was head of the provincial Education Association and continued to be influential in educational affairs until 1926. He and his friends had established some seventy lower primary schools in Nan-t'ung by 1910.[9]

Some progressive clans also opened modern schools. The Chus of Kiangsu converted an academy into a lower primary school in 1908; the P'ans of Ta-fu even took funds out of the clan's charitable estate to pay the new school's expenses.[10]

In many regions, founders of modern schools tried to solve shortages of money and personnel by using the resources of the traditional schools. The Society for the Improvement of Private Tutor Schools, organized by Shen Lian-chi of Shanghai in 1904, was an example of an organization that aimed at converting old-fashioned schools into new *hsüeh-t'ang*. This group was influential not only in Kiangsu but also in neighboring Anhwei and Kiangsi.[11]

Ogawa Yoshiko has identified thirty-two Shanghai charitable schools that were converted into modern lower primary schools (*hsiao hsüeh-t'ang*). The transition from old to new is epitomized by the fact that the last charitable school on her list was founded in 1902, the first year that such schools in Shanghai began to be converted into *hsiao hsüeh-t'ang*.[12] There was thus a very close and continuous development of elementary schools, accompanied by the conversion of the traditional charitable schools into their modern counterparts, a process largely completed by 1907. In Kiangsu, Chen-yang county created 45 percent of its modern schools by converting former charitable schools, and similar cases can be found elsewhere.[13] Both the physical plants and the endowments of the charitable schools could thus be transferred to support the new school system.[14]

Teacher Training

The modern school system was hindered by its limited ability to train qualified teachers. This difficulty had at first been ignored by Chang Chih-tung, who predicted that "any scholar who had already demonstrated high intellectual ability" could study books on Western learning and be able to teach primary school after only three months.[15] Perhaps the same sort of attitude lay behind Liu K'un-i's rejection in 1901 of a proposal by Chang Chien to incorporate teacher-training schools into plans for the new school system. Eventually, Chang Chien personally financed the Nan-t'ung Normal School, which opened in 1903.[16]

The first normal school in China was established in Shanghai in 1897 by Nanyang College, which used it to train its own teachers. Another was opened in Peking before the turn of the century.[17] In view of the shortage of trained teachers to fill posts in the new schools, Japanese were initially hired to fill the gap. This also reflected a general Chinese interest in Japan as a model for educational reform. The report of the 1903 commission on national public education had advocated the Japanese system rather than the alternatives presented by the missionary-backed Educational Association of China. Japanese advisers were used by the Educational Bureau of Shansi province to create its modern schools during the first decade of the twentieth century; and by 1904, there were about 165 Japanese teachers in China, many of them in modern science.[18]

Since there were far too few modern teachers for them to have any appreciable impact on primary school education, the movement toward modern schools was also accompanied by attempts to retrain old teachers. Sidney Gamble described such a program in Peking:

> Although teachers were at first trained by "short courses," by 1907 a number of normal schools with four or five year courses

> had been established. The subjects taught included psychology and pedagogy as well as those designed to fit a man to teach the required work in the government schools of primary grade, arithmetic, history, nature study, science and manual training. The pupils of these schools were, many of them, middle-aged or old men who had been teachers of the Chinese Classics.[19]

This sort of program suffered from obvious limitations imposed by the small number of qualified personnel who could be found to train new teachers, the long period of training normally required, and the relatively few old-style teachers who could be retrained within a short period of time. Even when training courses were cut to two or three months, resistance to changing methods and curriculum persisted.[20]

What were the new teachers to teach? Chang Chih-tung, when initially contemplating the problem, had suggested that they could use the printed materials on Western subjects then being issued in great quantities from Shanghai. Since the turn of the century, a tremendous amount of educational literature had been published in China. The Commercial Press, established in Shanghai at the close of the century, was publishing some sixty different Chinese-language textbooks and numerous other books on education. In addition, about twenty newspapers and magazines dealing with education were being issued in this period.[21] The old-fashioned schoolmaster was "retooled" with such materials before stepping into the classroom of the new lower primary school.

For the first time in China, teachers' manuals accompanied elementary textbooks. The *First Grade Chinese Reader for Primary Schools (Tsui-hsin ch'u-teng hsiao-hsüeh Kuo-wen chiao-k'o shu)* published by the Commercial Press, for example, had a ten-volume supplement entitled *A Method for Teaching Chinese National Readers (Ch'u-teng hsiao-hsüeh Kuo-wen chiao-k'o shu chiao-shou fa)*, which told the teacher how to present the lessons. According to one reviewer, "every lesson in the pupil's text-book has a corresponding lesson in the teacher's manual. He is instructed to begin by: (1) 'Pointing out' the leading principle of the lesson; (2) recognising the progressive order of thought; (3) developing the principle of comparison; (4) catechetical [*sic*]."[22]

In the traditional system, a teacher had no need for such guidance. He may have been an ineffective teacher from the viewpoint of modern educators, but he taught in a stable cultural order where classroom lessons reinforced values learned from parents, family, and society. Although earlier writers had quarreled with specific texts, few ever questioned the methods of instruction.[23]

By contrast, Chinese education underwent enormous changes in both teaching methods and curriculum content during the early twentieth century. As one writer put it, under the old system, "the teacher sat at his ease, generally smoking a water-pipe, while the scholar bawled the (to him) unmeaning sounds which constituted a lesson. Under the new system the scholar sits comfortably at his desk while the teacher has the floor and strives by simple lecture, by appropriate gesture, and by apt illustration to convey the meaning of the book to his pupils."[24]

This shift in emphasis was another notion derived from Western educational methods, and was perhaps further encouraged by the divergence of the new textbooks from the persistent themes in Chinese society itself. No longer could the hours in class be viewed as but one part of a coherent lesson in one's life roles. Given the uncertainty that so many Chinese had about the ultimate dimensions of the new world toward which China was moving, disparities among stated goals served to exacerbate the intellectual confusion of the times. It was natural for the new school system, in stressing the need for effective communication, to begin by concentrating on teaching methods.

The first two decades of the twentieth century brought significant changes, among them an official commitment to a national school system built on Western models and outlined in new regulations. Official reform efforts, along with private support, created a hierarchy of new schools that extended from the kindergarten to the university,[25] while numerous publications presented Western educational techniques and subjects for incorporation into the new curriculum. Yet establishing a modern Education Ministry and publishing detailed regulations for a national school system were not sufficient in themselves to bring about the desired changes. The difficulties of implementing the educational edicts of the late Ch'ing and early Republic were outlined by J. MacGowan: "China, taken as a whole, is still carrying on the system of education that has been in existence during the past ages. How, indeed, could it be otherwise? It will take long before men trained to teach the new educational methods can be obtained for the countless schools throughout the empire. These must remain very much as they have always been until sufficient teachers are available."[26]

The shortage of qualified teachers meant that outside the cities many schools were modern in name only, and right up into the 1920s and 1930s continued to use classical texts as well as traditional methods of rote learning and recitation. In many rural areas, the gap between modern and traditional schools was therefore much narrower than might be supposed. In the early 1930s, in a village only seventeen miles from Peking, for example, J. Stewart Burgess found the "modern" school still conducted along traditional lines.[27]

Traditional Schools

In the cities, and to an even greater extent in the villages, traditional schools persisted throughout the Republican period. An article on primary schools published in 1933 stated, "In most of the cities and villages in China, if not in every one, there are old-fashioned schools. These are carried on along the time-honored classical lines."[28]

Information from various sources confirms this statement. A 1927 survey found that even in Li-ch'eng county, a center for educational modernization in Shantung, there were 194 old-style primary schools (*szu-shu*) coexisting with the 325 modern lower primary schools.[29] T'ai-ch'u Liao's study of Wenshang county, Shantung, during the mid-1930s, and Ch'engtu, Szechwan, a decade later, showed numerous private traditional schools in existence.[30] Daniel Kulp's work on Phenix Village, Kwangtung; Martin Yang's study of Taitou, Shantung; and Japanese surveys of Hou Hsiao Chai, Shantung, all show that these villages had traditional schools during the Republican period. In Hopei, Sha-ching village also had a traditional school, as did villages less than twenty miles from Peking.[31] Thus, particularly in rural areas, there was an underlying continuity in education that ran counter to discontinuities in government policy.

Although incomplete government statistics underestimate the extent to which primary education was affected by the presence of traditional schools, they nevertheless provide a minimal estimate of private old-fashioned schools in the year 1935. They report that private schools (*szu-shu*) then constituted over 40 percent of the primary schools in the national system, and enrolled over 14 percent of the nation's students. Private schoolteachers represented about 19 percent of all primary school personnel. Only 37 percent of the private schools had been "improved." What this means in terms of curriculum and modes of instruction is made clearer by statistics on teacher training: a mere 9 percent of the private schoolteachers had a normal school education, and only 22 percent were graduates of the new primary or middle schools, while the great majority (69 percent) were themselves products of private schools.[32]

The downward bias of these government statistics stems not only from the incomplete coverage of administrative units (a problem noted in the report) but also from the fact that traditional schools frequently escaped counting of any kind. As Ida Belle Lewis noted, "It is impossible to register schools of the type with the Government, but they abound in all parts of the country."[33] This suggests that traditional schools were too numerous and perhaps too small to be counted in government statistics. In some areas, however, evasion was deliberate: Liao, studying traditional schools in Wenshang, observed that they had "gone underground" after 1929, when the government tried to close all such schools. Founders, teachers, and students were threatened with punishment and, "as a result, all *szu shu* in Wenshang emerged in the form of some kind of secret society so that nobody but a friend was allowed to knock at its door."[34] Despite the investigative problems imposed by such secrecy, Liao counted a total of 156 private traditional schools in the course of visiting 220 villages in the county. The schools were evenly dispersed and enrolled approximately three times the number of students attending government schools.[35]

Why were traditional schools so popular in Wenshang? According to Liao, it was because they answered the demands of rural families more effectively than did the new government schools. First, the teachers of the *szu-shu* fit the traditional model much more closely than did the government schoolteachers. During the Ch'ing dynasty, local teachers had usually been *t'ung-sheng* or *sheng-yüan* who had to earn a living while pursuing higher degrees. The traditional schools of the 1930s were staffed by older, traditionally educated men who enjoyed higher status than government schoolteachers. Liao noted that 60 percent of the private teachers over age sixty were retired government officials. The average age of the private schoolteachers was higher: 48 percent were between forty and sixty years of age, and 26 percent over sixty, as compared with government schoolteachers, 70 percent of whom were under the age of thirty.[36] Moreover, private schoolteachers possessed more of the knowledge most prized by rural dwellers. Their qualifications, as compared with those of government schoolteachers, were "definitely superior, especially in their knowledge of the Chinese language, of the Chinese rites and their experience in dealing with people. In rural China these two phases of human knowledge have long been and are still considered as most important, practical and fundamental among all human learning."[37] Indeed, private schoolmasters were moving into activities formerly dominated by the local elites—representing village interests in negotiations with officials, acting as advisers for individuals involved in litigation, and providing customary help in naming children, reading and writing letters, and supplying medical aid.[38]

A second major reason for the popularity of private traditional schools was that preference for the traditional curriculum and teaching methods continued in rural areas. According to Liao,

> The things taught and the measures of discipline in the szu shu were what people expected. . . . The learning of how to read and write Chinese and a few items of practical knowledge which could be applied in real life situations immediately were taught. . . . Whereas the things taught in the new school were many, but none of them was taught long enough to enable people to make any practical use of it. Subjects such as singing, games, [and] athletics were not considered by the people as part of human knowledge that has any decency.[39]

The traditional teaching methods and the arrangement of school terms held additional advantages for villagers. Since pupils were taught separately and not strictly classified into grades, parents could keep their children out of school for farm work without completely disrupting their education, whereas students in the new schools frequently had to wait for a new term if they missed too many classes. Private school holidays were geared to local festivals, unlike the government school terms, which adhered to a national schedule. Furthermore, traditional schools may well have charged lower tuition fees: in Phenix Village, Kwangtung, fees at the traditional school were only $3.50 per pupil, as opposed to $8.00 at the modern private school.[40]

Liao's study of private schools in Wenshang reveals that traditional education was thriving in the 1930s because it matched still unchanged rural attitudes and values. The extent to which these attitudes toward educational content and methodology remained unchanged in the Chinese countryside before 1949 can be seen not only in Wenshang, but in the attempts at mass education discussed later in this chapter.

The popularity of traditional schools reveals both general funding and personnel shortages in the modern sector and a specific rural rejection of an externally imposed school system. Liao suggested that part of this attitude stemmed from an anti-government bias traditionally common among peasants, but the rejection was not narrowly political. Indeed, what was being repudiated was a Western-based educational system that simply did not meet Chinese villagers' needs.[41]

Like their Ch'ing counterparts, the traditional schools were an integral part of the rural social fabric. The founders of these schools were local leaders—men with money, prestige, and land who still held to the belief "that the mere act of the gathering of younger members together and providing them with an education is the wisest and best contribution that one could make."[42] Teachers were selected from residents in the community or through personal ties with local leaders.[43] The integration of traditional schools into rural society simply intensified the barriers confronting government schools: to the persistence of traditional norms concerning educational content was added the difficulty of breaking through a system of education sponsored and staffed by the local elite.

Local resistance to modern schools was accompanied by a

general breakdown of government control over the rural sector and its local leaders, which probably arose as a result of government failure to control disorder—in itself evidence of a weakness that encouraged the semiautonomy of rural areas. To such military and political weakness was added a failure to win the loyalty of the local elites. As Lloyd Eastman notes, the alienation between the KMT government and local elites was an outcome of their competition for local control over police, militia, and taxation; these were traditional central government prerogatives that had been gradually usurped by local elites in many areas during the late Ch'ing and warlord periods. Local leaders naturally resisted subsequent attempts by the central government to regain control.[44]

The growing alienation between higher and lower level elites in China reflected a cultural gap that widened during this period. The Revolution of 1911 had destroyed the traditional consensus but failed to replace it with a new one. Whereas the Confucian curriculum and examination system provided traditional Ch'ing society with a unified basis for hierarchically structuring and organizing its elite, Republican society was characterized by a dichotomy between modern Western-oriented cities and a still traditional countryside. The national elite was composed of military leaders, capitalists, and individuals with a modern education.

According to Martin Bernal, with the shift to a Western system of education came a narrowed basis of recruitment for the national elite, since urban study and travel abroad were too expensive for most families.[45] The basis for local authority continued to be landholding and old-style learning, yet local leaders were no longer simply the lower end of a continuum of power and prestige, as had previously been the case: they were now, as a group, sharply differentiated from national leaders by their education and values. Rejection of the new education in the villages during Republican times sounds a theme that echoes through today's discussions of urban-rural tensions in the People's Republic.

We can thus trace a pattern in the Chinese response to major educational reforms as outlined in the new regulations of the late Ch'ing and Republican periods. New schools were accepted and made headway among groups of the urban elite, but in rural areas such schools were frequently rejected in favor of those in the traditional system. The extent to which rural areas resisted change can be seen in Liao's study of schools in Ch'engtu, Szechwan, in 1945–46. Here, in a county that bordered the major metropolis of Ch'engtu, old-fashioned private schools still existed, although most of them were located in small villages. In the market centers, private schools had emerged with combined traditional and modern courses of study and enrollments of several hundred students.[46] Over thirty years after the fall of the Ch'ing dynasty, the educational regulations of the modern school system had not yet been fully implemented, and this in a district that was more open to urban and hence modern influences than most.

Mass Education before 1949

Beginning in the 1920s, the Mass Education movement under Jimmy Yen, the Shantung rural reconstruction program under Liang Shu-ming, the programs of T'ao Hsing-chih, and the rural programs of the Chinese Communist Party all attacked the problem of educating and transforming rural Chinese. By and large, these efforts met the same kinds of constraints that limited the KMT administrators, but in a more exacerbated form. What evolved as temporary solutions were flexible mass education programs that responded to local demands for specific kinds of knowledge and used the local supply of semiliterates as teachers.

The founder of perhaps the best known and earliest program in mass education was Yen Yang-ch'u, better known in the West as Jimmy Yen. A Szechwanese born in 1893, Yen was raised as a Christian. After graduation from Yale University in 1918, he took a position with the War Work Council of the American YMCA to work with Chinese laborers in France. There he developed a program to teach a small number of basic characters to adult illiterates and started a periodical using these characters for workers to read. After graduate study in the United States, Yen returned to China in 1921. Under YMCA auspices he successfully tested his adult education program in Changsha in 1922. Success there and in other cities led to the organization of the National Association of the Mass Education Movement (*Chung-kuo chiao-yü tsu-chin hui*), which remained active until 1950. The Association's most famous program was its rural reconstruction effort in Ting county, Hopei, carried on from the mid-1920s until the war with Japan.[47]

T'ao Hsing-chih (1891–1946)[48] studied under John Dewey from 1915 to 1917 and returned to China to participate in the educational efforts of the New Culture movement. Like Yen, he believed that the key to a new China was education for all the people, for a literate citizenry was essential to build a democracy. From Wang Yang-ming, T'ao took the notion that knowledge and action are one, and that knowledge must have practical consequences. He combined this concept with Dewey's idea that all forms of human activity are instruments for problem solving. T'ao's educational philosophy, implemented in his rural experiment at Hsiao-chuang village and subsequently in urban experiments, stressed "living" rather than "learning" education. Society was a classroom: students should not merely sit passively in schools in order to learn. The distinction between manual and mental work, long upheld in Chinese tradition, must be broken down; and teaching, learning, and doing should be combined as part of a truly educational process.

In 1927, T'ao Hsing-chih opened a school in Hsiao-chuang, a village outside Nanking where he carried out many of his ideas. The Hsiao-chuang School, intended to train teachers for rural areas, was unlike orthodox training institutes. T'ao required students to farm small plots and perform all of the menial work in running the school. He proposed that "one who cannot plant vegetables is not a student, and one who cannot cook cannot graduate."[49] The curriculum thus sought to combine "teaching-learning-doing" into a unified process. Its unorthodoxy aroused KMT suspicions, and the school was forced to close in 1930.

By 1932, T'ao had turned to work among urban populations. In that year, he established a "work-study" system among factory workers in a suburb of Shanghai. The "work-study" system was designed to help the masses help themselves. One of its features was the "little teacher" system of using school children to teach illiterate adults, thus ameliorating the teacher shortage and implementing T'ao's personal educational philosophy. By 1934, the "work-study" system had spread to twenty-one provinces.[50]

Unlike T'ao, who came from a peasant background, Liang

Shu-ming came from a family of officials.[51] An early revolutionary, Liang had turned to Buddhism by 1913. As a professor at Peking University from 1917 to 1924, he participated in philosophical debates concerning the merits of both Eastern and Western civilization. By 1927, Liang had identified rural reconstruction as the key to the growth of a new China: he believed that for rural reconstruction to succeed, intellectuals must go back to the villages, mingle with the masses, and join them in creating a new and vital Chinese culture. In this belief—and in his notion that education, politics, and economics should not be compartmentalized but combined into one entity—Liang moved in directions parallel to those later travelled by Mao, although Liang, unlike Mao, rejected governmental direction of rural reconstruction.[52]

Liang's most important rural reconstruction project took place in Tsou-p'ing county, Shantung. There, through the Shantung Rural Reconstruction Institute, founded in 1931, an experimental station was opened that carried on extension work in agriculture and the rural economy similar to that of Jimmy Yen's Ting hsien project. A training program was established for students, who would then go back to the rural areas to work. Adult education was thus combined with rural reconstruction.[53]

Similar programs of rural reconstruction were to be found in other regions, and even in Kwangsi under the warlords.[54] By 1933, the National Convention of Rural Reconstruction Workers attracted sixty-three leaders representing forty different public and private organizations. A year later, at the peak of the movement, 151 delegates from seventy-six organizations in eleven provinces attended the national convention.[55]

The 1920s and 1930s were a period when mass education and rural reconstruction had stimulated widespread interest. The national organizations brought people together from various parts of China and permitted them to exchange ideas and experiences. T'ao Hsing-chih worked closely with Jimmy Yen in founding the Mass Education Association in 1923; Liang Shu-ming toured T'ao's Hsiao-chuang School in 1928 and called it a realization of his own educational ideals.[56] In view of their contacts with each other, it is not surprising that the programs instituted in Ting hsien, Tsou-p'ing, and Kiangsu bore many points of resemblance.

When we examine Mao Tse-tung's educational philosophies and programs in this historical context, we can see the extent to which persons of vastly divergent ideological commitments concurred in the solutions offered for persistent financing problems and personnel shortages. Mao himself gradually shifted his views on education as a result of his experiences with peasants. He had advocated instruction in vernacular Chinese during an early period, and had initially seen the modern school system as the appropriate model for future programs. After 1925, however, when he began organizing Hunan peasants, he discovered that the modern schools were too urban in orientation and taught subjects unsuited to rural needs.[57] Thenceforth, Mao moved toward an increasingly flexible policy on curriculum, which must have been at least partly dictated by the shortage of teachers and teaching materials.

Mao does not seem to have relied heavily on ideological criteria for selecting primers in this early period. For example, when educating soldiers in the People's Liberation Army (PLA), which was directed by political departments within the organization, Mao wrote that the primers published by the Commercial Press, the Mass Education movement's *Thousand-Character Book,* and similar textbooks could be consulted.[58]

New textbooks as well as traditional primers were probably in short supply in the Kiangsi Soviet. Both were inappropriate for short-term courses in basic literacy. During the early 1930s, Mao advocated abandoning the orthodox primers and modern textbooks in favor of what was at hand: newspapers, posters, and children's books; even books written by the students themselves were acceptable texts if the peasants found them interesting. In a night school for illiterate adults, students supplied their own reading matter. The first group studied newspapers and arithmetic; the second, adult reading materials; and the third, children's readers.

Spare-time schools (*shih-tzu pan*) designed to reach those who could not even attend the night schools, did not have textbooks. Instead, the teacher would write a character, which was then copied by each student into a personal notebook to be turned in and periodically corrected. Mao recommended that the characters taught begin with "table, chair, board, stool, pig, cow, chicken, duck"—in other words, with the names of objects familiar to all villagers. The goal of these classes was to teach from 450 to 750 characters.[59] In its reliance on vernacular materials and its emphasis on a reading vocabulary closely related to daily life, the basic mass education classes directed by the Chinese Communist Party during the Kiangsi Soviet days thus did not differ radically from classes conducted under other auspices.

Personnel shortages dictated similar compromises when selecting instructors. In Ch'ang-kang hsien, for example, seven of the nine teachers in night schools were also representatives of the Kiangsi Soviet. School principals were illiterate "older comrades," many of them women, whose job it was to exhort absentees to attend the classes. The "older comrades" were also pesonally enrolled as students. In the "spare-time schools," classes could be formed with groups as small as three persons. Most of the teachers who served as group leaders were, according to Mao, students in the night schools. In this way, learners could teach others who were illiterate.[60] All of the teaching was voluntary.

The methods used in the Kiangsi Soviet to recruit teachers and school principals resembled those of the Mass Education movement. Both reflected an understanding of the dynamics of rural society. According to Jimmy Yen,

> In order that the People's School may be an institution not only *of* the farmers and *for* the farmers but also *by* the farmers, the Mass Education Movement has from the very outset followed the principle of making every village, however poor, responsible for its own finances and—wherever there are literate members in the village—its own teachers.[61]

It was believed that rural schools should belong to the villagers. Unlike the externally imposed government schools, these programs, by bringing local leaders into participation, ensured their acceptance by the community. As Liang Shu-ming succinctly pointed out: "If you want to promote these [schools] in the countryside, there is no way to be successful without first obtaining the consent and agreement of the rural leaders."[62] Just as the enrollment of illiterate leading comrades in the Kiangsi Soviet set an example for others, an example as effective as any verbal exhortations they might have delivered, Yen's efforts to recruit literate persons from the community as teachers mobilized the most effective combination of talent and effort possible. These programs attempted to replicate the traditional conditions described by Liao in Wenshang—schools that were founded and operated by the villagers themselves.

In Yenan, the Chinese Communist Party refined the mass education lessons it had learned in Kiangsi. By 1942, the orthodox educational system, which had been applied in the Border Region since the late 1930s, had demonstrated its failure to penetrate rural areas and poor households. The "mass line" in education, which accompanied CCP efforts to mobilize production and defense in the war against Japan, shifted emphasis in curriculum to basic literacy and political indoctrination, and the responsibility for education from a professional education ministry to village leaders.[63] According to a 1944 Border Region government directive:

> As for the popular-management elementary school system and educational content, we should respect the opinion of the masses and refer to their own demands; the length of the course, the number of class hours a day, need not be uniform. The curriculum can also fall in with the desires of the masses, and temporarily excise those items which are not urgent—if the masses only want to learn to read, write, and do arithmetic, don't teach other things.[64]

There was potential conflict between the goal of political indoctrination and this policy of responding to popular desires. Unlike the Kiangsi Soviet policy of using teaching materials to suit the villagers' interests, the 1944 directive order that if peasants wished to use books like the *tsa-tzu* and the traditional *Hundred Names,* texts "in the old form but with new content" could be written. Selection of teachers was also modified so that in addition to local cadre or labor heroes, popular-management schools were given the attention of higher-level cadres and students who helped train local teachers.[65]

The Yenan programs in mass education reflected increased CCP control over the content of what was to be taught. This did not differ fundamentally from Jimmy Yen's attempts to incorporate "training for democracy" into his Ting hsien experiment. The use of drama, folk songs, and dances for the reeducation of the people appeared in both programs.[66] Those who study post-1949 China will see a continuity in the themes developed in these earlier mass education programs, not only in the media they used, but in their insistence on practical learning as well as political indoctrination, their accommodation of school hours to the needs of a laboring population, and their policy of flexibility and adaptability to specific conditions.[67]

The Yenan educational programs and their successors in the People's Republic of China represent a successful synthesis of the dual and often conflicting goals of "learning from the masses" while transforming mass behavior and values within the fundamental constraints imposed by shortages of funds and personnel. In contrast to the Republican period, when local elites and private organizations dominated, the Yenan and post-1949 periods reveal the ability of the political authority to control the direction and content of the new learning. From a historian's point of view, this situation is also not without its precedents. One is tempted to say that the CCP has merely succeeded in reintegrating polity and education after a transitional period of disruption in the early decades of the twentieth century. Of course, the resemblance of CCP priorities on education to those of past Chinese regimes does not alter the overriding importance of its new orientations and values. The success of the CCP in achieving the narrower goal of mass literacy and the broader aim of cultural transformation marks a new period in China's educational history.

Educational Materials

The reform of educational texts, like other changes in education, proceeded most rapidly in urban areas and lagged behind in rural and poor regions. Although the new textbooks that accompanied the modern school system were used in some schools during the period 1905–49, traditional schools continued to use old primers and Ch'ing texts, while the mass education programs for adult illiterates developed textbooks partially derived from traditional vernacular materials. Thus, only a few of the students used modern textbooks.

After 1900, more and more new textbooks were created to meet the needs of a revised curriculum. The *New National Readers* described by Cyrus Peake, printed in 1904–05, and the Commercial Press readers cited by John Darroch for the same period were typical efforts.[68] These books introduced new subjects: science, technology, foreign relations, and topics reflecting the new nationalism. At the same time, they often continued the older tradition of displaying a heavily moralistic tone. *Elementary Ethics (Tsui-hsin ch'u-teng hsiao-hsüeh hsiu-shen k'o liao shu)*, a Commercial Press reader for lower primary schools, states in its preface:

> It is constantly said that moral culture, mental culture and physical culture constitute true education. This is true, but moral culture is the root of all; on this, ancient and modern, Chinese and foreign, are all agreed. . . . This book selects the wise sayings of the ancients and their brave acts and sets these forth as examples for the children of today.[69]

Based on European, American, and Japanese models, the new textbooks introduced methods intended to break with traditional rote memorization, oral recitation, and individualized instruction. Like the traditional primers that they were intended to replace, they were designed to lead a student from primary to advanced levels. The mass education texts, however, were structured very differently from the new primary school textbooks. Educators concerned with adult illiteracy tried to devise short courses that could provide basic literacy to a large number of people. Questions immediately arose: if only a limited number of characters were to be taught, how was that number to be selected? What method should be used to determine priority? Short courses could not use the orthodox elementary primers, which were designed for a long course of study and were organized along different principles of character selection. Furthermore, primers written for children often failed to arouse and sustain the interest of adults. The problem of maintaining reader interest while compressing materials in order to maximize the amount that could be learned within a short period dictated the creation of entirely new texts.

Jimmy Yen was a pioneer in the effort to produce new texts

for mass education. In France, when he first tried to teach adult illiterates, Yen used a textbook that was already available, an introduction to 600 common characters; but this text, *Liu-pai t'ung-su chiao-yü k'o-pen,* suffered from several deficiencies: it was written in classical Chinese, it was difficult for the laborers to understand, and it failed to interest them.[70] Better vernacular texts were needed, ones that included the most commonly used characters. Characters most frequently encountered in elite literature—for example, those in the orthodox primers—were not the same characters most commonly used in vernacular literature or in the activities of daily life. Thus, the identification of appropriate texts and vocabulary were primary problems in the effort to compile textbooks for mass education. At first, the selection of those characters that should be most useful in everyday life was intuitive: Jimmy Yen's first *Thousand-Character Book* (*Ch'ien tzu k'o*) was based on a selection of characters from dictionaries.[71] Such a method could hardly provide an accurate basis on which to choose or rank characters according to their usefulness.

Ch'en Ho-ch'in, whose work underlay the revised *Thousand-Character Book* published in 1923, tried to provide an empirical basis for selecting the small number of characters to be taught in adult education classes. He took vernacular materials of various kinds, including modern children's texts, mass newspapers, and excerpts from traditional novels like *Dream of the Red Chamber* and *Monkey,* then counted the characters appearing in them. Out of over half a million characters, this character count identified only 4,261 unique characters. When these were grouped in order of frequency of appearance, it was found that 41.9 percent appeared less than ten times, while 840 characters, or less than 20 percent of the total, appeared over a hundred times in the materials.[72] Although subsequent criticisms of the vernacular materials selected by Ch'en led to further studies of this sort, the method of counting character frequencies in representative vernacular materials continued to be used.

Under the auspices of the National Association of the Mass Education Movement, further efforts to compile better word lists were coupled with another line of inquiry, the attempt to identify the vocabulary essential for such daily activities as writing letters, keeping household accounts, reading notices, buying tickets, and reading contracts. Characters were ranked in order of their frequency of occurrence in two categories: their appearance in vernacular materials and their use in daily activities. There was surprisingly little overlap between the most frequently used characters in these two categories. The top twenty-one characters listed for daily activities included only seven of those most frequently found in vernacular materials.[73]

As the compilation of word lists and the identification of essential vocabulary proceeded, different *Thousand-Character Books* were published for urban dwellers, farmers, and soldiers—each intended to be completed during a four-month course. The successful graduate of these courses could read simple newspapers, write letters, and keep accounts.[74]

Beyond the four-month course, the broader goal of the Mass Education movement was expressed in its slogan: ''Eliminate illiteracy, make a new person.''[75] Limited literacy had to be fed with written materials that the graduates could read, not only to encourage successful retention of the characters they had learned, but to realize the goal of transforming these individuals into new citizens as well. This concern was not limited to Yen's group alone. Participants in the New Culture movement, which was not directly involved in mass education, were also writing about the small readership enjoyed by the journals written by intellectuals, and expressing the need to go beyond this limited audience in order to fulfill the goals of social transformation through education.[76]

Attempts to devise "what people should read" were accompanied by investigations to determine what people actually read. These efforts disclosed the continued popularity of traditional literature, particularly among poor and rural Chinese. Here was something reformers had to confront and, if possible, utilize for their own purposes.

Investigators observed that the new vocabulary in newspapers and other modern reading matter imposed severe barriers of understanding for potential readers. As Olga Lang notes:

> Even those classified as knowing how to read and write were for the most part unable to read a newspaper or book. The difficulty

> of Chinese script makes illiteracy more common than in the West and explains the high percentage of semiliterate people, acquainted with only a limited number of characters and unable to read current literature. Moreover, modern books and newspapers often employ foreign constructions and expressions and thus are difficult for the untrained.[77]

Chinese who continued to live in relatively unchanged traditional settings may also have found the older materials more interesting and relevant. This is supported by findings showing that preference for traditional reading matter was positively correlated with poverty and rural residence. In north China, only two persons among twenty-two farm laborer families, and five among twenty-four poor peasant and tenant families, read newspapers; but ten persons read the classics and old popular novels. Not a single member of twelve poor and middle-level Fukien peasant families read newspapers or modern books, but twelve persons read old-style books. The few literate women found in Fukien and Hopei surveys did not read modern works, but they did read old books.[78] Japanese investigations cited by Ramon Myers also observed that newspapers did not circulate widely in the Hopei and Shantung villages studied.[79]

Even in the early 1930s in Shanghai, a city that was the quintessence of the new China, newspaper readers tended to be intellectuals or middle-class residents, as distinguished from children, store clerks, housewives, workers, and prostitutes—all of whom patronized vendors of traditionally popular genres. Housewives and other readers favored comic book serials, issued in installments of about ten sheets at a time, which could be rented for one cash or less per volume. The existence of a regular audience for these *lien-huan t'u-hua,* which included tales of knights-errant, love tragedies, and ghost stories, can be seen from Hsü Hsü's finding that in 1933 over 500 such serials were being published and distributed throughout the city by roughly 1,100 to 1,200 vendors. Most vendors dealt with a regular clientele, whom they recognized and to whom they frequently extended credit.[80]

Without further analysis of these serials, however, we do not know to what extent (if any) the content of traditional literary genres had been modified by the changing times. Traditional orthodox primers still retained some appeal for these nonelite readers. Hsü notes that the book vendors sold the *Trimetrical Classic,* the *Thousand-Character Classic,* the *Hundred Names,* the Confucian Four Books, and children's illustrated glossaries.[81]

Tsa-tzu survived the shift into the twentieth century by including new terms and concepts. Because the simplest *tsa-tzu* were illustrated glossaries, they could easily accommodate new words. Transitional *tsa-tzu* like the *Hui-t'u ssu-ch'ien tzu wen* (Illustrated 4,000-character glossary) were published in editions that also presented five, six, and seven thousand characters respectively;[82] and a similar glossary, the *Hui-t'u shih-tzu shih-tsai i* (Easy illustrated reading primer),[83] added new words to the old lists while retaining the traditional categories of organization. The *Hui-t'u shih-tzu shih-tsai i* was typical, with its blend of Chinese mythical animals alongside a map of Europe, and Western fedoras placed next to depictions of traditional Chinese headgear. As figure 3 shows, some items were borrowed from the Japanese.

The *tsa-tzu* discussed above were simple illustrated glossaries without substantive written texts. Traditionally, unillustrated *tsa-tzu* had been of two kinds: those written in the vernacular (which were fairly rare) and those written in rhymed couplets. The *Thousand-Character Readers* published by the Mass Education movement represented the modern development of vernacular *tsa-tzu* and dominated mass education in the Republican period. The rhymed couplet form of *tsa-tzu* did not disappear and continues to be published, as shown by the 1964 printing of *Hsin-pien ssu-yen tsa-tzu* (Newly compiled four-character glossary) issued by the Kiangsi Educational Press.

Like the traditional *tsa-tzu,* the *Newly Compiled Four-Character Glossary* was explicitly intended for mass education. It was a revised and expanded version of a book issued for use in the *min-pan hsiao-hsüeh* (locally-managed elementary schools) a year earlier, and had itself been modeled on a version published by the Hunan People's Press. According to its preface, the new work contains 2,400 characters, including 500 commonly used in village life.[84] Since some of the campaigns to eradicate adult illiteracy had initially established mastery of 1,000 and then of 1,500 characters as their goal, the 2,400 characters in this work represent a large

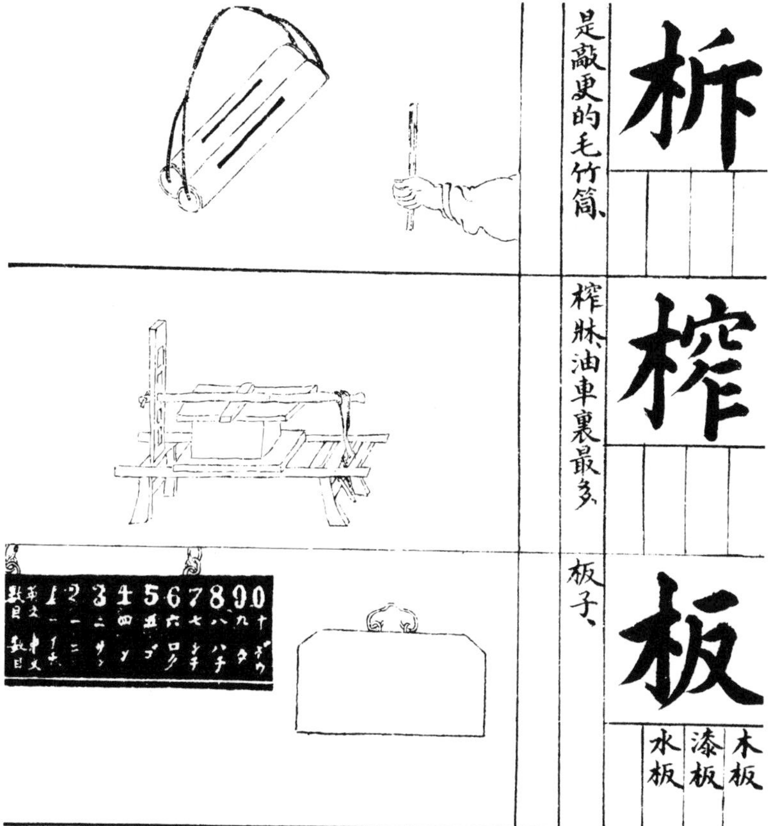

Fig. 3. Page from the *Hui-t'u shih-tzu shih-tsai i* (Easy illustrated reading primer), compiled by Shih Ch'ung-en (Shanghai, 1918), 3.17b. Notice the arabic numerals and Japanese syllabary accompanying the numbers on the board. (Courtesy of Asia Library, University of Michigan)

number for rural readers to learn.[85] The book is divided into twenty-eight chapters that incorporate political indoctrination with practical information on agriculture. Political chapters such as "The Three-Sided Red Flag" carry specific messages: "The liberation of the country, the revolutionary victory [is due to] the alliance of workers and peasants, class dictatorship, . . . "[86] Other chapters consist of little more than lists of objects used in daily life.[87] This blend of the ideological and the practical is in keeping with Chairman Mao's directive that "teaching materials must be local in nature," an injunction that stimulates the production of aids ranging from *Long Live Chairman Mao* to lists of farm implements.[88]

If we compare traditional *tsa-tzu* and popular genres such as short stories, ballads, and comic books with their post-1949 counterparts, we can appreciate not only how an old genre can serve the needs of a modernizing nation, but also the continuities in rural life, where the requisite characters useful for daily routines are frequently the same as those used a century or more ago. Here again, the significant difference between post-1949 materials and their traditional predecessors lies in the unified political culture that now controls even popular genres. Unlike the traditional world, where popular literature often served as a vehicle for the transmission of non-Confucian values, Chinese society today is one in which political authority has come to effectively control all media. From this point of view, Chairman Mao may indeed have been the most successful teacher China has ever known.

Appendices

Appendix 1

Estimates of the Late Nineteenth-Century School Population

Since formal schooling in Ch'ing society was largely limited to males, any estimate of the late nineteenth century school population must first exclude females from population totals. As P. T. Ho notes, women made up less than half of the population, with the practice of female infanticide probably contributing to the preponderance of men. The proportion of females in the population in 1953—48.18 percent—was probably higher than would have been the case in the late nineteenth century. Even surveys from the 1930s show a higher proportion of males, with females representing from 45 to 47.7 percent of the population;[1] the estimate of 47.7 percent will be used in the following calculations.

As noted in chapter 2, boys began schooling at the age of seven, and those who did not go on to advanced levels ended their schooling at age fourteen (fifteen *sui*). Several sources state that poor students who had to begin earning a living at age eleven or twelve could only obtain a maximum of four to five years of schooling, which was still probably more than most students received.

If the ages from seven to fourteen are taken as the school-going age, what percentage of the male population fell into this group? There are no contemporary statistics that provide information of this sort.[2] Traditional records presented by P. T. Ho, however, provide a range of figures for the proportion of the total population (males and females) under age sixteen; this group, in Chihli for example, constituted from 31.4 to 38.3 percent of the population.[3]

Early twentieth century surveys produced similar figures. For example, Chi-ming Chiao found that 36.3 percent of the male and 34 percent of the female population in north China were under age fifteen.[4] If these figures are adjusted to include those aged fifteen, we obtain an estimate of 37 percent of the population under age sixteen,[5] a figure that fits into Ho's range. The Chiao age and sex breakdowns for 1929–31 are used in the following calculations as an approximation of late nineteenth century figures for China.

In order to obtain an estimate of the number of males between the ages of seven and fourteen, females are first subtracted from the total population of approximately 430 million persons in about 1850. Of the remaining 225 million, 17.92 percent, or 40.3 million persons, are males between ages seven and fourteen.[6]

The total number of active schools reported in local histories and listed in table 18 is 5,846. With an average enrollment of 23 students per school (see table 2), a total of 134,000 students could be accommodated. The significance of this sum depends on what percentage of the 40.3 million boys of school-going age fell into the category of "poor" sons whose parents could not afford to pay for schooling. Information on socio-economic stratification is of course unavailable, but if we assume that 90 percent of the populace was rural and accept the estimate that 68 percent of farming households in the 1930s were poor peasants as an approximation of late Ch'ing figures, then 24.7 million boys would fall into the category of those eligible to attend charitable schools. The available schools then provided negligible opportunities for education.[7]

As noted in chapter 4, the reported figures for charitable schools are of questionable accuracy: the actual number of schools in Chungking prefecture, Szechwan, for example, was as much as forty times the total reported in the gazetteer. It is exceedingly unlikely that community and charitable schools were underreported to this extent throughout the whole empire, however, and even if the numbers of schools were ten times the figures reported, the extent to which the schools could accommodate eligible students would remain negligible on the national level.

The availability of free education varied considerably on the provincial and sub-provincial level, as shown by table 19, which gives the percentage of boys of school-going age who could be accommodated in the schools within each province. As chapter 4 described, county-level distribution of schools in some cases could provide higher access to free education than the provincial or national figures suggest.

Fuller analysis of these data must await the compilation of sufficient information on social stratification in Ch'ing society to permit a more accurate estimate of the size of the group who were too poor to pay for their schooling, as well as more knowledge on the extent of clan schools than is presently available. Scrutiny of the available figures on community and charitable schools suggests that only a minority of the provinces succeeded in providing educational facilities for the poor to any meaningful extent.

TABLE 18
Charitable Schools Reported in Late Ch'ing China, by Province

Place	Number of *I-hsüeh*		Number of *She-hsüeh*		Total Number of Active Schools
	Total	Defunct	Total	Defunct	
1. Anhwei	26	2	0	0	24
2. Chekiang	11	0	420	0	431
3. Chihli	946	94	138	74	916
4. Fukien	42	0	464	0	506
5. Honan	200	0	32	0	232
6. Hunan	341	2	1	0	340
7. Hupei	266	40	62	39	249
8. Kansu	27	0	35	0	62
9. Kiangsi	5	0	231	0	236
10. Kiangsu	255[a]	46	42	8	243
11. Kwangsi	120	58	109	92	79
12. Kwangtung	0	0	748	0	748
13. Kweichow	77	1	0	0	76
14. Shansi	547	190	22	12	367
15. Shantung	169	0	0	0	169
16. Shensi	435	11	158	6	582
17. Szechwan	45	2	11	7	47
18. Yunnan	539	0	0	0	539

Sources:

1. 1877 TC, chüan 92.
2. 1899 TC, chüan 25–29.
3. 1884 TC, chüan 114–17.
4. 1829 TC, chüan 62–66.
5. Reprint of 1869 TC, 43.46a–49b.
6. 1885 TC, chüan 68–70.
7. 1921 TC, chüan 59.
8. 1736 TC, chüan 9.
9. 1881 TC, chüan 81–82.
10. Kiangsu data are derived from the following gazetteers: *Chiang-ning* FC, 1880 ed., 5.8b, 7.16b–17b; *Su-chou* FC, 1882 ed., chüan 24–25; *Sung-chiang* FC, 1817 ed., pp. 682–714; *Wu-chin, Yang-hu* HC, 1879 ed., 5.7a–8b; *Wu-hsi, Chin-kuei* HC, 1881 ed., pp. 117–18; *Chiang-yin* HC, 1920 ed., p. 376; *I-hsing* HC, 1882 ed., p. 691; *Ching-chiang* HC, 1876 ed., 6.35a; *Tan-t'u* HC, 1879 ed., pp. 354–55; *Tan-yang* HC, 1885 ed., 10.10b; *Huai-an* FC, 1852 reprint of 1748 ed., chüan 10; *Yang-chou* FC, 1874 ed., chüan 3; *Hsü-chou* FC, 1874 ed., chüan 15; and *T'ung-chou chih-li chou* 1875 ed., chüan 5.
11. 1800 TC, chüan 133–40.
12. Liu Po-chi, *Kuang-tung shu-yüan chih-tu,* pp. 90–91.
13. 1741 TC, chüan 9.
14. 1892 TC, chüan 76.
15. Total for the Tao-kuang period, 1821–50, taken from county and departmental gazetteers: Nakamura Jihei, "Shindai Santō nōson no gigaku," *Tōyō shigaku* 15(1956):10.
16. 1934 TC, chüan 37–38.
17. 1816 TC, chüan 79.
18. Information from 1730 TC, cited by Ogawa Yoshiko, "Shindai ni okeru gigaku setsuritsu no kiban," in *Kinsei Chūgoku kyōiku shi kenkyū,* edited by Hayashi Tomoharu, p. 279.

[a]Incomplete coverage of all administrative units.

TABLE 19
Charitable Schools and School-Age Boys, by Province

Province	Number of Active Schools	Estimated Student Body	Number of Boys Aged 7–14 (x 1,000)	Percentage of Boys Entering Schools
Anhwei	24	552	4,089	0.01
Chekiang	431	9,913	3,265	0.30
Chihli	916	21,068	2,544	0.83
Fukien	506	11,638	1,306	0.89
Honan	232	5,336	2,602	0.20
Hunan	340	7,820	2,241	0.35
Hupei	249	5,727	3,668	0.16
Kansu	62	1,426	1,648[a]	0.09
Kiangsi	236	5,428	2,666	0.20
Kiangsu	243	5,589	4,801	0.12
Kwangsi	79	1,817	851	0.21
Kwangtung	748	17,204	3,064	0.56
Kweichow	76	1,748	561[a]	0.31
Shansi	367	8,441	1,645	0.51
Shantung	169	3,887	3,602	0.11
Shensi	582	13,386	1,316	1.02
Szechwan	47	1,081	4,802	0.02
Yunnan	539	12,397	376[a]	3.30

Sources: "Number of Active Schools" is from table 18; figures for "Estimated Student Body" were obtained by multiplying the "Number of Active Schools" by 23 (the average class size); "Percentage of Boys Entering Schools" was obtained by dividing "Estimated Student Body" by "Number of Boys Aged 7–14."

[a]While other figures were derived from the 1850 totals in Ping-ti Ho, *Studies on the Population of China* (appendix 2, p. 283), these were derived from the 1787 totals in an attempt to approximate the population at the time of the eighteenth century gazetteers that provided information on school numbers. No attempt was made to estimate the smaller total of poor boys eligible for school admission.

Appendix 2

The System of Elementary Education in South Chihli

Although private schools were the most important elementary educational institutions in Ch'ing times, absence of information on the private sector dictates that most of this study focus on public education. Three valuable documents dating from the late Ch'ing make it possible to partially repair this omission, however, by permitting an evaluation of the relative importance of private and public schools in three regions of south Chihli.[1]

These documents—the "Ch'ing hsien ts'un-t'u," the "Shen-chou ts'un-t'u," and the "Cheng-ting hsien ts'un-t'u"—are held in Japan, and are fully described in a 1941 article by Momose Hiromu.[2] The *ts'un-t'u* ("village records") were reports apparently held at local government offices and used as reference materials, perhaps as basic sources for the compilation of gazetteers. Their contents were of obvious value to administrators, for these documents include village-by-village details of population, cultivated land, marketing, and schools. The information provided for each village under the jurisdiction of the administrative unit also includes a listing of all officials' households, names of degree winners, and number of *i-hsüeh* (charitable schools) and *hsiang-shu* (rural schools), usually with the name of the school teacher, and often with the number of pupils attending each type of school. Since *hsiang-shu* were private schools that charged attendance fees (see chapter 2), these data permit us to count all primary educational facilities except for those within individual households where the family engaged a private tutor.

The three *ts'un-t'u* all date from the 1870s and 1880s: the "Ch'ing hsien ts'un-t'u," about 1880; the "Shen-chou ts'un-t'u," between about 1873 and 1875; and the "Cheng-ting hsien ts'un-t'u," around 1885 or 1886. Table 20 presents the actual numbers of villages included in each work. Only the "Ch'ing hsien ts'un-t'u" is complete, while the "Shen-chou ts'un-t'u" includes approximately 80 percent of the villages in the department, and the "Cheng-ting hsien ts'un-t'u" covers only the east circuit and the county seat—or approximately 13 percent of the total units in the county.

TABLE 20
Availability of Elementary Education in Three South Chihli Areas

Place	Schools			Villages			School-Age Boys (7–14)			
	I-hsüeh (A)	*Hsiang-shu* (B)	Total (C)	Total (D)	Schools per Village (average) (E)	Percentage with Schools (F)	Total[a] (G)	Schools per 1,000 (H)	Number in School (I)	Percentage in School (J)
Ch'ing hsien	11	371	382	435[b]	0.88	52.0	13,624	28.0	1,958	14.4
Shen-chou	141	429	570	415	1.37	66.3	20,427	27.9		
Cheng-ting hsien	4	18	22	28	0.78	21.4	1,097	20.0	243	22.2

[a]Figures for *hsiao-nan* (immature males) were added to obtain a total for all boys aged 0–16. The age distribution in Chi-ming Chiao's "A Study of the Chinese Population" (p. 92) was used to calculate that approximately 49.58 percent of this group would have been aged 7–14—defined as the ages of school attendance (see Appendix 1 for discussion). This method was used to calculate figures for Ch'ing hsien and Cheng-ting hsien; for Shen-chou, where figures for immature males were not provided, Chiao's age distribution table was again consulted and it was assumed that 18 percent of the male population would have been aged 7–14.

[b]Including the hsien city. My count differs from that of Momose Hiromu, who cites 436 units in his "Shinmatsu Chokurei-shō no sonzu san shu ni tsuite" (p. 847).

The three regions differed in their access to wealth derived from trade. Ch'ing county was favorably located on the highly urbanized strip adjoining the Grand Canal south of Peking. Cheng-ting county, which was also the seat of the prefectural government, was situated inland, southwest of Peking on the major overland route leading westward from the capital.[3] Shen-chou lay inland in southern Chihli, ostensibly in the least favorable location for long distance trade.

In the 1870s and 1880s, parts of southern Chihli had still not recovered from the devastation of the Taiping and Nien rebellions. The eastern Nien rebels, who practiced mobile warfare against imperial troops in this region, were not suppressed until the winter of 1867,[4] and Momose ascribes the drastic decline in Ch'ing county's population to the unrest brought about by these campaigns. A comparison of the early nineteenth century population of 260,017 with the 148,166 figure found in the *ts'un-t'u* indicates the extent and long-term nature of this disruption.[5] Shen-chou, which also felt the devastation, was affected to a slighter degree.

Population loss, declining villages, and concomitant economic phenomena thus form the context for an evaluation of the data presented in table 20. A comparison of the numbers of private schools (*hsiang-shu*) with public charitable schools (*i-hsüeh*) supports the point made in earlier chapters that private education was the most important channel for schooling in Ch'ing society. Even in Shen-chou, which benefited from the efforts of an energetic early nineteenth century magistrate who endowed it with 245 *i-hsüeh*,[6] private schools were several times more numerous than charitable schools. The ratio of private to public schools is 33.7:1 for Ch'ing hsien, 3:1 for Shen-chou, and 4.5:1 for Cheng-ting hsien.

As table 20 also shows, there was an average of over one school per village in Shen-chou, and slightly less than one per village in Ch'ing hsien and Cheng-ting hsien. Items G and H attempt first to estimate the number of boys of school-going age in each of these administrative units, then to calculate the number of schools per thousand boys of school-going age. The actual number of students enrolled in the schools is presented first in absolute numbers (item I) and then as a percentage of the number of boys of school-going age (item J). It was not possible to calculate items I and J for Shen-chou because information on the number of students was available for only 14.4 percent of *hsiang-shu* and 30.5 percent of *i-hsüeh*.

The figures in table 20 reveal that even in regions that had suffered the effects of rebellion, there was a substantial network of public and private schools. The number of students attending these schools amounted to 14.4 percent of the eligible school-going population in Ch'ing hsien and over 22 percent of the eligible population in Cheng-ting hsien. Since boys attended school for an average of only two to three years, the number of males who were exposed to schooling with the facilities that existed was much larger. For example, with the schools in Ch'ing county, 57.6 percent of the boys of school-going age could attend school for two years each; if attendance were for three years, 38.4 percent of the boys of school-going age could attend school.

Information in the *ts'un-t'u* also allows us to analyze regional distribution of schools more precisely. As item F in table 20 indicates, educational opportunities were not uniformly distributed. Schools were concentrated in some villages and absent in others. Thus, although there was an average of 1.37 schools per village in Shen-chou, only 66.3 percent of the villages and other units in the department actually had schools. In Cheng-ting hsien, only 21 percent of the units had schools, but this high concentration reflects the relatively small number of villages included in the *ts'un-t'u* and the excessive importance thus placed on the city, which was the seat of both the county and the prefectural governments.

What factors influenced school location? Some have already been discussed in chapter 4. Since private education depended on the ability to pay, wealth was certainly important. So was the supply of teachers. The more urban a place, the more likely it was to attract scholars, among them potential teachers. Residents of towns and market centers were also more likely to be able to pay the tuition fees charged by private schools. Thus preferences for urban residence on the part of the educated, coupled with the surplus generated by trade, tended to ensure that urban places had a disproportionate share of educational facilities.

The three south Chihli regions had very few towns of any size. The largest was the prefectural seat of Cheng-ting, with a population of over 15,000—far more than the 4,014 residents of Ch'ing county's seat, not to mention Shen-chou's 2,620 inhabitants.[7] Only in Ch'ing county was there a town outside the administrative center that equaled or surpassed it in size. For the most part, the important central places outside the administrative center were standard markets with populations of 3,000 or less, and hence low in the central place hierarchy.[8]

Standard markets with less than 3,000 population varied in the extent of the marketing area that they dominated. In Ch'ing hsien, the presence of cheap water transport via the Grand Canal enabled relatively few standard markets to serve large communities, as compared to an interior landlocked area such as Shen-chou. There were only nine standard markets in Ch'ing county as opposed to forty-three in Shen-chou. The largest market in Ch'ing county served a population of 35,600 scattered over ninety-two villages, while Shen-chou's largest market served only 17,196 people living in forty-two villages.[9] The volume of commerce and surplus derived from trade was probably higher in Ch'ing county standard markets than in the other regions.

Table 21 examines the number of schools in market and administrative centers, and confirms our expectation that the surplus generated by trade would attract educational facilities. Most of the central places in the three areas had more than one school: only one market in Ch'ing county, two in

TABLE 21

Markets and School Locations in Three South Chihli Areas

Place	Number of *I-hsüeh*	Number of *Hsiang-shu*	Total Number of Schools	Number of Markets	Schools per Market (average)	Percentage of Schools Located in Settlements with Markets
Ch'ing hsien	1	50	51	9	5.7	13.4
Shen-chou	30	108	138	43	3.2	24.2
Cheng-ting hsien	4	15	19	4	4.8	86.4

Shen-chou, and two in Cheng-ting county had no schools whatsoever. The last column in the table, however, shows that—with the exception of Cheng-ting county[10]—the schools operating in these central places constituted only a fraction of the total number of schools in each region and that educational facilities had penetrated well below the market centers in both Ch'ing county and Shen-chou.

Ch'ing county and Shen-chou thus possessed substantial numbers of rural schools. Table 22 presents information showing that larger villages were more likely than smaller ones to have schools. In Ch'ing county and Shen-chou, both the average and the median number of households in a village were markedly higher for villages with schools than for those without them. The larger the village, the more children there were of school-going age and the better able the village was to support a schoolteacher.

TABLE 22
Settlement Size and School Distribution in Three South Chihli Areas

	Settlements			
	With Schools		Without Schools	
Place	Average Number of Households	Median Number of Households	Average Number of Households	Median Number of Households
Ch'ing hsien	77.5	60	47.8	39.0
Shen-chou	114.2	94	49.8	40.0
Cheng-ting hsien	1,517.5	40	72.2	59.5

Note: All units in the administrative areas listed in each *ts'un-t'u* were counted, including the markets presented in table 21. As is clear from table 21, few settlements were markets; most of the units in Ch'ing hsien and Shen-chou were rural villages.

TABLE 23
Educational Background of Schoolteachers in Three South Chihli Areas

		Teachers for Whom Data is Known					
			Teachers (in percent) with Degrees				Teachers without Degrees
Place	Total Number of Teachers	Number	*T'ung-sheng*	*Sheng-yüan*	Other Degrees	Total	(in percent)
Ch'ing hsien	382	376		23.7	2.6	26.3	73.7
Shen-chou	570	311	30.9	24.1	7.1	62.1	37.9
Cheng-ting hsien	23	23		69.6		69.6	30.4

Note: Only "Shen-chou ts'un-t'u" gives information for *t'ung-sheng*. If a degree was not cited or a teacher was not on the list of *sheng-yüan*, he was counted among those without degrees. The gap in information on *t'ung-sheng* is undoubtedly responsible for the high percentage of Ch'ing hsien teachers listed above as being without degrees; had such information been available, this percentage would have been much lower.

Who were the private school teachers? Information in the *ts'un-t'u* presented in table 23 confirms the statements made in chapters 2 and 4 that failed scholars provided an important part of the teaching force in elementary education. In Shen-chou, where information on *t'ung-sheng* was provided, over 62 percent of the teachers came from the scholar or failed-scholar group.

Conclusion

The "Ch'ing hsien ts'un-t'u," "Shen-chou ts'un-t'u," and "Cheng-ting hsien ts'un-t'u" provide information on educational facilities in a part of north China during the last half of the nineteenth century. These sources demonstrate that despite the ravages wrought by rebellion, there were enough private and charitable schools—located not only in market towns, but in hundreds of rural villages as well—to enable from 38 to over 50 percent of all males in these areas of south Chihli to obtain some schooling. Information from the *ts'un-t'u* also shows that scholars and failed scholars made up a large part of the teaching force in these regions.

Abbreviations for Tables and Notes

CC	*chou-chih;* gazetteer for a department
FC	*fu-chih;* prefectural gazetteer
HC	*hsien-chih;* county gazetteer
TC	*t'ung-chih;* provincial gazetteer

Notes

Chapter 1

1. Carlo Cipolla, *Literacy and Development in the West* (Harmondsworth, 1969), pp. 12–13.
2. Ping-ti Ho, *The Ladder of Success in Imperial China* (New York, 1964); and Chung-li Chang, *The Chinese Gentry: Studies on Their Role in Nineteenth Century Chinese Society* (Seattle, 1955) offer two of the most important English-language treatments of this subject for the Ch'ing period.
3. From Abbé Huc, *The Chinese Empire* (London, 1855), cited by Victor Purcell, *Problems of Chinese Education* (London, 1936), p. 25, n. 2.
4. Joshua Dukes Edwin, *Everyday Life in China; or, Scenes Along River and Road in Fuh-kien* (London, n.d.), pp. 194–95.
5. Ibid., pp. 196, 198. Cornelius Osgood, *Village Life in Old China: A Community Study of Kao Yao, Yunnan* (New York, 1963), also raises the question of the quality of literacy.
6. Sidney Gamble, *Ting Hsien: A North China Rural Community* (New York, 1954), pp. 185–86. The Mass Education movement was led by Y. C. James Yen, whose biography is in *Biographical Dictionary of Republican China,* ed. Howard Boorman and Richard Howard (New York, 1971), 4:52–54. See Y. C. James Yen, "New Citizens for China," *Yale Review* 18 (1928–29):266–67.
7. Gamble, *Ting Hsien,* pp. 185–86.
8. Ibid. Y. C. James Yen, "New Citizens for China," pp. 266–67, cites a foundation vocabulary of 1,300 characters.
9. John N. Hawkins, *Mao Tse-tung and Education: His Thoughts and Teachings* (Hamden, Conn., 1974), pp. 98–100, 147.
10. Vincent T. C. Lin, "Adult Education in People's Republic of China, 1950–1958," (Ph.D. diss., University of California at Berkeley, 1963), pp. 141–43.
11. Arthur H. Smith, *Village Life in China* (1899; reprint ed., Boston, 1970), pp. 57–68.
12. Jack Goody and Ian Watt, "The Consequences of Literacy," *Comparative Studies in Society and History* 5.3(1963):313. The authors cite mastery of 3,000 characters as a minimum for literacy and estimate it takes twenty years to reach full literacy in Chinese.
13. Chung-li Chang, *Chinese Gentry,* pp. 186–87; and Maurice Freedman, *Chinese Lineage and Society: Fukien and Kwangtung* (New

York, 1966), p. 75. See also Kung-ch'üan Hsiao, *Rural China: Imperial Control in the Nineteenth Century* (Seattle, 1960), pp. 250–52.

14. Kung-ch'üan Hsiao, *Rural China*, pp. 250–52, cites evidence to support his contention that rural inhabitants of Ch'ing society were largely illiterate. Richard H. Solomon, *Mao's Revolution and the Chinese Political Culture* (Berkeley, 1971), p. 82, also argues that few Chinese were literate. For a direct rebuttal of Solomon's contention that only 1–2 percent of the Chinese population between 1600 and 1900 was literate, see Frederick W. Mote, "China's Past in the Study of China Today—Some Comments on the Recent Work of Richard Solomon," *Journal of Asian Studies* 32.1(1972):107–110.
15. Denis Twitchett, review of Joseph Needham, *Science and Civilization in China*, vol. 3 (Cambridge, 1959), *Bulletin of the School of Oriental and African Studies* 25.1(1962):188.
16. Ronald P. Dore, *Education in Tokugawa Japan* (London, 1965).
17. Paul Wheatley, *The Pivot of the Four Quarters* (Chicago, 1971), p. 380. On Tunhuang manuscripts, see Denis Twitchett, "Chinese Social History from the Seventh to the Tenth Centuries," *Past and Present* 35(1966):43–44. Kenneth K. S. Ch'en, *The Chinese Transformation of Buddhism* (Princeton, 1973), pp. 288–89, cites Tunhuang manuscripts that were notices of various societies. These included a tenth century document from a society of fifteen women devoted to the promotion of friendship among women. Were these women literate? If not, who wrote the document?
18. Joanna F. Handlin, "Lü K'un's New Audience: The Influence of Women's Literacy on Sixteenth Century Thought," in *Women in Chinese Society*, ed. Margery Wolf and Roxane Witke (Stanford, 1975), pp. 16, 28–29, 37.
19. *Chinese Repository* 1 (1832–33):306, 2(1833–34):252, 4(1835–36):7, 6(1837–38):234; John Lossing Buck, *Land Utilization in China* (Nanking, 1937), 1:373 (table 10), 374 (table 11). See his vol. 1 for details on areas surveyed.
20. Cited in John E. Reinecke, *Language and Dialect in Hawaii: A Sociolinguistic History to 1935* (Honolulu, 1969), p. 120 (table 12). Similarly high rates for female literacy are recorded for Hong Kong and Kowloon in a 1931 unpublished "Census of Occupations of Hong Kong," pp. 138–39 (tables 32, 33); my thanks to Professor Janet Salaff for this material.
21. Arthur Waley, *Yuan Mei: Eighteenth Century Poet* (Stanford, 1970), pp. 77, 179, 183. The *Nü lun-yü* and other similar titles are presented in Chang Chih-kung's bibliography in *Ch'uan-t'ung yü-wen chiao-yü ch'u-t'an* (Shanghai, 1962); see pp. 158–59 and 165–66 for examples. The *Nü ssu-tzu ching* is in the collection of the former Cabinet Library (Naikaku bunko) in Tokyo.

22. Handlin, "Lü K'un," p. 27; Waley, *Yuan Mei*, pp. 11, 37–38, 119; Ping-ti Ho, *Ladder of Success*, case 5, pp. 274–76; Philip C. Huang, *Liang Ch'i-ch'ao and Modern Chinese Liberalism* (Seattle, 1972), p. 11; Olga Lang, *Pa Chin and His Writings: Chinese Youth between the Two Revolutions* (Cambridge, Mass., 1967), p. 13; Pichon Loh, *The Early Chiang Kai-shek: A Study of His Personality and Politics, 1887–1924* (New York, 1971), p. 6.
23. See discussions of *t'an-tz'u* in Cheng Chen-to, *Chung-kuo su-wen-hsüeh shih* (Shanghai, 1938), pp. 370–81; Ch'en Ju-heng, *Shuo-shu shih-hua* (Peking, 1958), pp. 170, 205–19. On the literacy of storytellers, see Vera Hrdlickova, "The Professional Training of Chinese Storytellers and the Storytellers' Guilds," *Archiv orientalni* 33.2(1965):232–33.
24. Handlin, "Lü K'un," p. 16; Marjorie Topley, "Marriage Resistance in Rural Kwangtung," in *Women in Chinese Society*, ed. Margery Wolf and Roxane Witke (Stanford, 1975), pp. 75, 78; Daniel Harrison Kulp, *Country Life in South China: The Sociology of Familism* (1925; reprint ed., Taipei, 1966), p. 279.
25. Smith, *Village Life*, p. 202.
26. Translated from the Chiang clan rules by Hui-chen Wang Liu, *The Traditional Chinese Clan Rules* (Locust Valley, 1959), p. 165.
27. T'ung-tsu Ch'ü, *Local Government in China under the Ch'ing* (Cambridge, Mass., 1962), pp. 39, 43–44. The figure of 300,000 is based on taking 200 as the average number of clerks per unit, and multiplying that by 1,503—the number of basic units (departments and counties) in China during the Ch'ien-lung period (1736–95): Ch'ü, p. 2 (table 1).
28. Ibid., pp. 77–86. The number of personal servants in a county or department varied from five to about thirty (p. 77); if we take ten as an average and multiply it by 1,503 (Ch'ü, p. 2 [table 1]), we get an estimate of 15,030 personal servants employed at any one time during the period 1736–95. This does not consider the pool of such servants that must have existed.
29. Ping-ti Ho, "The Salt Merchants of Yang-chou: A Study of Commercial Capitalism in Eighteenth Century China," *Harvard Journal of Asiatic Studies* 17(1954):130–68; *Ta Ch'ing lü-li hui-t'ung hsin tsuan*, section on markets, 14.1a–3b. A detailed description of price reporting is provided by Endymion P. Wilkinson, "Studies in Chinese Price History" (Ph.D. diss., Princeton University, 1970), chap. 4.
30. Such regulations are found in *Hu-nan sheng-li ch'eng-an*; they have been studied for Kiangsi by Yokoyama Suguru, "Shindai Kōsei-shō ni okeru unyugyō no kikō," *Hiroshima daigaku bungakubu kiyō* 18(1960):49–89. See Edward H. Parker, "The Yangtze Gorges and Rapids in Hu-pei," *The China Review* 9(1880–81):173. Contracts are

discussed in Shiba Yoshinobu, *Commerce and Society in Sung China,* trans. Mark Elvin (Ann Arbor, 1970), pp. 36–37.

31. Contract forms for these transactions are included in the *jih-yung lei-shu;* see Sakai Tadao, "Mindai no nichiyō ruisho to shomin kyōiku," in *Kinsei Chūgoku kyōiku shi kenkyū,* ed. Hayashi Tomoharu (Tokyo, 1958). One of these books is described in English in *Chinese Repository* 7(1838–39):402, 10(1841):613–18.
32. Jonathan D. Spence, *Emperor of China* (New York, 1974), p. 40.
33. See Lien-sheng Yang, *Money and Credit in China* (Cambridge, Mass., 1952), p. 99, on Chekiang regulations in 1780. Such regulations are also found in collections of provincial regulations such as the *Fu-chien sheng-li.* The schedules of carrying charges for porters alluded to previously is another example of government regulation of enterprises designed to ensure consumer protection.
34. Such regulations occupy a prominent place in collections of stone inscriptions, such as *Chiang-su sheng Ming Ch'ing i-lai pei-k'o tzu-liao hsüan-chi,* compiled by the Kiangsu Provincial Museum (Chiang-su sheng po-wu kuan [1959; reprint ed., Tokyo, 1967]). The guilds themselves circulated written pay scales to members; see Meng T'ien-p'ei and Sidney Gamble, *Prices, Wages, and the Standard of Living in Peking, 1900–1924,* 1926 Supplement to *Chinese Social and Political Science Review* (Peking, 1926), p. 90.
35. Roswell S. Britton, *The Chinese Periodical Press, 1800–1912* (Shanghai, 1933), p. 4.
36. Gazettes could also be rented (ibid., pp. 7–8). In Canton, the provincial gazette (sold for one or two cash a sheet) was printed from wax blocks, but elsewhere gazettes were issued in manuscript form (ibid., p. 14). See Justus Doolittle, *Social Life of the Chinese . . .* (New York, 1865), 1:332. According to the *Chinese Repository* 1(1832–33):506–7, the *Peking Gazette* itself came in different editions for officials of different ranks.
37. *Chinese Repository* 1 (1832–33):492–93. Quote from Britton, *Chinese Periodical Press,* p. 6; Britton also describes (p. 4) how newspapers were printed on clay blocks and wax blocks that could be cut more quickly than wood and later reused.
38. Reported by the Lazarist priest Joseph Gabet in Britton, *Chinese Periodical Press,* pp. 6–7.
39. D. J. MacGowan, "Chinese Guilds or Chambers of Commerce and Trades Unions," *Journal of the North China Branch of the Royal Asiatic Society* 21 (1886):170. Britton, *Chinese Periodical Press,* p. 7, citing an "Old China Hand." Talcott Williams, "Silver in China—and Its Relation to Chinese Copper Coinage," *Annals of the American Academy of Political and Social Science* 9(1897):367 (footnote). The Chinese postal system has been studied by Ying-wen Cheng,

Postal Communication in China and Its Modernization (Cambridge, Mass., 1970); see also Doolittle, *Social Life,* 1:332; and W. H. Medhurst, *The Foreigner in Far Cathay* (New York, 1873), p. 119. Hosea B. Morse, *The Trade and Administration of the Chinese Empire* (London, 1908), pp. 413–14, writes that "very strong letter hongs have been developed, utilising every means of conveyance, and meeting in every way the wishes of the public." The *Chinese Repository* 9(1840):636 also reported that "there is great confidence reposed in the postmen and carriers by the community."

40. Britton, *Chinese Periodical Press,* p. 3; Reverend Milne, writing in the *Chinese Repository* 16(1847):19–20; G. M. H. [Playfair], "Guild Terrorism," *Journal of the North China-Branch of the Royal Asiatic Society* 20(1885):181–82.
41. *Chinese Repository* 2(1833–34):252; 1(1832–33):306; 4(1835–36):7, 9.
42. Ibid., 9(1840):80; 2(1833–34):252.
43. Ibid., 4(1835–36):190. These lending libraries still exist; see chap. 8.
44. Ibid., 4(1835–36):431; two such books are introduced in ibid., 6(1837–38):276–79, and in William C. Hunter, *The "Fan Kwae" at Canton before Treaty Days, 1825–1844, by an Old Resident,* 2d ed. (Shanghai, 1911), pp. 63–64.
45. Hunter, "*Fan Kwae,*" notes that the cost of such books was a penny or two; this was approximately 7–14 Chinese copper cash in the 1830s. See *Chinese Repository* 3(1834–35):468, where .1 liang = 14 cents. We assume 1 liang = 1,000 copper cash in the calculation. See also "Jargon Spoken at Canton," *Chinese Repository 4(1835–36):428–35.*
46. Doolittle, *Social Life,* 2:331–36, 339.
47. Jean Chesneaux, *Secret Societies in China in the Nineteenth and Twentieth Centuries,* trans. Gillian Nettle (Ann Arbor, 1971), p. 14, describes the initiation ceremony of a Triad branch in Singapore in 1824. *Chinese Repository* 18(1849):287–88.
48. Susan Naquin, *Millenarian Rebellion in China: The Eight Trigrams Uprising of 1813* (New Haven, 1976), pp. 18–23.
49. Yu-wen Jen, *The Taiping Revolutionary Movement* (New Haven, 1973), pp. 32, 48, 153–54.
50. Kung-ch'üan Hsiao, *Rural China,* chap. 3–especially pp. 43–44.
51. Ibid., pp. 71–72, 80; regulations excluded gentry from holding the posts (p. 68), but pp. 70–71 is devoted to a discussion of how gentry often cooperated with officials to keep the system operating. Hsiao's view differs from that of T'ung-tsu Ch'ü (*Local Government,* p. 153), who observes that in general the gentry did not participate in the administration of *pao-chia.* See Derk Bodde and Clarence Morris, *Law in Imperial China* (Cambridge, Mass., 1967), pp. 246–47, for a case of "unauthorized assumption" of *pao-chia* posts.

52. T'ung-tsu Ch'ü, *Local Government,* pp. 136–37; Kung-ch'üan Hsiao, *Rural China,* describes this on p. 96, and the *li-chia* system in chap. 4.
53. See Kung-ch'üan Hsiao, *Rural China,* chaps. 3–4, and T'ung-tsu Ch'ü, *Local Government,* pp. 151–53.
54. Doolittle, *Social Life,* 1:332–33. For Sung practices, see Brian E. McKnight, *Village and Bureaucracy in Southern Sung China* (Chicago, 1971), pp. 62–70.
55. Mark Elvin, *The Pattern of the Chinese Past* (Stanford, 1973), p. 115.
56. Jonathan Spence, "Chang Po-hsing and the K'ang-hsi Emperor," *Ch'ing-shih wen-t'i* 1.8(1968):5.
57. Ch'ing Sheng-tsu, *The Sacred Edict, with a Translation of the Colloquial Rendering,* trans. F. W. Baller (Shanghai, 1907). The colloquial version was the work of an official named Wang Yo-p'u.
58. Wang Hui-tsu, *Hsüeh-chih i-shuo,* cited in Etienne Balazs, *Political Theory and Administrative Reality in Traditional China* (London, 1965), p. 56.
59. Emily Ahern, *The Cult of the Dead in a Chinese Village* (Stanford, 1973), pp. 79–80; Yang clan rules, presented by Hsien-chin Hu, *The Common Descent Group in China and Its Functions* (New York, 1948), app. 58, p. 184.
60. Hsien-chin Hu, *Common Descent Group,* app. 53, p. 171.
61. In an introduction to Smith, *Village Life,* p. xv. See Martin C. Yang, *A Chinese Village: Taitou, Shantung Province* (New York, 1965), pp. 106–8 for descriptions of marriage customs; pp. 86–89 for funeral customs. The *fen-tan,* or document specifying the distribution of property among sons, is described by Niida Noboru, *Chūgoku no nōson kazoku* (Tokyo, 1966), pp. 15, 89, 90, 93, 106, 133, 189; see also Ramon Myers, *The Chinese Peasant Economy: Agricultural Development in Hopei and Shantung, 1890–1949* (Cambridge, Mass., 1970), pp. 59, 97, 115.
62. Morita Akira, *Shindai suiri shi kenkyū* (Tokyo, 1974), pp. 399–405; Ramon Myers, "Economic Organization and Cooperation in Modern China: Irrigation Management in Xing-tai County, Ho-bei Province," in Ko Muramatsu Yūji Kyōju tsuitō rombunshū—*Chūgoku no seiji to keizai,* comp. Ko Muramatsu Yūji Kyōju tsuitō jigyōkai (Tokyo, 1975), pp. 197–204.
63. Yu-wen Jen, *Taiping Revolutionary Movement,* p. 24.
64. *Chinese Repository* 6 (1837–38):236.
65. Excerpt from *Annales de la Propagation de la Foi,* in *Chinese Repository* 9(1840):246; Smith, *Village Life,* pp. 52–53; Doolittle, *Social Life,* 1:376–77; J. MacGowan, *Men and Manners of Modern China* (London, 1912), p. 77.

66. Huc's *The Chinese Empire* (London, 1855) is cited in Purcell, *Problems of Chinese Education,* p. 25, n. 2. According to Sakai Tadao, "Confucianism and Popular Educational Works," in *Self and Society in Ming Thought,* ed. William T. de Bary (New York, 1970), pp. 336–38, the broadening of the social base for literacy dates from Ming times.
67. Freedman, *Chinese Lineage and Society,* p. 76; p. 10, n.5; on p. 11 of his *Lineage Organization in Southeastern China* (London, 1958), Freedman cites Buck's statistics for twelve counties of Fukien and Kwangtung, where the percentage of net income from nonfarm sources ranged from 1 to 43 percent. Buck, *Land Utilization,* 3:309–10, table 6, gives 15.6 percent as the percentage of net income from other than farm sources derived from sixty-eight localities in the wheat region. The corresponding figure for eighty-four localities in the rice region was 12.9 percent. In individual localities, this figure could be much higher: in Ch'ang-shu, Kiangsu, for example, the Shanghai Research Department of the South Manchurian Railroad discovered in the 1930s that over half the residents in some villages were no longer engaged in agricuture: Minami Manshū tetsudō kabushiki kaisha, Shanhai jimusho, *Kōso-shō Jōjuku-ken nōson jittai chōsa hōkokusho* (Shanghai, 1939), p. 23 (table 10). Dwight Perkins discusses rural marketing on pp. 114–15 of his *Agricultural Development in China, 1368–1968* (Chicago, 1969).
68. *Chinese Repository* 6(1837–38):234.
69. Data from Hawaiian Census of 1896, cited by Reinecke, *Language and Dialect,* p. 120 (table 12). Reinecke compares the 49.84 percent for illiterate Chinese males to the 41.6 percent for illiterate Japanese males in Hawaii that same year.
70. Imperial Maritime Customs, *Decennial Reports,* 1882–1891, cited by Dwight H. Perkins, "Introduction: The Persistence of the Past," in *China's Modern Economy in Historical Perspective,* ed. D. H. Perkins (Stanford, 1975), p. 4, footnote. Perkins also compares the Buck data with these figures. Similar estimates appear in the 1892–1901 ed. of the *Decennial Reports* (2 vols.).
71. Horace E. Chandler, "The Work of the American Presbyterian Mission from 1918 to 1941 toward the Lessening of Adult Illiteracy in Shantung Province, China" (Ph.D. diss., University of Pittsburgh, 1943), pp. 9–10.
72. Kan Yü-yüan, *Hsiang-ts'un min-chung chiao-yü* (Shanghai, 1934–35), pp. 47–49. In Kwangtung, the figure might have been much higher: C. K. Yang, *A Chinese Village in Early Communist Transition* (Cambridge, Mass., 1959), p. 181, writes that a 1950 survey of Nanching village showed 65 percent of the men and 80 percent of the women were literate; see Yang's comments, pp. 184–85.

73. Jen-chi Chang, *Pre-Communist China's Rural School and Community* (Boston, 1960), p. 77; see also pp. 78, 79 (table 21), 80–81 (table 22).
74. Osgood, *Village Life*, p. 95.
75. Myers, *Chinese Peasant Economy*, pp. 62, 82, 102, 119; on written documents: pp. 77, 93, 94, 97, 113, 115; on village schools: pp. 62, 101, 119. Martin C. Yang, *Chinese Village*, pp. 137, 144.
76. David Crook and Isabel Crook, *Revolution in a Chinese Village: Ten Mile Inn* (London, 1959), p. 12–13.
77. Alan P. L. Liu, *Communications and National Integration in Communist China* (Berkeley, 1971), p. 22. Victor C. Falkenheim, "County Administration in Fukien," *China Quarterly* 59(1974):528, gives a figure of 4.3 million illiterates ca. 1952 in Fukien; taking 13.1 million as the provincial population in 1953 (Nai-ruenn Chen, *Chinese Economic Statistics* [Chicago, 1967], p. 132), this results in a literacy rate of 66.2 percent of the population.
78. Hawkins, *Mao Tse-tung and Education*, p. 208, n. 4; Hsi-sheng Ch'i, *Warlord Politics in China, 1916–1928* (Stanford, 1976), p. 109, footnote; Gamble, *Ting Hsien*, p. 188 (for data on literacy by occupation), p. 187 (by family income and age).
79. Naikaku sōri daijin kanbō chōsa shitsu, ed. *Chūkyō tekkōgyō chōsa hōkokusho (kigyō hen)* (Tokyo, 1956), 1:98; *Ta kung pao* (Hong Kong), March 23, 1953; John Gardner, "The Wu-fan Campaign in Shanghai," in *Chinese Communist Politics in Action*, ed. A Doak Barnett (Seattle, 1969), pp. 498–99; for a general estimate, see Peter J. Seybolt, *Revolutionary Education in China: Documents and Commentary* (White Plains, 1974), p. xx, as well as Vincent T. C. Lin, "Adult Education," pp. 223, 243.
80. Manshū kaihatsu yonjūnen shi kankō kai, *Manshū kaihatsu yonjūnen shi* (Tokyo, 1964–65), 3:80; traditional nineteenth century schools are described by Robert H. G. Lee, *The Manchurian Frontier in Ch'ing History* (Cambridge, Mass., 1970), p. 104. Frederick W. Mote, "The Rural 'Haw' [Yunnanese Chinese] of Northern Thailand," in *SEA Tribes, Minorities, and Nations*, ed. Peter Kunstadter (Princeton, 1967), 2:500.
81. Crook and Crook, *Revolution*, p. 72.
82. See Ping-ti Ho, *Ladder of Success*, pp. 267–318.
83. Ibid., p. 314; Tachibana Shiraki, *Shina shakai kenkyū* (Tokyo, 1936), p. 453—and my thanks to Andrew Nathan who pointed out this source to me.
84. Agnes Smedley, *The Great Road: The Life and Times of Chu Teh* (New York, 1972), p. 36.
85. Yü-yüan Kan, *Min-chung chiao-yü*, pp. 47–49.
86. Martin Yang, *Chinese Village*, p. 144.

87. Morton H. Fried, *Fabric of Chinese Society* (New York, 1953), p. 51.
88. Peter J. Seybolt, "The Yenan Revolution in Mass Education," *China Quarterly* 48(1971):644–45. The opposite phenomenon, persistence of the notion that education was the first step up the ladder of success, is cited for the same area and period by Mark Selden, *The Yenan Way in Revolutionary China* (Cambridge, Mass., 1971), p. 270. C. K. Yang, *Chinese Village*, pp. 181–82, writes that "literacy and traditional book knowledge had very limited practical significance in the personal life of the majority of the peasants," but cites (p. 181) a 1950 survey showing that 65 percent of the males in Nanching were literate, and describes the peasants' eager response to adult evening classes held in 1948 (p. 184), in contrast to the Yenan peasant attitude reported by Seybolt.

Chapter 2

1. These schools are described by Chung-li Chang, *Chinese Gentry*, pp. 4–5, and Ping-ti Ho, *Ladder of Success*, pp. 169–73.
2. Chung-li Chang, *Chinese Gentry*, p. 4, n. 5; Ping-ti Ho, *Ladder of Success*, p. 194.
3. In *Yeh* HC, 2.17a. Ch'ing academies are treated in Ping-ti Ho, *Ladder of Success*, pp. 200–203, and Ōkubo Hideko, "Shindai no shōin to shakai," in *Kinsei Ajia kyōiku shi kenkyū*, ed. Taga Akigorō (Tokyo, 1966), pp. 645–90.
4. For Ming developments, see Tilemann Grimm, *Erziehung und Politik im konfuzianischen China der Ming-Zeit (1368–1644)* (Hamburg, 1960).
5. Arthur Waley, *Yuan Mei*, p. 11. Unless explicitly stated in *sui* (Western age + 1 year), ages are in Western years.
6. Ch'en Tung-yüan, *Chung-kuo k'o-hsüeh shih-tai chih chiao-yü* (Shanghai, 1934–35), pp. 49–50, and his *Chung-kuo chiao-yü shih* (1937; reprint ed., Taipei, 1966), pp. 427–28; and Chang Chih-kung, *Yü-wen chiao-yü*, p. 3, all discuss the number of characters needed before beginning to read books.
7. Doolittle, *Social Life*, 1:376–77. The different kinds of schools are described in T'ung Chen-chia, "Ch'ing-mo hsiao-hsüeh chiao-yü chih yen-pien," *Shih-ta yüeh-k'an* 21(1935):126; Ch'en Tung-yüan, *Chung-kuo chiao-yü shih*, p. 425; and Taga Akigorō, 'Shinmatsu kakyo haishi zen sōzoku keiei no gakkō kyōiku ni tsuite," *Nihon no kyōiku shigaku* (Tokyo, 1958), pp. 95–96.
8. On Yen Yüan, see Arthur W. Hummel, ed., *Eminent Chinese of the Ch'ing Period* (Washington, 1943–44), 2:912–15. Shen Kuan-ch'ün, *Chung-kuo ku-tai chiao-yü ho chiao-yü ssu-hsiang* (Wuhan, 1956), pp. 145–46, describes Tai Chen's work as an elementary school-

teacher, an item omitted from his biography in Hummel, *Eminent Chinese,* 2:695–700, which does mention that Tai Chen worked as a private tutor at one time. Chung-li Chang's biographies are presented in *The Income of the Chinese Gentry* (Seattle, 1962), app. 4.

9. The contract form is in a rare book held by the Tōyō bunka kenkyūjo, University of Tokyo: *Hsin tseng yu-hsüeh i-chih kao-t'ou tsa-tzu ta-ch'üan,* last chüan, 9b. A similar form is in a book held by the former Cabinet Library in Tokyo: *Hsin ch'ieh Tseng T'ai-shih hui-tsüan su weng ch'i-meng cho-yü ao-t'ou,* fourth section; this is in the form of a hand-copied Japanese manuscript with unnumbered pages. On *tsa-tzu,* see Sakai Tadao, "Mindai no nichiyō ruisho to shomin kyōiku," pp. 125–31.
10. "Description of the City of Canton," *Chinese Repository* 2(1833–34):250; "Education among the Chinese," *Chinese Repository* 4(1835–36):9; "First Annual Report of the Morrison Education Society," *Chinese Repository* 6(1837–38):236; J. MacGowan, *Men and Manners,* pp. 80–81; Edwin, *Everyday Life in China,* p. 201.
11. Smith, *Village Life,* p. 65.
12. Ibid., pp. 52–53; quotation from p. 51.
13. Robert H. G. Lee, *Manchurian Frontier,* p. 104, describing the late nineteenth century; *Manshū kaihatsu,* 3:80.
14. Smith, *Village Life,* p. 53.
15. Chung-li Chang, *Income of the Chinese Gentry,* pp. 99–100. See further discussion in my chap. 4.
16. Doolittle, *Social Life,* 1:61.
17. Smith, *Village Life,* p. 52. Mexican dollars converted to taels using Maritime Customs data for the 1890s: Liang-lin Hsiao, *China's Foreign Trade Statistics, 1864–1949* (Cambridge, 1974), p. 191 (table 9a).
18. Cited by Kung-ch'üan Hsiao, *Rural China,* p. 252.
19. Kulp, *Country Life in South China,* pp. 224–26; Lillian M. Li, "Kiangnan and the Silk Export Trade, 1842–1937" (Ph.D. diss., Harvard University, 1975), p. 123; Y. K. Leong and L. K. Tao, *Village and Town Life in China* (London, 1915), pp. 96–97.
20. *Liu-yang* HC, 8.36b–37a.
21. *Kuang-hsi* TC, 1800 ed., 133.20ab. This is part of a plea for support of elementary education in Kwangsi.
22. "First Annual Report of the Morrison Education Society," *Chinese Repository* 6(1837–38):235.
23. Hsien-chin Hu, *The Common Descent Group in China and Its Functions* (New York, 1948), p. 70. In *Traditional Chinese Clan Rules,* pp. 160–61, Hui-chen Wang Liu found that 128 of 151 clan rules published in the twentieth century stressed study as the preferred vocation for clan members. See the 1689 ed. of *Ta-kang Chao-shih*

tsu-p'u, 6.4b; the 1850 *Fan-shih chia-ch'eng*, 15.38b–39a; and the 1808 ed. of *Ching-k'ou Ting-shih tsu-p'u*, 3.6ab.

24. The Wang clan in Chen-chiang, Kiangsu, cited by Hsien-chin Hu, *Common Descent Group*, p. 71; such provision is also made in *Yün-yang Yin-shih ch'ung-hsiu tsu-p'u* (1798), 14.1b.
25. *Yung-chia* HC, 6.13a. The verb used is t'ung, meaning "to know, to be well versed in."
26. Hsien-chin Hu, *Common Descent Group*, pp. 77–78; Ping-ti Ho, *Ladder of Success*, pp. 210–12; Hui-chen Wang Liu, *Traditional Chinese Clan Rules*, p. 126.
27. *Yao-shih chia-ch'eng*, in Taga, "Shinmatsu kakyo," pp. 118–19, n. 26; *Ta-fu P'an-shih chih-p'u*, 21.22ab.
28. *P'i-ling T'u-shih chih-p'u*, in Taga, "Shinmatsu kakyo," pp. 120–21, n. 32, provided clothing in addition to the items listed in the text. *Lu-shih feng-men chih-p'u*, regulation 7, in Taga Akigorō, *Sōfu no kenkyū* (Tokyo, 1960), p. 587, provided free school supplies as well as free tuition and board. *Hua-t'ing Ku-shih tsung-p'u*, ibid., p. 586, and *An-yang Ma-shih tz'u-t'ang t'iao-kuei*, ibid., p. 584, gave school supplies as prizes at the regular inspections.
29. *Yao-shih chia-ch'eng*, in Taga, "Shinmatsu kakyo," pp. 118–19, n. 26; Hsien-chin Hu, *Common Descent Group*, app. 47, p. 166 and app. 37, p. 144 respectively. *P'ing-yüan p'ai Sung-yüan Lu-shih tsung-p'u*, 1874 ed., 20.18ab; this clan also provided grants which increased as pupils advanced in their lessons.
30. Hsien-chin Hu, *Common Descent Group*, app. 11, p. 120. A similar grant of one picul of grain a year for those beginning study is found in the regulations of *Wu-shih chih-p'u*, 1882 ed., 12.9a, regulation dated 1648.
31. Hsien-chin Hu, *Common Descent Group*, app. 46, p. 165; *Lu-shih feng-men chih-p'u*, in Taga, *Sōfu no kenkyū*, pp. 586–87; *Ling-hu Wang-shih chih-p'u*, in Taga, "Shinmatsu kakyo," pp. 124–25, n. 60; and Shimizu Taiji, *Shina no kazoku to sonraku no tokushitsu* (Tokyo, 1927), pp. 67–68. See Ogawa Yoshiko, "Chūgoku kinsei no zokujuku ni tsuite," in *Ishikawa Ken hakase kanreki kinen ronbunshū—kyōiku no shiteki tenkai*, contributed by Ishiyama Shūhei et al. (Tokyo, 1952), p. 542.
32. *Hua-t'ing Ku-shih tsung-p'u*, in Taga, *Sōfu no kenkyū*, pp. 584–86, has regulations for a *chia-shu* open to all males in the clan; *P'i-ling T'u-shih chih-p'u*, in Taga, "Shinmatsu kakyo," pp. 120–21, n. 32, has regulations for a *chia-shu* specifically established for fatherless boys in the clan. *I-shu* specifically aimed at poor clan boys are found in *Yao-shih chia-ch'eng*, ibid., pp. 118–19, n. 26; and *Ta-kang Chao-shih tsu-p'u*, 6.3a. An *i-shu* which was open to all clan males is found in *Yün-shih chia-ch'eng* (1859 ed.), 11.23ab. Other names for

clan schools were *tz'u-t'ang hsiao-hsüeh* (ancestral hall elementary school), *An-yang Ma-shih tz'u-t'ang t'iao-kuei*, in Taga, *Sōfu no kenkyū*, p. 584; *chuang-shu* (estate school), in *Lu-shih feng-men chih-p'u*, ibid., p. 501; *i-hsüeh*, *Ching-k'ou Ting-shih tsu-p'u*, 3.6ab; and *i-kuan* (charitable house), *Yün-yang Yin-shih ch'ung-hsiu tsu-p'u*, 14.2a. The subject of variant names for clan schools is discussed in Taga, "Shinmatsu kakyo," p. 96, and Ogawa, "Chūgoku zokujuku," p. 542.

33. Ogawa, "Chūgoku zokujuku," pp. 545–46. According to Hsien-chin Hu, *Common Descent Group*, p. 71, the *i-hsüeh* "as a rule is not restricted to members of one tsu, but where the tsu is well integrated this is often the case in practice." *Yao-shih chia-ch'eng*, in Taga, "Shinmatsu kakyo," pp. 118–19, n. 26.

34. Eight *sui* is specifically cited in the following clan school regulations: *P'i-ling T'u-shih chih-p'u*, in Taga, "Shinmatsu kakyo," pp. 120–21, n. 32; *An-yang Ma-shih tz'u-t'ang t'iao-kuei*, in Taga, *Sōfu no kenkyū*, p. 584; and *Fan-shih chia-ch'eng*, 1746 ed., ibid., p. 581. *Yün-shih chia-ch'eng*, 1.23b, indicates that younger boys were also admitted; *Lu-shih feng-men chih-p'u*, in Taga, *Sōfu no kenkyū*, p. 587, that the age of admission was nine *sui*. See Ogawa Yoshiko, "Sōzoku-nai no kyōiku," in *Kyōikugaku ronshū*, ed. Nihon kyōiku gakkai (Tokyo, 1951), p. 228.

35. Ogawa, "Sōzoku-nai," p. 228. This was a division found in other kinds of elementary schools: see Ch'en Tung-yüan, *Chung-kuo chiao-yü shih*, p. 425. In the Yao clan school the lower was called the western division and the upper the eastern division: *Yao-shih chia-ch'eng*, in Taga, "Shinmatsu kakyo," pp. 118–19, n. 26.

36. *Lu-shih feng-men chih-p'u*, in Taga, *Sōfu no kenkyū*, p. 587; *P'i-ling T'u-shih chih-p'u*, in Taga, "Shinmatsu kakyo," pp. 120–21, n. 32; and *Yao-shih chia-ch'eng*, ibid., pp. 118–19, n. 26, all cite ten students as the upper limit. *An-yang Ma-shih tz'u-t'ang t'iao-kuei*, in Taga, *Sōfu no kenkyū*, p. 584, lists a maximum of twenty. Ogawa, "Chūgoku zokujuku," p. 542, puts class size at eight to ten students.

37. *P'i-ling T'u-shih chih-p'u*, in Taga, "Shinmatsu kakyo," pp. 120–21, n. 32; and *Yao-shih chia-ch'eng*, ibid., pp. 118–19, n. 26, note that if there is a clansman of upright character and good scholarship who is willing to teach, he should be hired "no matter what his generation."

38. *Yao-shih chia-ch'eng*, in Taga, "Shinmatsu kakyo," pp. 118–19, n. 26; *An-yang Ma-shih tz'u-t'ang t'iao-kuei*, in Taga, *Sōfu no kenkyū*, p. 584; and *Lu-shih feng-men chih-p'u*, ibid., p. 587, all cite estate managers as supervising clan schools, while *P'i-ling T'u-shih chih-p'u*, in Taga, "Shinmatsu kakyo," pp. 120–21, n. 32, mentions a specially designated supervisor. *Ta-fu P'an-shih chih-p'u*, 21.22ab, cites lineage branch heads as school supervisors.

39. *Hua-t'ing Ku-shih tsung-p'u,* in Taga, *Sōfu no kenkyū,* p. 585. *Lu-shih feng-men chih-p'u,* ibid., p. 587, listed holidays for six festivals.
40. Regulations on pupil and (occasionally) teacher attendance are included in *Yao-shih chia-ch'eng,* in Taga, "Shinmatsu kakyo," pp. 118–19, n. 26; *Ling-hu Wang-shih chih-p'u,* ibid., pp. 124–25, n. 60; *An-yang Ma-shih tz'u-t'ang t'iao-kuei,* in Taga, *Sōfu no kenkyū,* p. 584; and *Hua-t'ing Ku-shih tsung-p'u,* ibid., p. 585.
41. *Fan-shih chia-ch'eng,* in Taga, *Sōfu no kenkyū,* p. 581; *An-yang Ma-shih tz'u-t'ang t'iao-kuei,* ibid., p. 584; and *Wu-shih chih-te chih* (1876 ed.), 10.8b—10b.
42. The Hsiang clan rules are in *Yung-chia* HC, 6.13a; *P'i-ling T'u-shih chih-p'u,* in Taga, "Shinmatsu kakyo," pp. 120–21, n.32. Clan school regulations which stipulate fifteen *sui* include *Yao-shih chia-ch'eng,* ibid., pp. 118–19, n. 26; *An-yang Ma-shih tz'u-t'ang t'iao-kuei,* in Taga, *Sōfu no kenkyū,* p. 584; *Lu-shih feng-men chih-p'u,* ibid., p. 587; and *Ching-chiang Chang-shih tsung-p'u,* 6.7ab. The Chaos of Ch'ang-shu, Kiangsu, suggest that this decision be made for orphans at the age of nine: Hsien-chin Hu, *Common Descent Group,* app. 37, p. 144.
43. Hsien-chin Hu, *Common Descent Group,* app. 47, p. 166. The Chaos of Ch'ang-shu, ibid., app. 37, p. 144, provided an annual allowance of two ounces of silver for those sent to learn a trade; *Yao-shih chia-ch'eng,* in Taga, "Shinmatsu kakyo," pp. 118–19, n. 26, states that 5,000 cash should be given to those entering trade.
44. *Fan-shih chia-ch'eng,* 15.38b–39a; the *Wu-shih chih-p'u,* 12.9a, states that if the income from 100 *mou* of school lands is insufficient, other revenues should be used.
45. *Ching-k'ou Ting-shih tsu-p'u,* 3.6ab, and *Ta-kang Chao-shih tsu-p'u,* 6.4b. See Hsien-chin Hu, *Common Descent Group,* pp. 88–89.
46. See Tilemann Grimm, *Erziehung,* pp. 139–43 for discussion; also Ping-ti Ho, *Ladder of Success,* pp. 194–97, and Nakamura Jihei, "Shindai Santō nōson no gigaku," *Tōyō shigaku* 15(1956):1–3.
47. *Ch'in-ting hsüeh-cheng ch'üan-shu,* 60.1a.
48. Ibid., 69.2ab. These are all spelled out in an edict dated 1715. See Donald J. Munro, *The Concept of Man in Early China* (Stanford, 1969), pp. vii, viii, 15–16, 21–22, 81–83, for detailed discussion of the centrality of education in Confucian solutions to social and political problems.
49. *Ch'in-ting hsüeh-cheng ch'üan-shu,* 69.2ab. Kung-ch'üan Hsiao, *Rural China,* pp. 237–38; Nakamura Jihei, "Shindai Santō nōson no gigaku," pp. 3–5; Ogawa Yoshiko, "Shindai no okeru gigaku setsuritsu no kiban," in *Kinsei Chūgoku kyōiku shi kenkyū,* ed. Hayashi Tomoharu (Tokyo, 1958), p. 280.
50. Decrees dated 1725, 1727, 1730, 1732, 1735, 1737, 1740, 1742, 1745, 1746, 1751, 1761 in *Ch'in-ting hsüeh-cheng ch'üan-shu,* chüan 60.

51. Ibid., 60.2ab. Described in Kung-ch'üan Hsiao, *Rural China*, pp. 238–40.
52. *Ch'in-ting hsüeh-cheng ch'üan-shu*, 60.6ab.
53. *Shang-ch'eng* HC, 6.3a. In this district, charitable schoolteachers were directed to recite the *Sacred Edicts* and to give the *hsiang-yüeh*.
54. See Kung-ch'üan Hsiao, *Rural China*, pp. 253–54, although Hsiao concludes that the rural schools failed in their aim to spread ideological control.
55. (Ch'ien-t'ang) Ch'en Wen-shu's regulations for charitable schools, in Yü Chih, *Te-i lu*, chüan 10.3, .1ab. This is a common theme running through the charitable school regulations.
56. In *Chūgoku kyōiku shi* (Tokyo, 1955), pp. 100–101, Taga Akigorō tries to distinguish between the two in terms of financing and size. He says *i-hsüeh* were semipublic in funding and much larger than *she-hsüeh*, which were publicly funded. Kung-ch'üan Hsiao, *Rural China*, pp. 238–39, raises and dismisses two other possible distinctions: one that the *she-hsüeh* were for Han Chinese and the *i-hsüeh* for ethnic minorities, and secondly that the *she-hsüeh* were rural based as opposed to the *i-hsüeh*, which could be either urban or rural. See Higashikawa Tokuji, *Nan-Shi ni okeru kyōiku oyobi shūkyō no hensen* (Taipei, 1919), p. 98, for another version.
57. *Ch'in-ting hsüeh-cheng ch'üan-shu*, chüan 60; Kung-ch'üan Hsiao, *Rural China*, pp. 238–39.
58. (*Hsü-hsiu*) *Ch'ü-wu* HC (Shansi), 8.28a. The same explanation is given in *I-hsing* HC, p. 691. Regional distribution of elementary schools is discussed in chap. 4.
59. *Kuang-tung shu-yüan chih-tu* (Shanghai, 1938), pp. 46, 81.
60. The 1786 edition of *Ku-shih* HC (Honan), 6.50a, notes: "This school was originally a *kuan-shu* but Mr. Wu made contributions of land and fixed up the school building. . . ." The school's current name was *i-hsüeh*. *Chih-chiang* HC (Hunan), 12.41a, states "A *kuan-hsüeh* is another name for an *i-hsüeh*" and justifies the name by explaining that students were expected to study the ancients and enter officialdom, thus glorifying their names. Not all *i-shu* were elementary schools: see *Hua-yang* HC, 15.44a, for an exception. *Tsao-ch'iang* HC, p. 92, lists a *shu-yüan* with the comment that "it is called a *shu-yüan* but in reality is merely an *i-hsüeh*."
61. Fu-jen charitable school regulations, in Shu Hsin-ch'eng, *Chung-kuo chin-tai chiao-yü shih tzu-liao* (Peking, 1962), 1:92.
62. *Meng-kuan* and *ching-kuan* are noted in *T'ai-shun* HC, 3.15a; *Kuang-hsi* TC, 137.19a; (*Ch'ung tsuan*) *Fu-chien* TC, 64.21b; *T'ung* CC, 1879 ed., 5.24a; *Chi-fu* TC, 114.84b–85a; *Shan-hsi* TC, 1892 ed., 76.35a. *Ting-yuan* HC, 11.29b, lists a charitable school for the "al-

ready capped" and another for the "uncapped" pupils, designating an upper and lower division: the capping ceremony normally took place at age twenty. The conversion of charitable schools to academies is noted in many areas of Fukien in the provincial gazetteer; see 64.25b, 64.29a, 64.31a–32a, 65.31a. This is distinguished from charitable schools maintained or supervised by academies.

63. Sources citing age six or seven include *Hsü-chou* FC, 15.17a; *Shang-jao* HC, 7.76a; Yü Chih, *Te-i lu,* 10.4.5b; Smith, *Village Life,* p. 57. Nakamura Jihei, "Shindai Santō nōson no gigaku," p. 30, finds that some students were admitted when only four or five years old. Fu-jen charitable school regulations, pp. 92–93. *Hsü-chou* FC, 15.18a, ruled that students who failed to perform well could be replaced after one year with new students.

64. *Hsü-chou* FC, 15.17a; Yü Chih, *Te-i lu,* 10.4.5b. Nakamura Jihei, "Shindai Santō nōson no gigaku," p. 30, cites a cut-off at age eleven or twelve, except when the school had an upper division. In that case, students up to age nineteen could be accommodated.

65. *Shang-jao* HC, 7.76ab; *Yen-ch'ing* CC, 4.41a. *Ku-ch'eng* HC, 3.38ab, mentions that especially bright students could either be entered in the upper division or put into an academy. Also see *Tan-t'u* HC, 19.44b.

66. *Ku-ch'eng* HC, 3.38b; Fu-jen charitable school regulations, p. 92.

67. *Man-ch'eng* HC, 4.32ab. The general notion is repeated in almost every reference to charitable schools in local gazetteers. For examples, see *An-hui* TC, 1830 ed., 70.26ab; *Ch'ang-t'ing* HC, p. 157; *Chi-fu* TC, 116.83a; *Chia-hsing* FC, p. 223; *Chih-chiang* HC, 1870 ed., 12.37b, 15.13a; *Lo-ch'ing* HC, 4.50b; *Mien* HC, pp. 142–43; *T'ai-ku* HC, 2.37b; and *T'ai-p'ing* HC, 1775 ed., 2.13b.

68. *Ku-ch'eng* HC, 3.36a; parents can pay according to their convenience if they can afford it; if they are poor, nothing need be paid. Also in *Yen-ch'ing* CC, 4.40b; *Shang-ch'eng* HC, 6.2b–3a. Teachers' salaries are discussed in chap. 3. One study of the actual class composition of an *i-hsüeh* records that both poor peasants and the son of the second richest landlord were in attendance: see Wu Hsün li-shih tiao-ch'a tuan, *Wu Hsün li-shih tiao-ch'a chi* (Peking, 1951), pp. 45–46.

69. *Ku-ch'eng* HC, 3.34b; *Shang-jao* HC, 4.75a; Fu-jen charitable school regulations, p. 92; Yü Chih, *Te-i lu,* 10.3.3b, 19.4.5b–6a; *Tan-t'u* HC, 19.45a, describes a charitable school for poor widows' sons which provided books, ink, paper, and one free meal a day.

70. *Shang-jao* HC, 7.74b; *Hsü-chou* FC, 15.18a.

71. Nakamura Jihei, "Shindai Santō nōson no gigaku," p. 22; Ogawa Yoshiko, "Shindai ni okeru gigaku," p. 284.

72. *An-hui* TC, 70.12b; *Luan-ch'eng* HC, 6.17a–19a; five of the eighteen

charitable schools founded in the Tao-kuang period originated through local petition.

73. *Hsü hsiu Ch'ü-wu* HC, 8.28b–29a; Ch'ung-yang hsien in Hupei, *Hupei* TC, 59.55b–56a, lists four schools publicly established by a *pao* unit in the police security system; *Ch'eng-k'ou t'ing-chih,* 10.70a–76a; Nakamura Jihei, "Shindai Santō nōson no gigaku," pp. 25–26 gives several Shantung examples.
74. Ogawa Yoshiko, "Shindai ni okeru gigaku," p. 278, n. 2; Ping-ti Ho, *Ladder of Success,* p. 196. Negishi Tadashi, *Chūgoku no girudo* (Tokyo, 1953), p. 170, describes charitable schools run by landmannschaften (*hui-kuan*). *Wu Hsün li-shih tiao-ch'a chi,* pp. 21–38. Wu, however, had little interest in elementary schools, and his schools were advanced divisions; see p. 44. On the anti-Wu Hsün campaign conducted in 1951, see James P. Harrison, *The Communists and Chinese Peasant Rebellions* (New York, 1968), pp. 239–40.
75. The various terms for school manager appear in (*Ch'ung-hsiu*) *Ku-shih* HC, 6.50a (*chang-chiao*); Ch'en Wen-shu's charitable school regulations, 10.3.3b in Yü Chih, *Te-i lu* and *Yen-ch'ing* CC, 4.40a (*tung-shih*); *Shang-ch'eng* HC 6.2b (*ssu-hsüeh*); *Shang-jao* HC, 7.74a (*ching-li*). According to Nakamura Jihei, "Shindai Santō nōson no gigaku," p. 29, Shantung terms for school manager were *shou-shih, ssu-shih,* and *tung-shih*. Chung-li Chang, *Income of the Chinese Gentry,* p. 55, comments briefly on management of charitable schools as a source of gentry income. In "Shindai ni okeru gigaku," pp. 299–304, Ogawa Yoshiko presents detailed information on the backgrounds of forty-one school managers in Hsi-p'ing county, Honan; almost every one was an official, a *chien-sheng,* or a *sheng-yüan*. See also *Shang-ch'eng* HC, 6.2b.
76. *Ku-ch'eng* HC, 3.35b–36a. Wealth is also cited as a qualification in charitable school regulations for Kwangtung, Yü Chih, *Te-i lu,* 10.4.4b.
77. Managerial duties are described in sources cited in n.75 above; see also Ogawa Yoshiko, "Shindai ni okeru gigaku," pp. 295–97. The two-year term is cited in (*Ch'ung-hsiu*)*Ku-shih* HC, 6.50a. *Yen-ch'ing* CC, 4.40a, lists the manager's salary.
78. Ogawa Yoshiko, "Shindai ni okeru gigaku," pp. 295–97; *Yen-ch'ing* CC, 4.40a, and regulations for Kwangtung charitable schools in Yü Chih, *Te-i lu,* 10.4.4b–5a. *T'ai-ku* HC, 6.48b, provides a case where supervision was delegated to the Confucian school. In *Hsü-chou* FC, 15.18a, the supervisor is the educational official. *Chih-chiang* HC, 1870 ed., 12.41b, names the Sub-Director of Schools on the county level to supervise its ten charitable schools.
79. *Luan-ch'eng* HC, 6.11b–12a, article in academy regulations, dated 1836: in this instance charitable school lands had been shifted to the

jurisdiction of the academy but were still to be used for their initial purpose. Also *Luan* CC, 1898 ed., 12.83a.

80. Yü Chih, *Te-i lu,* 10.4.3b.
81. *Shang-jao* HC, 7.74b. See also *Shang-ch'eng* HC, 6.4ab. On occasion, the process of taking over public buildings for schools could be reversed; see the petition, dated 1775, on prohibiting use of the school building for government offices, in *An-i* HC, 4.44a–46a.
82. Nakamura Jihei, "Shindai Santō nōson no gigaku," p. 29; *Wen-an* HC, 2.36ab; *T'ung-chou chih,* 1879 ed., 5.24a–25a; *Shang-ch'eng* HC, 6.4ab; *Ting-yüan* HC, 11.29a–31b. See Kung-ch'üan Hsiao, *Rural China,* p. 240; Y. K. Leong and L. K. Tao, *Village and Town Life,* pp. 96–97. Ping-ti Ho, *Ladder of Success,* p. 195, notes that this was true in Ming times.
83. *Kuang-hsi* TC, 137.11a, 138.31a; smaller schools are also listed. *Su-chou* FC, 1824 ed., 24.36b, 24.39a. Nakamura Jihei, "Shindai Santō nōson no gigaku," p. 28.
84. *Shang-ch'eng* HC, 6.18b–25b; *Ch'eng-k'ou t'ing-chih,* 10.70a–76a. *Man-ch'eng* HC, 4.31a; *Nan-kung* HC, 3.33a–34a; *Hsü-hsiu Ch'ü-wu* HC, 8.28a. The average size of schools in Ch'ü-wu county was 4.6 rooms (ibid., 8.28b–29a).
85. *Yen-ch'ing* CC, 4.41a; *Chih-chiang* HC, 1870 ed., 12.41a.
86. 1687 regulations in *Li* HC, 3.25b; Yü Chih, *Te-i lu,* 10.4.5a.
87. For details on the different degrees, see Chung-li Chang, *Chinese Gentry,* pp. 3–30, and Ping-ti Ho, *Ladder of Success,* pp. 26–41.
88. *Ch'in-ting hsüeh-cheng ch'üan shu,* 64.3a, .4a, .5ab, .7a, .8a, representing edicts dated 1723, 1728, 1730, 1735, 1740, and 1745. See also *Chih-chiang* HC, 1870 ed., 12.35b.
89. Selection of an elementary schoolteacher from the local *sheng-yüan* is mentioned in: *Kuang-hsi* TC, 166.18b; 1671 *Shu-lu wu-chih ho-k'an,* 2.30b; *Hsiang-yang* FC, 8.26ab; *Shang-jao* HC, 7.74a; *Shan-hsi* TC, 1892 ed., 76.34b–35a; *Ku-ch'eng* HC, 3.35ab. The 1736 ed., *Huo-lu* HC, 6.12a, mentions hiring a *sui-kung-shen* and *sheng-yüan* as teachers in a charitable school; while *Tsao-ch'iang* HC, 18.33b–34a, presents a report by a magistrate who says he filled teaching posts with military and civil *sheng-yüan.*
90. *Ku-ch'eng* HC, 3.35ab.
91. *T'ai-ku* HC, 6.48a.
92. *Luan* CC, 12.82b–83a; the school term is stipulated in *Chiang-tu* HC, p. 900; *Chih-chiang* HC, 1870 ed. 12.35a, 12.41a; *Hsü-chou* FC, 15.18a; and *Yen-ch'ing* CC, 4.41a, as well.
93. Yü Chih, *Te-i lu,* 10.4.5b. For descriptions of the school day, see "Description of the City of Canton," *Chinese Repository* 2(1833–34):250–51; J. MacGowan, *Men and Manners,* pp. 84–85; Purcell, *Problems of Chinese Education,* p. 18.

94. Ku clan regulations, in Taga Akigorō, *Sōfu no kenkyū,* p. 585. Other descriptions are found in *Yün-shih chia-ch'eng* 1.24a. Regulations for charitable schools reprinted in Shu Hsin-ch'eng, *Chung-kuo chin-tai chiao-yü shih tzu-liao,* 1:89–90.
95. Ku clan regulations, in Taga Akigorō, *Sōfu no kenkyū.* p. 586; see also p. 584 for Ma clan regulations and p. 587 for Lu clan rules.
96. In *Meng-hsüeh lu,* cited in Ch'en Tung-yüan, *Chung-kuo k'o-hsüeh shih-tai,* p. 50. Many school regulations invoke punishments for noisy classroom behavior.
97. Ritual observances for Confucius or Chu Hsi are cited in Yü Chih, *Te-i lu,* 10.3a, 10.5.6a; regulations reprinted in Shu Hsin-ch'eng, *Chung-kuo chin-tai chiao-yü shih tzu-liao,* 1:86, 89, 90; and clan rules reprinted in Taga Akigorō, *Sōfu no kenkyū,* pp. 584, 586–87; also see Smith, *Village Life,* p. 54, and Doolittle, *Social Life,* 1:136–37.
98. See clan regulations reprinted in Taga Akigorō, "Shinmatsu kakyo," pp. 120–21, n. 32, and pp. 124–25, n. 60.
99. Yü Chih, *Te-i lu,* 10.4.6a; Shu Hsin-ch'eng, *Chung-kuo chin-tai chiao-yü shih tzu-liao,* pp. 89–90; clan rules reprinted in Taga Akigorō, *Sōfu no kenkyū,* p. 584, and his "Shinmatsu kakyo," pp. 124–25, n. 60.
100. Mote, "China's Past," p. 112.
101. A detailed description of this process is provided in Yee Chiang, *Chinese Calligraphy* (Cambridge, Mass., 1973), pp. 189–91.
102. Ch'en Tung-yüan, *Chung-kuo chiao-yü shih,* p. 429; Miyazaki Ichisada, *Kakyo* (Tokyo, 1963), p. 11; Wang Feng-chieh, *Chung-kuo chiao-yü shih* (Taipei, 1954), p. 165.
103. *Yün-shih chia-ch'eng,* 1.23b.
104. "In the afternoon take the brush and practice writing proverbs by copying 100 characters," Yü Chih, *Te-i lu,* 10.5.8a. See Miyazaki Ichisada, *Kakyo,* p. 11, and Smith, *Village Life,* p. 62. According to Smith, later writing lessons consisted of characters from T'ang poetry, resulting in ignorance of characters useful in everyday life: he does note that the initial lessons present "characters at once simple and common."
105. See Yee Chiang, *Chinese Calligraphy,* p. 191. *Ling-hu Wang-shih chih-p'u,* in Taga Akigorō, "Shinmatsu kakyo," pp. 124–25, n. 60, warns against the writing of "grass script" by students. This genealogy directs students under age fourteen who are being examined by the supervisors of study to write one sheet of large characters or write from a copy-book while students fifteen and older can increase the copying to 100 characters. Yee Chiang, p. 197, states that pupils over age ten wrote 10–20 middle-sized characters and 50 or more small characters a day, while those under ten wrote only middle-sized characters. Yü Chih, *Te-i lu,* 10.5.8a mentions writing 100

characters daily; *Yün-shih chia-ch'eng,* 1.23b, says that when copying characters, a day's lesson should not exceed 110 characters. The "squared paper" is described by Yee Chiang, *Chinese Calligraphy,* pp. 189–91.

106. Doolittle, *Social Life,* 2:385.

107. Chang Chih-kung, *Yü-wen chiao-yü,* p. 3, citing Wang Yun's "On teaching boys"; see also *Hsü-chou* FC, 15.17ab, which presents much the same kind of method for teaching characters.

108. Ch'en Tung-yüan, *Chung-kuo k'o-hsüeh shih-tai,* pp. 49–50; this anticipates that the quick-witted child (aged 3–4 *sui*) will learn ten characters a day.

109. *P'i-ling T'u-shih chih-p'u,* reprinted in Taga Akigorō, "Shinmatsu kakyo," pp. 120–21, n. 32; Ch'en Tung-yüan, *Chung-kuo chiao-yü shih,* pp. 427–28.

110. Ch'en Tung-yüan, *Chung-kuo chiao-yü shih,* pp. 427–28; at the rate of ten new characters a day, only 200 days would be required to learn 2,000 characters, and the school term, described in the text, was much longer than 200 days. Chang Chih-kung, *Yü-wen chiao-yü,* p. 3, also notes that 2,000 characters were taught for recognition purposes in the first year.

111. T'ung Chen-chia, "Ch'ing-mo hsiao-hsüeh," p. 127; Wang Feng-chieh, *Chung-kuo chiao-yü shih,* p. 165; Ch'en Tung-yüan, *Chung-kuo chiao-yü shih,* pp. 427–28. The most detailed discussion of the origins and subsequent revisions of these texts is provided by Chang Chih-kung, *Yü-wen chiao-yü,* chap. 1, especially pp. 6–25. The widespread acceptance of these primers is shown by the Taiping rebels, who issued their own versions when they opened an elementary school in Nanking: Chiang Shun-hsing, "I-chien nung-min ko-ming ti pao-kuei wen-hsien—tu Hung Hsiu-ch'üan pien *Ch'ien tzu wen,*" *Wen-wu* 11(1974):47–50.

112. Chang Chih-kung, *Yü-wen chiao-yü,* pp. 6–10, 11–16, 154–57. H. A. Giles has a wonderful story about popular acquaintance with the *Thousand-Character Classic*: "A bookcase, or similar article of furniture, which has been taken to pieces and reduced to chaos by a carpenter at one end of China, for purposes of travelling, can be rapidly and accurately restored by any carpenter at the other end of China. The various parts are marked with the opening characters of the familiar *Ch'ien-tzu-wen* . . . in such a way that a perfect key is provided to what might otherwise prove an awkward puzzle." "Thousand Character Numerals Used by Artisans," *Journal of the China Branch of the Royal Asiatic Society* 20(1885):279.

113. Chang Chih-kung, *Yü-wen chiao-yü,* pp. 16–21; list of versions of the *Trimetrical Classic* on pp. 158–59; for *Hundred Names,* see pp. 21–25, 157–58.

114. Ibid., pp. 32–35.
115. Ibid., pp. 32–36.
116. Ibid., pp. 37–38; on p. 39, Chang tries to analyze features of elementary education. See Smith, *Village Life*, p. 62, and Wang Feng-chieh, *Chung-kuo chiao-yü shih*, p. 165, for examples. The same issue was discussed during 1950–51 by Communist educators: see Vincent T. C. Lin, "Adult Education," pp. 241–44.
117. The program of study for those preparing to take the civil service examinations is described by Ch'en Tung-yüan, *Chung-kuo k'o-hsüeh shih-tai*, pp. 52–59.
118. *Yün-shih chia-ch'eng*, 1.23a.
119. *Shang-ch'eng* HC, 6.3b. Also Ch'en Tung-yüan, *Chung-kuo k'o-hsüeh shih-tai*, p. 61.
120. On the ideological indoctrination of the Chinese elite, see Chung-li Chang, *Chinese Gentry*, pp. 197–202.
121. Chang Chih-kung, *Yü-wen chiao-yü*, pp. 40–41.
122. *Shang-ch'eng* HC, 6.3b.
123. Chang Chih-kung, *Yü-wen chiao-yü*, chap. 2, pp. 40–86. Cheng Chen-to's description of these reading materials is cited in Meng Hsien-ch'eng et al., comps., *Chung-kuo ku-tai chiao-yü shih tzu-liao* (Peking, 1961), p. 269. *Chih-chiang* HC, 1870 ed., 12.41ab.
124. Regulations dated 1687, in *Li* HC, 3.26b–27a.
125. In Taga Akigorō, *Sōfu no kenkyū*, p. 584.
126. *Ku-ch'eng* HC, 3.37ab; although the *Hsiao-erh yü* and *Hsiao-hsüeh shih-li* were to be used, this regulation notes: "It does not do to permit ignorant people to study the *Shen-t'ung shih*, wine poems, and such profitless books." The *Shen-t'ung shih* is discussed in Chang Chih-kung, *Yü-wen chiao-yü*, pp. 95–97; a variant, the *Hsü Shen-t'ung shih*, was recommended by several writers for use in elementary schools: see Yü Chih, *Te-i lu*, 10.4.6b–7a, 10.5.7b–8a. The *Hsiao-erh yü* is described in Chang Chih-kung, *Yü-wen chiao-yü*, p. 51, and is included on his bibliographical list, p. 165; the *Hsiao-hsüeh shih-li* is also on p. 165.
127. The *Hsiao-hsüeh* in its initial version was compiled by Chu Hsi: see Chang Chih-kung, *Yü-wen chiao-yü*, pp. 41–43. It was very popular with scholars and appeared in many schools: see *Shang-ch'eng* HC, 6.3b; clan regulations in Taga Akigorō, "Shinmatsu kakyo," pp. 120–21, n. 32, and pp. 124–25, n. 60; *Chih-chiang* HC, 1870 ed., 12.41ab; and Nakamura Jihei, "Shindai Santō nōson no gigaku," p. 30. On the *Hsiao-hsüeh yün-yü*, see Chang Chih-kung, *Yü-wen chiao-yü*, pp. 47, 166. Cited in *Shang-jao* HC, 7.75ab.
128. Described in Chang Chih-kung, *Yü-wen chiao-yü*, p. 47; listed on p. 166. In Ma clan regulations, in Taga Akigorō, *Sōfu no kenkyū*, p. 584.

129. Ch'en Wen-shu's list of seven morality books is part of his school regulations, reprinted in Yü Chih, *Te-i lu,* 10.3.3a; also see 10.4.6b–7a, 10.5.7b–8a, which repeat many of the books recommended. For a detailed discussion of the *Yin-chih wen,* see Sakai Tadao, *Chūgoku zensho no kenkyū* (Tokyo, 1960), chap. 6.
130. *Shang-ch'eng* HC, 6.3b, notes that the yamen will contribute part of the *Hsiao-hsüeh* to each school; the teacher can order students either to buy one or study from a handwritten copy. *Ku-ch'eng* HC, 3.37ab states that the prefecture will give 100 copies of the first three elementary texts to each charitable school. *Shang-jao* HC, 7.75ab, and *Chih-chiang* HC, 12.41ab, also have books provided by officials. See Kung-ch'üan Hsiao, *Rural China,* p. 241.
131. Yü Chih, *Te-i lu,* 10.4.6b–7a; as *Wu-chi* HC, 1.10b put it: "what is studied in the rural schools, outside of the Four Books, is vulgar lowbrow books."
132. T'u clan rules, reprinted in Taga Akigorō, "Shinmatsu kakyo," pp. 120–21, n. 32.
133. *Yün-shih chia-ch'eng,* 1.23a.
134. *Jun-tung Piao-lin Chu-shih t'ung-hsiu tsung-p'u,* 1.3b–4a; the same idea appears in the Wang clan regulations presented in Taga Akigorō, "Shinmatsu kakyo," pp. 124–25, n. 60.
135. *Yün-shih chia-ch'eng,* 1.22b, 1.24b.
136. *Jun-tung Piao-lin Chu-shih t'ung-hsiu tsung-p'u,* 1.3b–4a.
137. Lu clan regulations, reprinted in Taga Akigorō, *Sōfu no kenkyū,* pp. 586–87. Also in *Li* HC, 3.26b–27a. The same procedures of careful review and repetition are described in "Methods of child reading," in *Shih-lin kuang-chi, ting-chi,* .16a.
138. *Hsü-chou* FC, 15.17b. Also in *Yün-shih chia-ch'eng,* 1.23a.
139. *Hsü-chou* FC, 15.17b.
140. Ibid.
141. T'u clan regulations, reprinted in Taga Akigorō, "Shinmatsu kakyo," pp. 120–21, n. 32.
142. *Country Life in South China,* pp. 224–26.
143. John Stewart Burgess, *The Guilds of Peking* (1928; reprint ed., New York, 1970), p. 165; *Pei-ching Jui-fu-hsiang* (Peking, 1959), p. 35.
144. *Tien-yeh hsü-chih,* a manual for pawnbrokers presented in Yang Lien-sheng, "Tien-yeh hsü-chih," *Shih-huo yüeh-k'an,* n.s. 1.4(1971):241.

Chapter 3

1. In Ts'ang-chou, 1880, 48.7 per cent of the annual income was used for the teacher's salary: *(Ch'ung-hsiu) T'ien-chin* FC, 35.31b.

Schools whose total annual income went to pay the teacher's salary include: Shang-ch'eng, Honan (HC, 6.18b–25b); Shu-lu, and Ching-hai, Chihli (HC, 1799 ed., 5.64b; *Chi-fu* TC, 115.49ab).

2. *Chinese Repository* 2(1833–34):250.
3. Taga Akigorō, "Shinmatsu kakyo," pp. 120–21, n. 32. *Wu Hsün li-shih tiao-ch'a chi,* pp. 44–45, states that students had to present gifts of 400 cash twice a year.
4. Ogawa Yoshiko, "Chūgoku zokujuku," p. 543.
5. See She, Luan chou, and T'ai-ku in table 3.
6. Descriptions of school buildings often mention a room for the teacher. *Ku-ch'eng* HC, 3.34b, states: "Set up a sleeping room and kitchen for the teacher." A discussion of meal provisions is in the rules for establishing charitable elementary schools in Kwangtung: Yü Chih, *Te-i lu,* 10.4.5b.
7. (*Ch'ung-hsiu*) *Feng-hsiang* FC, 6.24a; *Chi-fu* TC, 117.28ab.
8. *Shang-ch'eng* HC, 6.1b.
9. *Feng-huang t'ing-chih,* 11.50ab; *Yung-sui chih-li t'ing-chih,* 2.12a; *Kan-chou t'ing-chih,* 4.69b–70a; all had special schools for non-Han peoples. See Ping-ti Ho, *Studies on the Population of China* (Cambridge, Mass., 1959), pp. 149–53, on migration into the Han River highlands.
10. *Feng-huang t'ing-chih,* 11.50ab; *Yung-sui chih-li t'ing-chih,* 2.12a.
11. All of the information provided below is presented in table 3. "Urban" is used here to include all administrative centers.
12. *Yen-ch'ing* CC, 4.40a; *Kuang-hsi* TC, 166.21a; although *chang-chiao* is technically the term for manager, it is not used in any other of the thirteen schools listed in the TC. It is possible that this was a misprint for teacher and the salary listed may actually be a teacher's salary; note that the supplementary monetary gift for opening school customarily given to a teacher is attached to this item.
13. Cited by Chung-li Chang, *Income of the Chinese Gentry,* pp. 56, 94.
14. (*Ch'ung-hsiu*) *T'ien-chin* FC, 35.32a.
15. *Su-chou* FC, 1824 ed., 26.36ab, .38b–39a. According to *Chen-tse* HC, p. 184, P'ing-wang chen is over 40 li from the hsien city.
16. *Ch'eng-k'ou t'ing-chih,* 10.70a–71b.
17. *T'ai-ku* HC, 6.47b–48a; *Chi-fu* TC, 115.4ab; *Huang-kang* HC, p. 734.
18. *Tan-t'u* HC, 19.43a.
19. An example is a school in the Feng clan hall, Chin-t'ang hsien, Szechwan, founded in 1803 by a local resident named Ch'iu: *Ssu-ch'uan* TC, 79.4a.
20. 10 percent of the annual income was set aside in Ta-i, Szechwan: *Ch'iu chou chih-li* CC, 9.33ab. 13 percent was set aside in T'ai-ku: *T'ai-ku* HC, 6.48a.

21. Yao clan rules, reprinted in Taga Akigorō, "Shinmatsu kakyo," pp. 118–19, n. 25, assuming a school term of eleven months.
22. *Ch'iu chou chih-li* CC, 9.33a; *Kuang-hsi* TC, 166.13b–26b, lists various student stipends for *i-hsüeh,* but these seem to be really higher level schools accommodating *sheng-yüan* and *t'ung-sheng*—i.e., academies. Another elementary school with student stipends is listed in *Lo-ch'ing* HC, 4.50b.
23. *Kuang-hsi* TC, 166.15a. Judging from the regulations, there must have been many schools with such funds.
24. Yü Chih, *Te-i lu,* 10.4.5b.
25. "The summer days are long; in the school prepare *tien-hsin* [tea pastries] and congee; from the Dragonboat festival [fifth day of the fifth lunar month] to the fifteenth day of the eighth lunar month, if finances are ample, add a noon meal": *Ling-hu Wang-shih chih-p'u,* in Taga Akigorō, "Shinmatsu kakyo," p. 125, n. 60; see also the T'u clan regulations, ibid., p. 121, n. 32.
26. Wu Ching-tzu, *The Scholars,* trans. Hsien-yi Yang and Gladys Yang (New York, 1972), p. 355.
27. Daniel Overmyer, *Folk Buddhist Religion: Dissenting Sects in Late Traditional China* (Cambridge, Mass., 1976), p. 117; *Chinese Repository* 3(1834–35):468. In the following calculation, a school term of 300 days is assumed. 1,000 copper cash = 1 tael. Susan Naquin also gives cost-of-living data in *Millenarian Rebellion in China,* app. 3, p. 280.
28. Shu Hsin-ch'eng, ed., *Chung-kuo chin-tai chiao-yü shih tzu-liao,* p. 90.
29. For example, Liu Po-chi, *Kuang-tung shu-yüan chih-tu,* pp. 204–5, lists thirty-eight sources of academy income.
30. *Tsao-ch'iang* HC, p. 309: this is part of a record of academy lands, but the same considerations applied to all school lands.
31. See, for example, complaints in *Ning-hua* HC, p. 272, *Feng-chieh* HC, 18.3a–5b.
32. Nakamura Jihei, "Shindai Santō no gakuden," *Shien* 64(1955):54–55.
33. *Liu-yang* HC, 8.25ab, a total of nine charitable schools and nineteen clan elementary schools; *Wu-hsi, Chin-kuei* HC, pp. 117–18, with a total of eleven public and eleven clan schools.
34. *Wu-hsi, Chin-kuei* HC, pp. 525–28; three of the charitable estates also had schools, with separate school lands in some cases. According to data presented by Muramatsu Yūji, rents on privately owned lands in Soochow ranged from .7 to over 1 *shih* (husked rice) per *mou*: see Evelyn Rawski, *Agricultural Change and the Peasant Economy of South China* (Cambridge, Mass., 1972), table 24, p. 153. The school lands section of *Wu-hsi, Chin-kuei* HC, p. 115, lists rents

of over 1 *shih* per *mou* for the mid-eighteenth century, but rent data presented in Dwight Perkins, *Agricultural Development in China, 1368–1968* (Chicago, 1969), table G.4, pp. 318–19, result in a figure of .75 *shih/mou* (husked rice). The figure used in the calculations is .7 *shih/mou*. Yeh-chien Wang, "The Secular Trend of Prices during the Ch'ing Period" (Chinese University of Hong Kong) *Journal of the Institute of Chinese Studies* 5.2(1972):359, cites 1.35 taels per *shih* as the Shanghai price in 1854, and estimates (p. 359, n. 21) that the Wu-hsi price was 93 percent of the Shanghai one. This gives us an estimate of 1.25 taels per *shih* as the price of rice in Wu-hsi, ca. 1854: if this is applied to a rent of .7 *shih/mou*, the figure cited in the text is obtained.

35. Yeh-chien Wang, "Secular Trend," p. 359, cites 2.15 taels per *shih* as the price of rice in Shanghai, 1873–77; assuming a rent of .7 *shih/mou* results in a cash income of 97.97 taels, converted to copper cash at a rate of 982 cash per silver *liang* (Frank H. H. King, *Money and Monetary Policy in China* [Cambridge, Mass., 1965], p. 62, taking the midpoint). A cash income of 96,206 cash from 65.1 *mou* would be equivalent to a rent of 1,478 cash per *mou*, a figure which falls within the range of cash rents cited for Ju-kao county's school lands: see *Ju-kao* HC, pp. 182–83.
36. Assuming a rent of .6 *shih/mou* (husked rice) derived from Perkins, *Agricultural Development in China*, Table G.4, pp. 318–19.
37. Yeh-chien Wang, "Secular Trend," p. 359, n. 21, gives a price of 1.6 to 1.7 taels per *shih* for Shanghai in the mid-eighteenth century: the figures in the text were obtained by assuming a rent of .7 *shih* per *mou*.
38. Ibid., table 5, p. 357, has the rice price in Shanghai during 1866–69 at from 121 to 160 percent of the 1875 price (p. 359, n. 21) of about 2.15 taels/*shih*; at a rent of .7 *shih/mou*, 24.6 to 32.6 *mou* would be required to pay a salary of 58,300 cash, assuming 982 cash to the tael.
39. *Shang-ch'eng* HC, 6.4b–17a. The average holding for the forty schools with land was 17.6 *mou*; for parcels stipulating rents but not acreage, an estimated acreage was used, based on the average rent of 1.31 *shih/mou* derived from thirty items in this source that gave both the rent and acreage.
40. *Yung-ch'ing* HC, 15.16ab; *(Ch'ung-hsiu)T'ien-chin* FC, 1898 ed., 35.31b; *Ting-hsing* HC, p. 98.
41. At the price of 3.44 taels per *mou* cited in *(Ch'ung-hsiu) T'ien-chin* FC, 35.31b.
42. Nakamura Jihei, "Shindai Santō no gakuden," p. 53, gives an average of 97.1 *mou* for selected Shantung schools in the eighteenth century, and average holdings of 79.2 *mou* per school during the

Ch'ing up to 1850 (p. 55); these figures can be compared with the discussion in his "Shindai Santō nōson no gigaku," p. 34.

43. *Chinese Repository* 3(1834–35):468–70; in academy financing, too, urban real estate played a minor role: see Liu Po-chi, *Kuang-tung shu-yüan,* pp. 204–6.
44. *Tung-t'ai* HC, p. 531; *(Ch'ung-hsiu)T'ien-chin* FC, 35.13b.
45. Lien-sheng Yang, *Money and Credit,* pp. 98–99; the legal ceiling for pawnbrokers was 3 percent a month in the eighteenth century and 2 percent in the nineteenth. Public funds entrusted to pawnbrokers and salt merchants drew an average of 2 percent interest a month in the eighteenth century, 1 percent a month in the nineteenth century. Hunter, "*Fan Kwae,*" pp. 39–40, writes that "2–3 per cent on temporary loans per month was common."
46. *Wu-ning* HC, 16.35a, for example, forbids moving the school's capital into investment with pawnbrokers.
47. Examples of direct allocations are cited in table 7; *Chi-fu* TC, 114.66a cites schools in Ch'ing-yüan county obtaining funds from the prefectural allotment for Confucian schools; *Wen-an* HC, 12.23a, and *Ting-yüan* HC, 11.29b–31b both list schools financed by proceeds from local market taxes. *(Ch'ung-hsiu)T'ien-chin* FC, 35.11b, 13a, provide examples of schools using funds from salt revenues.
48. Data from Ch'en-chou, Hunan, dated 1825, cited in Lien-sheng Yang, *Money and Credit,* pp. 101–3.
49. Purchase price and rent data in *Tsao-ch'iang* HC, p. 314; *(Ch'ung-hsiu)T'ien-chin* FC, 35.31b; *Ch'eng-k'ou t'ing-chih,* 10.70b–71b; in Ch'eng-k'ou, rents given in maize were converted to money using the price for maize, 300–400 cash per .1 *shih,* found in 6.14ab. This price is identical to one cited by Yen Ju-i, *San-sheng shan-nei feng-t'u tsa-chih* (Shanghai, 1936), p. 25.
50. Yeh-chien Wang, *Land Taxation in Imperial China, 1750–1911* (Cambridge, Mass., 1973), table 6.8, p. 127, presents value of yield per *mou* and land value for Wu-ch'ing, Chihli (1888), Lai-chou prefecture, Shantung (1888) and Shanghai (1907): these result in annual rates of return of 15 percent, 4.7 percent, and 12–15 percent respectively, assuming rent was 50 percent of output.
51. Given a teacher's (cash) salary of 24 taels or (grain) salary of 25.5 shih (see table 3). The grain salary is an average of the items in table 3. Three plots with purchase price information were used to calculate range given in text (*Shang-ch'eng* HC, 6.11a–12b). An interest rate of 1 percent a month (see table 10) was used to calculate the required cash endowment.
52. In Ts'ang-chou the rate of exchange is taken at 1 tael = 1,604 cash, as stipulated in P'eng Hsin-wei, *Chung-kuo huo-pi shih* (Shanghai, 1958), p. 588 (for 1880). If rates as high as 21.4 percent could be

obtained from land, the relatively greater security of this form of investment might have made it preferable to deposits with a pawnshop. On the other hand, these high returns were obtained on mountain land, growing maize, and it is possible that such lands underwent rapid declines in fertility due to their marginal quality and poor soil maintenance. See Ping-ti Ho, *Studies on the Population,* pp. 149–51.

53. *An-hui* TC, 70.26b. A similar case is reported in the 1864 *I-ch'ang* FC, 6.15b.
54. *I-yang* HC, 5.9b.
55. If we assume that the money was invested, a minimum of 189.3 taels was needed to start a school in Shang-ch'eng in 1802. P'eng Hsin-wei, *Chung-kuo huo-pi,* p. 577, cites an exchange rate of 1,400 cash per silver tael for Honan in 1829: this would result in a minimum of 265,020 cash per school.
56. *Chi-fu* TC, 114.47b.
57. Chung-li Chang, *Income of the Chinese Gentry,* pp. 138–39.
58. Lien-sheng Yang, *Money and Credit,* pp. 98–100.
59. Ibid., p. 100: this is the 1844 rate in Peking; in Soochow, monthly rates were .6 percent. Yang states that interest rates in large cities were lowered substantially in the first part of the nineteenth century.
60. Yü Chih, *Te-i lu,* 10.4.4a.
61. Ping-ti Ho, *Ladder of Success,* chapter on "Factors in Social Mobility."
62. Yü Chih, *Te-i lu,* 10.5.9b.
63. Hummel, *Eminent Chinese* 1:86–87. See the long report in *Ch'üan Tien i-hsüeh hui-chi.*
64. Many of the donations listed in *Wu-ning* HC, 1824 ed., 7.14a–16b (also in 1870 ed., 16.29a–36b) are less than one *mou* in size. *Ch'ung-yang* HC, 3.51a–53a; Nakamura Jihei, "Shindai Santō nōson no gigaku," table 4, p. 31; *Hsü Ch'ü-wu* HC, 8.28a–29a; *Ch'eng-k'ou t'ing-chih,* 10.70a–76a.
65. *Shang-ch'eng* HC, 6.9a.
66. Yü Chih, *Te-i lu,* 10.5.3b–4a.
67. Chung-li Chang, *Income of the Chinese Gentry,* p. 146.
68. Ibid., p. 51.
69. "The rural markets gather at temples, in a year they must contribute up to several hundred taels for dramatic performances," *Liu-yang* HC, 8.36a.
70. Chung-li Chang, *Income of the Chinese Gentry,* table 15, p. 40.

Chapter 4

1. These gaps are clearly reflected in the standard bibliographies for Chinese local gazetteers, in particular Chu Shih-chia's *Chung-kuo*

ti-fang chih tsung-lu (rev. ed., 1958; reprint ed., Tokyo, 1968) and the National Diet Library's *Nihon shuyō toshokan kenkyūjo shozō Chūgoku chihō shi sōgō mokuroku* (Tokyo, 1969).

2. *Ssu-ch'uan* TC, 79.10ab; *Ch'ung-ch'ing* FC, 5.6b–15a.
3. As in *Liu-yang* HC, 8.24b–25b, or *T'ai-ku* HC, 2.37b.
4. Johanna M. Meskill, "The Chinese Genealogy as a Research Source," in *Family and Kinship in Chinese Society*, ed. Maurice Freedman (Stanford, 1970), p. 141.
5. See discussion in chap. 2.
6. Meskill, "Chinese Genealogy," p. 147.
7. Jack M. Potter, "Land and Lineage in Traditional China," in *Family and Kinship in Chinese Society*, ed. Maurice Freedman (Stanford, 1970), pp. 130–31.
8. Niida Noboru, *Chūgoku no nōson kazoku*, pp. 64–65; Makino Tatsumi, *Kinsei Chūgoku sōzoku kenkyū* (Tokyo, 1949), table 2, pp. 208–9, presented this information slightly differently: 80 out of 169 (47.3 percent) of the villages in T'an-yüan hsiang were single-surname villages. Hsien-chin Hu, *Common Descent Group*, p. 14.
9. See table in Taga Akigorō, *Sōfu no kenkyū*, p. 63, which includes genealogies from Heilungkiang, Kirin, Fengtien, Chichihar, and Mongolia. Also Taga Akigorō, "Kindai Chūgoku ni okeru zokujuku no seikaku," *Kindai Chūgoku kenkyū* 5(1963):208.
10. Martin C. Yang, *Chinese Village*, pp. 137, 144. On clan financing of education, see pp. 139–41. Crook and Crook, *Revolution*, p. 12. Not all classes held in ancestral halls were in clan schools, and there are examples of ordinary village schools meeting in a clan hall. See (*Hsü-hsiu*)*Ch'ü-wu* HC, 8.28a–29a; *Ssu-ch'uan* TC, 79.4a.
11. *Ting-hsing* HC, p. 102; the school was endowed with a six-room house and 40 *mou* of land.
12. *Ting-yüan* HC, 11.29a–31b.
13. "Record of the Shang clan living together for eight generations," *Shu-lu* HC, 1872 ed., p. 1235; the family numbered several hundred persons in the 1860s when this was written.
14. Niida Noboru, *Chūgoku no nōson kazoku*, p. 75, using information from genealogies.
15. Hui-chen Wang Liu, *Traditional Chinese Clan Rules*, table 1, pp. 211–12, 108, 116.
16. Investigation of 79 genealogies held by the National Diet Library and the Toyo bunko in Tokyo for lineages in Kiangsu produced only ten with direct information on schools and three with related information on schools. In one genealogy, the *Hsi-shan tung-li Hou-shih liu-hsiu tsung-p'u* (Taga Akigorō, *Sōfu no kenkyū* bibliography #414), there are no school regulations or other documents pertaining to a clan

school, except for a list at the very end, noting the location of copies, one of which was left at the school.

17. *Su-chou* FC, 1824 ed., 2.14b–15a.
18. Ibid., 25.23b, lists the Fan clan school, which seems to have been defunct, while the 1882 ed. lists schools under *i-chuang,* 24.28b, 35ab. Soochow genealogies listed in Taga Akigorō, *Sōfu no kenkyū,* with direct information on clan schools are his #5, #227, #479, #802, #804, #812, and #1031.
19. *Sung-chiang* FC, p. 696, 706, 713–14; genealogies #854, #1192 in Taga Akigorō, *Sōfu no kenkyū* bibliography. *Wu-hsi, Chin-kuei* HC, pp. 117–18, 525, 527.
20. Both Taga Akigorō, *Chūgoku kyōiku shi,* p. 110, and Ogawa Yoshiko, "Sōzoku-nai no kyōiku," p. 225, present this information.
21. *Liu-yang* HC, 8.35b.
22. Ibid., 8.24b–25b.
23. *Hu-pei* TC, 59.55b–56a lists eight clan schools for Ch'ung-yang hsien, and 59.57ab, three clan schools for Huang-kang hsien. The 1866 edition of *Ch'ung-yang* HC, 3.51a–53a, lists nine clan schools, which amount to 47.4 percent of the total schools listed.
24. Han-seng Ch'en, *Landlord and Peasant in China: A Study of the Agrarian Crisis in South China* (New York, 1936), pp. 34–35, 37. According to Ch'en, clan landholdings were lowest in southwest Kwangtung and highest in the Pearl River delta, where one-half of the cultivated land was owned by lineages. Freedman, *Lineage Organization in Southeastern China,* p. 11, reproduces a table from the *Chinese Economic Journal* surveying landholdings along the East River in Kwangtung, which shows considerable variance in lineage holdings. Here again distinctions between ritual or ancestral land and school lands were not very rigid, and Han-seng Ch'en, *Landlord and Peasant,* p. 27, notes that income from ancestral lands was used for education as well as for worship.
25. Shimizu Taiji, *Shina no kazoku to sonraku no tokushitsu* (Tokyo, 1927), pp. 67–68. Shimizu also saw actual schools in operation, pp. 68–69.
26. Frederic Wakeman, Jr., *Strangers at the Gate: Social Disorder in South China, 1839–1861* (Berkeley, 1966), pp. 62–65.
27. *Chinese Repository* 6(1837–38):236; Freedman, *Chinese Lineage and Society,* p. 73, citing an 1859 report.
28. Hugh D. R. Baker, *A Chinese Lineage Village: Sheung Shui* (London, 1968), pp. 72–73.
29. Liu Hsing-t'ang, "Fu-chien ti hsüeh-tsu tsu-chih," *Shih-huo* 4.8(1936):37.
30. Fried, *Fabric of Chinese Society,* p. 134.
31. Nakamura Jihei, "Shindai Santō nōson no gigaku," p. 10; table 1,

shows a total of 135 elementary schools active in the K'ang-hsi and Yung-cheng periods, while his table 2, derived from lower level gazetteers and extending into the early nineteenth century, shows a total of 169 schools.

32. Only 71 percent of the schools listed in *Chi-fu* TC, chüan 114–17, presented information on the date they were founded; if only these are counted, 59.8 percent of the schools were founded in the K'ang-hsi period.
33. On agricultural disturbances caused by flood or drought, see Myers, *Chinese Peasant Economy*, pp. 274–75.
34. Mary Wright, *The Last Stand of Chinese Conservatism: The T'ung-chih Restoration, 1862–1874* (Stanford, 1957), pp. 129–33, describes the efforts to revive scholarship and learning.
35. The numerous communications concerning charitable schools in Ting Jih-ch'ang's collected works testify to his concern: see *Fu-wu kung-tu* (1877; reprint ed., Taipei, n.d.), 1:307–12, 355–57, 424–26, 478–79; 2:562–64, 618–19, 712, 753–54, 763–65, 817–18, 849–51, 864–65, 916–18; 3:1165–66, 1195, 1322–24, 1502–4, 1537–38, 1590. Also see *Su-chou* FC, 16.18b, 46b, 51ab, 27.15b, 17b; *Feng-hsien* HC, pp. 348–349.
36. *Yang-chou* FC, 3.15a; *Hsü-chou* FC, 15.11b; *Su-chou* FC, 24.16b.
37. See preface to Hang-chou Fu-jen charitable school by Wu Hsü, reprinted in Shu Hsin-ch'eng, ed., *Chung-kuo chin-tai chiao-yü shih tzu-liao*, pp. 91–92.
38. *Tan-t'u* HC, pp. 354–55; *Tan-yang* HC, 10.10b; *Su-chou* FC, chüan 24–27; *Wu-chin, Yang-hu* HC, 5.7a–8b; *Wu-hsi, Chin-kuei* HC, pp. 117–18; *Chiang-yin* HC, p. 376; *I-hsing* HC, pp. 691, 1003; *Ching-chiang* HC, 6.35a; *Yang-chou* FC, 3.15a–20a; *Feng-hsien* HC, pp. 348–49. According to Ogawa Yoshiko, "Shindai ni okeru gigaku," pp. 275–77, 25 percent of the Shanghai charitable schools were founded in the T'ung-chih period, a figure exceeded only by the number founded in the Kuang-hsü period (1875–1908).
39. Shu Hsin-ch'eng, ed., *Chung-kuo chin-tai chiao-yü shih tzu-liao*, pp. 91–92.
40. Reported in *Shan-hsi* TC, 76.39b as 123 schools, in *Hsü Kao-p'ing* HC, 5.5a as 121 schools, founded in 1865 and 1867.
41. *Wen-an* HC, 12.22b–23a; in Shanghai, as noted by Ogawa Yoshiko, "Shindai ni okeru gigaku," pp. 275–77, this was the peak for establishing charitable schools. See *(Ch'ung-hsiu)T'ien-chin* FC, 1898–99 ed., 35.11b–46b, which provides information on school expansion during the Kuang-hsü period.
42. Wang Lan-yin, "Ming-tai chih she-hsüeh," *Shih-ta yüeh-k'an* 5.4(1935):80, data on pp. 81–102.
43. *Ho-nan* TC, 43.46a–59b; 34 per cent of i-hsüeh and 34.4 percent of

she-hsüeh were in rural areas; *Ssu-ch'uan* TC, chüan 79; remaining schools in Szechwan could not be classified; *Che-chiang* TC, chüan 25–29, and here 46.2 percent of the schools could not be classified. Gazetteers generally give the location of the school. Schools set within a walled prefectural or county seat were identified as urban; those located in *ts'un, chuang,* or other designations for village, were identified as rural.

44. *Hu-pei* TC, chüan 59, where 22.9 percent of *i-hsüeh* and 53.2 percent of *she-hsüeh* listed defied classification. *She-hsüeh* represented only 18.9 percent of the total number of schools.
45. *Chi-fu* TC, chüan 114–17. There was no basis for classifying 3.5 percent of *i-hsüeh* and 27.5 percent of *she-hsüeh*. Information in district gazetteers reinforces the picture of rural dominance provided by the provincial figures: see *Luan-ch'eng* HC, 6.17b, *Nan-kung* HC, 3.31b–34a; *T'ang* HC, 4.40a–42a; *Tsao-ch'iang* HC, 10.23b; and *Wen-an* HC, 2.36ab. For Honan, *Yeh* HC, 2.11a–16b, *Wu-an* HC, 7.32a, and *Shang-ch'eng* HC, 6.18b–25b; for Shansi, *Chao-ch'eng* HC, 17.22a–23a, (*Hsü-hsiu*)*Ch'ü-wu* HC, 8.28b–29a; and *Lin-fen* HC, 5.6ab.
46. Nakamura Jihei, "Shindai Santō nōson no gigaku," p. 5 (table 1) and p. 10 (table 2).
47. *Ch'ung-ch'ing* FC, 5.6b–15a. 12.9 percent of the schools could not be classified.
48. Liu Po-chi, *Kuang-tung shu-yüan,* pp. 89–91.
49. The range was from 0 schools (12 units) to 40 schools (2 units). Prefectural and *chou* units were separately counted in addition to counties, since schools were often separately listed for a *fu* and *chou* city. Data taken from *Chi-fu* TC, chüan 114–17.
50. Gilbert Rozman, *Urban Networks in Ch'ing China and Tokugawa Japan* (Princeton, 1973), provides a summary of his discussion of Chihli's urban network on pp. 198–201. For definition of the levels, see p. 60. On major cities, see p. 151.
51. *Fu-chien* TC, chüan 62–66. T'ing-chou had 69 schools as compared to 66 for Foochow. According to Rozman, *Urban Networks,* p. 240, Foochow was the second largest city in southeast China, a port which had long enjoyed commercial prosperity.
52. *Hu-nan* TC, chüan 68–70. Shui-sui had 44 schools, while Ch'ang-sha prefecture had 30. Ch'ang-sha was the second largest city in central China, according to Rozman, *Urban Networks,* pp. 230, 233; see p. 234 on Hsiang-t'an.
53. Yu-wen Jen, *Taiping Revolutionary Movement,* pp. 13, 19, 22–23, 217–18; Philip C. Huang, *Liang Ch'i-ch'ao,* p. 11; Diana Lary, *Region and Nation: the Kwangsi Clique in Chinese Politics, 1925–37* (Cambridge, 1974), pp. 35–36; Ping-ti Ho, *Ladder of Success,* Ap-

pendix, cases, 1, 5, 7, 11, 14, 17, 20, 22, 26. Tachibana Shiraki, *Shina shakai kenkyū,* p. 452, describes a village schoolteacher with a *chü-jen* degree, but this must have been unusual.

54. *Wu Hsün li-shih tiao-ch'a chi,* pp. 42–43, 46.
55. Chung-li Chang, *Chinese Gentry,* p. 137; 1850 population total of 430 million taken from Ping-ti Ho, *Studies on the Population,* p. 64.
56. Cipolla, *Literacy and Development in the West,* p. 26; see his table 5, on numbers of elementary schoolteachers in relation to the total population of selected countries, pp. 28–29. Chung-li Chang, *Chinese Gentry,* pp. 90–92.
57. See appendix 1 for calculations leading to this estimate.
58. Ping-ti Ho, *Ladder of Success,* pp. 122–25, 262.
59. Chung-li Chang, *Income of the Chinese Gentry,* p. 114, estimates that the total number of students who resided in academies was 112,500 with another 90,000 who attended lectures and examinations but were "free to engage in teaching" and other activities. If the first group is subtracted from the total number of potential teachers, we are still left with almost 2.8 million, a figure which is 0.6 per cent of the total population ca. 1850.
60. Ping-ti Ho, *Ladder of Success,* pp. 200–203. Some academies provided room and board; many provided "ink and paper" money to those sitting in the examinations as well as "food money" in other instances. These are frequently discussed in detail in academy regulations. Rankings were usually compiled on the occasion of "official examinations" (*kuan-k'o*) held as often as twice a month (*Lüeh-yang* HC, 2.26a).
61. There were usually two categories of students, the first one including *sheng-yüan, chien-sheng,* and *kung-sheng* and the second for *t'ung-sheng.* See Liu Po-chi, *Kuang-tung shu-yüan,* p. 310; more rarely, *chü-jen* were also admitted, pp. 310–11. In addition the two categories could be divided into a "regular" and "supplementary" quota, which were differentiated in terms of stipends and prize money.
62. Ibid., pp. 319–21 presents information on stipends from 38 Kwangtung academies. The table assumes that a student will succeed in retaining his rank in the "regular" quota in each of the official examinations. If he does not, his stipend will either decline or be omitted. Since prizes to the highest ranked student in each category were often the equivalent of his monthly stipend (for example, in *T'ang* HC, 4.33a, and *Ch'ung-jen* HC, 4.3.4b–5a), prizes could be an important income supplement.
63. With the exception of 1800–25 in table 14, median stipends were substantially less than half the median teachers' salaries; in 1800–25, median stipends were 58 percent of median teachers' salaries. This

would be even more true for *t'ung-sheng* who received smaller stipends and prizes: in Liu Po-chi, *Kuang-tung shu-yüan,* pp. 319–21, 28 percent of the academies with stipends for both *t'ung-sheng* and *sheng-yüan* gave smaller stipends to the former. See table 13 for other examples.

64. *Luan-ch'eng* HC, 6.9a, 11b–12a.
65. *Luan* CC, 12.78b, 82b.
66. *Lüeh-yang* HC, 2.26a, 32a.
67. Ibid., 2.28b, 26a.
68. *Nan-ch'ang* HC, 1870 ed., 6.50b, 48ab.
69. *T'ung* CC, 5.11b; *Ch'ang-p'ing* HC, 12.14b–15a, where the *chai-fu* who watched the gate, performed janitorial services, looked after the academy head, and cooked each received 2,000 "big cash" a month as opposed to the 1,200 paid to a *sheng-yüan.*
70. Ping-ti Ho, *Ladder of Success,* pp. 201–3; Chung-li Chang, *Income of the Chinese Gentry,* pp. 115, 117.
71. *Luan-ch'eng* HC, 6.9b, calculated from food allowance.
72. Wu Ching-tzu, *The Scholars,* p. 454.
73. Ibid.
74. Ping-ti Ho, *Ladder of Success,* pp. 36–37, 303.
75. Bodde and Morris, *Law in Imperial China,* pp. 246–47, 413–17. Chung-li Chang, *Income of the Chinese Gentry,* pp. 45–46, discusses handling of lawsuits and local disputes by gentry members.
76. Ch'ing Sheng-tsu, *Sacred Edict,* trans. F. W. Baller, pp. 137, 134–36. For a missionary description of "strolling quacks," see J. MacGowan, *Men and Manners,* pp. 185–88.
77. Chung-li Chang, *Income of the Chinese Gentry,* pp. 117–22.
78. Doolittle, *Social Life,* 2:331–36, 339; the method of fortune-telling is described more fully on pp. 340–44.
79. Ch'en Tung-yüan, *Chung-kuo chiao-yü shih,* pp. 425–26, citing *Hsing-shih yin-yüan.*
80. Yu-wen Jen, *Taiping Revolutionary Movement,* pp. 30–31. Feng was eventually rescued from his lowly occupation by his employer, and later hired as a private tutor.
81. Chung-li Chang, *Income of the Chinese Gentry,* pp. 89–91. Yet another example of the depths to which indigent scholars were reduced is given by Smith, *Village Life,* p. 76, who describes the "Strolling Scholars" who tried to sell paper, pictures, pens, ink, and lithographs of tablets. According to Smith, "These individuals are not to be confounded with travelling pedlars, who, though they deal in the same articles, make no pretension to learning, and generally convey their goods on a wheelbarrow, whereas the Strolling Scholar cannot manage anything larger than a pack."
82. Wang's case cited in Ping-ti Ho, *Ladder of Success,* p. 293. Canton

data from *Chinese Repository* 3(1834–35):368–69, with conversion being cited in the text, namely .1 liang = 14 cents. Conversions were made on the basis of the western calendar. For information on median teachers' salaries see table 4.

83. Private teachers' income obtained from the "First Annual Report of the Morrison Education Society," *Chinese Repository* 6(1837–38):237, which states that a teacher with twenty pupils ordinarily receives half or two-thirds of a dollar a month from each. At a half-dollar a month, assuming a school year of ten months, a private teacher would earn $100 or about 71 taels. At $.66 a month, he would earn $132, or 94.3 taels. This estimate seems to be for urban schools; the report goes on to state that pupils in some village schools pay only $2–3 a year, or from 1.4 to 2.1 taels a year.
84. Doolittle, *Social Life,* 1:61. The wages themselves are in dollars, converted into taels at the rate of $1.33 = 1 tael (p. xxxiv), 1000 cash =$1 (2:145). Since clerks, accountants, field workers and personal servants worked for a wage plus board, they may well have earned more than a schoolteacher, who got only "30 to 60 dollars" a year, plus small presents. Servants and field workers receiving board earned 3 dollars a month less than the same job paid if they boarded themselves; if we assume that the resulting $36 a year represents what it would have cost a teacher to board himself, it is clear that he earned less than a clerk or accountant who received $10–$30 a year, plus board, and personal servants and fieldworkers who could earn from $1–$3 a month or $12 to $36 a year with board. Of course, the field worker's wages undoubtedly fluctuated according to the agricultural demand for labor, and it may never have been possible for persons in this category to earn $36 a year.
85. Smith, *Village Life,* p. 52; see chap. 2, n. 17.
86. J. Martin Miller, cited in Chung-li Chang, *Income of the Chinese Gentry,* pp. 101–2. Teachers' salaries cited by Miller went from 30 taels to almost 150 taels, as compared to 10 taels a year for laborers. See also p. 102. A household account book for the 1860s–1870s from a landlord family on Taiwan shows that the Yens paid about 17,600 cash for the initial schooling of two sons in 1868. By the next year, fees had risen to 22,000 cash for a better teacher and more advanced lessons: see Huang Tien-ch'üan, *Ku chang yen-chiu i-li,* T'ai-wan shih-shih yen-chiu, vol. 2 (Tainan, 1959), table 5, pp. 38, 72–73. These fees were quite close to the median salaries for charitable school teachers as presented in table 4.
87. Chung-li Chang, *Income of the Chinese Gentry,* p. 101; some combined teaching and medicine, pp. 99–100.
88. *Chinese Repository* 6(1837–38):237.
89. Chung-li Chang, *Income of the Chinese Gentry,* pp. 99–100; Nym

Wales, *Red Dust* (Stanford, 1952), pp. 44–45 assuming 1 dollar = .72 tael (King, *Money and Monetary Policy*, p. 88); Smedley, *The Great Road*, pp. 36–37.

90. This is especially the case because these groups received board as well as a money wage, so that although 2.2 taels represents 8 per cent of the money wage, it is a much smaller fraction of the whole wage, were boarding costs included.
91. Smedley, *The Great Road*, p. 36.
92. Ibid., pp. 14–15, 36–39; a *hsiu-ts'ai* is a sheng-yüan.
93. Ibid., pp. 36–45. Ping-ti Ho's cases are presented in *Ladder of Success*, appendix.
94. Yu-wen Jen, *Taiping Revolutionary Movement*, pp. 12–13.
95. Ibid., pp. 13, 19, 26, for descriptions of Hung's teaching career; pp. 23, 30–31 on Feng Yün-shan.
96. Ping-ti Ho, *Ladder of Success*, pp. 310–13; Lary, *Region and Nation*, pp. 35–37.
97. Ping-to Ho, *Ladder of Success*, pp. 316–18.
98. Edgar Snow, *Red Star Over China* (New York, 1938), pp. 131, 133; Stuart Schram, *Mao Tse-tung* (New York, 1966), pp. 15–17.
99. Wales, *Red Dust*, pp. 44–45, 190–91, 48–49; the same story is told about his grandfather by Chung Kun-ai, a descendant of Cantonese immigrants to Hawaii, in *The Sandalwood Mountains: Readings and Stories of the Early Chinese in Hawaii*, ed. Tin-yuke Char (Honolulu, 1975), p. 256.
100. Wales, *Red Dust*, p. 77.
101. Roxane Witke, "Chiang Ch'ing's Coming of Age," in *Women in Chinese Society*, ed. Margery Wolf and Roxane Witke (Stanford, 1975), p. 173.

Chapter 5

1. See Elizabeth Eisenstein, "Some Conjectures about the Impact of Printing on Western Society and Thought," *Journal of Modern History* 40.1(1968):1–56; and her "The Advent of Printing and the Problem of the Renaissance," *Past and Present* 45(1969):19–89, in which she discusses the advent of typographical culture and examines its repercussions on scholarship and modes of thought: rationalization, individuation, and the shift to modern forms of consciousness.
2. Ping-ti Ho, *Ladder of Success*, p. 214. K. T. Wu, "Chinese Printing under Four Alien Dynasties (916–1368 A.D.)," *Harvard Journal of Asiatic Studies* 13(1950):463–75, 477, 490, discusses printing in Yüan times.
3. See Chu Yün's biography in Hummel, *Eminent Chinese*, 1:198–99; L. Carrington Goodrich, *The Literary Inquisition of Ch'ien-lung*

(Baltimore, 1935), points to the negative effects of this vast compilation project. Another major imperially-sponsored compilation was the encyclopedia, *Ku-chin t'u-shu chi-ch'eng*, presented to the emperor in 1725, the largest such work besides a fourteenth century encyclopedia: see Ssu-yü Teng and Knight Biggerstaff, comps., *An Annotated Bibliography of Selected Chinese Reference Works* (Cambridge, Mass., 1950), pp. 126–28.

4. Ping-ti Ho, *Ladder of Success*, p. 212; Kōjirō Yoshikawa, *An Introduction to Sung Poetry*, trans. Burton Watson (Cambridge, Mass., 1967), p. 183.
5. Ping-ti Ho, *Ladder of Success*, p. 212. According to K. T. Wu, "Chinese Printing," p. 497, the small number of copies is explained by the limited demand and inadequate facilities for shipping books over long distances.
6. On movable type, see Thomas F. Carter, *The Invention of Printing in China and Its Spread Westward*, rev. L. C. Goodrich (New York, 1955), chap. 4. See K. T. Wu, "Chinese Printing," pp. 469–70; Yeh Te-hui, *Shu-lin ch'ing-hua* (N.p., 1920), 7.7a–8a, discusses Yüan expenses in cutting the woodblocks and comments, "The labor of printing books has probably never been more expensive than this." For Ming costs, see Yeh's discussion, 7.13b–15a, where he states that, in sharp contrast to the Yüan, early Ming printing was extremely cheap. See Ping-ti Ho, *Ladder of Success*, p. 214.
7. Accounts of the most famous Ch'ing literati printers are to be found in Wang Hsiu, "Pan-pen shu," *Che-chiang t'u-shu-kuan kuan-k'an* 3.3(1934):6, and Nagasawa Kikuya, *Wa-Kan sho no insatsu to sono rekishi* (Tokyo, 1952), p. 87.
8. Biographies of these men are to be found in Hummel, *Eminent Chinese*: for Huang P'ei-lieh, 1:340–41; Mao Chin, 1:565; Pao T'ing-po, 2:612–13. See Cheuk-woon Taam, *The Development of Chinese Libraries under the Ch'ing Dynasty, 1644–1911* (Shanghai, 1935), pp. 15–17; for a discussion of the historiographical school in Ch'ing scholarship, see Liang Ch'i-ch'ao, *Intellectual Trends in the Ch'ing Period*, trans. Immanuel Hsü (Cambridge, Mass., 1959), pp. 51–79. The atmosphere in which these bibliophiles worked is conveyed by Nancy Lee Swann, "Seven Intimate Library Owners," *Harvard Journal of Asiatic Studies* 1(1936):363–90, on eighteenth century book collectors in Hangchow. Note that only two of the men in the group did not reprint or print books.
9. According to Ping-ti Ho, *Ladder of Success*, pp. 214–15, reproduction of the basic texts in large numbers helped those in humble circumstances, but Ch'ing reproductions of specialized and expensive works, beyond the reach of the poor, gave the well-to-do an advantage in their studies and preparation for the civil service examinations.

10. The printing of winning examination papers began in the sixteenth century in Soochow and Hangchow. In 1587 the Supervisorate of Rites suggested that the best papers be printed by local schools to serve as good examples and models for students: K. T. Wu, "Ming Printing and Printers," *Harvard Journal of Asiatic Studies* 7 (1943):250. For discussion of how these fit into Ch'ing education, see Ch'en Tung-yüan, *Chung-kuo k'o-hsüeh shih-tai*, pp. 54–59.
11. Burton Watson, *Chinese Lyricism: Shih Poetry from the Second to the Twelfth Century* (New York, 1971), pp. 199, 209–10, 212–13.
12. Kōjirō Yoshikawa, *Introduction to Sung Poetry*, pp. 171–73, 175–76, 177–78, 183.
13. Vera Hrdlickova, "The Professional Training of Chinese Storytellers," pp. 225–48. The topic of popular fiction and its links to storytellers is a controversial one: see Glen Dudbridge, *The Hsi-yu Chi: A Study of Antecedents to the Sixteenth Century Chinese Novel* (Cambridge, 1970), pp. 9–10; Jaroslav Prusek, "The Beginnings of Popular Chinese Literature: Urban Centres—the Cradle of Popular Fiction," *Archiv orientalni* 36(1968):67–121; and his *The Origins and the Authors of the "Hua-pen"* (Prague, 1967); W. L. Idema, "Storytelling and the Short Story in China," *T'oung Pao* 59(1973):1–67, for a range of opinions. In his *The Chinese Short Story: Studies in Dating, Authorship, and Composition* (Cambridge, Mass., 1973), Patrick Hanan comments on the link between spoken and written forms of popular entertainment: "We have seen that there was a reading public in the Yüan, and probably earlier, for popular fiction in the vernacular. As a possible parallel, we may note that there was a mass reading public during the Ch'ing dynasty and after even for such uncompromising *chantefable* forms as the *pao-chüan* and the *t'an-tz'u*."
14. Patrick Hanan, "Sung and Yüan Vernacular Fiction: A Critique of Modern Methods of Dating," *Harvard Journal of Asiatic Studies* 30(1970):167.
15. Liu Ts'un-yan, *Chinese Popular Fiction in Two London Libraries* (Hong Kong, 1967), pp. 25–27.
16. Jaroslav Prusek, "P'u Sung-ling and His Work," *Chinese History and Literature* (Dordrecht, 1970), p. 109.
17. Colin Mackerras, *The Rise of the Peking Opera 1770–1870* (Oxford, 1972), pp. 20–26, 33–40, 116–24, 154–61 and app. C, pp. 258–66; Colin Mackerras, "The Theatre in Yang-chou in the Late Eighteenth Century," *Papers on Far Eastern History* 1(1970):1–30; Tanaka Issei, "Chōsen shisetsu En kōro-tei ni okeru Shindai shoki kōgyō engeki no keisei" (Kumamoto daigaku hōbun gakkai) *Hōbun ronsō* 25(1970):36–69.
18. Wolfram Eberhard, *Cantonese Ballads* (*Munich State Library Col-*

lection), Asian Folklore and Social Life Monographs, vol. 30 (Taipei, 1972). See also Cheng Chen-to, *Chung-kuo su-wen-hsüeh shih*, chaps. 12, 13, pp. 238–406; Ch'en Ju-heng, *Shuo-shu shih-hua*, pp. 130–31, 170–71, 205, 219–25, 253–55.

19. Cheng Chen-to, *Chung-kuo su-wen-hsüeh shih*, pp. 353–54, 407–62; Ch'en Ju-heng, *Shuo-shu shih-hua*, p. 205.

20. See W. L. Idema, *Chinese Vernacular Fiction: The Formative Period* (Leiden, 1974), pp. xi–xii, xvii, lxi, 133–34. Perhaps the most famous ghost stories are the *Liao-chai chih i* (Strange Stories from a Chinese Studio) by P'u Sung-ling (1640–1715), discussed by Shou-yi Ch'en, *Chinese Literature: A Historical Introduction* (New York, 1961), pp. 573–75. Lu Hsün, *A Brief History of Chinese Fiction*, trans. Hsien-yi Yang and Gladys Yang (Peking, 1964), pp. 269–75; pp. 355–71 describes Ch'ing adventure and detective novels.

21. For the pseudohistories, see Harold L. Kahn, *Monarchy in the Emperor's Eyes: Image and Reality in the Ch'ien-lung Reign* (Cambridge, Mass., 1971), pp. 50–59.

22. Sakai Tadao, *Chūgoku zensho no kenkyū*: "Ledgers of Merit and Demerit" are treated in chap. 5, pp. 356–403, and *Meritorious Deeds at No Cost* on pp. 395–98; Sakai Tadao, "Confucianism and Popular Educational Works," in *Self and Society in Ming Thought*, ed. William T. de Bary (New York, 1970), pp. 331–66.

23. See Idema, "Storytelling and the Short Story," pp. 34–35. Okuzaki Hiroshi, "En Ryōhan no shisō—Mindai makki no shisō shiteki kosatsu," *Shakai bunka shigaku* 3(1967):18, tries to link both the morality books and *pao-chüan* to Yüan Huang and his emphasis on the possibility of self-improvement through everyday action, and (pp. 21–23) to late Ming social changes.

24. The religious significance of *pao-chüan* is outlined in Wei-pang Chao, "Secret Religious Societies in North China in the Ming," *Folklore Studies* 7(1948):107–12; Hsiang Ta, "Ming-Ch'ing chih-chi chih pao-chüan wen-hsüeh yü Pai-lien chiao," *T'ang-tai Ch'ang-an yü hsi-yü wen-ming* (Peking, 1957), pp. 600–616.

25. Cheng Chen-to, *Chung-kuo su-wen-hsüeh shih*, pp. 306–47; Ch'en Ju-heng, *Shuo-shu shih-hua*, pp. 123–29; Li Shih-yü, *Pao-chüan tsung-lu* (Shanghai, 1961), pp. 1–11.

26. Sakai Tadao, "Confucianism and Popular Educational Works," pp. 334–35; Sakai's "Mindai no nichiyō ruisho to shomin kyōiku" is still the most comprehensive introduction to this subject.

27. Niida Noboru drew heavily on these in his "Gen Min jidai no mura no kiyaku to kosaku shōsho nado—nichiyō hyakka-zensho no rui nijusshu no naka kara," *Tōyō bunka kenkyūjo kiyō* 8(1956):123–66. The "report of robbers" on the theft of an ox is found in books formerly in Niida's private collection: *Hsin-shou yu-hsüeh i-chih*

shu-li pien-lan, last page, and *Ch'i-shu wen-yüeh tien-p'i ch'eng chieh chuang hun ch'i-chu wen pien-lan,* last chüan, 10b. Both books are described by Sakai Tadao, "Mindai no nichiyō ruisho to shomin kyōiku," p. 125.

28. Sakai Tadao, "Mindai no nichiyō ruisho to shomin kyōiku," p. 119.
29. A Ying (Ch'ien Hsing-ts'un), *Chung-kuo lien-huan t'u-hua shih-hua* (Peking, 1957), pp. 1–14; my thanks to Perry Link, who pointed out this source.
30. Ibid., pp. 15–17.
31. Ibid., pp. 24–29; Gino Nebiolo, "Introduction," p. xii in *The People's Comic Book,* trans. Endymion Wilkinson (New York, 1973).
32. See chap. 1; also see A Ying, *Chung-kuo lien-huan,* p. 27.
33. A Ying, *Chung-kuo lien-huan,* pp. 17–23.
34. Endymion Wilkinson, *The History of Imperial China: A Research Guide* (Cambridge, Mass., 1973), pp. 122–24, lists some important guides and secondary sources on this genre; see pp. 159–63 for similar treatment of agricultural and technological treatises.
35. The history of these Fukien printing centers is presented in K. T. Wu, "Chinese Printing," pp. 486–90, and in his "Ming Printing," pp. 232–36; Ch'en Yen, "Fu-chien pan-pen chih," included in *Fu-chien hsin t'ung-chih,* 1922 ed.; and Yeh Ch'ang-ch'ing, "Min pen k'ao," *T'u-shu-kuan hsüeh chi-k'an* 2.1(1927):115–61. On quality production, see K. T. Wu, "Ming Printing," pp. 232–54.
36. K. T. Wu, "Ming Printing," pp. 229–30.
37. K. T. Wu, "Chinese Printing," pp. 490, 495; K. T. Wu, "Ming Printing," pp. 207, 236. Sun K'ai-ti, *Jih-pen Tung-ching so-chien Chung-kuo hsiao-shuo shu-mu* (Shanghai, 1953), pp. 133–34, discusses various works of fiction printed by Yü Hsiang-tou. Sakai Tadao, "Mindai no nichiyō ruisho to shomin kyōiku," pp. 141–47, discusses Yü and others; see Liu Ts'un-yan, *Chinese Popular Fiction,* pp. 68–69.
38. Ch'ü Wan-li and Ch'ang Pi-te, *T'u-shu pan-pen hsüeh yao lüeh* (Taipei, 1954), p. 61; Lo Chin-t'ang, *Li-tai t'u-shu pan-pen chih-yao* (Taipei, 1958), p. 80.
39. Liu Ts'un-yan, *Chinese Popular Fiction,* pp. 38–39; very little is known about these bookstores (p. 36), and their location is often a mystery. On pp. 39–42, he lists the bookstores encountered in his survey of popular fiction, noting locations when these are known, and the approximate dates these stores existed. A similar list of producers of *pao-chüan* is provided by Li Shih-yü, *Pao-chüan tsung-lu,* pp. 11–13, although not all were printing firms.
40. Nagasawa Kikuya, *Wa-Kan sho,* p. 87; see his list of important printing centers, p. 30. On Chekiang printers, see the "Che-chiang

sheng wen-hsien lan-hui chüan-tsai," *Wen-lan hsüeh-pao*, 2.3–4(1936):327–50, which has a bibliography of famous printers and editions. Mao Ch'un-hsiang, "Che-chiang sheng-li t'u-shu-kuan ts'ang shu-pan chi," *Che-chiang t'u-shu-kuan kuan-k'an* 4.3 (1935):19–20, lists the printing houses whose woodblocks have been donated to the Chekiang Provincial Library, providing a glimpse of the active printing firms there.

41. Nagasawa Kikuya, *Wa-Kan sho*, pp. 86–87, states that printing in Peking was limited to elite private printing or local materials.
42. Ibid., pp. 61, 87; Yeh Te-hui, *Shu-lin ch'ing-hua*, 9.22b–23b; Ch'ü Wan-li and Ch'ang Pi-te, *T'u-shu pan-pen hsüeh yao-lüeh*, p. 60, also names printing centers in Shantung, Kansu, Honan, and Chihli.
43. *Shun-te* HC, 3.50a.
44. See Liu Ts'un-yan's discussion of popular fiction printed at Fo-shan and elsewhere in *Chinese Popular Fiction*, pp. 32–36, and his list of Kwangtung bookstores, pp. 40–41.
45. According to Nagasawa Kikuya, *Wa-Kan sho*, p. 88, the Ma-kang books were coarse pocket editions; on p. 87 he cites the use of female labor in printing. See also Yeh Te-hui, *Shu-lin ch'ing-hua*, 7.13b–15a.
46. Sun Yü-hsiu, *Chung-kuo tiao-pan yüan-liu k'ao* (Shanghai, 1926), pp. 38–39. In contrast, as noted by K. T. Wu, "Ming Printing," p. 254, books printed in Peking were three times more expensive than those printed in Chekiang because of the high cost of paper.
47. Most of the information on Peking bookstores comes from *Liu-li-ch'ang shu-ssu-chi*, an account dated 1769 by Li Wen-tsao (1730–78): see Hummel, *Eminent Chinese* 1:175. Wang Yeh-ch'iu, *Liu-li-ch'ang shih-hua* (Peking, 1963) brings together these and other materials on the history of this street. See pp. 21, 41 for information on regional origins of dealers, a topic treated by Yeh Te-hui, *Shu-lin ch'ing-hua*, 9.26b–32b. Essays of this kind on book districts, by Yeh and others, have been collected in Yeh Te-hui et al., *Shu-lin chang-ku* (Hong King, 1972), but since most bibliophiles were primarily interested in rare books, the essays do not provide much information on the lower echelons of the market.
48. Ch'ing regulations for printing firms are printed in *Ch'in-ting hsüeh-cheng ch'üan shu*, chüan 14. For a typical exposition of the official objections to such works, see "Hsiao-hsüeh i-shu yü-lun," in Wang Hsiao-ch'uan, *Yüan Ming Ch'ing san-tai chin-hui hsiao-shuo hsi-ch'ü shih-liao* (Peking, 1958), which also contains the best collection of orders banning these publications. Prohibitions of the same kind are also found in compendia of local regulations such as the *Fu-chien sheng-li* (Taipei, 1964), pp. 1019–20, *Hsi-chiang hsüeh-cheng*, first ts'e, 4b–5a, 22a–23a; Chiang-su-sheng po-wu-kuan,

comp., *Chiang-su-sheng Ming Ch'ing i-lai pei-k'o tzu-liao hsüan chi,* sec. 15.

49. Wang Hsiao-ch'uan, *Yüan Ming Ch'ing,* pp. 111–12.
50. Ibid., pp. 156–57. One of the bookstores signing this agreement, the Sao-yeh shan fang, is cited by Sun Yü-hsiu, *Chung-kuo tiao-pan,* p. 38, as the Ch'ing bookstore printing the largest number of books.
51. "To prohibit Soochow prints of lascivious books and fiction," in Wang Hsiao-ch'uan, *Yüan Ming Ch'ing,* pp. 112–13, 220.
52. In Cheuk-woon Taam, *Development of Chinese Libraries,* p. 11.
53. Huang P'ei-lieh, ed., *Shih-li chü Huang-shih ts'ung-shu* (N.p., n.d. [ca. 1800]) includes the *Chi-ku ko chen-ts'ang mi-pen shu-mu* drawn up by Mao Chin's son.
54. The most expensive item was a manuscript copy of Sung poetry in the *tz'u* form (ibid., 25a); Mao's printed books included some for which he paid as little as .1 tael (about 100 cash). Calculation of the average price cited in the text omits all manuscripts.
55. Sun K'ai-ti, *Jih-pen Tung-ching,* pp. 118–22. See Idema, *Chinese Vernacular Fiction,* pp. lviii–lxi, for a discussion of the contrast between the deluxe editions of "literary novels" and the cheaper "chapbooks."
56. The work is a Fukien imprint, cited by K. T. Wu, "Ming Printing," p. 235. See also Sakai Tadao, "Mindai no nichiyō ruisho to shomin kyōiku," p. 151.
57. Sakai Tadao, "Mindai no nichiyō ruisho to shomin kyōiku," p. 151.
58. Chang Te-ch'ang, *Ch'ing-chi i-ko ching-kuan ti sheng-huo* (Hong Kong, 1970), itemizes various books purchased by the official Li Tz'u-ming in 1863, 1864, and 1875, on pp. 106–7, 112–13, 156. In 1875, for example, Li purchased two books at an average cost of 3.5 taels.
59. Carter, *Invention of Printing,* pp. 26–27. Movable type printing is treated by R.C. Rudolph, "Chinese Moveable Type Printing in the Eighteenth Century," in *Silver Jubilee Volume of the Zinbun-kagaku-kenkyusyo, Kyoto University,* ed. Kaizuka Shigeki (Kyoto, 1954), pp. 317–35.
60. *Chinese Repository* 1 (1832–33):420.
61. Ibid., p. 419. Government printing bureaus usually stored the blocks, as did private printers. Yüan Mei, for example, left his blocks to his heirs, who could thus reprint and derive future income from them: Waley, *Yuan Mei,* pp. 108–9, 200. Liu Ts'un-yan, *Chinese Popular Fiction,* p. 30, discusses the sale of printing blocks. This was not new: Carter, *Invention of Printing,* p. 59, cites the renting of blocks in a twelfth century account book.
62. Carter, *Invention of Printing,* p. 27.
63. K. T. Wu, "Ming Printing," p. 233. Perhaps the best way to glimpse

some of the niceties of materials in fine printing is to read accounts by bibliophiles: see Achilles Fang, "Bookman's Decalogue (*Ts'ang shu shih-yüeh*) by Yeh Te-hui," *Harvard Journal of Asiatic Studies* 13(1950):132–73, and "Bookman's Manual (*Ts'ang shu chi-yao*) by Sun Ts'ung-t'ien," *Harvard Journal of Asiatic Studies* 14(1951):215–60.

64. *T'ai-yüan chia-p'u*, #37 in Taga Akigorō, *Sōfu no kenkyū*, bibliography. The genealogy is dated 1802 but the itemized expenses for printing are clearly dated 1772–73; last chüan, 26b, cites price of ink; see 37b–38b, list of costs, and 32a–36a for an itemized chart of carving fees for the text, maps, genealogical charts, etc.

65. *T'ai-yüan chia-p'u*, Taga #38, in ibid. The genealogy is dated 1828 but the itemized expenditures for printing are dated 1789–90 and 1802. Last chüan, 57a, for paper costs. This approximates the cost of the paper used in the 1772–73 printing, which was 1.7 cash per sheet (last chüan, 1802 ed., 26b); paper used in printing another Kiangsu genealogy, *Tung-t'ing Tung-shan Wang-shih tsung-p'u* (1765 ed., Taga #608) was 1.5 cash per sheet (12.49a). According to this source, one sheet was cut to produce 3 folios or 6 pages.

66. Memorial by Chin Chien, presented in Ching Yu, "Ch'ing-tai yin-shuai-shih hsiao-chi," in Chang Ching-lu, ed., *Chung-kuo chin-tai ch'u-pan shih-liao* (Shanghai, 1962) 2:358, n.2. The estimated cost of woodblock printing was compared with movable wooden type, which was eventually the method adopted.

67. *Chinese Repository* 15(1846):424. Since Yeh Te-hui, *Shu-lin ch'ing-hua*, 7.13b–15a, says that in Hunan the cost of carving was 50–60 cash in the early years of the Kuang-hsü period (1874–1908), in 1846 the charge of 68 cash may well be higher than the minimum.

68. Yeh Te-hui, *Shu-lin ch'ing-hua*, 7.13b–15a.

69. If Yeh's first citation, carving charges in the late seventeenth century, is taken as 100 and an index made of subsequent changes in charges, the resulting series can be compared with the general index of prices prepared by Yeh-chien Wang, table 6, p. 361 in his "Secular Trend of Prices during the Ch'ing Period," which takes 1682 as the base year. The index number of 250–300 for carving woodblocks ca. 1875 is slightly higher than Wang's number of 240 for that year, while the carving cost of 650 ca. 1908 is slightly higher than Wang's index number of 600, but in general this comparison suggests that carving charges did not rise substantially in a real sense.

70. Yeh Te-hui, *Shu-lin ch'ing-hua*, 7.13b–15a; charges for female carvers were only 20–30 cash per hundred characters, in the early twentieth century.

71. When a bowl of noodles cost eight cash, as cited by Wu Ching-tzu, *The Scholars*, p. 353.

72. Smith, *Village Life*, pp. 69, 71.
73. *Chinese Repository* 1(1832–33):420–21, suggested distributing religious tracts by itinerant printers. Most towns must have had some printing activity to accommodate purely local markets, even if they did not produce books for long-distance trade. As we have noted, the simple techniques and tools used for woodblock printing permitted small-scale production.
74. Achilles Fang, "Bookman's Decalogue," pp. 148–49; a biography of Yeh that emphasizes his political activities is found in Boorman and Howard, *Biographical Dictionary of Republican China*, 4:35–37.
75. *Shang-ch'eng* HC, 6.3b.
76. Book rental stores are cited in Wang Hsiao-ch'uan, *Yüan Ming Ch'ing*, pp. 112–13; see chap. 1 for description of the Canton book rental peddlers.
77. Olga Lang, *Chinese Family and Society* (New Haven, 1946), pp. 73, 85, 91, 96.
78. Leo Lowenthal, *Literature, Popular Culture, and Society* (Englewood Cliffs, 1961), p. 52.
79. Ibid., pp. 52–108.
80. Chung Kun-ai, cited in Char, ed., *Sandalwood Mountains*, p. 257; J. MacGowan, *Men and Manners* p. 206, makes the same observation.

Chapter 6

1. Joseph Needham, *Science and Civilization in China* (Cambridge, 1959), vol. 3, sec. 19.
2. Smith, *Village Life*, p. 74.
3. Ibid.
4. Li Yen, *Shih-san, shih-ssu shih-chi Chung-kuo min-chien shu-hsüeh* (Peking, 1957), pp. 1–4, 60–65. Some of the rhymes that are simplified methods for multiplication and division are explained in English by Yoemon Yamazaki, "History of Instrumental Multiplication and Division in China—from the Reckoning-blocks to the Abacus," *Memoirs of the Research Department of the Toyo Bunko* 21(1962):133–44.
5. Yoemon Yamazaki, "History of Instrumental Multiplication," pp. 145–46, states that the reckoning blocks were used chiefly by tax officials and mathematicians, while the cruder abacus was popular "among the masses, the less intellectual tradesmen." Debates concerning the early history of the abacus are reported in Needham, *Science and Civilization*, 3:74–80.
6. A typical Ming arithmetic book is included in a popular encyclopedia (*Shih min*)*Wan-yung cheng-tsung pu ch'iu jen* (Orthodox teachings with myriad uses for scholars and commoners), a rare book owned by the Library of Congress. The chapter on arithmetic is chüan 14.

Others are included in *P'u Tseng t'ai-shih hui-tsuan ao-t'ou cho-yü tsa-tzu,* chüan 1; *Hsin ch'ieh Tseng t'ai-shih hui-tsuan su weng ch'i-meng cho-yü ao-t'ou,* a Japanese copy of a Ming work, sec. 2; the eighteenth century *Chin-ch'ang Tan-shan t'ang hsin-k'o tseng-ting shih-i ching-shu pien-yung t'ung-k'ao tsa-tzu,* and the virtually identical work issued by the San-huai t'ang, *Chin-ch'ang San-huai t'ang hsin-k'o tseng-ting shih-i ching-shu pien-yung t'ung-k'ao tsa-tzu,* which has an arithmetic section in the last chüan. See Cargill G. Knott, "The Abacus, in Its Historic and Scientific Aspects," *Transactions of the Asiatic Society of Japan* 14(1886):67. Yoemon Yamazaki, "History of Instrumental Multiplication," p. 133, describes the *chiu-kuei* as a new Sung method of seeking the quotient by means of the supplementary number of the divisor. See pp. 133–43 for descriptions of *chiu-kuei* and *kuei-ch'u.* According to Yamazaki, the *kuei-ch'u* appeared in the Yüan period as an improved revision of the *chiu-kuei* to use when the divisor was two or more places.

7. Smith, *Village Life,* pp. 34–35.
8. See concluding section, chap. 4, for details.
9. Sakai Tadao, "Mindai no nichiyō ruisho to shomin kyōiku," pp. 125–26; *tsa-tzu* are also studied by Chang Chih-kung, *Yü-wen chiao-yü,* pp. 27–32, and listed, pp. 159–61, in his bibliography. As explained in chap. 2, lessons for character recognition were separate from writing lessons.
10. P'u Sung-ling, preface, "Jih-yung su-tzu," *P'u Sung-ling chi* (Peking, 1962), p. 733. Chang Chih-kung, *Yü-wen chiao-yü,* p. 22; Ch'en Tung-yüan, *Chung-kuo k'o-hsüeh shih-tai,* p. 50; see Jaroslav Prusek's chapter, "P'u Sung-ling and His Work," *Chinese History and Literature,* p. 137.
11. *Shang-jao* HC, 7.75ab.
12. Chang Chih-kung, *Yü-wen chiao-yü,* pp. 27–28.
13. The linkage of *tsa-tzu* to the "square blocks" was suggested to me by my colleague Cho-yun Hsü.
14. Chang Chih-kung, *Yü-wen chiao-yü,* p. 27.
15. The first page of the text notes that it was newly printed by the Wang Chin-yu shu-t'ang of Nanking in Hung-wu, cyclical year *hsin-hai,* i.e. 1371. Reprinted in facsimile reproduction in Tokyo, 1920.
16. *Hsin-pien Tui-hsiang Szu-yen: 15th Century Illustrated Chinese Primer, with Introduction and Notes by L. Carrington Goodrich* (Hong Kong, 1967).
17. Held by the Cabinet Library, Tokyo, this edition notes on the first page that it was by the Sheng-te t'ang of Wu-men (Soochow). The catalog (*Naikaku bunko Kanseki bunrui mokuroku* [Tokyo, 1971] p. 51) states that it is a Ch'ing edition.
18. The catalog of the Tōyō bunko, which holds this book, lists it as a

Ch'ing publication; its inside page states that it was cut in the cyclical year *keng-shen* by the Wen-hua t'ang. The years corresponding to this cyclical designation in Ch'ing times were 1680, 1740, 1800, and 1860. The cyclical date and name of the printing house are repeated at the end of the work. The illustrated glossary appears in the second of three chüan.

19. This book belonged to the late Niida Noboru, who described it in his "Gen Min jidai no mura no kiyaku to kosaku shōsho nado," p. 161. Although it is undated, Niida suggested that the contract forms in it pointed to its being a late Ming product. The illustrated glossary appears as the first of three sections.
20. Although undated, this work is a Ch'ing publication, as can be seen by its use of the Yung-cheng reign name (1723–35) in a sample form: see upper column, last chüan, 41b. The illustrated glossary appears as the first of several sections. This book is held by the Harvard-Yenching Library.
21. This book also belonged to Niida Noboru and is discussed on pp. 162–63 of his "Gen Min jidai no mura no kiyaku to kosaku shōsho nado;" Niida guessed that it was a 1675–76 edition, corresponding to the cyclical year *ping-chen* which is printed on the cover. The Wen-hua t'ang which has its name printed on the inside cover is the same firm which produced text (A) in this group. The illustrated glossary section, which is the first of several parts, is identical with the illustrated glossary in text (B), except that this one is dated by the cyclical year *yi-mao,* which may be 1699.
22. L. Carrington Goodrich, "Introduction," *Hsin-pien Tui-hsiang.*
23. The "Eight Diagrams" were eight sets of trigrams (three broken and unbroken lines) used by Taoists in divination. Needham, *Science and Civilization,* 3:140, discusses a method of calculation connected with the *pa-kua*; for information on the secret society of that name, see Chesneaux, *Secret Societies,* pp. 38–40.
24. For example, in *K'an-t'u shih-tzu* (Shanghai, 1972).
25. The character *ling* which means "spirit," is present in the Group II illustrated glossaries but only as part of the compound *ling chih* referring to orchids. This is the only possible exception to the generalization.
26. *San Tzu Ching: Elementary Chinese,* trans. and annotated by Herbert A. Giles (New York, 1963) was the text used for the comparison. In his preface, p. v, Giles estimates that the book contains about 500 different characters out of a total of 1,068 characters. Citation comes from pp. 1–4.
27. Ibid., pp. 147–48.
28. If the characters in variant editions, included in the appendices by Giles, are counted, *i* appears eight times in the text.

29. Francis W. Paar, ed., *Ch'ien Tzu Wen: The Thousand Character Classic* (New York, 1963), p. 3. This edition was used for the comparison of characters that follows.
30. Ibid., p. 27.
31. Sakai Tadao, "Mindai no nichiyō ruisho to shomin kyōiku," p. 143, lists the firm as also publishing popular encyclopedias; it is not the Nanking firm of the same name cited by K. T. Wu, "Ming Printing," p. 236.
32. See category 21, 23a–28a.
33. *Chin yao tzu,* 2a.
34. Chang Chih-kung, *Yü-wen chiao-yü,* pp. 30–31. Copies of these works are not available in the United States. The title of the *Shantung nung-chuang jih-yung tsa-tzu* cited by Chang sounds very much like the *Nung-chuang tsa-tzu* that P'u Sung-ling mentioned: see n. 10.
35. Chang Chih-kung, *Yü-wen chiao-yü,* p. 31.
36. This work is held by the Cabinet Library, Tokyo, and is a Ming publication.
37. "Fourth Annual Report, Society for the Diffusion of Useful Knowledge in China," *Chinese Repository* 7(1838–39):402.
38. Olga Lang, *Pa Chin and His Writings,* p. 12.
39. Niida Noboru, "Gen Min jidai no mura no kiyaku;" Sakai Tadao, "Mindai no nichiyō ruisho to shomin kyōiku."

Chapter 7

1. If 30 percent of the men (males representing 52.3 percent of the population [see appendix 1]) were literate, they would constitute 15.7 percent of the population. If to this are added the 2–10 percent of Chinese women also estimated to be literate, then from 16.6 to 20.5 percent of the total population was literate. But if 45 percent of the men were literate, 24–28 percent of the total population would have been literate. Since average family size in China was probably close to five members each, there would thus have been an average of approximately one literate person per family. See appendix 1 for a discussion of the sex ratios on which these estimates are based.
2. Edwin O. Reischauer and John K. Fairbank, *East Asia: The Great Tradition* (Boston, 1960), 1:43. See Kristofer M Schipper, "The Written Memorial in Taoist Ceremonies," in *Religion and Ritual in Chinese Society,* ed. Arthur Wolf (Stanford, 1974), p. 324.
3. Mark Mancall, "The Ch'ing Tribute System: An Interpretive Essay," in *The Chinese World Order,* ed. J. K. Fairbank (Cambridge, Mass., 1968), p. 65. According to Mancall, the political expression of this importance was that Chinese valued the credentials and letter

carried by an ambassador more highly than his person, in contradiction to the Western concept that an emissary partook of his master's official personality. Such divergent concepts could provoke international misunderstandings.

4. Doolittle, *Social Life,* 2:169–70, describes these societies, which propagated the belief that those desecrating written papers might be punished by being born blind in their next reincarnation.
5. Mote, "The Rural 'Haw' of Northern Thailand," 2:516.
6. Noted by Owen Lattimore, "Chinese Colonization in Inner Mongolia: Its History and Development," in *Pioneer Settlement: Cooperative Studies by Twenty-six Authors,* ed. W. L. G. Joerg, American Geographical Society Special Publication, no. 14 (New York, 1932), p. 307.
7. J. J. M. de Groot, *The Religious System of China* (Leiden, 1892), 5:905; on pp. 918–19, de Groot describes various written charms. For example, a piece of paper with the character "to kill" would be hidden in someone's clothing in an attempt to kill him and his entire family; characters for diseases, insects, spectres, etc., could also be used in the same manner. Yu-wen Jen, *Taiping Revolutionary Movement,* pp. 102–3, describes the importance of seals among these rebels.
8. David Jordan, *Gods, Ghosts, and Ancestors* (Berkeley, 1972), pp. 64–67, describes such a method of divination still practiced on Taiwan.
9. C. K. Yang, *Religion in Chinese Society* (Berkeley, 1967), p. 17; see his explanation, pp. 135–36, of the assumptions lying behind the concept of "lucky" and "unlucky" days. See also Kulp, *Country Life in South China,* pp. 186–87, 278–79.
10. Discussed by Laurence G. Thompson, *Chinese Religion: An Introduction* (Belmont, Calif., 1969), pp. 23–25.
11. Hok-lam Chan, "The White Lotus—Maitreya Doctrine and Popular Uprisings in Ming and Ch'ing China," *Sinologica* 10(1969):217–18, discusses the visual cryptograms used in the White Lotus prophecy that Niu Pa (lit. "Cow Eight") would overthrow the Manchus and restore the Ming dynasty. The two characters "Cow" (*niu*) and "Eight" (*pa*) when combined form the character "Chu," the surname of the Ming ruling house. Similar cryptograms are described by Chesneaux, *Secret Societies,* pp. 30, 55, 56. See Yu-wen Jen, *Taiping Revolutionary Movement,* pp. 153–54, which discusses Taiping publications.
12. T. J. Newbold and F. W. Wilson, "The Chinese Triad Society of the Tien-ti-huih," *Journal of the Royal Asiatic Society of Great Britain and Ireland* 6(1841):120–58. See also Stanford M. Lyman, W. E. Willmott, and Berching Ho, "Rules of a Secret Society in British

Columbia," *Bulletin of the School of Oriental and African Studies* 27(1964):530–39.

13. J. J. M. de Groot, "Inscriptions on Red Paper, Pictures etc. on Chinese Street-doors," *The China Review* 9(1880–81):20; W. H. Medhurst, *the Foreigner in Far Cathay* (New York, 1873), pp. 144–45.
14. Cipolla, *Literacy and Development in the West,* pp. 12–13.
15. The importance of boxing masters as a link between various groups in a rebellion is described by John W. Dardess, "The Transformations of Messianic Revolt and the Founding of the Ming Dynasty," *Journal of Asian Studies* 29.3(1970):542, and Jerome Ch'en, "The Origin of the Boxers," in *Studies in the Social History of China and Southeast Asia: Essays in Memory of Victor Purcell,* ed. Jerome Ch'en and Nicholas Tarling (Cambridge, 1970), pp. 70–72.
16. G. William Skinner, "Chinese Peasants and the Closed Community: An Open and Shut Case," *Comparative Studies in Society and History* 13.3(1971):275, 277 cites this as one of the distinguishing characteristics of Chinese society.
17. Discussed in Ping-ti Ho, *Studies on the Population of China,* pp. 136–63.
18. Eisenstein, "Advent of Printing and the Problem of the Renaissance"; Einsenstein, "Some Conjectures About the Impact of Printing on Western Society and Thought"; Elizabeth L. Eisenstein, "The Advent of Printing in Historical Literature: Notes and Comments on an Elusive Transformation," *American Historical Review* 74.3(1970):727–43. The impact of printing on Tudor science is described by Antonia McLean, *Humanism and the Rise of Science in Tudor England* (New York, 1972), pp. 91–102.
19. Cheuk-woon Taam, *The Development of Chinese Libraries,* pp. 15–17.
20. This is the subject of Leo Lowenthal's "The Debate Over Art and Popular Culture: English Eighteenth Century as a Case Study," in his *Literature, Popular Culture, and Society,* pp. 52–108.
21. Natalie Davis, "Printing and the People," in her *Society and Culture in Early Modern France* (Stanford, 1975), pp. 193–94, 211–18.
22. Ibid., pp. 195, 210.
23. Ibid., p. 209.
24. R. M. Hartwell discusses various positions in the debate in his *The Industrial Revolution and Economic Growth* (London, 1971), pp. 226–44. More recently, evidence cited by Michael Sanderson, "Literacy and Social Mobility in the Industrial Revolution in England," *Past and Present* 56(1972):75–104, supports the conclusion that a decline in literacy was brought about by social and demographic factors linked with the Industrial Revolution. Evaluation of illiteracy

in marriage registers, taken from a random sample of 274 parishes, 1754–1840, leads R. S. Schofield to conclude that the English case does not support the thesis that there is a positive relationship between education and economic growth: "Dimensions of Illiteracy, 1750–1850," *Explorations in Economic History* 10.4(1973):437–54.

25. Alex Inkeles and David H. Smith, *Becoming Modern* (Cambridge, Mass., 1974), p. 174. See chaps. 9, 11.
26. Sidney Pollard, "Factory Discipline in the Industrial Revolution," *Economic History Review*, 2d ser., 16.2(1963):254–59, 267–70.
27. Philippe Aries, *Centuries of Childhood,* trans. Robert Baldick (New York, 1962), p. 309; also pp. 312–13, 334–35. See also Richard Johnson, "Educational Policy and Social Control in Early Victorian England," *Past and Present* 49(1970):96–119.
28. Dore, *Education in Tokugawa Japan,* chap. 10, pp. 101–4.
29. M. B. Jansen and L. Stone, "Education and Modernization in Japan and England," *Comparative Studies in Society and History* 9.2(1967):219–23, compares mid-seventeenth century England and mid-nineteenth century Japan, each on the eve of a revolution, and notes that the male literacy rate for adults in both societies was about one-third. This essay states (p. 228) that "the very high rate of literacy in the mid-nineteenth century clearly put Japan in a class by itself compared with any other non-Western country."
30. In addition to Dore's *Education in Tokugawa Japan,* see his essay, "The Legacy of Tokugawa Education," in *Changing Japanese Attitudes Toward Modernization,* ed. Marius B. Jansen (Princeton, 1965), pp. 99–131; Dore's estimates of the percentage of Japanese receiving schooling are discussed in his *Education in Tokugawa Japan,* app. 1, pp. 317–22. If one takes his estimate that 43 percent of the boys and 10 percent of the girls received some sort of schooling, on the basis of the 1852 sex ratio approximately 27 percent of the Japanese population would have received some sort of schooling in late Tokugawa times. Sex ratio from Irene B. Taeuber, *The Population of Japan* (Princeton, 1958), p. 22, table 3. Marius Jansen, "Tokugawa and Modern Japan," in *Studies in the Institutional History of Early Modern Japan,* ed. J. W. Hall and M. B. Jansen (Princeton, 1968), p. 325, cites over 35 percent as a possible figure.
31. E. Sydney Crawcour, "The Tokugawa Heritage," in *The State and Economic Enterprise in Japan,* ed. W. W. Lockwood (Princeton, 1965), p. 34. Jansen and Stone, "Education and Modernization in Japan and England," pp. 208–32, discuss rates of literacy rather than schooling. Jansen's essay on "Tokugawa and Modern Japan" also refers to Japan's literacy rate. The dangers of equating education or school attendance with literacy are ably discussed by Cipolla in his *Literacy and Development in the West,* chap. 1; and (for

Japan) by Koji Taira, "Education and Literacy in Meiji Japan: An Interpretation," *Explorations in Economic History* 8.4(1971):371–94.

32. Kazushi Ohkawa and Henry Rosovsky, *Japanese Economic Growth: Trend Acceleration in the Twentieth Century* (Stanford, 1973), table 3.6, p. 56.
33. Tokugawa attitudes toward education are discussed by Dore, "The Legacy of Tokugawa Education," pp. 105–8, and by Jansen, "Tokugawa and Modern Japan," pp. 326–27.
34. Dore, *Education in Tokugawa Japan,* chaps. 3, 4, 9. Jansen and Stone point out that since the same Confucian texts used in Chinese academies did not "on balance, produce 'ministers of modernization' in the same way," it may be difficult to say more than that "Tokugawa Confucian education, *per se,* did not rule out modernization," see their "Education and Modernization in Japan and England," p. 211.
35. Suzuki Kenichi, "Min Shin shakai to Edo bakufu no minshū kyōka shisō—Roku yu o ichirei to shite," *Rekishi kyōiku* 15.9–10 (1967):148–49.
36. This is described by Dore, "The Legacy of Tokugawa Education," p. 103; see chap. 1 for descriptions of Chinese government practices.
37. These are areas identified in ibid., pp. 101–4. It should be clear from previous discussions of the Chinese civil service examination system, notably in Ping-ti Ho, *The Ladder of Success,* that Chinese education was oriented to selection for government service, permitted significant social mobility, and encouraged positive attitudes toward acquiring knowledge.
38. Perkins, "Introduction: The Persistence of the Past," pp. 1–18.
39. Dwight H. Perkins makes this comparison in "Government as an Obstacle to Industrialization: The Case of Nineteenth Century China," *Journal of Economic History* 27.4(1967):487. Perkins estimates that central government revenues in China were 1 or 2 per cent of GNP, as compared with the Meiji government's revenues, which were 25–27 percent of Japan's national income: see Crawcour, "Tokugawa Heritage," p. 31.

Chapter 8

1. Cited by Lawrence Stone, "Literacy and Education in England, 1640–1900," *Past and Present* 42(1969):83–84. See Arthur Wright, "Propaganda and Persuasion in Imperial and Contemporary China," *Rice University Studies* 59.4(1973):11–15.
2. Hao Chang, *Liang Ch'i-ch'ao and Intellectual Transition in China, 1890–1907* (Cambridge, Mass., 1971), discusses the "new citizen"

in chaps. 6, 8, 9, and 10. See Philip Huang, *Liang Ch'i-ch'ao*, pp. 30–31, 164–65.

3. On KMT programs, see Lloyd Eastman, *The Abortive Revolution: China under Nationalist Rule, 1927–1937* (Cambridge, Mass., 1974), pp. 48–50. Benjamin I. Schwartz, *Communism and China: Ideology in Flux* (Cambridge, Mass., 1968), p. 175, identifies "the enormous emphasis on the power of spiritual transformation" to bring about collectivist society as one of the characteristics of the Maoist vision. See his discussion, pp. 15–16, 41–42, 86, on the doctrine of remolding thought, and p. 177 on the links between this spiritual transformation and the overcoming of material barriers to progress. The continuity between post-1949 emphases on education and traditional attitudes is demonstrated in Donald J. Munro, *Concept of Man in Early China*, pp. 165–74. Stuart Schram, "The Cultural Revolution in Historical Perspective," in *Authority, Participation, and Cultural Change in China*, ed. S. Schram (Cambridge, 1973), p. 57.
4. Kulp, *Country Life in South China*, pp. 218–19; at the same time, Kulp noted, p. 228, that 44 percent of the children of school age were attending school. See also Herbert Lamson, "The Effect of Industrialization upon Village Livelihood," *Chinese Economic Journal* 9.4(1931):1069–72.
5. William Ayers, *Chang Chih-tung and Educational Reform in China* (Cambridge, Mass. 1971), pp. 210–11, 215–16, 220; David Buck, "Educational Modernization in Tsinan, 1899–1937," in *The Chinese City Between Two Worlds*, ed. M. Elvin and G. W. Skinner (Stanford, 1970), pp. 182–83.
6. Theodore E. Hsiao, *The History of Modern Education in China* (Shanghai, 1935), p. 34.
7. In addition to those listed in ibid., there were the modern primary and middle schools founded in Chuchow and Wenchow, noted in Mary B. Rankin, *Early Chinese Revolutionaries: Radical Intellectuals in Shanghai and Chekiang, 1902–1911* (Cambridge, Mass., 1971), pp. 140–41. In addition, Gamble, *Ting Hsien*, p. 188, states that the first modern school in Ting county, Chihli, was opened in 1894; but it is not clear whether this was a primary school.
8. Rankin, *Early Chinese Revolutionaries*, pp. 140–41.
9. Samuel Chu, *Reformer in Modern China* (New York, 1965), pp. 95–96, 98, 105; see also pp. 100–101.
10. This topic is covered by Taga Akigorō in part two of "Kindai Chūgoku ni okeru zokujuku no seikaku" pp. 225–36. *Ssu-ming Chu-shih chih-p'u nei-wai pien*, 15.1a; *Ta-fu P'an-shih chih-p'u*, 30.23a. Kulp, *Country Life in South China*, p. 124, relates that village income from public land was used to reward graduates of modern middle schools and colleges.

11. Theodore E. Hsiao, *History of Modern Education*, pp. 33–34.
12. Ogawa Yoshiko, "Shindai ni okeru gigaku," pp. 275–77. Of thirty-two charitable schools listed, seven or about 22 percent, were not converted but were abolished or otherwise closed. The bulk of the schools were converted into modern primary schools in 1905–7.
13. Nakamura Tsune, "Shinmatsu gakudō setsuritsu o meguru—Kō Setsu nōson shakai no ichi danmen," *Rekishi kyōiku* 10.11(1962):76, table 4. Since there was a general expansion in schools during this period, many new schools were created, including most of the 199 elementary schools for Shu-lu hsien, Chihli: *Shu-lu wu-chih ho-k'an* #5, 9.2b–10b. But another Chihli county, Wen-an, recorded that in 1906 its old charitable school was abolished and a lower primary school established: *Wen-an* HC, 12.23a. In Kiangsu, T'ung-shan county recorded a total of 61 elementary schools established 1907–11, mostly new ones: *T'ung-shan* HC, 16.9a–13a. I-hsing county in the same province lists 2 charitable schools that were converted to modern primary schools in 1907–8: *I-hsing* HC, p. 1003. Of the 84 primary schools listed in *Chiang-yin* HC, pp. 378–98, 17 were former charitable schools, 1 was a former private school, and another a former academy. Of a total of 25 lower and combined primary schools founded from 1905–11 in She hsien, Anhwei, some used temples, others used former academy buildings, and one was housed in a former charitable school: *She* HC, 2.11a–12b. In Shensi, the *Pao-chi* HC, 4.7a, notes that the 16 charitable schools which had been revived in 1872–73 by a district magistrate were all converted in 1908–9 into modern lower primary schools by a successor.
14. T'ai-ch'u Liao, "School Land: A Problem of Educational Finance," *Yenching Journal of Social Studies* 2.2(1940):214–16, 228–33. The shifting of charitable school funds to the modern primary schools is frequently cited in gazetteers. For examples, see *Wen-an* HC, 12.23a; *Chiang-yin* HC, pp. 378–98.
15. Ayers, *Chang Chih-tung*, pp. 163–64. Chang subsequently discovered (pp. 233–34) that he had been overoptimistic.
16. Samuel Chu, *Reformer in Modern China*, p. 94.
17. Theodore E. Hsiao, *History of Modern Education*, pp. 45–47.
18. Cyrus Peake, *Nationalism and Education in Modern China* (New York, 1932), pp. 43–46, 50–51; Samuel Chu, *Reformer in Modern China*, pp. 92–93. Sidney Gamble, *Peking: A Social Survey* (Peking, 1921), p. 131, writes that the Japanese teachers were gradually replaced by Chinese returned students, and most of the Japanese had gone by 1910.
19. Gamble, *Peking*, p. 131.
20. David Buck, "Educational Modernization," pp. 186–87, reporting on Huang Yen-p'ei's tour of 1914.

21. Peake, *Nationalism and Education,* pp. 52–53. In app. 1, pp. 159–93, Peake identifies and briefly describes the contents of some popular textbooks used in primary and middle schools, 1905–29.
22. John Darroch, "Chinese Textbooks," *Journal of the North China Branch of the Royal Asiatic Society* 37(1906):214.
23. An exception to this generalization is the late Ming–early Ch'ing philosopher Yen Yüan (1635–1704), who criticized Sung and Ming schools and educational methods, including the emphasis on reading and quiet sitting in conventional classrooms, for producing the physically weak scholar whom farmers and soldiers ridiculed. See Shen Kuan-ch'ün, *Chung-kuo ku-tai chiao-yü ho chiao-yü ssu-hsiang* (Wuhan, 1956), pp. 129–33; Meng Hsien-ch'eng et al., comp. *Chung-kuo ku-tai chiao-yü shih tzu-liao* (Peking, 1961), pp. 400–405 present excerpts of Yüan's ideas on education.
24. Darroch, "Chinese Textbooks," p. 210.
25. The hierarchy of national schools endorsed by the Ministry of Education changed from time to time: see Theodore E. Hsiao, *History of Modern Education,* pp. 34–35.
26. J. MacGowan, *Men and Manners,* pp. 89–90. Another possible hindrance to the spread of modern education was its cost. According to Hsiang-po Lee, "Rural-Mass Education Movement in China, 1923–1937," (Ph.D. diss., Ohio State University, 1970), pp. 97–98, elementary school fees were $50–$100 (Chinese $) a year in 1930, a sum which represented from 14 to 30 percent of average monthly incomes for households in cities such as Nanking, Shanghai, Canton, and Peking. Lee concludes that most people could not afford to send their children to school. Sidney Gamble, *The Household Accounts of Two Chinese Families* (New York, 1931), p. 20, found tuition charges of only $25 per child per year in Peking in 1924, so Lee's figures may be upwardly biased. Of course, tuition fees of $25 a year were still beyond the reach of most Chinese, since the average income of a farmer, ca. 1923, was only $44.25 (Hsiang-po Lee, "Rural-Mass Education," p. 98).
27. J. Stewart Burgess, "Some Observations on Chinese Village Life," *Social Forces* 11.3(1933):408. David Buck, "Educational Modernization," p. 192.
28. Ida Belle Lewis, "A Study of Primary Schools," in *China,* ed. Orville A. Petty (New York, 1933), pp. 618–19.
29. David Buck, "Educational Modernization," pp. 195–96.
30. T'ai-ch'u Liao, "Rural Education in Transition: A Study of Old-fashioned Chinese Schools (Szu Shu) in Shantung and Szechwan," *Yenching Journal of Social Studies* 4.2(1949):19–67. This study was called to my attention by G. W. Skinner.
31. Kulp, *Country Life in South China,* pp. 221–24; Martin C. Yang,

Chinese Village, p. 146; Myers, *Chinese Peasant Economy*, pp. 62, 119. Sidney Gamble, *North China Villages: Social, Political and Economic Activities before 1933* (Berkeley, 1963), Village "H" on pp. 238–39; Burgess, "Some Observations," p. 408, on the village of San Chia Tien.

32. Hsing cheng yüan, Chu chi ch'u, T'ung-chi chü, comp., "Nien-ssu nien tu ch'üan-kuo ssu-shu t'ung-chi," *T'ung-chi chi-pao* 8(1936):2–4. Statistics from Hunan, the Manchurian provinces, Sinkiang, and areas like Weihaiwei were not included in these figures. In addition, statistics from Kiangsi, Hupei, Yunnan, Shantung, Szechwan, and Kweichow were incompletely reported, with only 33 to over 50 percent of returns completed. In all, 18 percent of the counties and directly administered municipalities in the twenty provinces covered by the statistics failed to report. The representation of private schools in the national system is obtained by including appended totals for private schools in Anhwei and Shensi, p. 4, and using the comparative national school totals provided for 1933 on p. 4.
33. Lewis, "A Study of Primary Schools," p. 619. David Buck, "Educational Modernization," pp. 210–11 describes Wenshang as shifting from espousal to rejection of modern education in the middle and late 1920s. At the same time, the number of modern schools in Wenshang before the mid-1920s was so small that it could not have fundamentally altered traditional dominance in education.
34. T'ai-ch'u Liao, "Rural Education," p. 22.
35. Ibid., pp. 22, 48. A similar bias in enrollments is noted by Burgess, "Some Observations," p. 408, who found that the three private traditional schools in San Chia Tien enrolled twice the number of students as the modern primary school.
36. T'ai-ch'u Liao, "Rural Education," pp. 27, 36; the two modern school-teachers in Kulp's village were both higher primary school graduates under age 30: *Country Life in South China*, p. 233.
37. T'ai-ch'u Liao, "Rural Education," p. 37; Kulp, *Country Life in South China*, p. 221.
38. T'ai-ch'u Liao, "Rural Education," p. 49; Kulp, *Country Life in South China*, pp. 112–13; Jen-chi Chang, *Pre-Communist China's Rural School and Community*, writes on the basis of his work with the Kiangsi Rural Welfare Service in the 1930s. But a contrary view is expressed by J. Stewart Burgess, "Community Organization in China," *Far Eastern Survey* 14.25(1945):372, who says only men with a modern education could provide the village with leadership as changing regulations affected local areas.
39. T'ai-ch'u Liao, "Rural Education," pp. 46–47.
40. Ibid.; Kulp, *Country Life in South China*, pp. 229–30; Hsiao-t'ung

Fei, *Peasant Life in China: A Field Study of Country Life in the Yangtze Valley* (London, 1939), pp. 39–40.

41. T'ai-ch'u Liao, "Rural Education," pp. 46–47; this rejection is especially noteworthy because the government schools were free (p. 45) while the private schools charged tuition (p. 38).
42. Ibid., p. 33.
43. Ibid., p. 35. 83 percent of the teachers were natives of Wenshang county, 65 percent being members of the same village or township in which they taught.
44. See Eastman, *Abortive Revolution*, pp. 240–43. David Buck, "Educational Modernization," pp. 200–201, notes that such a breakdown of control occurred in parts of Shantung during the Republican period.
45. Martin Bernal, *Chinese Socialism to 1907* (Ithaca, N. Y., 1976), p. 130.
46. T'ai-ch'u Liao, "Rural Education," pp. 55, 58–60. The modern subjects occupied about a quarter of the curriculum.
47. See Yen's biography in Boorman and Howard, *Biographical Dictionary of Republican China*, 4:52–54.
48. Ibid., 3:243–248; see Hsiang-po Lee, "Rural-Mass Education," pp. 162–84, 247–67.
49. Hsiang-po Lee, "Rural-Mass Education," p. 171.
50. Boorman and Howard, *Biographical Dictionary of Republican China*, 3:246.
51. Ibid., 2:357–359. See also Hsiang-po Lee, "Rural-Mass Education," pp. 184–204, 231–47, and Guy S. Alitto, "Rural Reconstruction during the Nanking Decade: Confucian Collectivism in Shantung," *China Quarterly* 66(1976):213–46.
52. Hsiang-po Lee, "Rural-Mass Education," p. 246, Alitto, "Rural Reconstruction," pp. 242–43; Wen-shun Chi, "Liang Shu-ming and Chinese Communism," *China Quarterly* 41(1970):79–80.
53. Alitto, "Rural Reconstruction," pp. 217–36.
54. According to Lary, *Region and Nation*, pp. 181–82, the basic educational movement was one of the successes in the reconstruction movement carried out by this province's warlords.
55. Hsiang-po Lee, "Rural-Mass Education," pp. 119–30.
56. Ibid., pp. 116, 241.
57. Hawkins, *Mao Tse-tung and Education*, pp. 98–99.
58. See Mao Tse-tung, *Mo Taku-to shū*, comp. Takeuchi Minoru (Tokyo, 1972), 2:117 (written in 1929).
59. Hawkins, *Mao Tse-tung and Education*, pp. 98–100, 147. Many of the citations are from Mao's "Ch'ang-kang hsiang tiao-ch'a," reprinted in Mao Tse-tung, *Mo Taku-to shū*, 4:158–59.
60. Taken from "Ch'ang-kang hsiang tiao-ch'a," in Mao Tse-tung, *Mo Taku-to shū*, 4:158–159.

61. Y. C. James Yen, "New Citizens for China," p. 273.
62. Cited in David Buck, "Educational Modernization," p. 207; Liang Shu-ming's program has been studied by Harry Lamley, "Liang Shu-ming, Rural Reconstruction, and the Rural Work Discussion Society, 1933–35," *Chung Chi Journal* 8.2(1969):50–61.
63. This is the subject of Seybolt, "The Yenan Revolution in Mass Education." The popular education movement is also treated by Selden, *The Yenan Way in Revolutionary China*, pp. 267–74.
64. "Pien-ch'ü cheng-fu kuan-yü t'i ch'ang yen-chiu fan-li chi shih-hsing min-pan hsiao-hsüeh ti chih-shih-hsin," *Shen-Kan-Ning pien-ch'ü chiao-yü fang-chi* (April 1944), pp. 7–8, translated in *Chinese Education* 4.4(1971–72):269–75; but the translation used is my own. I am indebted to Peter Seybolt and Nicholas Lardy who provided me with copies of the original text. This text is also cited in Hawkins, *Mao Tse-tung and Education*, p. 101.
65. Selden, *The Yenan Way*, pp. 270–271. On the need for literate cadres see p. 159.
66. Ibid., p. 268; Y. C. James Yen, "China's New Scholar-Farmer," *Asia* 29(1929):160.
67. Vincent T. C. Lin, "Adult Education," pp. 179–200 (winter schools for peasants), 203–21 (people's schools for peasants), 222–51 (workers' spare-time schools).
68. Peake, *Nationalism and Education*, app. 1, pp. 159–93, provides some examples of popular textbooks; also see Darroch, "Chinese Textbooks."
69. Darroch, "Chinese Textbooks," p. 208.
70. T'ang Mao-ju, "Ch'eng-shih p'ing-min hsüeh-hsiao ti chiao-ts'ai," *Chiao-yü tsa-chih* 19.10(1927):1–2. The sources cited in discussing mass education texts were brought to my attention by Charles Hayford.
71. Ibid., p. 2.
72. Ch'en Ho-ch'in, comp., *Yü-t'i wen ying-yung tzu-hui* (Shanghai, 1931), pp. 6–11. Ch'en's first character list was criticized for leaving out some major terms while including less important characters. This defect may have partially arisen from the fact that two of his categories of vernacular materials, which compromised over 30 percent of the characters counted, were primary school materials, written for an orthodox and longer educational sequence.
73. Liu Te-wen, "P'ing chiao tsung-hui *Kai-pien ch'ien tzu k'o* chien-tzu kung-tso ti ching-kuo," *Chiao-yü tsa-chih* 18.12(1926):10–12.
74. Y. C. James Yen, "New Citizens for China," pp. 266–68. The *Thousand-Character Readers* were also used in missionary programs: see Horace Chandler, "The Work of the American Presbyterian Mission."

75. T'ang Mao-ju, "Ch'eng-shih p'ing-min," p. 3; Y. C. James Yen, "New Citizens for China," p. 275.
76. Barry Keenan, "Educational Reform and Politics in Early Republican China," *Journal of Asian Studies* 33.2(1974):230, writes about Chiang Meng-lin's advocacy of popular education as a goal within the New Culture movement.
77. Lang, *Chinese Family and Society*, pp. 72–73.
78. Ibid., footnote, p. 73; further information is provided on pp. 85, 91, 96, and footnote, pp. 96–97. See Kulp, *Country Life in South China*, pp. 278–79, but Phenix Village was unusual because it had a public reading room, stocked with a Swatow newspaper and magazines from Canton and Shanghai (p. 246).
79. Myers, *Chinese Peasant Economy*, p. 62, on Sha-ching village; and p. 119, on Hou Hsia Chai.
80. Hsü Hsü, "Shanghai hsiao shu-pao t'an tiao-ch'a," in his *T'u-shu-kuan yü min-chung chiao-yü* (Ch'ang-sha, 1941): bookvendor survey, pp. 142–80; newsvendor survey, pp. 181–213. New serials were the most expensive, at one cash per volume. Old issues rented for one cash per two or three volumes or five to six cash for a whole set (p. 159). The evolution of comic book rentals is treated by A Ying, *Chung-kuo lien-huan*, p. 27, who states that the distribution network was established by publishers who expanded their operations to include not only markets in China but in Southeast Asia as well. Wolfram Eberhard, "Notes on Chinese Story Tellers," *Fabula* 11(1970):26–27, describes such lending stalls in Taipei in 1967.
81. Hsü Hsü, "Shanghai hsiao shu-pao," p. 155; Hsü's table, pp. 156–57, shows that these primers represented 5–10 percent of the stock.
82. Although undated, the glossaries edited by Sung Hao-ling seem to be late Ch'ing or early Republican publications, resembling the 1918 *Hui-t'u shih-tzu shih-tsai-i* closely; these are the *Hui-t'u ssu-ch'ien tzu wen; Hui-t'u wu-ch'ien tzu wen; Hui-t'u liu-ch'ien tzu wen*, and *Chu shih hui-t'u ch'i-ch'ien tzu wen*. Another very similar work, also undated, is the "Newly expanded illustrated ten-thousand character glossary" (*Hsin tseng hiu-t'u yi-wan tzu wen*), published by the Wen-hsing book firm.
83. This is a ten-volume work edited by Shih Ch'ung-en and published in Shanghai in 1918.
84. Words for artisans' crafts were also included.
85. Munemitsu Abe, "Spare-time Education in Communist China: A General Survey," in *Education and Communism in China*, ed. Stewart E. Fraser (London, 1971), pp. 245–46. According to Paul Harper, "Problems of Spare-time Schools," pp. 261–62 in the same volume, a higher standard of 2,000 characters was set for workers.
86. *Hsin-pien ssu-yen tsa-tzu* (Nan-ch'ang, 1964), p. 1.

87. For example, chapters on articles of clothing, common utensils, and the like.
88. Trans. Seybolt, in his *Revolutionary Education in China: Documents and Commentary*, p. 195.

Appendix 1

1. Ping-ti Ho, *Studies on the Population*, pp. 57–62; Frank Notestein and Chi-ming Chiao, "Population," in *Land Utilization*, by John Lossing Buck, 1:376, table 12; Ch'eng-hsin Chao, "Familism as a Factor in the Chinese Population Balance," *Yenching Journal of Social Studies* 3.1(1940):15, table 4, presents data from other sources. The 47.7 percent figure is taken from Chi-ming Chiao, "A Study of the Chinese Population," *Milbank Memorial Fund Quarterly Bulletin* 12.1(1934):96, table 12. This is the sex ratio for the total population: as Chiao shows, table 11, p. 95, the sex ratio varies considerably when broken down by age group, and especially favors males in ages 5–19.
2. Ping-ti Ho, *Studies on the Population*, p. 57.
3. Ibid., table 14, pp. 58–59. Chihli figures on p. 58.
4. Chi-ming Chiao, "Study of the Chinese Population," table 10, p. 92. These figures are quite similar to those presented by Irene B. Taeuber, "The Families of Chinese Farmers," in *Family and Kinship in Chinese Society*, ed. Maurice Freedman (Stanford, 1970), table 3, p. 70, (for "Northern Plain"), which were 35 percent for males and 32.9 percent for females below age fifteen.
5. Assuming that the 9.6 percent of males aged 15–19 were evenly distributed through each of the five years covered, an estimated 1.9 percent would be added on to the 36.3 percent of males aged 0–14: see Chi-ming Chiao, "Study of the Chinese Population," table 10, p. 92. The same procedure was followed for females, and resulted in a figure of 38.2 percent of males and 35.8 percent of females aged 0–15. If these figures are applied to Chiao's sex ratio (109), it follows that 37 percent of the total population was under age 16.
6. Here a procedure like the one described in the preceding footnote was used to obtain an estimate of the percentage of males aged 7–9, using the data in Chi-ming Chiao, ibid. The "All China" figures were used. This was added to the percentage of males aged 10–14 to obtain the figure of 17.9 percent.
7. Nai-ruenn Chen and Walter Galenson, *The Chinese Economy under Communism* (Chicago, 1969), p. 4. There was of course considerable regional diversity in social-economic stratification: in northern Kiangsu in 1939, for example, poor peasants and rural laborers combined constituted less than 50 percent of the rural population: Robert Ash,

"Economic Aspects of Land Reform in Kiangsu, 1949–52," *China Quarterly* 66(1976):268, table.

Appendix 2

1. With special thanks to Gilbert Rozman, who introduced me to these documents, held in microfilm by Princeton's Gest Library and the Hoover Library, Stanford University.
2. Momose Hiromu, "Shinmatsu Chokurei-shō no sonzu san shu ni tsuite," in *Katō Hakase kanreki kinen: Tōyō shi shūsetsu,* ed. Katō Hakase kanreki kinen ronbunshū kankō kai (Tokyo, 1941), pp. 841–60.
3. See Rozman, *Urban Networks,* pp. 174–75, 151, 168–70.
4. According to Yu-wen Jen, *Taiping Revolutionary Movement,* pp. 181–82, the Taiping rebels entered Chihli in 1853, capturing Shen-chou and eventually moving east and north to take Ts'ang-chou then Ching-hai, cities on the Grand Canal directly south and north of Ch'ing hsien: see Jen's map, p. 568.
5. Momose Hiromu, "Shinmatsu Chokurei-shō son-chin kokō shōkō," *Tōhōgakuhō* (Tokyo) 12.3(1941):108–9. The disturbance also explains why most of the largest settlements are in spots distant from the Grand Canal and the hsien city, where the bulk of rebel action took place. Momose's figure of 145,810 for the *ts'un-t'u* population total is wrong; the figure 148,166 was obtained from Gilbert Rozman, who has been working extensively with these materials.
6. *Shen-chou feng-t'u chi,* 1900 ed., pp. 231–32. A list of the charitable schools in operation ca. 1866, when Chang Ying-ling was serving as assistant chou magistrate (*chou-p'an*), indicates that there were 219 schools at that time, and only 141 a decade later (see table 20). In this chou the number of *i-hsüeh* thus declined through the nineteenth century: pp. 434, 233–39.
7. Data obtained from the *ts'un-t'u.* Shen-chou's population is undercounted because the "Shen-chou ts'un-t'u" lacks information on the eastern quarter of the city. According to the definitions for levels of central places presented in Rozman, *Urban Networks,* table 3, p. 60, Cheng-ting was a level 4; Ch'ing hsien, a level 5; and Shen-chou, a level 7 central place.
8. These would all be level 7 central places according to Rozman's definition.
9. Data for Ch'ing hsien was taken from Momose Hiromu, "Shinmatsu Chokurei-shō Sei-ken shijō kyōdōtai zakkō," *Tōyō shi kenkyū* 27.3(1968):318–32, which lists each market affecting Ch'ing county villages.
10. Because the "Cheng-ting hsien ts'un-t'u" includes so few villages, this statistic probably reflects not a different distribution of schools but the fragmentation of the *ts'un-t'u* record.

Glossary

chang-chiao 掌教
chi-t'ien 祭田
chia-shu 家塾
chien-sheng 監生
Ch'ien-tzu wen 千字文
ching-kuan 經館
ching-li 經理
Ching-pao 京報
ching-shu 經塾
chiu-kuei 九歸
chüan 卷
chuang 莊
Chuang-nung tsa-tzu 莊農雜字
chuang-shu 莊塾

fang-tzu 方字
fu-t'ou 埠頭

hsiang-shu 鄉塾
Hsiao-erh yü 小兒語
Hsiao-hsüeh 小學
Hsiao-hsüeh shih-li 小學詩禮
hsiao hsüeh-t'ang 小學堂
Hsiao-hsüeh yün-yü 小學韻語
hsin-wen-chih 新聞紙
Hsien-hsien hsiao-hsüeh 先賢小學
hsüeh-t'ang 學堂

i-hsüeh 義學
i-kuan 義館
I-pao 驛報
i-shu 義塾
i-t'ien 義田

jih-yung lei-shu 日用類書

k'ai-shu 楷書
Keng-chih t'u 耕織圖
ku-tz'u 鼓詞
kuan-hsüeh 官學
kuan-shu 官塾
kuei-ch'u 歸除
kung-sheng 貢生

lien-huan t'u-hua 連環圖畫

meng-kuan 蒙館
meng-shu 蒙塾
mou 畝

nien-hua 年畫
Nü hsiao-ching 女孝經
Nü lun-yü 女論語
Nü ssu-tzu ching 女四字經

pao-chüan 寶卷

shan-shu 善書
she-hsüeh 社學
shen-shih 紳士
sheng-yüan 生員
shih-hua 詩話
shih-tzu pan 識字班
shu-fang 書房
Shu-fang chen 書房鎮
shu-shih 書室
shu wu 書屋
shu-yüan 書院
ssu-hsüeh 司學
ssu-shu 私塾
Suan-fa ju-men 算法入門
sui-kung-sheng 歲貢生

t'an-tz'u 彈詞
t'ang pao 塘報
terakoya 寺子屋
Ti-tzu kuei 弟子規
tsa-tzu 雜字
tsu-shu 族塾
ts'un 村
ts'un-t'u 村圖
t'ung-sheng 童生
tung-shih 董事
tz'u-t'ang hsiao-hsüeh 祠堂小學

wen-yen 文言

ya-hang 牙行
yang-lien 養廉
Yu-hsüeh i-chih chia-li tsa-tzu 幼學易知家禮雜字

Bibliography

Primary Chinese Sources

Clan Genealogies

These clan genealogies for Kiangsu province are held by the Tōyō bunko and the National Diet Library in Tokyo, Japan. The numbers are those found in the bibliography of genealogies compiled by Taga Akigorō, *Sōfu no kenkyū* (Tokyo, 1960), to which readers can turn for more detailed bibliographic information.

Chao-shih fen-p'u 趙氏分譜. 1830 ed. Taga #983.
Ch'ao-shih tsung-p'u 巢氏宗譜. 1837 ed. Taga #620.
Ch'en-shih tsu-p'u 陳氏族譜. 1833 ed. Taga #769.
Ch'en-shih tsung-p'u 陳氏宗譜. 1902 ed. Taga #761.
(*Ch'ung-hsiu*) *Cheng-shih shih-p'u* 重修鄭氏世譜. 1794 ed. Taga #1071.
Chi-shih tsung-p'u 季氏宗譜. 1821 ed. Taga #385.
Chiang-shih ch'ung-hsiu tsu-p'u 蔣氏重修族譜. 1849 ed. Taga #1057.
Chiang-shih tsung-p'u 江氏宗譜. 1784 ed. Taga #177.
Chiang-tu Pien-shih tsu-p'u 江都卞氏族譜. 1830 ed. Taga #90.
Chiang-yin Liu-shih tsung-p'u 江陰六氏宗譜. 1896 ed. Taga #88.
Ch'ien-shih tsung-p'u 錢氏宗譜. 1880 ed. Taga #1097.
Ching-chiang Chang-shih tsung-p'u 京江張氏宗譜. 1866 ed. Taga #636.
Ching-chiang Ho-shih chih-p'u 京江何氏支譜. 1836 ed. Taga #192.
Ching-chiang Liu-shih tsung-p'u 京江柳氏宗譜. 1825 ed. Taga #440.
Ching-chiang Ma-shih tsung-p'u 京江馬氏宗譜. 1839 ed. Taga #489.
Ching-chiang Sui-shih chih-p'u 京江眭氏支譜. 1851 ed. Taga #823.
Ching-chiang Yang-shih tsu-p'u 京江楊氏族譜. 1851 ed. Taga #917.
(*Ching-chiang*) *Yen-shih tsung-p'u* (京江)嚴氏宗譜. 1779 ed. Taga #1172.
Ching-k'ou Chang-shih ch'ung-hsiu tsu-p'u 京口張氏重修族譜. 1837 ed. Taga #669.
Ching-k'ou Mao-shih tsung-p'u 京口茅氏宗譜. 1829 ed. Taga #475.
Ching-k'ou Ting-shih tsu-p'u 京口丁氏族譜. 1808 ed. Taga #5.

Chu-shih chia-p'u 朱氏家譜. 1793 ed. Taga #149.
Chuang-shih tsung-p'u 莊氏宗譜. 1802 ed. Taga #717.
Ch'un-hui Han-shih tsung-p'u 春暉韓氏宗譜. 1896 ed. Taga #169.
Fan-shih chia-ch'eng 范氏家乘. 1850 ed. Taga #479.
Fu-ch'i Hsü-shih shih chen-chi 洑溪徐氏珍集. 1833 ed. Taga #566.
Fu-ch'iao Huang-shih tsung-p'u 浮橋黃氏宗譜. 1852 ed. Taga #833.
Fu-ch'un Sun-shih tsu-p'u 富春孫氏族譜. 1871 ed. Taga #551.
Hai-ling Hu-shih chih-p'u 海陵胡氏支譜. 1859 ed. Taga #465.
Hai-yü P'ang-shih chia-p'u 海虞龐氏家譜. 1827 ed. Taga #1169.
Ho-tung shih-p'u Chin-ch'eng t'ang hsin-chi 河東世譜盡誠堂新集. 1802 ed. Taga #1115.
Hsi-shan tung-li Hou-shih liu-hsiu tsung-p'u 錫山東里侯氏六修宗譜. 1842 ed. Taga #414.
Hsi-ying Liu-shih chia-p'u 西營劉氏家譜. 1718 ed. Taga #998.
Hsia-shih tsung-p'u 夏氏宗譜. 1816 ed. Taga #534.
Hsü Ch'ien-hsüeh chia-p'u 徐乾學家譜. Manuscript. Taga #576.
Hsü-shih tsung-p'u 徐氏宗譜. 1814 ed. Taga #569.
I-t'ai Chang-shih fen ch'ien Shao-po chih-p'u 義台張氏分遷邵伯支譜. 1811 ed. Taga #681.
Jun-chou Liu-shih K'ang-hsi tsung-p'u 潤州柳氏康熙宗譜. 1697 ed. Taga #444.
Jun-chou Yao-shih tsung-p'u 潤州姚氏宗譜. 1813 ed. Taga #426.
Jun-tung Piao-lin Chu-shih t'ung-hsiu tsung-p'u 潤東彪林朱氏統修宗譜. 1846 ed. Taga #165.
Kao-shih tsu-p'u 高氏族譜. 1857 ed. Taga #509.
Kao-yang Hsü-shih Tung-t'ang shu chih-p'u 高陽許氏東唐墅支譜. Chia-ch'ing date. Taga #723.
Ku-jun Ku-shih tsung-p'u 古潤顧氏宗譜. 1841 ed. Taga #1185.
Liu-shih tsung-p'u 劉氏宗譜. 1808 ed. Taga #1011.
Liu-shih tsung-p'u 劉氏宗譜. 1868 ed. Taga #85.
Mei-shih tsu-p'u 梅氏族譜. 1849 ed. Taga #702.
P'an-shih ch'ung-hsiu tsu-p'u 潘氏重修族譜. 1844 ed. Taga #1040.
Pao-shan hou-pu-chih-lu Fei-shih chih-p'u 包山後埠支陸費氏支譜. Kuang-hsü date. Taga #802.
P'eng-shih tsung-p'u 彭氏宗譜. 1854 ed. Taga #861.
(*Hsü hsiu*) *P'i-ling Meng-shih tsung-p'u* 續修毘陵孟氏宗譜. 1850 ed. Taga #406.
P'i-ling Sha-shih tsu-p'u 毘陵沙氏族譜. 1859 ed. Taga #325.
(*P'ing-chiang*) *Sheng-shih chia-ch'eng* (平江)盛氏家乘. 1874 ed. Taga #819.
P'ing-yüan p'ai Sung-ling Lu-shih tsung-p'u 平原派松陵陸氏宗譜. 1874 ed. Taga #804.
P'ing-yüan tsung-p'u 平原宗譜. 1825 ed. Taga #803.
P'u-lu ho-pien 譜錄合編. 1693 ed. Taga #121. (This is a Shih family genealogy.)
Shang-hai Chu-shih tsu-p'u 上海朱氏族譜. 1802 ed. Taga #135.

Shao-tai Shih-shih ch'ung-hsiu tsung-p'u 邵埭史氏重修宗譜. 1825 ed. Taga #120.
Shen-shih tsung-p'u 沈氏宗譜. 1860 ed. Taga #331.
Ssu-ming Chu-shih chih-p'u nei-wai pien 四明朱氏支譜內外編. 1936 ed. Taga #140.
Ta-fu P'an-shih chih-p'u 大阜潘氏支譜. 1887 ed., 1908–09 ed. Taga #1031, 1032.
Ta-kang Chao-shih tsu-p'u 大港趙氏族譜. 1689–90 ed. Taga #973.
T'ai-yüan chia-p'u 太原家譜. 1802 ed., 1828 ed. Taga #37, 38.
T'ai-yüan Wang-shih Kao-ch'iao chih-p'u 太原王氏臯橋支譜. 1921 ed. Taga #35.
Tan-t'u Chiang-shih tsung-p'u 丹徒蔣氏宗譜. 1819 ed. Taga #1047.
Ting-kou Chang-shih tsu-p'u 丁溝張氏族譜. 1897 ed. Taga #624.
Ting-shih tsung-p'u 丁氏宗譜. 1792 ed. Taga #1138.
Tung-hsing Miao-shih tsung-p'u 東興繆氏宗譜. 1715 ed. Taga #1108.
Tung-t'ing Tung-shan Weng-shih tsung-p'u 洞庭東山翁氏宗譜. 1765 ed. Taga #608.
Wang-shih tsu-p'u 王氏族譜. 1817 ed. Taga #52.
Wang-shih tsung-p'u 王氏宗譜. 1821 ed. Taga #44.
Wu-chiang Chin-shih chia-p'u 吳江金氏家譜. 1798 ed. Taga #350.
Wu-chiang Yang-shih tsung-p'u 吳江楊氏宗譜. 1917 ed. Taga #922.
Wu-chün Lu-shih Tou-hsiang chih shih-hsi t'u-piao 吳郡陸氏竇巷支世系圖表. 1933 ed. Taga #806.
Wu-ling Ku-shih chih-p'u 武陵顧氏支譜. 1820 ed. Taga #1188.
Wu-men Yüan-shih chia-p'u 吳門袁氏家譜. 1920 ed. Taga #522.
Wu-shih chih-p'u 吳氏支譜. 1882 ed. Taga #217.
Wu-shih chih-te chih 吳氏至德志. 1876–77 ed. Taga #227.
Wu-Yüeh Ch'ien-shih Ching-chiang fen chih liu-hsiu tsung-p'u 吳越錢氏京江分支六修宗譜. 1848 ed. Taga #1087.
Yang-chou Juan-shih tsu-p'u 楊州阮氏族譜. 1840 ed. Taga #348.
Yen-shih tsung-p'u 嚴氏宗譜. 1833 ed. Taga #1177.
Yü-shih chia-ch'eng 郁氏家乘. 1933 ed. Taga #486.
Yün-shih chia-ch'eng 惲氏家乘. 1859 ed. Taga #870.
Yün-yang tung-men chi-chuang P'eng-shih ch'ung-hsiu tsu-p'u 雲陽東門基庄彭氏重修族譜. 1792 ed. Taga #867.
Yün-yang Yin-shih ch'ung-hsiu tsu-p'u 雲陽尹氏重修族譜. 1798 ed. Taga #100.

Gazetteers

Abbreviations used in this section are:

TC (*t'ung-chih*) 通志
FC (*fu-chih*) 府志
HC (*hsien-chih*) 縣志
CC (*chou-chih*) 州志

These gazetteers were consulted in libraries in Japan and the United States. Readers desiring further bibliographic details should consult Chu Shih-chia, *Chung-kuo ti-fang-chih tsung-lu* (Shanghai, 1958), and the *Nihon shuyō toshokan kenkyūjo shozō Chūgoku chihōshi sōgō mokuroku*, compiled by the National Diet Library (Tokyo, 1969).

The gazetteers listed below were selected (1) to obtain provincial-level coverage, by consulting a provincial gazetteer for every Ch'ing province within the Great Wall—with the exception of Kwangtung, Shantung, and Yunnan, for which figures had already been produced by other scholars; and (2) to examine schools in selected areas in greater depth, by sifting through numerous lower-level gazetteers. For example, over 110 Chihli gazetteers were examined, and of this number only 41 (listed below) provided relevant information. Over 40 Kiangsi gazetteers were studied, but only 13 (also listed below) yielded information. Similarly, the following list includes 34 Kiangsu, 21 Shensi, 19 Szechwan, 18 Hunan, and 18 Shansi gazetteers. Kwangtung and Shantung gazetteers were bypassed because of the already published work of Liu Po-chi on Kwangtung and Nakamura Jihei on Shantung schools. These gazetteers and secondary sources provided information on provinces scattered throughout China, representing widely varying geographical and economic conditions.

An-hui TC 安徽. 1830 ed., 1877 ed.
An-i HC 安義. 1871 ed.
Ch'ang-an HC 長安. 1872 ed.
Ch'ang-chou FC 常州. 1886 reprint of K'ang-hsi ed.
Ch'ang-lo HC 長樂. 1875 ed.
Ch'ang-p'ing CC 昌平. 1886 ed.
Ch'ang-sha hsien hsüeh-kung chih 長沙縣學宮志. 1867 ed.
Ch'ang-t'ing HC 長汀. 1879 ed.
Ch'ang-yüan HC 長垣. 1810 ed.
Chao-ch'eng HC 趙城. 1827 ed.
Chao-chou shu-i chih 趙州屬邑志. 1897 ed.
Che-chiang TC 浙江. 1899 ed.
Chen-an HC 鎮安. 1753 ed.
Chen-chiang FC 鎮江. 1750 ed.
Chen-tse HC 震澤. 1893 reprint of 1746 ed.
Cheng-ting HC 正定. 1762 ed.
Ch'eng-k'ou t'ing-chih 城口廳志. 1844 ed.
Ch'eng-ku HC 城固. 1878 ed.
Ch'eng-tu HC 成都. 1815–16 ed.
Chi-fu TC 畿輔. 1884 ed.
Ch'i-yang HC 祁陽. 1870 ed.
Chia-hsing FC 嘉興. 1879 ed.
Chia-ting HC 嘉定. 1882 ed.
(*Chih-li*) *Chiang* CC 直隸絳. 1765 ed., 1879 ed.

Chiang-hsi TC 江西. 1880–81 ed.
Chiang-hsia HC 江夏. 1869 ed.
Chiang-nan TC 江南. 1967 reprint of 1736–37 ed.
(*Hsü tsuan*) *Chiang-ning* FC 續纂江甯. 1880 ed.
Chiang-tu hsien hsü-chih 江都縣續志. 1883 ed.
Chiang-yin hsien hsü-chih 江陰縣續志. 1920 ed.
Ch'ien-chiang HC 黔江. 1894 ed.
Chih-chiang HC 芷江. 1760 ed., 1870 ed.
Chin-chiang HC 晉江. 1765 ed.
Chin-ch'i HC 金谿. 1870 ed.
Chin CC 晉. 1860 ed.
Chin-hsien HC 進賢. 1871 ed.
Ching-chiang HC 靖江. 1876 ed.
Ch'ing-p'u HC 青浦. 1879 ed.
Ch'ing-yüan HC 淸苑. 1873 ed.
Ch'iu chou chih-li CC 邛州直隸. 1818 ed.
Cho CC 涿. 1765 ed.
Chu-shan HC 竹山. 1785 ed., 1807 ed.
Chü-lu HC 鉅鹿. 1886 ed.
(*Hsü-hsiu*) *Ch'ü-wu* HC 續修曲沃. 1880 ed.
Ch'üan-chou FC 泉州. 1763 ed.
Ch'ung-ch'ing FC 重慶. 1843 ed.
Ch'ung-jen HC 崇仁. 1873 ed.
Ch'ung-yang HC 崇陽. 1866 ed.
Fang HC 房. 1866 ed.
Fen-yang HC 汾陽. 1851 ed.
Feng HC 鳳. 1892 ed.
Feng-chieh HC 奉節. 1893 ed.
(*Ch'ung-hsiu*) *Feng-hsiang* FC 重修鳳翔. 1766–7 ed.
Feng-hsien HC 奉賢. 1878 ed.
Feng-huang t'ing-chih 鳳凰廳志 1881 ed.
Fu-an HC 福安. 1783 ed.
(*Ch'ung-tsuan*) *Fu-chien* TC 重纂福建. 1829 ed.
Han-tan HC 邯鄲. 1756 ed.
Han-yin t'ing-chih 漢陰廳志. 1818 ed.
Hao-feng CC 鶴峯. 1867 ed.
Heng-chou FC 衡州. 1875 reprint of 1763 ed.
Heng-shan HC 衡山. 1875 ed.
Ho-nan FC 河南. 1867 ed.
Ho-nan TC 河南. 1914 ed.
Ho-nei HC 河內. 1825 ed.
Hsi-an FC 西安. 1779 ed.
Hsi-an HC 西安. 1811 ed.
Hsiang-hsiang HC 湘鄉. 1874 ed.
Hsiang-ling HC 襄陵. 1881 ed.

Hsiang-shan HC　香山. 1828 ed.
Hsiang-t'an HC　湘潭. 1781 ed., 1888–89 ed.
Hsiang-yang FC　襄陽. 1760 ed.
Hsiao HC　蕭. 1875 ed.
Hsin-ch'eng HC　新城. 1870 ed.
Hsing-an HC　興安. 1871 ed.
Hsü-chou FC　徐州. 1874 ed.
(*Pu hsiu*) *Hsü-kou* HC　補修徐溝. 1881 ed.
Hsün-yang HC　洵陽. 1904 ed.
Hu-nan TC　湖南. 1885 ed.
Hu-pei TC　湖北. 1921 ed.
(*Ch'ung-hsiu*) *Hua-t'ing* HC　重修華亭. 1878 ed.
Hua-yang HC　華陽. 1816 ed.
Huai-an FC　淮安. 1852 reprint of 1748 ed.
Huai-an HC　懷安. 1876 ed.
Huai-ning HC　懷寧. 1916 ed.
Huang-kang HC　黄岡. 1882 ed.
Huo-lu HC　獲鹿. 1736 ed., 1881 ed.
I-ch'ang FC　宜昌. 1864 ed.
I-hsing HC　宜興. 1965 Taipei reprint of three Ch'ing eds.
I-wu HC　義烏. 1802 ed.
I-yang HC　宜陽. 1881 ed.
Ju-kao HC　如皐. 1808 ed., 1873 ed.
Jui-an HC　瑞安. 1809 ed.
K'ai HC　開. 1746 ed.
Kan-chou t'ing-chih　乾州廳志. 1877 ed.
Kan-su TC　甘肅. 1736 ed.
Kan-yü HC　贛榆. 1888 ed.
Kao-ch'eng HC　藁城. 1720 ed.
Kao-i HC　高邑. 1811 ed.
(*Hsü*) *Kao-p'ing* HC　續高平. 1880 ed.
Kao-yu CC　高郵. 1845 ed.
Ku-ch'eng HC　槀城. 1867 ed.
(*Ch'ung-hsiu*) *Ku-shih* HC　重修固始. 1786 ed.
Kuang CC　光. 1887 ed.

Kuang-hsi TC　廣西. 1800 ed.
Kuang-hsi TC *chi-yao*　廣西通志輯要. 1889 ed.
Kuang-yüan HC　廣元. 1757 ed.
Kuei-chou TC　貴州. 1741 ed.
K'uei-chou FC　夔州. 1747 ed.
K'un-Hsin liang-hsien hsü-hsiu ho-chih　崑新兩縣續修合志. 1880 ed.
(*Chih-li*) *Li-chou chih-lin*　直隷澧州志林. 1752 ed.
Li HC　蠡. 1876–77 ed.
(*Tseng hsiu*) *Li-ling* HC　增修醴陵. 1744 ed.
Lin-ch'uan HC　臨川. 1870 ed.

Lin-fen HC 臨汾. 1779 ed.
Ling HC 酃. 1873 ed.
Liu-pa t'ing-chih 留壩廳志. 1842 ed.
Liu-yang HC 瀏陽. 1873 ed.
Lo-ch'ing HC 樂淸. 1901 ed.
Lo-nan HC 雒南. 1746 ed.
Lo-t'ien HC 羅田. 1876 ed.
Lu-ling HC 盧陵. 1873 ed.
Luan CC 灤. 1810 ed., 1898 ed.
*Luan-ch'eng*HC 欒城. 1872-73 ed.
Lüeh-yang HC 略陽. 1904 ed.
Lung-yen HC 龍巖. 1890 ed.
Man-ch'eng HC 滿城. 1780 ed.
Meng HC 孟. 1881 ed.
Mien HC 沔. Reprint of 1883 ed.
Min-hou HC 閩侯. 1933 ed.
Nan-ch'ang HC 南昌. 1849 ed.
Nan-chao HC 南召. 1746 ed.
Nan-ch'eng HC 南城. 1873 ed.
Nan-kung HC 南宮. 1831 ed.
Nan-p'i HC 南皮. 1888 ed.
Ning-ch'iang CC 寧羌. 1888 ed.
Ning-hsiang HC 寧鄉. 1882 ed.
Ning-hua HC 寧化. 1869 ed.
Ning-po FC 寧波. 1846 ed.
Pa HC 霸. 1923 ed.
Pa HC 巴. 1867 ed.
Pai-ho HC 白河. 1801 ed.
Pao-an CC 保安. 1835 ed.
Pao-chi HC 寶雞. 1922 ed.
Pao-ching HC 保靖. 1871 ed.
Pao-ning FC 保寧. 1821 ed.
Pao-shan HC 寶山. 1882 ed.
P'ing-yang HC 平陽. 1760 ed.
P'ing-yao HC 平遙. 1883 ed.
Shan-hsi TC 山西. 1811 reprint of 1734 ed., 1892 ed.
Shang-ch'eng HC 商城. 1803 ed.
Hsü Shang CC 續商. 1744 ed., 1758 ed.
Shang-hai hsien hsü chih 上海縣續志. 1918 ed.
Shang-jao HC 上饒. 1873 ed.
Shang-nan HC 商南. 1752 ed.
Shao-wu FC 邵武. 1900 ed.
She HC 歙. 1937 ed.
Shen CC 深. 1697 ed.
Shen-chou feng-t'u chi 深州風土記. 1900 ed.

(*Hsü hsiu*) *Shen-hsi sheng* TC *kao* 續修陝西省通志稿. 1934 ed.
Shou-yang HC 壽陽. 1882 ed.
Shu-lu wu-chih ho-k'an 束鹿五志合栞. 1938 reprint of five Ch'ing eds.
Shun-te HC 順德. 1853 ed·
Ssu-ch'uan TC 四川. 1816 ed.
Su-chou FC 蘇州. 1824 ed., 1882 ed.
Sung-chiang FC 松江. Reprint of 1817 ed.
Sung-chiang fu shu chiu-chih erh-chung 松江府屬舊志二種. 1932 reprint of two Ming eds.
Ta HC 達. 1815 ed.
Ta-ming HC 大名. 1790 ed.
Ta-ning HC 大甯. 1885 ed.
T'ai CC 泰. 1908 ed.
T'ai-ku HC 太谷. 1886 ed.
T'ai-p'ing HC 太平. 1725 ed., 1775 ed. (Shansi county.)
T'ai-p'ing HC 太平. 1795 ed. (Szechwan county.)
T'ai-shun HC 泰順. 1729 ed.
Tan-t'u HC 丹徒. 1879 ed.
Tan-yang HC 丹陽. 1885 ed.
T'ang HC 唐. 1906 reprint of 1878 ed.
(*Ch'ung-hsiu*) *T'ien-chin* FC 重修天津. 1898–99 ed.
T'ien-chin hsien hsin-chih 天津縣新志. 1930–31 ed.
T'ien-chin shih kai-yao 天津市概要. 1934 ed.
T'ing-chou FC 汀州. 1867 ed.
Ting-hsing HC 定興. 1890 ed.
Ting-yüan HC 定遠. 1879 ed.
Tsao-ch'iang HC *pu-cheng* 棗強縣志補正. 1876 ed.
T'ung CC 通. 1783 ed., 1879 ed. (Chihli department.)
T'ung chou chih-li CC 通州直隸. 1876 ed. (Kiangsu department.)
Tung-ming HC 東明. 1924 ed. (Includes reprint of 1756 ed.)
T'ung-shan HC 銅山. 1926 ed.
Tung-t'ai HC 東臺. 1817 ed.
Tz'u CC 磁. 1703 ed. (Bound with 1874 *Tz'u chou hsü-chih* 磁州續志.)
Tz'u-ch'i HC 慈谿. 1730 ed.
Tzu-yang HC 紫陽. 1843 ed.
Wan HC 萬. 1866 ed.
Wen-an HC 文安. 1703 ed., 1922 ed.
Wen-chou FC 温州. 1866 reprint of 1762 ed.
Wen-hsi HC 聞喜. 1766 ed
Wu-an HC 武安. 1739 ed.
Wu-chi HC 無極. Combines 1757 and 1893 eds.
Wu-ch'iang hsien hsin-chih 武強縣新志. 1831 ed.
Wu-ch'iao HC 吳橋. 1875 ed.
Wu-chin, Yang-hu HC 武進陽湖. 1879 ed.
Wu-hsi, Chin-kuei HC 無錫金匱. 1881 ed.

Wu-ning HC 武甯. 1824 ed., 1870 ed.
Wu-shan HC 巫山. 1715 ed.
(*Hsü tsuan*) *Yang-chou* FC 續纂揚州. 1874 ed.
Yeh HC 葉. 1872 ed.
Yen-an FC 延安. 1884 ed.
Yen-ch'ing CC 延慶. 1881 ed.
Yen-p'ing HC 延平. 1873 ed.
Yü-tz'u HC 榆次. 1862 ed.
Yün HC 鄖. 1866 ed.
Yün-yang chih 鄖陽. 1870 ed.
Yün-yang HC 雲陽. 1854 ed.
Yung-chia HC 永嘉. 1881–82 ed.
Yung-ch'ing HC 永清. 1875 ed.
Yung-sui chih-li t'ing-chih 永綏直隸廳志. 1862 ed.
Yung-sui t'ing-chih 永綏廳志. 1909 ed.

Tsa-tzu *and Other Educational Texts*

The location of rare editions is denoted as follows: Library of Congress: DLC; Harvard-Yenching Library: H-Y; Naikaku bunko: NK; Tōyō bunko: TB; and Tōyō bunka kenkyūjo: TYBKK.

(*Ch'eng-chung meng-hsüeh t'ang*) *Tzu k'o t'u-shuo* (澄衷蒙學堂) 字課圖說 [(Ch'eng-chung School's) Illustrated primer]. N.p., 1904.

Chia-shu meng-ch'iu 家塾蒙求 [School primer]. Compiled by K'ang Chi-yüan 康基淵. 1826. Reprint. N.p., 1867.

Ch'i-shu wen-yüeh tien-p'i ch'eng chieh chuang hun ch'i-chu wen pien-lan 契書文約佃批呈結狀婚啓祝文便覽 [Guide to contracts, agreements, tenancies, petitions, accusations, and marriage congratulations]. N.p., n.d. (Eleven folios, bound into one volume with two other items, under TYBKK #20357.)

Chin-ch'ang San-huai t'ang hsin-k'o tseng-ting shih-i ching-shu pien-yung t'ung-k'ao tsa-tzu 金閶三槐堂新刻增訂釋義經書便用通考雜字 [Comprehensive miscellany explaining the classics, newly published in an enlarged edition by Wu county's San-huai Studio]. Compiled by Hsü San-sheng 徐三省, supplemented by Tai Ch'i-ta 戴啓達. N.p., n.d. (Held by NK.)

Chin-ch'ang Tan-shan t'ang hsin-k'o tseng-ting shih-i ching-shu pien-yung t'ung-k'ao tsa-tzu 金閶丹山堂新刻增訂釋義經書便用通考雜字 [Comprehensive miscellany for use in explaining the classics, newly published in an enlarged edition by Wu county's Tan-shan Studio]. Compiled by Hsü San-sheng 徐三省, supplemented by Tai Ch'i-ta 戴啓達. N.p., n.d. (Preface dated 1765. Held by NK.)

Chin-yao tzu 緊要字 [Important words]. Compiled by Yang An-ch'eng 楊安城. N.p., 1778 (Held by NK.)

Hsin-ch'ieh Tseng t'ai-shih hui-tsuan su-weng ch'i-meng cho-yü ao-t'ou 新鍥曾太史彙纂素翁啓蒙琢玉鼇頭 [A new edition of Compiler Tseng's annotated elementary primer]. Compiled by Tseng Ch'u-ch'ing 曾楚卿. N.d. (Japanese manuscript copy; unnumbered pages. Held by NK.)

Hsin-chien tseng-pu lei-tsuan che-yao ao-t'ou tsa-tzu 新鐫增補類纂摘要鰲頭雜字 [New expanded annotated selected glossary]. N.p., n.d. (Ming ed. Held by NK.)

Hsin-chien yu-hsüeh i-chih shu-cha pien-lan 新鐫幼學易知書札便覽 [New guide for easy elementary instruction in letters]. N.p., n.d. (Five folios, bound with two other items into one volume, under TYBKK #22673. According to Niida Noboru, "Gen Min jidai," pp. 162–163, likely to be a 1675–76 ed.)

(*Hsin-k'an kuang-chi*) *Chü-chia chin-yao jih-yung tsa-tzu* (新刊廣輯)居家緊要日用雜字 [Householder's essential glossary for daily use (in a new enlarged edition)]. N.d. Reprint. N.p.: Wan-chüan lou 萬卷樓, n.d. (Ming ed. Held by NK.)

(*Hsin-k'o*) *Nü ssu-tzu ching* (新刻)女四字經 [Female's four-character classic (New edition)]. Collated by the Hu shih wen-hui t'ang 胡氏文會堂. N.p., n.d. (Ming ed. Held by NK.)

Hsin-k'o shih-i ch'ün-shu liu-yen lien-chu tsa-tzu 新刻釋義群書六言聯珠雜字 [A newly edited annotated glossary in six-word phrases for a host of books]. Compiled by Hsieh Jung-teng 謝榮登. N.p., n.d. (Ming ed., printed in Fukien. Held by NK.)

(*Hsin-k'o*) *Ssu-yen tsa-tzu* (新刻) 四言雜字. [(New edition of the) Four-character glossary]. Hangchow: n.p., n.d. (Ming ed. Held by NK.)

Hsin-k'o tseng-chiao ch'ieh-yung cheng-yin hsiang-t'an tsa-tzu ta-ch'üan 新刻增校切用正音鄉談雜字大全 [New expanded glossary of standard and rural terms]. N.d. (Japanese manuscript copy; unnumbered pages. Held by NK.)

Hsin-pien ssu-yen tsa-tzu 新編四言雜字 [Newly compiled four-character glossary]. Nan-ch'ang: Kiangsi chiao-yü ch'u-pan she 江西教育出版社, 1964.

Hsin-pien Tui-hsiang Szu-yen 新編對相四言: *15th Century Illustrated Chinese Primer, with Introduction and Notes by L. Carrington Goodrich*. Hong Kong: University of Hong Kong Press, 1967.

Hsin-pien yu-erh shih-tzu 新編幼兒識字 [Newly compiled children's reader]. 2 vols. Hong Kong: Educational Book Company, 1972.

Hsin-tseng hui-t'u i-wan tzu wen 新增繪圖一萬字文 [New expanded 10,000-character illustrated glossary]. N.p.: Wen-sheng shu-chü 文盛書局, n.d.

Hsin-tseng yu-hsüeh i-chih kao-t'ou tsa-tzu ta-ch'üan 新增幼學易知高頭雜字大全 [Newly enlarged and complete easy glossary for elementary instruction]. N.p., n.d. (Bound with two other works into one volume, under TYBKK #22673. According to Niida, "Gen Min jidai," pp. 162–63, this is a 1675–76 ed.)

Hsin-tseng yu-hsüeh ku-shih ch'iung-lin 新增幼學故事瓊林 [Newly expanded collection of stories for elementary instruction]. By Ch'eng Yüan-sheng 程元升. N.p., n.d. (Held by DLC.)

K'an-t'u shih-tzu 看圖識字 [Illustrated reading primer]. Compiled by Huang I-te 黃一德. Shanghai: Jen shih-chien ch'u-pan she 人世間出版社, 1951.

K'an-t'u shih-tzu 看图识字 [Illustrated reading primer]. Shanghai: Jen-min ch'u-pan she 人民出版社, 1972.

(*Kuan-pan*) *Tzu hsüeh ch'i-chung* (官板)字學七種 [(Officially printed) Seven-category character studies]. Edited by Li Chung-fen 李鍾份, collated by Chang Pang-t'ai 張邦泰. N.p., 1837. (Japanese edition of early [Tao-kuang] nineteenth century book. Held by NK.)

Lei-shu tsuan-yao 類書纂要 [Reference book]. Compiled by Chou Lu 周魯. Soochow: San-huai t'ang 三槐堂, 1664. (Held by NK.)

"Li Cho-wu hsien-sheng chiao shih-min ch'ieh-yao t'ieh-shih shou-ching" 李卓吾先生校士民切要帖式手鏡 [Guide to important document forms for scholars and commoners collated by Mr. Li Cho-wu]. N.d. (Handwritten manuscript; unnumbered pages. Held by NK.)

Li-tai tseng-pu su-weng chih-chang tsa-tzu 歷代增補素翁指掌雜字 [Historically expanded easy glossary]. N.p., n.d. (Held by NK.)

Ni jen-shih ma? 你认识吗 [Can you read?]. Shanghai: Jen-min ch'u-pan she 人民出版社, 1972.

P'u Tseng t'ai-shih hui-tsuan ao-t'ou cho-yü tsa-tzu 莆曾太史彙纂鰲頭琢玉雜字 [Compiler Tseng's annotated glossary]. Collated by Tseng Ch'u-ch'ing 曾楚卿. N.p., n.d. (According to Sakai, "Mindai no nichiyō ruisho," p. 127, this is an early seventeenth century edition. Held by NK.)

San-tzu ching chu-t'u 三字經註圖 [Annotated and illustrated three-character classic]. N.p., 1878.

Shih Ch'ung-en 施崇恩, comp. *Hui-t'u shih-tzu shih-tsai i* 繪圖識字實在易 [Easy illustrated reading primer]. Shanghai: Piao-meng shu-shih 彪蒙書室, 1918.

(*Shih-min*) *Wan-yung cheng-tsung pu-ch'iu jen* (士民)萬用正宗不求人 [Orthodox teachings with myriad uses for scholars and commoners]. N.p., n.d. (Ming [Wan-li] ed. Held by DLC.)

Sung Hao-ling 宋鶴齡, comp. *Chu-shih hui-t'u ch'i-ch'ien tzu wen* 註釋繪圖七千字文 [Annotated illustrated 7,000-character glossary]. N.p., n.d.

———. *Hui-t'u liu-ch'ien tzu wen* 繪圖六千字文 [Illustrated 6,000-character glossary]. N.p., n.d.

———. *Hui-t'u ssu-ch'ien tzu wen* 繪圖四千字文 [Illustrated 4,000-character glossary]. N.p., n.d.

———. *Hui-t'u wu-ch'ien tzu wen* 繪圖五千字文 [Illustrated 5,000-character glossary]. N.p., n.d.

Tseng-kuang yu-hsüeh hsü-chih ao-t'ou tsa-tzu ta-ch'üan 增廣幼學須知鰲頭雜字大全 [Augmented and complete annotated glossary of knowledge essential for elementary schooling]. N.p., n.d. (Held by TB, which lists it as a Ch'ing *keng-shen* [cyclical date that coincided with 1680, 1740, 1800, or 1860] publication, by the Wen-hua t'ang 文華堂, which published TYBKK #22673.)

Tseng-pu i-chih tsa-tzu ch'üan shu 增補易知雜字全書 [Augmented complete easy glossary]. N.p., n.d. (This is part of three items bound into one volume. Held by TYBKK under #20357.)

(*Tseng-pu*) *Wan-pao ch'üan shu* (增補)萬寶全書 [(Enlarged) Complete "ten thousand treasures"]. N.p., 1739. (Held by DLC.)

(*Tseng-pu yin-shih*) *Shih-shih t'ung-k'ao tsa-tzu wan-hua ku* (增補音釋)世事通考雜字萬花谷 [(Expanded phonetic) encyclopedic glossary of difficult things]. Compiled by Ts'ao Ming 曹銘 and Hsü San-sheng 徐三省. N.p., n.d. (Early seventeenth century ed. Held by NK.)

Tseng-ting yu-hsüeh hsü-chih tsa-tzu ts'ai-chen 增訂幼學須知雜字采珍 [Expanded selected glossary of knowledge essential for elementary schooling]. N.p., n.d. (Ch'ing publication. Held by H-Y.)

Tsui-hsin hui-t'u shen t'ung shih 最新繪圖神童詩 [Latest illustrated *Shen t'ung shih*]. Shanghai: T'ien-pao shu-chü 天寶書局, n.d.

Tu Ping-ju 都冰如, comp. *K'an-t'u shih-tzu* 看圖識字 [Illustrated reading primer.. Vol. 1, N.p., n.d. (The cover illustration [a KMT star in a sun] and statement ["Authorized by the Ministry of Education; Standard kindergarten text"] suggest it is from the Republican period. Held by Columbia.)

Tui-hsiang ssu-yen 對相四言 [Illustrated four-character glossary]. Soochow: Sheng-te t'ang 聖德堂, n.d. (A Ch'ing publication, according to the NK catalog.)

Tui-hsiang ssu-yen tsa-tzu 對相四言雜字 [Illustrated four-character glossary]. 1371. Reprint. N.p., n.d.

Yu-hsüeh ch'iu-yüan 幼學求源 [Fundamentals of elementary instruction]. By Ch'eng Yüan-sheng 程元升. N.p., 1842.

Other Sources

"Cheng-ting hsien ts'un-t'u" 正定縣村圖 [Village records of Cheng-ting county]. N.d. (Manuscript; *ca.* 1885–86.)

Chiang-nan wen-chien lu 江南聞見錄 [Notes on Kiangnan]. Compiled by Economic Research Section, Bank of Taiwan. Taipei: Bank of Taiwan, 1967.

Chiang-ning fu ch'ung-hsiu p'u-yü ssu-t'ang chih 江寧府重修普育四堂志 [Revised records of four charitable *t'ang* in Chiang-ning prefecture]. Compiled by T'u Tsung-ying 涂宗瀛, revised by Sun Yün-chin 孫雲錦. 1886. Reprint. N.p., 1926.

Ch'in-ting hsüeh-cheng ch'üan-shu 欽定學政全書 [Official complete records of educational policy]. Compiled by T'ung Huang 童璜 et al. N.p., 1812.

"Ch'ing hsien ts'un-t'u" 青縣村圖 [Village records of Ch'ing county]. N.d. (Manuscript; *ca.* 1880.)

Ch'üan Tien i-hsüeh hui-chi 全滇義學彙記 [Collected records of Yunnan charitable schools]. Compiled by Ch'en Hung-mou 陳弘謀. N.p., 1738.

Fu-chien sheng-li 福建省例 [Collected regulations for Fukien]. Compiled by

Economic Research Section, Bank of Taiwan. 8 vols. Taipei: Bank of Taiwan, 1964.

Hsi-chiang hsüeh-cheng 西江學政 [Kiangsi educational regulations]. Edited by Kao Huang 高璜. N.p., 1682.

Hsin-k'o ting cheng chia ch'uan mi-chüeh, p'an-chu suan-fa shih-min li-yung 新刻訂正家傳秘訣盤珠算法士民利用 [New edition of the secretly transmitted orthodox methods of abacus calculation, for the convenience of scholars and commoners]. Collated by Hsü Hsin-lu 徐心魯. N.p., n.d. (Ming [Wan-li] ed. Held by NK.)

Hsin-pien chih-chih suan-fa tsuan-yao 新編直指算法纂要 [Newly compiled essentials of calculation methods]. Compiled by Ch'eng Ta-wei 程大位. N.p., n.d. (Ch'ing publication. Held by NK.)

Huan-chiang ts'ung-cheng lu 皖江從政錄 [Anhwei government regulations]. N.p., n.d. (1818 preface.)

Huang P'ei-lieh 黃丕烈, ed. *Shih-li chü Huang-shih ts'ung-shu: Chi-ku ko chen ts'ang mi-pen shu-mu* 士禮居黃氏叢書: 汲古閣珍藏秘本書目 [Mr. Huang's reprint series: catalogue of the rare books in the Chi-ku ko]. N.p., n.d. (*Ca.* 1800.)

P'u Sung-ling 蒲松齡. *P'u Sung-ling chi* 蒲松齡集 [Collected writings of P'u Sung-ling]. N.d. Reprint. Peking: n.p., 1962.

"Shen-chou ts'un-t'u" 深州村圖 [Village records of Shen-chou]. N.d. (Manuscript; *ca.* 1873–75.)

Shih-lin kuang-chi 事林廣記 [Notes on various matters]. Compiled by Ch'en Yüan-ching 陳元靚. N.p., n.d. (Yüan ed. Held by DLC.)

Ta Ch'ing lü-li hui-t'ung hsin tsuan 大清律例會通新纂 [Comprehensive new edition of the Great Ch'ing Code]. Edited by Yao Yü-hsiang 姚雨薌, with commentaries by Shen Chih-ch'i 沈之奇 and Hu Yang-shan 胡仰山. Peking: n.p., 1873.

Ting Jih-ch'ang 丁日昌. *Fu-wu kung-tu* 撫吳公牘 [Official writings of Ting Jih-ch'ang]. 3 vols. 1877. Reprint. N.p., n.d.

Yen Ju-i 嚴如熤. *San-sheng shan-nei feng-t'u tsa-chih* 三省山內風土雜識 [Notes on the local customs of the three-province highlands]. Shanghai: Commercial Press, 1936.

Yü Chih 余治. *Te-i lu* 得一錄 [Records of a purist]. N.p., 1869.

Secondary Sources

A Ying (Ch'ien Hsing-ts'un) 阿英(錢杏邨). *Chung-kuo lien-huan t'u-hua shih-hua* 中國連環圖畫史話 [History of Chinese comics]. Peking: Chung-kuo ku-tien i-shu ch'u-pan she 中國古典藝術出版社, 1957.

Ahern, Emily. *The Cult of the Dead in a Chinese Village*. Stanford: Stanford University Press, 1973.

Alitto, Guy S. "Rural Reconstruction during the Nanking Decade: Confucian Collectivism in Shantung," *China Quarterly* 66 (1976): 213–46.

Aries, Philippe. *Centuries of Childhood.* Translated by Robert Baldick. New York: Vintage paperback, 1962.

Ash, Robert. "Economic Aspects of Land Reform in Kiangsu, 1949–52," *China Quarterly* 66 (1976): 261–92.

Ayers, William. *Chang Chih-tung and Educational Reform in China.* Cambridge: Harvard University Press, 1971.

Baker, Hugh D. R. *A Chinese Lineage Village: Sheung Shui.* London: Frank Cass, 1968.

Balazs, Etienne. *Political Theory and Administrative Reality in Traditional China.* London: University of London, School of Oriental and African Studies, 1965.

Bayley, E.C. "On the Genealogy of Modern Numerals," *Journal of the Royal* Asiatic Society 14 (1883): 335; 15 (1883): 1.

Berkowitz, Morris, and Reed, John H. "Research into the Chinese Little Tradition," *Journal of Asian and African Studies* 6.3–4 (1971): 233–38.

Bernal, Martin. *Chinese Socialism to 1907.* Ithaca: Cornell University Press, 1976.

Biggerstaff, Knight. *The Earliest Modern Government Schools in China.* Ithaca: Cornell University Press, 1961.

———. "Modernization—and Early Modern China," *Journal of Asian Studies* 25.4 (1966): 607–21.

Bodde, Derk, and Morris, Clarence. *Law in Imperial China.* Cambridge: Harvard University Press, 1967.

Boorman, Howard, and Howard, Richard, eds. *Biographical Dictionary of Republican China.* 4 vols. New York: Columbia University Press, 1971.

Britton, Roswell S. *The Chinese Periodical Press, 1800–1912.* Shanghai: Kelly and Walsh, 1933.

Buck, David. "Educational Modernization in Tsinan, 1899–1937." In *The Chinese City between Two Worlds*, edited by Mark Elvin and G. W. Skinner, pp. 171–212. Stanford: Stanford University Press, 1974.

Buck, John Lossing. *Land Utilization in China.* 3 vols. Nanking: University of Nanking, 1937.

Budd, Josephine E. "Education for Women." In *China*, edited by Orville A. Petty, pp. 535–76. New York: Harper, 1933.

Burgess, John Stewart. "Community Organization in China," *Far Eastern Survey* 14.25 (1945): 371–73.

———. *The Guilds of Peking.* 1928. Reprint. New York: AMS Press, 1970.

———. "Some Observations on Chinese Village Life," *Social Forces* 11.3 (1933): 402–9.

Carter, Thomas F. *The Invention of Printing in China and Its Spread Westward.* Revised by L. C. Goodrich. New York: Columbia University Press, 1955.

Chan, Hok-lam. "The White Lotus—Maitreya Doctrine and Popular Uprisings in Ming and Ch'ing China," *Sinologica* 10 (1969): 211–33.

Chandler, Horace E. "The Work of the American Presbyterian Mission from 1918 to 1941 toward the Lessening of Adult Illiteracy in Shantung Province,

China." Ph.D. dissertation, University of Pittsburgh, 1943.

Chang Chih-kung 張志公. *Ch'uan-t'ung yü-wen chiao-yü ch'u-t'an* 傳統語文教育初探 [A preliminary study of traditional language primers]. Shanghai: Shanghai Educational Press, 1962.

Chang Ching-lu 張靜廬, ed. *Chung-kuo chin-tai ch'u-pan shih-liao* 中國近代出版史料 [Historical materials on modern Chinese publishing]. 2 vols. Shanghai: Shang-tsa ch'u-pan she 上雜出版社, 1962.

Chang, Chung-li. *The Chinese Gentry: Studies on Their Role in Nineteenth Century Chinese Society*. Seattle: University of Washington Press, 1955.

———. *The Income of the Chinese Gentry*. Seattle: University of Washington Press, 1962.

Chang, Hao. *Liang Ch'i-ch'ao and Intellectual Transition in China, 1890–1907*. Cambridge: Harvard University Press, 1971.

Chang, H. C. *Chinese Literature: Popular Fiction and Drama*. Edinburgh: University Press, 1973.

Chang, Jen-chi. *Pre-Communist China's Rural School and Community*. Boston: Christopher Publishing, 1960.

Chang Shun-hui 張舜徽. *Ch'ing-tai Yang-chou hsüeh chi* 清代揚州學記 [Records of Ch'ing schools in Yangchow]. Shanghai: Jen-min ch'u-pan she, 1962.

Chang Te-ch'ang 張德昌. *Ch'ing-chi i-ko ching-kuan ti sheng-huo* 清季一個京官的生活 [Life of a court official in the late Ch'ing dynasty]. Hong Kong: Chinese University Press, 1970.

Chang Ti-hua 張滌華. *Lei-shu liu-pieh* 類書流別 [On the different types of *lei-shu*]. Shanghai: Commercial Press, 1958.

Chao, Ch'eng-hsin. "Familism as a Factor in the Chinese Population Balance," *Yenching Journal of Social Studies* 3.1 (1940): 1–21.

Chao, Wei-pang. "Secret Religious Societies in North China in the Ming," *Folklore Studies* 7 (1948): 95–115.

Char, Tin-yuke, ed. and comp. *The Sandalwood Mountains: Readings and Stories of the Early Chinese in Hawaii*. Honolulu: University of Hawaii Press, 1975.

"Che-chiang sheng wen-hsien lan-hui chüan-tsai" 浙江省文獻覽會專載 [Special issue on Chekiang's cultural heritage], *Wen-lan hsüeh-pao* 文瀾學報 2.3–4 (1936), part 1.

Ch'en Chao-nan 陳昭南. *Yung-cheng Ch'ien-lung nien-chien ti yin-ch'ien pi-chia pien-tung* 雍正乾隆年間的銀錢比價變動 [Silver-copper price movements in the eighteenth century]. Institute of Economics Economic Monographs, no. 4. Taipei: Academia Sinica, 1966.

Ch'en, Han-seng. *Landlord and Peasant in China: A Study of the Agrarian Crisis in South China*. New York: International Publishers, 1936.

Ch'en Hao-ch'u 陳豪楚. "Ching-shan ssu k'o-ts'ang shu" 徑山寺刻藏迷 [Notes on the books of Ching-shan monastery], *Che-chiang t'u-shu-kuan kuan-k'an* 浙江圖書館館刊 4.6 (1935): 1–8.

Ch'en Ho-ch'in 陳鶴琴, comp. *Yü-t'i wen ying-yung tzu-hui* 語體文應用字

彙 [Characters for use in vernacular literature]. Shanghai: Commercial Press, 1931.

Ch'en, Jerome. "The Origin of the Boxers." In *Studies in the Social History of China and Southeast Asia: Essays in Memory of Victor Purcell*, edited by Jerome Ch'en and Nicholas Tarling, pp. 57–84. Cambridge: Cambridge University Press, 1970.

Ch'en Ju-heng 陳汝衡. *Shuo-shu shih-hua* 說書史話 [On the history of fiction]. Peking: Tso-chia ch'u-pan she 作家出版社, 1958.

Ch'en, Kenneth K. S. *The Chinese Transformation of Buddhism*. Princeton: Princeton University Press, 1973.

Chen, Nai-ruenn. *Chinese Economic Statistics*. Chicago: Aldine, 1967.

Ch'en Shao-hsing 陳紹馨. "Hsing-shih, tsu-p'u, tsung-ch'in hui" 姓氏·族譜·宗親會 [Surnames, genealogies, kin organization], *T'ai-wan wen-hsien* 臺灣文獻 9.3 (1958): 15–32.

Ch'en, Shou-yi. *Chinese Literature: A Historical Introduction*. New York: Columbia University Press, 1961.

Ch'en Tung-yüan 陳東原. *Chung-kuo chiao-yü shih* 中國教育史 [History of Chinese education]. 1937. Reprint. Taipei: Commercial Press, 1966.

———. *Chung-kuo k'o-hsüeh shih-tai chih chiao-yü* 中國科學時代之教育 [Education in China's scientific age]. Shanghai: Commercial Press, 1934–35.

Ch'en Yün-lo 陳允洛. "Hsi-shih Min-nan chih ssu-shu" 昔時閩南之私塾 [Private schools in south Fukien in former times], *Fu-chien wen-hsien* 福建文獻 4 (1968): 47–53

Cheng Chen-to 鄭振鐸. *Chung-kuo su-wen-hsüeh shih* 中國俗文學史 [History of Chinese popular literature]. Shanghai: Commercial Press, 1938.

Cheng, Ying-wen. *Postal Communication in China and Its Modernization*. Cambridge: Harvard University Press, 1970.

Chesneaux, Jean. *Secret Societies in China in the Nineteenth and Twentieth Centuries*. Translated by Gillian Nettle. Ann Arbor: University of Michigan Press, 1971.

Ch'i, Hsi-sheng. *Warlord Politics in China, 1916–1928*. Stanford: Stanford University Press, 1976.

Chi, Wen-shun. "Liang Shu-ming and Chinese Communism," *China Quarterly* 41 (1970): 64–82.

Chiang Shun-hsing 蔣順興. "I-chien nung-min ko-ming ti pao-kuei wen-hsien—tu Hung Hsiu-ch'üan pien *Ch'ien tzu wen*" 一件农民革命的宝貴文献—读洪秀全編〈千字文〉 [A valuable peasant rebellion document—Hung Hsiu-ch'üan's "Thousand-Character Reader"], *Wen-wu* 文物 11 (1974): 47–50.

Chiang, Yee. *Chinese Calligraphy*. Cambridge: Harvard University Press, 1973.

Chiang-su sheng po-wu kuan 江蘇省博物館, comp. *Chiang-su sheng Ming Ch'ing i-lai pei-k'o tzu-liao hsüan-chi* 江蘇省明清以來碑刻資料選集 [Selection of Kiangsu Ming and Ch'ing stone inscriptions]. 1959. Reprint. Tokyo: Daian 大安, 1967.

Chiao, Chi-ming. "A Study of the Chinese Population," *The Milbank Memorial Fund Quarterly Bulletin* 11.4 (1933): 325–41; 12.1 (1934): 85–96.

Chinese Repository, published in Macao and Canton, May 1832 to December 1851.

Ch'ing Sheng-tsu. *The Sacred Edict, with a Translation of the Colloquial Rendering*. Translated by F. W. Baller. Shanghai: Presbyterian Mission Press, 1907.

Chou Hung-tsu 周弘祖. *Ku-chin shu-k'o* 古今書刻 [Old and new book printings]. N.p., n.d. (Ming work).

Chu Ping-hsü 朱炳煦 and Yao Chih-hua 姚治華. "Ch'ing-tai hsüeh-chih piao-lüeh" 清代學制表略 [Outline of the Ch'ing school system], *Chung-hua chiao-yü chieh* 中華教育界 19.7 (1933): 43–52.

Chu, Samuel C. *Reformer in Modern China: Chang Chien, 1853–1926*. New York: Columbia University Press, 1965.

Chu Shih-chia 朱士嘉. *Chung-kuo ti-fang chih tsung-lu* 中國地方志綜錄 [Catalog of Chinese local histories]. Rev. ed., 1958. Reprint. Tokyo: Daian, 1968.

Ch'ü, T'ung-tsu. *Local Government in China under the Ch'ing*. Cambridge: Harvard University Press, 1962.

Ch'ü Wan-li 屈萬里 and Ch'ang Pi-te 昌彼得. *T'u-shu pan-pen hsüeh yao-lüeh* 圖書板本學要略 [Book printing and printed books in China: a general treatise]. Taipei: Institute of Chinese Culture, 1954.

Ch'üan Han-sheng 全漢昇. "Nan Sung ch'u-nien wu-chia ti ta-pien-tung" 南宋初年物價的大變動 [The great changes in commodity prices in early Southern Sung], *Kuo-li chung-yang yen-chiu yüan li-shih yü-yen yen-chiu so chi-k'an* 國立中央研究院歷史語言研究所集刊 11 (1947): 395–423.

Ch'üan Han-sheng 全漢昇 and Wang Yeh-chien 王業鍵. "Ch'ing Yung-cheng nien-chien ti mi-chia" 清雍正年間的米價 [Rice prices in the Yung-cheng reign period], *Chung-yang yen-chiu-yüan li-shih yü-yen yen-chiu so chi-k'an* 中央研究院歷史語言研究所集刊 30 (1959): 157–85.

Cipolla, Carlo M. *Literacy and Development in the West*. Harmondsworth: Penguin paperback, 1969.

Crawcour, E. Sydney. "The Tokugawa Heritage." In *The State and Economic Enterprise in Japan*, edited by William W. Lockwood, pp. 17–44. Princeton: Princeton University Press, 1965.

Crook, David, and Crook, Isabel. *Revolution in a Chinese Village: Ten Mile Inn*. London: Routledge and Kegan Paul, 1959.

Dardess, John W. "The Transformations of Messianic Revolt and the Founding of the Ming Dynasty," *Journal of Asian Studies* 29.3 (1970): 539–58.

Darroch, John. "Chinese Textbooks," *Journal of the North China Branch of the Royal Asiatic Society* 37 (1906): 208–14.

Davis, Natalie. "Printing and the People." In her *Society and Culture in Early Modern France*, pp. 189–226. Stanford: Stanford University Press, 1975.

de Groot, J. J. M. "Inscriptions on Red Paper, Pictures, etc., on Chinese Street-doors," *The China Review* 9 (1880–81): 20–28.

———. *The Religious System of China*. 6 vols. 1892. Reprint. Taipei: Literature House, 1964.

Doolittle, Justus. *Social Life of the Chinese—with Some Account of Their Religious, Governmental, Educational and Business Customs, and Opinions, with Special but not Exclusive Reference to Fuchau*. 2 vols. New York: Harper, 1865.

Dore, Henri. *Researches into Chinese Superstitions*. Translated by M. Kennelly, et al. 11 vols. 1914. Reprint. Taipei: Ch'eng-wen, 1965–67.

Dore, Ronald P. *Education in Tokugawa Japan*. London: Routledge and Kegan Paul, 1965.

———. "The Legacy of Tokugawa Education." In *Changing Japanese Attitudes toward Modernization*, edited by Marius B. Jansen, pp. 99–131. Princeton: Princeton University Press, 1965.

Dudbridge, Glen. *The Hsi-yu Chi: A Study of Antecedents to the Sixteenth Century Chinese Novel*. Cambridge: Cambridge University Press, 1970.

Eastlake, F. W. "The Arabic Numerals," *China Review* 9 (1880): 249–51.

———. "Finger Numerals," *China Review* 9 (1880): 319–20.

Eastman, Lloyd. *The Abortive Revolution: China under Nationalist Rule, 1927–1937*. Cambridge: Harvard University Press, 1974.

Eberhard, Wolfram. *Cantonese Ballads (Munich State Library Collection)*. Asian Folklore and Social Life Monographs, vol. 30. Taipei: Tung-fang wen-hua shu-chü 東方文化書局, 1972.

———. "Notes on Chinese Story Tellers," *Fabula* 11 (1970): 1–31.

———. *Social Mobility in Traditional China*. Leiden: Brill, 1962.

Edwin, Joshua Dukes. *Everyday Life in China; or, Scenes Along River and Road in Fuh-kien*. London: The Religious Tract Society, n.d.

Eisenstein, Elizabeth L. "The Advent of Printing and the Problem of the Renaissance," *Past and Present* 45 (1969): 19–89.

———. "The Advent of Printing in Historical Literature: Notes and Comments on an Elusive Transformation," *American Historical Review* 74.3 (1970): 727–43.

———. "Some Conjectures about the Impact of Printing on Western Society and Thought," *Journal of Modern History* 40.1 (1968): 1–56.

Elvin, Mark. *The Pattern of the Chinese Past*. Stanford: Stanford University Press, 1973.

Falkenheim, Victor C. "County Administration in Fukien," *China Quarterly* 59 (1974): 518–43.

Fang, Achilles. "Bookman's Decalogue (*Ts'ang shu shih-yüeh*) by Yeh Tehui," *Harvard Journal of Asiatic Studies* 13 (1950): 132–73.

———. "Bookman's Manual (*Ts'ang shu chi-yao*) by Sun Ts'ung-t'ien,"

Harvard Journal of Asiatic Studies 14 (1951): 215–60.

Fei, Hsiao-t'ung. *Peasant Life in China: A Field Study of Country Life in the Yangtze Valley*. London: Kegan Paul, 1939.

Firth, Raymond, et al. *Families and Their Relatives*. London: Routledge and Kegan Paul, 1969.

Fraser, Stewart E., ed. *Education and Communism in China: An Anthology of Commentary and Documents*. London: Pall Mall Press, 1971.

Freedman, Maurice. *Chinese Lineage and Society: Fukien and Kwangtung*. New York: Humanities Press, 1966.

———. *Lineage Organization in Southeastern China*. London: University of London, 1958.

Fried, Morton H. *Fabric of Chinese Society*. New York: Praeger, 1953.

"From The Revolutionary Past: Textbooks of China's Early Labor Movement," *China Reconstructs* 24.1 (1975): 33–35.

Fung Yu-lan. *A History of Chinese Philosophy*. Translated by Derk Bodde. 2 vols. London: Allen and Unwin, 1953.

Gamble, Sidney D. "Daily Wages of Unskilled Chinese Laborers, 1807–1902," *The Far Eastern Quarterly* 3.1 (1943): 41–73.

———. *The Household Accounts of Two Chinese Families*. New York: China Institute of America, 1931.

———. *North China Villages: Social, Political, and Economic Activities before 1933*. Berkeley: University of California Press, 1963.

———. *Peking: A Social Survey*. New York: Doran, 1921.

———. *Ting Hsien: A North China Rural Community*. New York: Institute of Pacific Relations, 1954.

Gardner, John. "The Wu-fan Campaign in Shanghai." In *Chinese Communist Politics in Action*, edited by A. Doak Barnett, pp. 477–539. Seattle: University of Washington Press, 1969.

Giles, H. A. "Thousand Character Numerals Used by Artisans," *Journal of the China Branch of the Royal Asiatic Society*, 20 (1885): 279.

Goodrich, L. Carrington. "The Abacus in China," *Isis* 39 (1948): 239.

———. *The Literary Inquisition of Ch'ien-lung*. Baltimore: Waverly Press, 1935.

Goody, Jack, ed. *Literacy in Traditional Societies*. Cambridge: Cambridge University Press, 1968.

Goody, Jack, and Watt, Ian. "The Consequences of Literacy," *Comparative Studies in Society and History*, 5.3 (1963): 304–45.

Grimm, Tilemann. *Erziehung und Politik im konfuzianischen China der Ming-Zeit (1368–1644)*. Hamburg: Gesellschaft für Natur- und Völkerkunde Ostasiens; Kommission suerlag O. Harrassowitz, 1960.

Hanan, Patrick. *The Chinese Short Story: Studies in Dating, Authorship, and Composition*. Cambridge: Harvard University Press, 1973.

———. "Sung and Yüan Vernacular Fiction: A Critique of Modern Methods of Dating," *Harvard Journal of Asiatic Studies* 30 (1970): 159–84.

Handlin, Joanna F. "Lü K'un's New Audience: The Influence of Women's

Literacy on Sixteenth Century Thought." In *Women in Chinese Society*, edited by Margery Wolf and Roxane Witke, pp. 13–38. Stanford: Stanford University Press, 1975.

Harrison, James P. *The Communists and Chinese Peasant Rebellions.* New York: Atheneum paperback, 1968.

Hartwell, R. M. *A Guide to Sources of Chinese Economic History.* Chicago: University of Chicago Press, 1964.

Hartwell, R. M. *The Industrial Revolution and Economic Growth.* London: Methuen, 1971.

Hawkins, John N. *Mao Tse-tung and Education: His Thoughts and Teachings.* Hamden, Conn.: Shoe String Press, 1974.

Hayashi Tomoharu 林友春, ed. *Kinsei Chūgoku kyōiku shi kenkyū—sono bunkyō seisaku to shomin kyōiku* 近世中國教育史研究—その文教政策と庶民教育 [Research on modern Chinese educational history—its educational policy and mass education]. Tokyo: Kokudosha 國土社, 1958.

Higashikawa Tokuji 東川德治. *Nan-Shi ni okeru kyōiku oyobi shūkyō no hensen* 南支ニ於ケル教育及ビ宗教ノ變遷 [Changes in education and religion in south China]. Taipei: Rinji Taiwan Kyūkan chōsa kai 臨時臺灣舊慣調査會, 1919.

Hirano Yoshitarō 平野義太郎. "Hoku-Shi sonraku no kiso yōso to shite no sōzoku oyobi sonbyō" 北支村落の基礎要素としての宗族及び村廟 [Lineage and temple, the basic elements of north China villages]. In *Shina nōson kankō chōsa hōkoku* 支那農村慣行調査報告 [Reports on rural customs in China], edited by Tōa kenkyūjo 東亞研究所, 1: 1–145. Tokyo: Tōa kenkyūjo 東亞研究所, 1943.

Ho, Ping-ti. *The Ladder of Success in Imperial China.* New York: John Wiley & Sons, 1964.

———. "The Salt Merchants of Yang-chou: A Study of Commercial Capitalism in Eighteenth Century China," *Harvard Journal of Asiatic Studies* 17 (1954): 130–68.

———. *Studies on the Population of China, 1368–1953.* Cambridge: Harvard University Press, 1959.

Hrdlickova, Vera. "The Professional Training of Chinese Storytellers and the Storytellers' Guilds," *Archiv orientalni* 33.2 (1965): 225–48.

Hsiang Ta 向達. "Ming Ch'ing chih-chi chih pao-chüan wen-hsüeh yü Pai-lien chiao" 明清之際之寶卷文學與白蓮教 [Ming and Ch'ing *pao-chüan* literature and the White Lotus movement]. In his *T'ang-tai Ch'ang-an yü hsi-yü wen-ming* 唐代長安與西域文明 [Culture in T'ang Ch'ang-an and the western regions], pp. 600–616. Peking: San-lien shu-tien 三聯書店, 1957.

Hsiao, Kung-ch'üan. *Rural China: Imperial Control in the Nineteenth Century.* Seattle: University of Washington Press, 1960.

Hsiao, Theodore E. *The History of Modern Education in China.* Shanghai: Commercial Press, 1935.

Hsieh Kuo-chen 謝國禎. "Ming Ch'ing pi-chi pai-ch'eng so-chien lu" 明清

筆記稗乘所見錄 [Notes on Ming and Ch'ing essays and fiction], *Wen-wu* 文物 3 (1961): 1–7.

Hsing-cheng yüan, Chu-chi ch'u, T'ung-chi chü 行政院，主計處，統計局, comp. "Nien-ssu nien tu ch'üan-kuo ssu-shu t'ung-chi" 廿四年度全國私塾統計 [Statistics on traditional private schools in China for 1935], *T'ung-chi chi-pao* 統計季報 8 (1936): 2–4.

Hsü Hsü 徐旭. "Shanghai hsiao shu-pao t'an tiao-ch'a" 上海小書報攤調查 [Survey of book and newspaper vendors in Shanghai]. In his *T'u-shu-kuan yü min-chung chiao-yü* 圖書館與民衆教育 [Libraries and mass education], pp. 142–213. Changsha: Shang-wu yin-shu kuan 商務印書館, 1941.

Hsüeh-pu tsung-wu ssu 學部總務司, comp. *Kuang-hsü san-shih-san nien-fen ti i-tz'u chiao-yü t'ung-chi t'u-piao* 光緒三十三年分第一次教育統計圖表 [The first educational statistics—1907]. Taipei: China Press, 1973.

Hu, Hsien-chin. *The Common Descent Group in China and Its Functions.* New York: Viking Fund, 1948.

Huang, Philip C. *Liang Ch'i-ch'ao and Modern Chinese Liberalism.* Seattle: University of Washington Press, 1972.

Huang Tien-ch'üan 黃典權. *Ku chang yen-chiu i li* 古帳研究一例 [An example of research on old account books]. T'ai-wan shih-shih yen-chiu 臺灣史事研究 [Taiwan historical research] vol. 2. Tainan: Hai-tung shan fang 海東山房, 1959.

Huang Yen-p'ei 黃炎培. "Ch'ing-chi ko-sheng hsing-hsüeh shih" 清季各省興學史 [History of Ch'ing schools in various provinces], *Jen-wen* 人文 1.7 (1930): 9–17; 1.9 (1930): 9–36; 1.10 (1930): 37–43.

Hummel, Arthur W., ed. *Eminent Chinese of the Ch'ing Period.* 2 vols. Washington, D. C.: Government Printing Office, 1943–44.

Hunter, William C. *The "Fan Kwae" at Canton before Treaty Days, 1825–1844, by an Old Resident.* 2d ed. Shanghai: Kelly and Walsh, 1911.

Idema, W. L. *Chinese Vernacular Fiction: The Formative Period.* Leiden: Brill, 1974.

———. "Storytelling and the Short Story in China," *T'oung Pao* 59 (1973): 1–67.

Inkeles, Alex, and Smith, David H. *Becoming Modern.* Cambridge: Harvard University Press, 1974.

Ishikawa Ken 石川謙. *Nihon shomin kyōiku shi* 日本庶民教育史 [History of popular education in Japan]. Tokyo: Tamagawa University Press, 1972.

———. *Terakoya—shomin kyōiku kikan* 寺小屋—庶民教育機關 [Temple schools—facilities for popular education]. Tokyo: Shibundō 至文堂, 1960.

Jansen, Marius. "Tokugawa and Modern Japan." In *Studies in the Institutional History of Early Modern Japan*, edited by J. W. Hall and M. B. Jansen, pp. 317–30. Princeton: Princeton University Press, 1968.

Jansen, Marius B., and Stone, Lawrence. "Education and Modernization in Japan and England," *Comperative Studies in Society and History* 9.2 (1967): 208–32.

Jen Shih-hsien 任時先. *Chung-kuo chiao-yü ssu-hsiang shih* 中國教育思想史

[History of Chinese educational theories]. 1937. Reprint. Taipei: Commercial Press, 1964.

Jen, Yu-wen. *The Taiping Revolutionary Movement*. New Haven: Yale University Press, 1973.

Johnson, Richard. "Educational Policy and Social Control in Early Victorian England," *Past and Present* 49 (1970): 96–119.

Jordan, David. *Gods, Ghosts and Ancestors*. Berkeley: University of California Press, 1972.

Kahn, Harold L. *Monarchy in the Emperor's Eyes: Image and Reality in the Ch'ien-lung Reign*. Cambridge: Harvard University Press, 1971.

Kan Yü-yüan 甘豫源. *Hsiang-ts'un min-chung chiao-yü* 鄉村民衆教育 [Rural mass education]. Shanghai: Commercial Press, 1934–35.

Keenan, Barry. "Educational Reform and Politics in Early Republican China," *Journal of Asian Studies* 33.2 (1974): 225–37.

King, Frank H. H. *Money and Monetary Policy in China: 1845–1895*. Cambridge: Harvard University Press, 1965.

Kinugawa Tsuyoshi 衣川強. "Kanryō to hōkyū—Sōdai no hōkyū ni tsuite zokkō" 官僚と俸給—宋代の俸給について續考 [Bureaucrats and salaries—a further study of Sung salaries], *Tōhōgakuhō* 東方學報 42 (1971): 177-208.

Knott, Cargill G. "The Abacus, in Its Historic and Scientific Aspects," *Transactions of the Asiatic Society of Japan* 14 (1886): 18–71.

Kulp, Daniel Harrison. *Country Life in South China: The Sociology of Familism*. 1925. Reprint. Taipei: Ch'eng-wen, 1966.

Lamley, Harry. "Liang Shu-ming, Rural Reconstruction, and the Rural Work Discussion Society, 1933–35," *Chung Chi Journal* 8.2 (1969): 50–61.

Lamson, Herbert. "The Effect of Industrialization upon Village Livelihood," *Chinese Economic Journal* 9.4 (1931): 1025–82.

Lang, Olga. *Chinese Family and Society*. New Haven: Yale University Press, 1946.

———. *Pa Chin and His Writings: Chinese Youth between the Two Revolutions*. Cambridge: Harvard University Press, 1967.

Lary, Diana. *Region and Nation: The Kwangsi Clique in Chinese Politics, 1925–37*. Cambridge: Cambridge University Press, 1974.

Lattimore, Owen. "Chinese Colonization in Inner Mongolia: Its History and Development." In *Pioneer Settlement: Cooperative Studies by Twenty-six Authors*, edited by W. L. G. Joerg, pp. 288–312. American Geographical Society Special Publication, no. 14. New York: American Geographical Society, 1932.

Lee, Hsiang-po. "Rural-Mass Education Movement in China, 1923–1937." Ph.D. dissertation, Ohio State University, 1970.

Lee, Robert H. G. *The Manchurian Frontier in Ch'ing History*. Cambridge: Harvard University Press, 1970.

Lemoine, J. G. "Les Anciens Procedes de Calcul sur les Doigts en Orient et en Occident," *Revue des études islamiques* 6 (1932): 1–58.

Leong, Y. K., and Tao, L. K. *Village and Town Life in China.* London: Allen and Unwin, 1915.

Lewis, Ida Belle. "A Study of Primary Schools." In *China,* edited by Orville A. Petty, pp. 615–54. New York: Harper, 1933.

Li, Lillian M. "Kiangnan and the Silk Export Trade, 1842–1937." Ph.D. dissertation, Harvard University, 1975.

Li Shih-yü 李世瑜. *Pao-chüan tsung-lu* 寶卷綜錄 [Catalog of *pao-chüan*]. Shanghai: Chung-hua shu-chü 中華書局, 1961.

Li Yen 李儼. "Ch'ing-tai shu-hsüeh chiao-yü chih-tu" 淸代數學教育制度 [The Ch'ing system of mathematics education], *Hsüeh-i* 學藝 13.4 (1934): 37–52; 13.5 (1934): 49–60; 13.6 (1934): 39–44.

———. *Shih-san, shih-ssu shih-chi Chung-kuo min-chien shu-hsüeh* 十三, 十四世紀中國民間數學 [Popular mathematics in China during the thirteenth and fourteenth centuries]. Peking: K'o-hsüeh ch'u-pan she 科學出版社, 1957.

Liang Ch'i-ch'ao. *Intellectual Trends in the Ch'ing Period.* Translated by Immanuel Hsü. Cambridge: Harvard University Press, 1959.

Liao, T'ai-ch'u. "Rural Education in Transition: A Study of Old-fashioned Chinese Schools (Szu Shu) in Shantung and Szechwan," *Yenching Journal of Social Studies* 4.2 (1949): 19–67.

———. "School Land: A Problem of Educational Finance," *Yenching Journal of Social Studies* 2.2 (1940): 212–33.

Lin, Vincent T. C. "Adult Education in People's Republic of China, 1950–1958." Ph.D. dissertation, University of California at Berkeley, 1963.

Lin, Yueh-hwa. *The Golden Wing: A Sociological Study of Chinese Familism.* London: Kegan Paul, 1947.

Liu, Alan P. L. *Communications and National Integration in Communist China.* Berkeley: University of California Press, 1971.

Liu Hsing-t'ang 劉興唐. "Fu-chien ti hsüeh-tsu tsu-chih" 福建的血族組織 [The structure of kinship groups in Fukien], *Shih-huo* 食貨 4.8 (1936): 35–46.

Liu, Hui-chen Wang. *The Traditional Chinese Clan Rules.* Locust Valley: J. J. Augustin, 1959.

Liu I-cheng 柳貽徵. "Chiang-su ko-ti ch'ien-liu-pai nien-chien chih mi-chia" 江蘇各地千六百年間之米價 [Kiangsu rice prices for the last 1,600 years], *Shih-hsüeh tsa-chih* 史學雜誌 2.3–4 (1930): 1–8.

Liu Kuo-chün 劉國鈞. *Chung-kuo shu-shih hua* 中國書史話 [History of Chinese books]. Hong Kong: Shanghai Bookstore, 1962.

Liu Po-chi 劉伯驥. *Kuang-tung shu-yüan chih-tu* 廣東書院制度 [Kwangtung academies]. Shanghai: Commercial Press, 1938.

Liu Te-wen 劉德文. "P'ing chiao tsung-hui *Kai-pien ch'ien-tzu k'o* chien-tzu kung-tso ti ching-kuo" 平教總會「改編千字課」檢字工作的經過 [Experiences of the National Association for the Advancement of Mass Education in simplifying characters for their "Revised Thousand-Character Reader"], *Chiao-yü tsa-chih* 教育雜誌 18.12 (1926): 1–14.

Liu Ts'un-yan. *Chinese Popular Fiction in Two London Libraries*. Hong Kong: Lung Men Bookstore, 1967.

Lo Chin-t'ang 羅錦堂. *Li-tai t'u-shu pan-pen chih-yao* 歷代圖書板本志要 [Outline of historical book printing]. Taipei: National History Museum, 1958.

Loh, Pichon. *The Early Chiang Kai-shek: A Study of His Personality and Politics, 1887–1924*. New York: Columbia University Press, 1971.

Lowenthal, Leo. *Literature, Popular Culture, and Society*. Englewood Cliffs: Spectrum paperback, 1961.

Lu Hsün. *A Brief History of Chinese Fiction*. Translated by Hsien-i Yang and Gladys Yang. Peking: Foreign Languages Press, 1964.

MacGowan, D. J. "Chinese Guilds or Chambers of Commerce and Trades Unions," *Journal of the North China Branch of the Royal Asiatic Society* 21 (1886): 133–92.

MacGowan, J. *Men and Manners of Modern China*. London: Fisher Unwin, 1912.

Mackerras, Colin. *The Rise of the Peking Opera 1770–1870*. Oxford: Oxford University Press, 1972.

———. "The Theatre in Yang-chou in the Late Eighteenth Century," *Papers on Far Eastern History* 1 (1970): 1–30.

McKnight, Brian E. *Village and Bureaucracy in Southern SungChina*. Chicago: University of Chicago Press, 1971.

McLean, Antonia. *Humanism and the Rise of Science in Tudor England*. New York: Neale Watson, 1972.

Makino Tatsumi 牧野巽. "Kanton gōzokushi to gōzokufu—shu to shite So-shi bukō shoin sefu ni tsuite" 廣東合族祠と合族譜—主として蘇氏武功書院世譜について [Kwangtung ancestral halls and genealogies—with special focus on the Su family's Wu-kung Academy genealogy]. In *Kindai Chūgoku kenkyū* 近代中國研究 [Studies on modern China], edited by Gakujutsu kenkyū kaigi, Gendai Chūgoku kenkyū tokubetsu iinkai 學術研究會議, 現代中國研究特別委員會, pp. 89–129. Tokyo: Kōgakusha 好學社, 1948.

———. *Kinsei Chūgoku sōzoku kenkyū* 近世中國宗族研究 [Research on modern Chinese lineages]. Tokyo: Nikkō shoin 日光書院, 1949.

———. *Shina kazoku no kenkyū* 支那家族の研究 [Research on Chinese families]. Tokyo: Seikatsusha 生活社, 1944.

Mancall, Mark. "The Ch'ing Tribute System: An Interpretive Essay." In *The Chinese World Order*, edited by J. K. Fairbank, pp. 63–89. Cambridge: Harvard University Press, 1968.

Manshū kaihatsu yonjūnen shi kankō kai 滿州開發四十年史刊行會, ed. *Manshū kaihatsu yonjūnen shi* 滿州開發四十年史 [Forty-year history of Manchurian development]. 3 vols. Tokyo: Manshū kaihatsu yonjūnen shi kankō kai 滿州開發四十年史刊行會, 1964–65.

Mao Ch'un-hsiang 毛春翔. "Che-chiang sheng-li t'u-shu-kuan ts'ang shu-pan chi" 浙江省立圖書館藏書版記 [The wooden printing blocks preserved in the Chekiang Provincial Library], *Che-chiang t'u-shu-kuan kuan-k'an* 浙江圖書館館刊 4.3 (1935): 1–20.

Mao Tse-tung 毛澤東. *Mo Taku-to shū* 毛泽东集 [Collected writings of Mao Tse-tung]. Compiled by Takeuchi Minoru 竹内実. 10 vols. Tokyo: Hokubōsha 北望社, 1972.

Medhurst, W. H. *The Foreigner in Far Cathay*. New York: Scribner, Armstrong, 1873.

Meng Hsien-ch'eng 孟憲承, et al., comp. *Chung-kuo ku-tai chiao-yü shih tzu-liao* 中國古代教育史資料 [Historical materials on education in ancient China]. Peking: Jen-min chiao-yü ch'u-pan she 人民教育出版社, 1961.

Meng T'ien-p'ei and Gamble, Sidney D. *Prices, Wages, and the Standard of Living in Peking, 1900–1924*. 1926 Supplement to *Chinese Social and Political Science Review*. Peking: Peking Express, 1926.

Meskill, Johanna M. "The Chinese Genealogy as a Research Source." In *Family and Kinship in Chinese Society*, edited by Maurice Freedman, pp. 139–61. Stanford: Stanford University Press, 1970.

Minami Manshū tetsudō kabushiki kaisha, Shanhai jimusho 南滿州鐵道株式會社, 上海事務所 [South Manchurian Railway Company, Shanghai Office], comp. *Kōso-shō Jōjuku-ken nōson jittai chōsa hōkokusho* 江蘇省常熟縣農村實態調查報告書 [Report of an agricultural survey of Ch'ang-shu hsien, Kiangsu]. Shanghai: South Manchurian Railway Company, 1939.

Miura Mitsuru 三浦滿. "Mindai no fu-shū-ken gaku no kōzō to sono seikaku—gakuden-sei ni tsuite" 明代の府州縣學の構造とその性格—學田制について [The structure of Ming prefectural, departmental, and county schools and their nature—the system of school lands], *Shakai bunka shigaku* 社會文化史學 3 (1967): 26–38.

Miyazaki Ichisada 宮崎市定. *Kakyo* 科擧 [The civil service examinations]. Tokyo: *Chūō kōron* 中央公論, 1963.

Momose Hiromu 百瀬弘. "Shinmatsu Chokurei-shō no sonzu san shu ni tsuite" 淸末直隷省の村圖三種について [On three late Ch'ing Chihli *ts'un-t'u*]. In *Katō Hakase kanreki kinen: Tōyō shi shūsetsu* 加藤博士還暦記念東洋史集說 [Festschrift commemorating Dr. Katō's sixty-first birthday: Collected articles on Oriental history], ed. Katō Hakase kanreki kinen ronbunshū kankō kai 加藤博士還暦記念論文集刊行會, pp. 841–60. Tokyo: Fuzanbō 冨山房, 1941.

———. "Shinmatsu Chokurei-shō Sei-ken shijō kyōdōtai zakkō" 淸末直隷省靑縣市場共同體雜考 [A note on the marketing community of Ch'ing hsien in Chihli province during the late Ch'ing], *Tōyō shi kenkyū* 東洋史研究 27.3 (1968): 318–32.

———. "Shinmatsu Chokurei-shō son-chin kokō shōkō" 淸末直隷省村鎭戶口小考 [Comments on village and market town population in late Ch'ing Chihli province], *Tōhōgakuhō* (Tokyo) 東方學報 12.3(1941): 99–112.

Morita Akira 森田明. *Shindai suiri shi kenkyū* 淸代水利史研究 [Research on Ch'ing water management history]. Tokyo: Aki shobō 亞紀書房, 1974.

Morse, Hosea B. *The Trade and Administration of the Chinese Empire*. London: Longmans, Green, 1908.

Mote, Frederick W. "China's Past in the Study of China Today—Some Comments on the Recent Work of Richard Solomon," *Journal of Asian Studies* 32.1 (1972): 107–20.

———. "The Rural 'Haw' of Northern Thailand." In *SEA Tribes, Minorities, and Nations*, edited by Peter Kunstadter, 2: 487–524. Princeton: Princeton University Press, 1967.

Munro, Donald J. *The Concept of Man in Early China*. Stanford: Stanford University Press, 1969.

Myers, Ramon. *The Chinese Peasant Economy: Agricultural Development in Hopei and Shantung, 1890–1949*. Cambridge: Harvard University Press, 1970.

———. "Economic Organization and Cooperation in Modern China: Irrigation Management in Xing-tai County, Ho-bei Province." In Ko Muramatsu Yūji Kyōju tsuitō rombunshū—*Chūgoku no seiji to keizai* 故村松祐次教授追悼論文集—中國の政治と經濟 [The polity and economy of China—commemoration volume for the late Professor Yūji Muramatsu], comp. Ko Muramatsu Yūji Kyōju tsuitō jigyōkai 故村松祐次教授追悼事業會, pp. 189–212. Tokyo: Tōyō keizai shinpōsha 東洋經濟新報社, 1975.

Nagasawa Kikuya 長澤規矩. *Wa-Kan sho no insatsu to sono rekishi* 和漢書の印刷とその歷史 [The printing of Japanese and Chinese books and their history]. Tokyo: Yoshikawa kōbunkan 吉川弘文館, 1952.

Naikaku sōri daijin kanbō chōsa shitsu 內閣總理大臣官房調查室. *Chūkyō tekkōgyō chōsa hōkokusho* (*kigyō hen*) 中共鉄鋼業調查報告書 (企業編) [Survey report on the steel industry of the People's Republic (Enterprises)]. 2 vols. Tokyo: Finance Ministry Printing Office, 1956.

Nakamura Jihei 中村治兵衞. "Shindai Santō no gakuden" 清代山東の學田 [School lands in Ch'ing Shantung], *Shien* 史淵 64 (1955): 43–64.

———. "Shindai Santō no gakuden no kosaku" 清代山東の學田の小作 [Tenants on school lands in Ch'ing Shantung], *Shien* 史淵 71 (1956): 55–77.

———. "Shindai Santō no shoin to tentō" 清代山東の書院と典當 [Academies and pawnshops in Ch'ing Shantung], *Tōhōgaku* 東方學 11 (1955): 100–109.

———. "Shindai Santō nōson no gigaku" 清代山東農村の義學 [Charitable schools in rural Shantung in Ch'ing times], *Tōyō shigaku* 東洋史學 15 (1956): 1–15; 16 (1956): 21–36.

Nakamura Tsune 中村恒. "Shinmatsu gakudō setsuritsu o meguru—Kō-Setsu nōson shakai no ichi danmen" 清末學堂設立をめぐる—江浙農村社會の一斷面 [The establishment of *hsüeh-t'ang* in late Ch'ing—an aspect of rural society in Kiangsu and Chekiang], *Rekishi kyōiku* 歷史教育 10.11 (1962): 72–85.

Naquin, Susan. *Millenarian Rebellion in China: The Eight Trigrams Uprising of 1813*. New Haven: Yale University Press, 1976.

Needham, Joseph. *Science and Civilization in China*. Vol. 3: *Mathematics and the Sciences of the Heavens and the Earth*. Cambridge: Cambridge University Press, 1959.

Negishi Tadashi 根岸佶. *Chūgoku no girudo* 中國のギルド [Chinese guilds]. Tokyo: Nihon hyōron shinsha 日本評論新社, 1953.

Newbold, T. J., and Wilson, F. W. "The Chinese Triad Society of the Tien-ti-huih," *Journal of the Royal Asiatic Society of Great Britain and Ireland* 6 (1841): 120–58.

Nihon shuyō toshokan kenkyūjo shozō Chūgoku chihōshi sōgō mokuroku 日本主要圖書館研究所所藏中國地方志總合目錄 [Union catalog of Chinese local gazetteers in Japanese major libraries and research institutes]. Tokyo: National Diet Library, Reference Department, 1969.

Niida Noboru 仁井田陞. *Chūgoku no nōson kazoku* 中國の農村家族 [China's rural households]. Tokyo: University of Tokyo Press, 1966.

———. "Gen Min jidai no mura no kiyaku to kosaku shōsho nado—nichiyō hyakka-zensho no rui nijusshu no naka kara" 元明時代の村の規約と小作證書など—日用百科全書の類二十種の中から [Yüan and Ming regulations of village and tenant bonds—from twenty encyclopedia of daily use], *Tōyō bunka kenkyūjo kiyō* 東洋文化研究所紀要 8 (1956): 123–66.

Ogawa Yoshiko 小川嘉子. "Chūgoku kinsei no zokujuku ni tsuite" 中國近世の族塾について [Modern clan schools in China]. In *Ishikawa Ken hakase kanreki kinen ronbunshū—kyōiku no shiteki tenkai* 石川謙博士還歷紀念論文集—教育の史的展開 [The historical development of education—essays in honor of Dr. Ken Ishikawa's sixty-first birthday], contributed by Ishiyama Shūhei 石山脩平 et al., pp. 533–49. Tokyo: Kōdansha 講談社, 1952.

———. "Shindai ni okeru gigaku setsuritsu no kiban" 清代における義學設立の基盤 [The basis for charitable school foundings in the Ch'ing]. In *Kinsei Chūgoku kyōiku shi kenkyū* 近世中國教育史研究 [Research on modern Chinese education], edited by Hayashi Tomoharu 林友春, pp. 273–308. Tokyo: Kokudosha, 1958.

———. "Sōzoku-nai no kyōiku" 宗族內の教育 [Education within the lineage]. In *Kyōikugaku ronshū* 教育學論集 [Essays on education], edited by Nihon kyōiku gakkai 日本教育學會, pp. 223–29. Tokyo: Meguro shoten 目黑書店, 1951.

Ohkawa, Kazushi, and Rosovsky, Henry. *Japanese Economic Growth: Trend Acceleration in the Twentieth Century*. Stanford: Stanford University Press, 1973.

Okuzaki Hiroshi 奥崎裕司. "En Ryō-han no shisō—Mindai makki no shisō shiteki kōsatsu" 袁了凡の思想—明代末期の思想史的考察 [On the thought of Yuan Huang—a study of late Ming thought], *Shakai bunka shigaku* 社會文化史學 3 (1967): 14–25.

Osgood, Cornelius. *Village Life in Old China: A Community Study of Kao Yao, Yunnan*. New York: Ronald Press, 1963.

Overmyer, Daniel L. *Folk Buddhist Religion: Dissenting Sects in Late Traditional China.* Cambridge: Harvard University Press, 1976.

Parker, Edward H. "The Yangtse Gorges and Rapids in Hu-pei," *The China Review* 9 (1880–81): 173–84.

Peake, Cyrus H. *Nationalism and Education in Modern China.* New York: Columbia University Press, 1932.

Pei-ching Jui-fu-hsiang 北京瑞蚨祥 [Peking's Jui-fu-hsiang]. Compiled by Economic Research Institute, Academia Sinica. Peking: San-lien shu-tien, 1959.

P'eng Hsin-wei 彭信威. *Chung-kuo huo-pi shih* 中國貨幣史 [History of Chinese currency]. Shanghai: Jen-min ch'u-pan she, 1958.

The People's Comic Book. Translated by Endymion Wilkinson. New York: Anchor paperback, 1973.

Perkins, Dwight H. *Agricultural Development in China, 1368–1968.* Chicago: Aldine, 1969.

———. "Government as an Obstacle to Industrialization: The Case of Nineteenth Century China," *Journal of Economic History* 27.4 (1967): 478–92.

———. "Introduction: The Persistence of the Past." In *China's Modern Economy in Historical Perspective*, edited by D. H. Perkins, pp. 1–18. Stanford: Stanford University Press, 1975.

[Playfair], G. M. H. "Guild Terrorism," *Journal of the North China Branch of the Royal Asiatic Society* 20 (1885): 181–82.

Pollard, Sidney, "Factory Discipline in the Industrial Revolution," *Economic History Review*, 2d ser. 16.2 (1963): 245–71.

Potter, Jack M. "Land and Lineage in Traditional China." In *Family and Kinship in Chinese Society*, edited by Maurice Freedman, pp. 121–38. Stanford: Stanford University Press, 1970.

Prusek, Jaroslav. "The Beginnings of Popular Chinese Literature: Urban Centres—the Cradle of Popular Fiction," *Archiv orientalni* 36 (1968): 67–121.

———. *Chinese History and Literature.* Dordrecht: Reidel, 1970.

———. *The Origins and Authors of the "Hua-pen."* Prague: Academia, 1967.

Purcell, Victor. *Problems of Chinese Education.* London: Kegan Paul, 1936.

Rankin, Mary B. *Early Chinese Revolutionaries: Radical Intellectuals in Shanghai and Chekiang, 1902–1911.* Cambridge: Harvard paperback, 1971.

Reinecke, John E. *Language and Dialect in Hawaii: A Sociolinguistic History to 1935.* Honolulu: University of Hawaii Press, 1969.

Rozman, Gilbert. *Urban Networks in Ch'ing China and Tokugawa Japan.* Princeton: Princeton University Press, 1973.

Rudolph, R. C. "Chinese Moveable Type Printing in the Eighteenth Century." In *Silver Jubilee Volume of the Zinbun-kagaku-kenkyusyo, Kyoto University*, edited by Kaizuka Shigeki 貝塚茂樹, pp. 317–35. Kyoto: Kyoto daigaku jinbun kagaku kenkyūjo 京都大學人文科學研究所, 1954.

Sakai Tadao 酒井忠夫. *Chūgoku zensho no kenkyū* 中國善書の研究 [Chinese popular morality books]. Tokyo: Kōbundō 弘文堂, 1960.

———. "Confucianism and Popular Educational Works." In *Self and Society in Ming Thought*, edited by William T. de Bary, pp. 331–66. New York: Columbia University Press, 1970.

———. "Mindai no nichiyō ruisho to shomin kyōiku" 明代の日用類書と庶民教育 [Ming encyclopedias of daily use and popular education]. In *Kinsei Chūgoku kyōiku shi kenkyū* 近世中國教育史研究 [History of modern Chinese education], edited by Hayashi Tomoharu 林友春, pp. 26–154. Tokyo: Kokudosha, 1958.

San Tzu Ching: Elementary Chinese. Translated and annotated by Herbert A. Giles. 1910. Reprint. New York: Ungar, 1963.

Sanderson, Michael. "Literacy and Social Mobility in the Industrial Revolution in England," *Past and Present* 56 (1972): 75–104.

Schipper, Kristofer M. "The Written Memorial in Taoist Ceremonies." In *Religion and Ritual in Chinese Society*, edited by Arthur Wolf, pp. 309–24. Stanford: Stanford University Press, 1974.

Schofield, R. "Dimensions of Illiteracy, 1750–1850," *Explorations in Economic History* 10.4 (1973): 437–54.

Schram, Stuart. "The Cultural Revolution in Historical Perspective." In *Authority, Participation, and Cultural Change in China*, edited by Stuart Schram, pp. 1–108. Cambridge: Cambridge University Press, 1973.

———. *Mao Tse-tung*. New York: Penguin paperback, 1966.

Schwartz, Benjamin I. *Communism and China: Ideology in Flux*. Cambridge: Harvard University Press, 1968.

Selden, Mark. *The Yenan Way in Revolutionary China*. Cambridge: Harvard University Press, 1971.

Seybolt, Peter J., ed. *Revolutionary Education in China: Documents and Commentary*. White Plains: International Arts and Sciences Press, 1974.

———. "The Yenan Revolution in Mass Education," *China Quarterly* 48 (1971): 641–69.

Shen Kuan-ch'ün 沈灌群. *Chung-kuo ku-tai chiao-yü ho chiao-yü ssu-hsiang* 中國古代教育和教育思想 [Education and educational philosophy in ancient China]. Wuhan: Jen-min ch'u-pan she 人民出版社, 1956.

Shiba Yoshinobu. *Commerce and Society in Sung China*. Translated by Mark Elvin. Ann Arbor: Center for Chinese Studies, University of Michigan, 1970.

Shimizu Morimitsu 清水盛光. "Chūgoku ni okeru giden seido no kigen to hattatsu—toku ni Han-shi giden no sōritsu to hatten no igi ni tsuite" 中國に於ける義田制度の起源と發達—特に范氏義田の創立と發展の意義について [On the origins and development of China's charitable-field system—with special focus on the Fan clan's charitable fields' establishment and development], *Shakaigaku kenkyū* 社會學研究 1.3 (1947): 100–131.

Shimizu Taiji 清水泰次. *Shina no kazoku to sonraku no tokushitsu* 支那の家族と村落の特質 [The special characteristics of Chinese households and villages]. Tokyo: Bunmei kyōkai 文明協會 1927.

Shu Hsin-ch'eng 舒新城, ed. *Chung-kuo chin-tai chiao-yü shih tzu-liao* 中國近代教育史資料 [Materials for the history of modern Chinese education]. 3 vols. Peking: Jen-min chiao-yü ch'u-pan she, 1962.

Skinner, G. William. "Chinese Peasants and the Closed Community: An Open and Shut Case," *Comparative Studies in Society and History* 13.3 (1971): 270–81.

Smedley, Agnes. *The Great Road: The Life and Times of Chu Teh.* New York: Monthly Review paperback, 1972.

Smith, Arthur H. *Village Life in China.* 1899. Reprint. Boston: Brown, 1970.

Solomon, Richard H. *Mao's Revolution and the Chinese Political Culture.* Berkeley: University of California Press, 1971.

Spence, Jonathan. "Chang Po-hsing and the K'ang-hsi Emperor," *Ch'ing-shih wen-t'i* 1.8 (1968): 3–9.

———. *Emperor of China: Self-portrait of K'ang-hsi.* New York: Knopf, 1974.

Stone, Lawrence. "Literacy and Education in England, 1640–1900," *Past and Present* 42 (1969): 69–139.

Sun K'ai-ti 孫楷第. *Jih-pen Tung-ching so-chien Chung-kuo hsiao-shuo shu-mu—fu Ta-lien t'u-shu-kuan so-chien Chung-kuo hsiao-shuo shu-mu* 日本東京所見中國小說書目—附大連圖書館所見中國小說書目 [Catalog of Chinese fiction found in Tokyo, Japan—with an appended list of Chinese fiction found in the Dairen library]. Shanghai: Shang-tsa ch'u-pan she, 1953.

Sun Yü-hsiu 孫毓修. *Chung-kuo tiao-pan yüan-liu k'ao* 中國雕板源流攷 [History of Chinese printing]. Shanghai: Commercial Press, 1926.

Suzuki Kenichi 鈴木健一. "Min Shin shakai to Edo bakufu no minshū kyōka shisō—Roku yu o ichirei to shite" 明清社會と江戸幕府の民衆教化思想—六諭を一例として [Ming and Ch'ing society and the Tokugawa shogunate's popular thought indoctrination—the example of the *Liu Yü*], *Rekishi kyōiku* 歷史教育 15.9–10 (1967): 144–50.

Swann, Nancy Lee. "Seven Intimate Library Owners," *Harvard Journal of Asiatic Studies* 1 (1936): 363–90.

Taam, Cheuk-woon. *The Development of Chinese Libraries under the Ch'ing Dynasty, 1644–1911.* Shanghai: Commercial Press, 1935.

Tachibana Shiraki 橘樸. *Shina shakai kenkyū* 支那社會研究 [Research on Chinese society]. Tokyo: Hyōronsha 評論社, 1936.

Taeuber, Irene B. "The Families of Chinese Farmers." In *Family and Kinship in Chinese Society*, edited by Maurice Freedman, pp. 63–85. Stanford: Stanford University Press, 1970.

———. *The Population of Japan.* Princeton: Princeton University Press, 1958.

Taga Akigorō 多賀秋五郎. *Chūgoku kyōiku shi* 中國教育史 [History of Chinese education]. Tokyo: Iwasaki shoten 岩崎書店, 1955.

———. *Kindai Chūgoku kyōiku shi shiryō—Shinmatsu hen* 近代中國教育史資料—清末編 [Historical materials for modern Chinese education—late

Ch'ing]. Tokyo: Japanese Association for the Advancement of Scholarship, 1972.

———. "Kindai Chūgoku ni okeru zokujuku no seikaku" 近代中國における族塾の性格 [On the character of modern Chinese clan schools], *Kindai Chūgoku kenkyū* 近代中國研究 5 (1963): 207–54.

———. ed. *Kinsei Ajia kyōiku shi kenkyū* 近世アジア教育史研究 [Studies on the history of modern Asian education]. Tokyo: Bunri shoin 文理書院, 1966.

———. "Shinmatsu kakyo haishi zen sōzoku keiei no gakkō kyōiku ni tsuite" 清末科學廢止前宗族經營の學校教育について [Late Ch'ing education in clan-managed schools before the ablition of the civil service examinations], *Kyōiku shigakkai kiyō; Nihon no kyōiku shigaku* 教育史學會紀要; 日本の教育史學 1 (1958): 95–125.

———. *Sōfu no kenkyū* 宗譜の研究 [Investigations of clan genealogies]. Tokyo: Tōyō bunko, 1960.

Taira, Koji. "Education and Literacy in Meiji Japan: An Interpretation," *Explorations in Economic History* 8.4 (1971): 371–94.

Tanaka Issei 田仲一成. "Chōsen shisetsu En kōro-tei ni okeru Shindai shoki kōgyō engeki no keisei" 朝鮮使節燕行路程における清代初期興行演劇の形成 [The form of early Ch'ing drama as seen in the Korean ambassador's travel account], (Kumamoto daigaku hōbun gakkai) *Hōbun ronsō* (熊本大學法文學會)法文論叢 25 (1970): 36–69.

T'ang Mao-ju 湯茂如. "Ch'eng-shih p'ing-min hsüeh-hsiao ti chiao ts'ai" 城市平民學校的教材 [Texts for urban mass education], *Chiao-yü tsa-chih* 教育雜誌 19.10 (1927): 1–10.

Thompson, Laurence G. *Chinese Religion: An Introduction*. Belmont, Calif.: Dickenson paperback, 1969.

Topley, Marjorie. "Marriage Resistance in Rural Kwangtung." In *Women in Chinese Society*, edited by Margery Wolf and Roxane Witke, pp. 67–88. Stanford: Stanford University Press, 1975.

T'ung Chen-chia 佟振家. "Ch'ing-mo hsiao-hsüeh chiao-yü chih yen-pien" 清末小學教育之演變 [The evolution of late Ch'ing elementary education], *Shih-ta yüeh-k'an* 師大月刊 21 (1935): 123–84.

Twitchett, Denis. "Chinese Social History from the Seventh to the Tenth Centuries," *Past and Present* 35 (1966): 28–53.

Wakeman, Frederic, Jr. *Strangers At the Gate: Social Disorder in South China, 1839–1861*. Berkeley: University of California Press, 1966.

Wales, Nym. *Red Dust*. Stanford: Stanford University Press, 1952.

Waley, Arthur. *Yuan Mei: Eighteenth Century Chinese Poet*. 1957. Reprint. Stanford: Stanford University Press, 1970.

Wang Feng-chieh 王鳳喈, ed. *Chung-kuo chiao-yü shih* 中國教育史 [History of Chinese education]. Taipei: Cheng-chung shu-chü 正中書局, 1954.

Wang Hsiao-ch'uan 王曉傳. *Yüan Ming Ch'ing san-tai chin-hui hsiao-shuo hsi-ch'ü shih-liao* 元明清三代禁毀小說戲曲史料 [Historical materials on banned fiction and drama during Yüan, Ming, and Ch'ing times]. Peking: Tso-chia ch'u-pan she, 1958.

Wang Hsiu 王修. "Pan-pen shu" 版本述 [On book printing], *Che-chiang t'u-shu-kuan kuan-k'an* 浙江圖書館館刊 3.3 (1934): 1–7; 3.4 (1934): 1–5.

Wang Lan-yin 王蘭蔭. "Ming-tai chih she-hsüeh" 明代之社學 [Community schools in the Ming], *Shih-ta yüeh-k'an* 師大月刊 5.4 (1935): 42–102.

Wang, Yeh-chien. *Land Taxation in Imperial China, 1750–1911*. Cambridge: Harvard University Press, 1973.

———. "The Secular Trend of Prices during the Ch'ing period (1644–1911)" (Chinese University of Hong Kong) *Journal of the Institute of Chinese Studies* 5.2 (1972): 347–71.

Wang Yeh-ch'iu 王冶秋. *Liu-li-ch'ang shih-hua* 琉璃廠史話 [Historical talks on Liu-li-ch'ang]. Peking: San-lien shu-tien, 1963.

Watson, Burton. *Chinese Lyricism: Shih Poetry from the Second to the Twelfth Century*. New York: Columbia University Press, 1971.

Wheatley, Paul. *The Pivot of the Four Quarters: A Preliminary Enquiry into the Origins and Character of the Ancient Chinese City*. Chicago: Aldine, 1971.

Wilkinson, Endymion P. *The History of Imperial China: A Research Guide*. Cambridge: Harvard University Press, 1973.

———. "Studies in Chinese Price History." Ph. D. dissertation, Princeton University, 1970.

Williams, Talcott. "Silver in China—and Its Relation to Chinese Copper Coinage," *Annals of the American Academy of Political and Social Science* 9 (1897): 359–79.

Witke, Roxane. "Chiang Ch'ing's Coming of Age." In *Women in Chinese Society*, edited by Margery Wolf and Roxane Witke, pp. 169–92. Stanford: Stanford University Press, 1975.

Wright, Authur. "Propaganda and Persuasion in Imperial and Contemporary China," *Rice University Studies* 59.4 (1973): 9–18.

Wright, Mary. *The Last Stand of Chinese Conservatism: the T'ung-chih Restoration, 1862–1874*. Stanford: Stanford University Press, 1957.

Wu Ching-tzu. *The Scholars*. Translated by Hsien-yi Yang and Gladys Yang. New York: Universal Library paperback, 1972.

Wu Hsün li-shih tiao-ch'a t'uan 武訓歷史調查團, comp. *Wu Hsün li-shih tiao-ch'a chi* 武訓歷史調查記 [Investigations in the history of Wu Hsün]. Peking: Jen-min ch'u-pan she, 1951.

Wu, K. T. "Chinese Printing under Four Alien Dynasties (916–1368 A.D.)," *Harvard Journal of Asiatic Studies* 13 (1950): 447–523.

———. "Ming Printing and Printers," *Harvard Journal of Asiatic Studies* 7 (1943): 203–60.

Yamazaki, Yoemon. "History of Instrumental Multiplication and Division in China—from the Reckoning-blocks to the Abacus," *Memoirs of the Research Department of the Tōyō Bunko* 21 (1962): 125–48.

Yang, C. K. *A Chinese Village in Early Communist Transition.* Cambridge: MIT Press, 1959.

———. *Religion in Chinese Society.* Berkeley: University of California Press, 1967.

Yang, Lien-sheng 楊聯陞. "K'o-chü shih-tai fu-k'ao lü-fei wen-t'i" 科擧時代赴考旅費問題 [On grants to cover the expenses of traveling to the examinations], *Ch'ing-hua hsüeh-pao* 清華學報 n.s. 2.2 (1961): 116–28.

———. *Money and Credit in China: A Short History.* Cambridge: Harvard University Press, 1952.

———. "Tien-yeh hsü-chih" 典業須知 [Pawnbrokers' guide], *Shih-huo yüeh-k'an* 食貨月刊 n.s. 1.4 (1971): 231–43.

Yang, Martin C. *A Chinese Village: Taitou, Shantung Province.* New York: Columbia University paperback, 1965.

Yeh Ch'ang-ch'ing 葉長青. "Min pen k'ao" 閩本考 [Fukien books], *T'u-shu-kuan hsüeh chi-k'an* 圖書館學季刊 2.1 (1927): 115–61.

Yeh Te-hui 葉德輝. *Shu-lin chang-ku* 書林掌故 [Historical records on books]. Hong Kong: Chungshan 中山, 1972.

———. *Shu-lin ch'ing-hua* 書林清話 [Chats on books]. 3d ed. N.p., 1920.

Yen, Y. C. James. "China's New Scholar-Farmer," *Asia* 29 (1929): 126–33, 158–60.

———. "New Citizens for China," *Yale Review* 18 (1928–29): 262–76.

Yokoyama Suguru 横山英. "Shindai Kōsei-shō ni okeru unyugyō no kikō" 清代江西省における運輸業の機構 [Structure of the carrying trade in Ch'ing Kiangsi], *Hiroshima daigaku bungakubu kiyō* 廣島大學文學部紀要 18 (1960): 49–89.

Yoshikawa, Kōjirō. *An Introduction to Sung Poetry.* Translated by Burton Watson. Cambridge: Harvard University Press, 1967.

Index